Joanne Buckley

Checkmate

A Writing Reference for Canadians

Second Edition

Australia Canada Mexico Singapore Spain United Kingdom United States

Checkmate: A Writing Reference for Canadians, Second Edition

by Joanne Buckley

Associate Vice President, Editorial Director:
Evelyn Veitch

Editor-in-Chief, Higher Education:
Anne Williams

Executive Acquisitions Editor:
Laura Macleod

Marketing Manager:
Sandra Green

Senior Developmental Editor:
Lesley Mann

Permissions Coordinator:
Cindy Howard

Content Production Manager:
Jaime Smith

Copy Editor:
Margaret Crammond

Proofreader:
Margaret Crammond

Indexer:
Dennis Mills

Technical Reviewers:
Patricia Buckley, MISt (Ch, 3)
Joan McKibbin (Ch 5–8)

Senior Production Coordinator:
Ferial Suleman

Design Director:
Ken Phipps

Interior Design:
Peter Papayanakis

Cover Design:
Peter Papayanakis

Compositor:
Carol Magee

Printer:
Transcontinental

Printed and bound in Canada
1 2 3 4 09 08 07 06

For more information contact Nelson, 1120 Birchmount Road, Toronto, Ontario, M1K 5G4. Or you can visit our Internet site at http://www.nelson.com

Library and Archives Canada Cataloguing in Publication Data

Buckley, Joanne, 1953–
Checkmate : A writing reference for Canadians / Joanne Buckley. — 2nd ed.

Includes index.
ISBN-13: 978-0-17-610361-3
ISBN-10: 0-17-610361-9

1. English language—Rhetoric—Handbooks, manuals, etc.
2. English language—Grammar—Handbooks, manuals, etc. I. Title.

PE1408.B818 2007 808'.042
C2006-905175-5

HOW TO USE THIS BOOK

Checkmate: A Writing Reference for Canadians, Second Edition, has been designed to save you time and effort in looking up answers to questions you have about your writing. Because the book lies flat, it is easy to use as a reference while you are editing and revising your work. Convenient section dividers enable you to reach the information you need as soon as you need it. These sections group chapters together according to five themes:

Writing Purpose (Chapters 1 and 2)
Research and Documentation (Chapters 3 to 8)
Writing Tools (Chapters 9 to 11)
Editing Tools (Chapters 12 to 14)
ESL (Chapter 15)

The Menu System

Inside the front cover, you will find the book's table of contents, laid out very simply. There are 15 chapters in the main menu, each of which leads to a tabbed divider that presents a brief menu on the first page and a more detailed menu, or table of contents, on the back.

Suppose you need to learn how to use commas between items in a list or series. First, you scan the main menu, where you will find the comma as the first entry under Chapter 11 ("Punctuation"). Then, you simply flip the book to the divider marked 11 and consult the more detailed menu there for the section you need (11-1d) and the page number.

The Index

If you aren't sure what topic to select from the main menu, you can easily consult the index at the back of the book. For instance, if you don't know what to call the problem of whether to use *imply* or *infer* (it's a word-choice problem, by the way), you can look up *Imply, infer* in the index at the back, and you will find the answer on the page listed.

The Glossary of Usage

If you are not sure about how to use a particular word (for example, *accept* or *except*, or *imply* or *infer*, or *phenomenon* or *phenomena*), you can flip to Chapter 13 ("Usage") and seek the answer in the alphabetical glossary provided for that purpose. The glossary may also direct you to a fuller explanation of the term located somewhere else in the book.

Sometimes a word may not appear in the Glossary of Usage, but will still be included in the index. If, for example, you want to understand how to use *he* versus *him*, which is a complicated question, that entry will appear in the index, with the page number you need.

Audio flashcards for all the items in the Glossary of Usage are available on the Companion Website that accompanies this book—see http://www.checkmate2e.nelson.com/student/. Now you can hear as well as read the glossary items. An announcer reads the glossary term as it is displayed on screen; then, after you've mentally checked your knowledge of the term, you can click on the "back" of the flashcard to see and hear the actual definition.

The Directories to Documentation Models

No one ever remembers all the details about how to document a research paper. That's what reference guides like these are for. An especially helpful change in the Second Edition is the use of separate tab dividers for the various documentation style guides: Modern Language Association (MLA), American Psychological Association (APA), Chicago Manual of Style (Chicago), Council of Science Editors (formerly the Council of Biology Editors/CBE) and Columbia Online Style (COS). These dividers make it easy for you to locate explanations and examples of the style you need to use for a particular assignment.

If English Is a Second Language

If your first language is not English, most of the advice you seek will appear in Chapter 15 ("ESL"). Other ESL advice occurs throughout the text and is flagged with a special icon. You can also find ESL advice by looking up *ESL* in the index at the back of the book.

Correction Symbols

A list of standard correction symbols is provided on the inside of the back cover. (Note, however, that some instructors use their own codes for correction.)

Checklists

You can download many of the checklists and boxes in this book from the Companion Website at http://www.checkmate2e.nelson.com/student/. This makes it easy for you to refer to guidelines such as the Structural Revision Checklist in Chapter 1 or the Things to Do to Avoid Plagiarism list from Chapter 4 as you write your papers and essays.

Brief Table of Contents

For a quick overview of the book's structure, consult the brief table of contents on page vi.

BRIEF TABLE OF CONTENTS

TABLE OF CONTENTS

CONTENTS

TO THE STUDENT

OR, WHAT CAN A HANDBOOK DO FOR ME AS A WRITER?

Handbooks are traditionally big, fat, expensive books that students buy under duress and sell as quickly as they can once a course is done. They are often among the most unread of books—a distinction they share with bestsellers like physicist Stephen Hawking's *A Brief History of Time*, which has been called the most popular unread book of all time.

This book isn't set up to add to your reading material. It is intended as a kind of recipe book (except without the pictures) to provide you with all the information you need to cook up great pieces of writing. You don't need to read it from cover to cover! That's the first good news.

The other good news is that knowing the kinds of information this book provides can raise your grades—about ten percent, generally speaking, since that is approximately how much is usually deductible for errors of correctness or style in any discipline. Obviously, though, the improvement may go further than that, because writing instructors in particular tend to mark impressionistically—not entirely unlike Olympic figure-skating judges, but with a certain regard for "artistic impression," a quality easily affected by a minor error or confusing sentence.

Why lose ten percent of your grade if you don't have to? Students today are encouraged to write and revise a number of drafts of papers, rather than completing them in one shot; your instructor may well allow you to—or demand that you—hand in an outline of your assignment or a working draft before you hand in the finished product. This is a great opportunity for you to mine the resources in this guide.

If, for example, you know that you have a weak understanding of research processes or source documentation, you can review the sections on these topics briefly, then keep the model essays and sample bibliographic entries near as you write your papers. You may never internalize all the details of MLA documentation, but you will know where to find the answers.

If you have identified problems with grammar or spelling in your work, this book will give you a tool to check your drafts with and protect your investment in your work. Hang on to this handbook and consult it whenever you have a question. Essays will seem easier to write as a result, and odds are your grades will be higher.

TO THE INSTRUCTOR

This clear, easy-to-use guide for students from all disciplines presents grammar and punctuation, style and usage—even documentation—in an often funny, always readable way. It is a truly Canadian handbook, rather than merely Canadianized, as will be seen in much of its content and many of its examples.

Beginning the Writing Process

Structured with the writing process in mind, the book takes a friendly, lighthearted approach to what can be a dry subject. In keeping with readers' needs, the book concentrates on writing in different contexts, not just writing in an academic setting. Throughout, it is written to be a convenient reference for students to use when revising drafts as well as during the composing process.

What's New in the Second Edition?

ORGANIZATION

The second edition of *Checkmate* has been reorganized to improve the flow of information. Five kinds of colour-coded tabs link similarly themed chapters:

- Writing Process (Chapters 1–2)
- Research and Documentation (Chapters 3–8)
- Writing Tools (Chapters 9–11)
- Editing Tools (Chapters 12–14)
- ESL (Chapter 15)

Chapters that deal with essay writing have been placed together at the beginning of the volume for greater continuity. This revision now treats the writing process from both an academic and a business perspective, with a dedicated chapter (2) on business formats, including report writing. Coverage of research papers and documentation is next, moved from the end of the book to reflect the importance of these topics. Dividers now separate the material on documentation systems, making it easy for students to locate discussion of the particular style required for an essay, whether it is MLA, APA, Chicago, CBE, or COS. The chapters on grammar have been reorganized to move from simple, common errors to more complex issues. The ESL chapter now concludes the book, with an overview of specialized issues.

Chapter Changes

- **Chapter 1—Composing a Document:** This chapter has been revised so it offers a more reader-friendly and realistic introduction to the purposes for which students write. The sample student essay illustrates the writing process from planning to outline to final draft, providing students with a clear understanding of the steps involved in creating a research paper. A new box provides hints for working with Microsoft Word.
- **Chapter 2—Business Writing:** The primary focus in this chapter is on business writing, including an expanded section on "Formatting Business Documents: What Employers Want." Additional student writing samples provide students with a variety of accepted formats for proposals, résumés, and business letters. The chapter continues to present basic information on setting up a document and comparison between business and academic writing approaches.
- **Chapter 3—Research Papers:** This key chapter has been heavily revised, moving from its position near the end of the previous edition and incorporating material on research papers transferred from the old Chapter 2. Students are given complete information on how to access the library's reference tools, including databases and computer catalogues, and advice on how and when to use the Internet for research purposes. Model essays following current manuscript formats will serve as style templates for student essays. In addition, the new edition stresses word-processing technology, online research, information about library databases, deep Internet searches, and electronic sources, explaining how to assess them for use in an academic context.
- **Chapter 4—Plagiarism and Documentation Overview:** The chapter's new title reflects the increased coverage of plagiarism demanded by the text's many reviewers. New content describes the importance of proper documentation. Techniques to avoid plagiarism are detailed (and can be downloaded from the text's website for easy student reference). The rest of the chapter presents an introduction to documentation, which has been moved to the front of the book to give it the prominence it deserves.

- **Chapters 5 to 8—Documentation Styles:** Manageable, separate chapters replace the first edition's mammoth 98-page unit on documentation styles. Students will be able to locate with ease all the information they need regarding the style required in their essays. Chapter 5 covers the Modern Language Association (MLA) style of documentation; Chapter 6, the American Psychological Association (APA) style; Chapter 7, the *Chicago Manual of Style*; and Chapter 8, the Council of Science Editors (CSE) and the Columbia Online Style (COS) manuals. The chapters have been closely revised and updated to reflect the latest versions of these guides, including the 15th edition of the *Chicago Manual* (2003), the 7th edition of CSE (2006), and the 2nd edition of COS (2006). More prominence is given to online documentation in each of these chapters, and dedicated essay examples are provided for the MLA, APA, and Chicago chapters.
- **Chapters 9 to 11—Grammar, Common Sentence Errors, and Punctuation:** The overall approach of these chapters has been geared toward the new theme, "Writing Tools." These are chapters students need to master before and during the writing of their essays. Special efforts have been made to ensure that topics are dealt with in the most logical chapter.
- **Chapters 12 to 14—Sentence Structure and Style, Usage, and Mechanics and Spelling:** These chapters have been revised with the new theme "Editing Tools" in mind. They are chapters that students should consult in preparing a final draft. Some material from the old "Common Sentence Errors" chapters has been moved to "Sentence Structure and Style," as reviewers felt it required more sophisticated explanation.
- **Chapter 15—ESL:** The chapter on English as a second language has been moved from the middle of the book to the very end. Representing an overview of very technical issues, it can easily be accessed by ESL students in this new location.

Design

To ensure students can easily read and locate information, the visual look of *Checkmate* has been significantly revised. Colour has been added to make material more appealing and to reinforce some rules and examples. Blue type has been used to highlight correct or recommended examples, while red signals examples that are erroneous or in need of improvement.

Pedagogy

Helpful Menus, Tabs, and Index: This resource is designed to help students without a firm knowledge of grammar terminology find quick answers to their questions. It will be useful to students not only before submitting a paper, but after it is returned, as they respond to their instructor's comments. The index and tabs make it easy for users of this book to find the information they need to check their work.

Teaching by Example: Numerous sample research papers and writing formats have been added to *Checkmate*. More illustrations are included—for example, new Statistics Canada figures and tables to illustrate proper documentation style and new screenshots to illustrate online library research tools. One important innovation is that following examples of effective writing by well-known authors, bibliographic details are now supplied. Instead of appending just the author's name and the item title, *Checkmate* includes the author's name, the poem or article name, the book name, and the place, publisher, and year of publication. This level of detail is supplied to indicate *Checkmate*'s emphasis on the seriousness of proper documentation.

Addressing ESL Issues

Chapter 15 alerts students to special problems with English. There are also ESL notes throughout the text to indicate areas of special concern for those learners for whom English is not the first language.

ACKNOWLEDGMENTS

I extend my thanks to Anne Williams, Editor-in-Chief, whose generosity and hard work made the writing process manageable and even pleasant. Thanks also go to Laura Macleod, Executive Acquisitions Editor; Jaime Smith, Content Production Manager; Ferial Suleman, Senior Production Coordinator; Peter Papayanakis, Designer; Margaret Crammond, Copy Editor and Proofreader; Cynthia Howard, Permissions Coordinator; and Sandra Green, Marketing Manager. All these people have done splendid work all throughout the process.

I am especially grateful to two specialists whose contributions ensured the second edition of *Checkmate* reflects the latest developments in research and documentation. Patricia Buckley, MISt (Master of Information Studies), reviewed the research chapter and offered many constructive suggestions for updating online research in particular. Joan McKibbin of St. Lawrence College contributed substantially to this edition with her intensive review of Chapters 5 to 8, ensuring documentation materials reflected the latest versions of the different style guides and that the information was presented clearly and accurately.

The reviewers, who took time to read and help me revise, are also responsible for the improvements and innovations in this edition of *Checkmate*. I would like to thank all of these people for their efforts:

Peter Auksi, University of Western Ontario
Janice Burke, Sault College
James French, Fanshawe College
Lorrie Graham, University of Ottawa
Kam Jugdev, Athabasca University
Chris Legebow, St. Clair College
Gary Lipschutz, Centennial College
Kazem Mashkournia, Grande Prairie Regional College
Sandi Mills, Centennial College
Richard Moll, University of Western Ontario
Nine Pyne, Sault College
Phyllis Rozendal, York University
Marilyn Sorensen, Medicine Hat College
Mary Clare Vautour, New Brunswick Community College—Moncton

Lastly, I particularly would like to thank the students whose fine work appears in this volume, including Marie Kamel, Sharon McCulloch, Dan McKeown, Daniel Rosenfield, and Caitlin Williams. As always, I would like to thank my patient and helpful mother, Mary Buckley.

1 COMPOSING A DOCUMENT

I love being a writer. What I can't stand is the paperwork.

— Peter De Vries

1

Composing a Document

1 Composing a Document

For many of us, the hardest part is starting to write. Standing in front of a blank canvas, we are faced with overwhelming choices, if not about the subject matter of our work, which may have been assigned, then about its style, its tone, its wording, and the general approach we should take. The best advice is to learn to "divide and conquer." The best—and calmest—writers start with the large issues (subject matter, important ideas, research methods) and move to the smaller yet significant issues as the work proceeds. We can't get caught up in the details at the early stage. We need to allow ourselves room for mistakes—and for creativity. That way, we say something we want to say, as well as something that fits the occasion for which we are writing.

1-1: PLANNING

For most writers, even professional ones, reaching the ultimate goal of a persuasive, polished document demands a complex writing process. The process varies among writers, but generally includes the following three major stages.

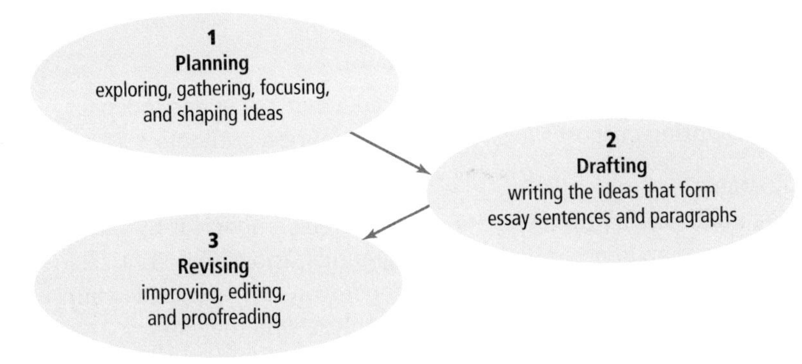

These stages often overlap as you develop and polish a piece of writing.

1-1A: ANALYZING THE WRITING TASK

The first step when planning any written document—and one that many fledgling writers neglect—is figuring out what is required.

Assessing the scope and requirements of the assignment or the goals of the finished document will help make the writing task manageable—even pleasurable—and, all-importantly, it will ensure that you satisfy your audience's expectations. Here are a few criteria and questions to consider as you analyze a writing task.

SUBJECT/TOPIC

The **subject** is what you are writing about. The **topic** is the specific aspect of the subject you will focus on in your writing.

- Has the topic been assigned, or are you free to explore your own topic?
- Why is this topic worth writing about? Why would you want to spend your time researching it and writing about it? And why would a reader want to spend his or her time reading about it?
- How do your own experiences, interests, and knowledge relate to the topic? What do you bring to the writing table?
- Does the topic need to be narrowed down to make it clearer and the writing task manageable?

PURPOSE

The **purpose** is what you are trying to accomplish in your writing.

- What is your writing purpose? To inform? Explain? Persuade? Express? Entertain? Or something else?
- Is it a combination of the above?
- If the writing topic has been assigned, what key words indicate the writing purposes (e.g., inform, summarize, outline)?

AUDIENCE

The **audience** is whom you are writing for. It's important to understand your audience members' backgrounds, knowledge, interests, attitudes, sensibilities, and expectations—you can't persuade your readers if you don't take the time to analyze who they are.

- Are you writing for a very specific audience, such as your instructor, or a wider audience, which could include your classmates or a wider readership?
- What might this audience already know about the topic?
- What is it important to tell them?
- How will you capture and maintain this particular audience's undivided attention and interest?

- How will you tell them about the important topic ideas and information? (It's not too early to start thinking about such writing considerations as formality of language and tone.)
- What writing features and techniques will most clearly communicate essential ideas and information to this specific audience?

SPECIFIC REQUIREMENTS

These are the considerations that help you make decisions about writing content, the way you spend your time, and even the appearance of your completed work.

DOCUMENT LENGTH

- How long is the written document required to be?
- If it's up to you to determine the length, what length would be appropriate, given the breadth of your topic and how deeply you intend to explore it? (Translation: Don't try to write the history of Christianity in 500 words.)

DEADLINES

- When is the document due? In large measure, this will determine the breadth and depth of content you can cover thoroughly. The deadline will also help you determine how much time to spend on each essential stage in the writing process.

DOCUMENT STYLE AND DESIGN

- Which document style and design does your audience or instructor require or prefer? Ask! Some subject instructors prefer the Modern Language Association (MLA) style, others the American Psychological Association (APA) or the *Chicago Manual of Style* (Chicago) style.
- Where do you find out about the preferred style and design specifications? Stay tuned. Our chapters on documentation will provide lots of specific advice on that score.

INFORMATION SOURCES

You're making headway. It's just about time to turn yourself loose on the topic.

- What kind of information will you need? Perhaps a literary work and critical commentary on that work, reports, text, or visuals from an Internet site, or your own experiences, observations, and insights?

- How should you acknowledge these information sources? Again, this book provides complete information. Maybe it's time to begin your research by scanning the book to find out what it offers and how it can meet your academic writing needs.

1-1B: GENERATING AND EXPLORING IDEAS

For any writer, just getting started can be intimidating. Accomplished writers often have a repertoire of strategies for generating and exploring ideas and, in some cases, starting to shape and connect thoughts to create new ideas. The idea-generating strategies outlined here include

- brainstorming and listing
- clustering and branching
- free-writing
- asking questions
- writing journal entries
- keeping a work diary

You are encouraged to try or at least consider them all. Then, choose the strategy or strategies that work best for you.

BRAINSTORMING AND LISTING

You might think of brainstorming as a group activity, but it can also be used while working alone to generate ideas for writing. It is similar to free-writing (see below), but it differs from free-writing in that what is written down is generally a list of phrases and, sometimes, just words.

If your writing topic has been established for you, start with it; or, if you can choose your topic, begin with a subject that interests you. Give yourself a set amount of time in which to list freely *all* the ideas relating to the subject that come into your mind. Don't try to censor or criticize any of the list items. At this point, your goal is quantity, not quality. Here is a brainstorm list on working dogs.

Working Dogs
- history of dogs
- breed characteristics
- hazardous situations
- avalanche rescue dogs
- fire protection dogs
- amazing sense of smell

- they hear extremely well, too
- dogs that sniff suitcases at airports
- pet visitation dogs at hospitals
- human–animal bond

When the time you have given yourself is up, and only then, take a critical look at your brainstormed list. Reject weak or irrelevant ideas, add any new ideas that occur to you, and start looking for idea patterns and linkages. This kind of shaping and organizing is a preliminary step to the writing outline.

CLUSTERING AND BRANCHING

The goal of clustering and branching is not just to put ideas on paper or on the screen, but to start showing possible relationships between ideas. To start clustering, put a key subject word at the top or centre of a blank page. Look for ideas related to the key word and connect them to it, and to other ideas, using circles and lines. Let your mind explore all possible associations freely. Here is a sample cluster to generate ideas for an essay on "People I Admire."

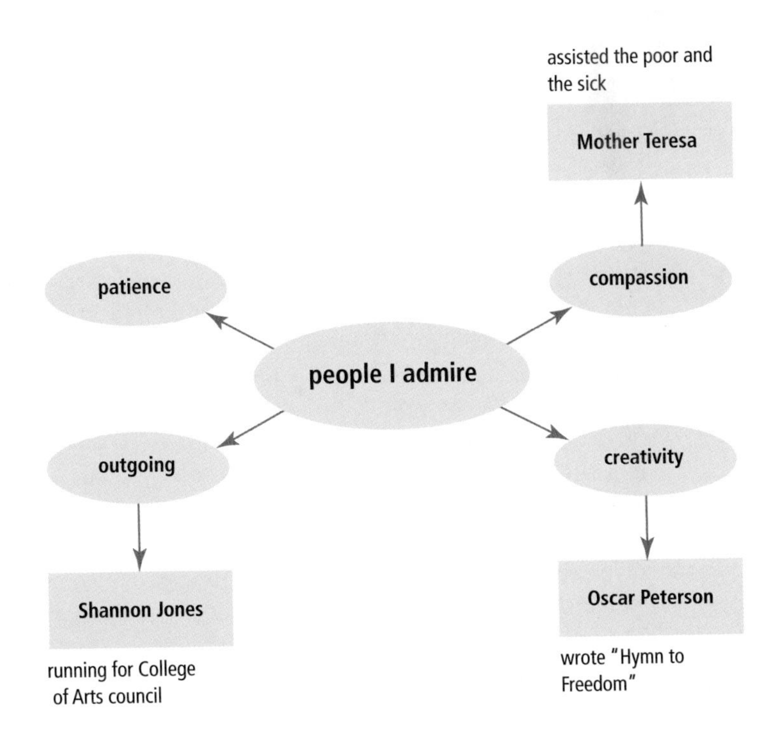

Note that the person who generated this cluster used different shapes to designate different types of ideas. Someone else might use colour-coding to group ideas and show the relationships between them.

Branching is another strategy for generating ideas and showing how they are linked. To create a branch diagram, put your topic at the top of a blank page, with your main ideas branching from it. Next, write in any supporting ideas and details on branches below each main idea. Extend the branching options as far as you think necessary.

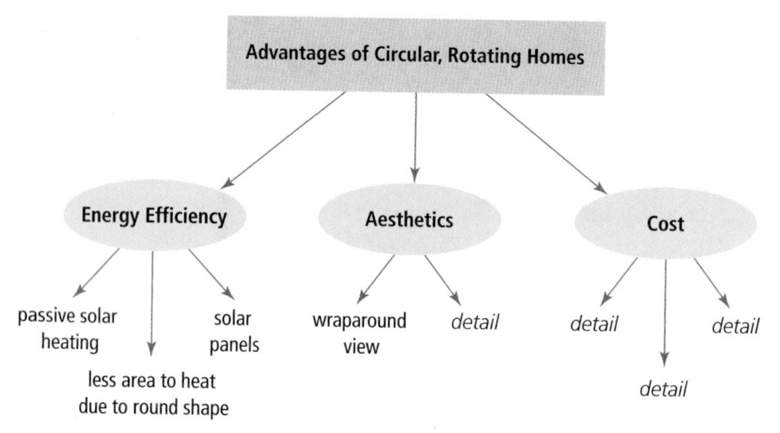

FREE-WRITING

Free-writing is writing freely for a set period of time—say, five to ten minutes—or in a given amount of space—say, part of a page or a whole page—about a very general subject. Ideas should flow out uncensored and without concern for spelling, grammar, or punctuation. The important goals are to keep going and to be open to a process of discovery. Then, after you've met your time or space quota, review what you've written and try to see any patterns, topics, or ideas that look interesting enough to develop in a piece of writing. You can free-write in longhand on paper or by typing into a computer. It's best to use the writing mode in which you are most proficient so you can keep the ideas flowing. One-fingered, incompetent typing defeats the purpose of rapid free-writing. If you're happy with the keyboard, though, it can ensure that your ideas are saved and secure.

ASKING QUESTIONS

At this initial stage of the writing process, it's a good idea to think like a journalist. Reporters are known for probing subjects by asking the 5 Ws and H, which is short for *who, what, where, when, why,* and *how.* Suppose you're writing an explanatory essay for an environmental studies course on a new, energy-efficient, circular, rotating home. Some questions you might ask are

Who designed this revolutionary home?

What are the environmental advantages of the new design?

Where would the home be most energy efficient?

When will it be available to the general public?

Why was it designed?

How does it work?

Your first set of questions can easily lead to other questions that will help you identify even more ideas. For instance, another *who* question might be this one:

Who will need the new product?

Often, academic disciplines have special questions that are asked consistently by researchers and analysts in these fields. For example, in English Literature, you might be asked "What is the central theme of the work?" Try to identify key questions in any discipline you're studying. They come in handy when generating ideas for papers in that discipline.

JOURNAL WRITING

Journal writing is similar to free-writing in that it gives you complete latitude to express yourself. The key goal is to get those ideas down on paper. The main difference is that your journal-writing entries are made on a regular basis. Entries might record

- your observations
- interesting ideas and facts learned from reading
- your reactions to course content
- connections you've made between ideas

These are just a few possibilities. Keeping a journal has many advantages.

1. It gives you practice articulating your thoughts.
2. It strengthens your powers of observation and memory.
3. It provides you with a record of ideas when you need them for writing assignments.

You may wish to experiment with ideas in your journal before you try incorporating them into a formal draft.

> *Oct 10.* The girl in biology I have a crush on said she was a real Robert Ludlum fan. I said I had a copy of his latest book that I could lend her. Of course, I didn't. I must have gone to every bookstore in Victoria looking for a copy. They were all sold out. Finally I got one in the local Shoppers Drug Mart. I dog-eared it so it looked like I'd read it about six times. When I gave the book to her, she was pretty cold. Suddenly I understood what James Joyce meant in "Araby" when he said, "I saw myself as a creature driven and derided by vanity." I now have a pretty good sense of what epiphany means too.

WORK DIARY

A work diary may include notes of what you are reading in preparation for writing. It is intended to catalogue the accumulated sources you delve into and your insights into them as you go along. Having the habit of keeping a work diary increases your awareness of how the things you are writing fit together into a whole.

1-1C: FOCUSING ON A THESIS OR A PURPOSE

After thinking broadly to collect as many ideas related to your writing topic as you can, it's time to begin focusing your thoughts to frame a controlling idea called a **thesis.** A **thesis statement** alerts your reader to the main argument of the essay and prepares him or her, in a general way, for the content that is to follow. A good thesis statement states your case as clearly as it can in a sentence or so. In an academic essay, a thesis statement should be just that—a statement—and not a question. It provides the answer, generally, to the questions you had in mind as you explored the topic. It presents your educated opinion on the topic, and ideally, has a controversial edge. You are writing, after all, to settle a question—perhaps not definitively, but to the best of your ability. An essay typically presents evidence to support your thesis statement. Hence, the thesis statement is an educated opinion about the facts, or the evidence, that you have found in your research and your thinking on the subject. The thesis will hold the entire essay together, so it needs to be a forcefully defended statement of your findings on a subject.

Developing such a focus is crucial in essays, but not just in essays. Even in report writing, the reader expects you to provide a purpose statement. In the purpose statement, you make your final recommendations in general known to the reader, upfront, without any suspense; the detailed report that follows is thus a defence of your recommendations and provides detailed support.

Let's look at a few examples of report purpose statements and essay thesis statements:

> This report will show how the new electronic filing system has benefited the company by increasing data storage and saving search time.

> Genetically modified foods need to be labelled in order to protect Canada's population from potential long-term dangers to health and to the environment.

> Yann Martel's *Life of Pi* demonstrates how magic realism has become a literary form that transcends cultural boundaries and the limits of contemporary time and place by reducing us to our limited humanity in the face of nature.

> The self-fulfilling prophecy helps shape social reality often through a combination of stereotypes and expectations based on ability in school.

Note that most writers of essays published in newspapers also have a thesis, but theirs may not follow the rigours of clarity demanded in an academic or business setting. In journalism, the reader is more apt to be voluntary rather than captive, and more willing to sort out meaning. Hence, you may find a great deal more latitude in published essays of a non-academic type. Unlike students, these writers may more freely use questions, broad implications, or sweeping statements to serve as the thesis or purpose statement in the writing.

When generating your preliminary thesis statement, you might ask the following questions, though you may not be able to satisfy all of these requirements.

- Does your thesis statement provide an **assertion** in which you state clearly your topic and your position on the topic?
- Is your thesis statement too broad, making it difficult to defend?

- Does it give a sense of your purpose (to persuade, explain, describe, entertain)?
- Does your thesis statement give the reader a sense of how you will organize and present your argument?
- Does your thesis statement relate to the themes and overall direction of the course materials assigned? In other words, does it fit the context of the course? Does it engage in the themes of the course?
- Does your thesis statement go beyond the facts to present an argument based on your educated opinion about the facts?

It's important to remember that you're engaged in a writing *process*. Good thesis statements don't just drop out of the sky. They're the result of ongoing revision and refinement.

As you progressively hone your outline and more precisely focus your ideas, you will probably need to refine your thesis statement.

Preliminary Thesis Statement
Circular, rotating homes offer users many advantages.

More Refined Thesis Statement
Circular, rotating homes offer significant advantages in terms of energy efficiency, building costs, and the aesthetics of design.

Notice that the words *significant* and *in terms of* limit the topic and focus it more precisely. To a large extent, a thesis statement frames the choices you make about content. The thesis statement usually comes within the first paragraph in the final sentence or sentences.

In certain writing situations, such as essays with a non-academic purpose, a thesis statement may be too confining, and writers may need more latitude to introduce a theme or spark a reader's interest. This can be seen in the following introduction from David Adams Richards's "My Old Newcastle."

> In Newcastle, New Brunswick, which I call home, we all played on the ice floes in the spring, spearing tommy-cod with stolen forks tied to sticks. More than one of us almost met our end slipping off the ice.
>
> —David Adams Richards, "My Old Newcastle" in *A Lad from Brantford and Other Essays* (Fredericton, NB: Broken Jaw Press, 1994).

1-1D: FORMULATING A WRITING PLAN

PRELIMINARY ORGANIZATIONAL PLAN

Now that you've generated writing ideas and a thesis statement to define your topic, you may want to create a preliminary outline to frame a general structure for ideas. In this first, tentative outline, organize your ideas into categories under your thesis statement.

> ***Thesis:*** Independent-study high schools provide a better education because they prepare students for university by combining freedom with responsibility.
>
> ***Disadvantages***
> - Immature students may take advantage of the greater freedom.
> - Students forfeit many opportunities for discussions and group projects.
> - The social element of the educational experience is limited.
>
> ***Advantages***
> - Students who have had educational difficulties are removed from the classroom context of failure.
> - Scheduling flexibility accommodates mature students or those who have had medical difficulties.
> - Students are better prepared for the university experience, where they will be largely unsupervised.
> - Students are allowed to take complete responsibility for their own learning.

If you completed a branching diagram to generate ideas, you'll have noticed that it's a small next step to a preliminary outline. Also, notice that this writer is starting to organize her ideas persuasively by placing her strongest points last. Tentative outlines can be used at a number of points in the writing process. For example, when drafting or revising, you might get a sense that there are problems with the logic or focus of your writing. Creating a rough outline will help you identify and fix these writing problems.

FORMAL WRITING OUTLINE

The formal outline differs from the preliminary outline in its level of detail. The formal outline should be flexible enough so as not to be too limiting, but it should show clearly the logical flow of your ideas or arguments. Like informal outlines, formal outlines are generally created in the planning stage of the writing process, but they can be created while drafting or even revising if you sense your writing is losing focus or logical flow.

Here is a formal outline for a very short persuasive essay on xenotransplantation (the use of animal organs in human transplants).

> ***Thesis:*** Transplanting organs from animals to humans is unacceptable because it is a cruel practice, it is unsafe, and it is unethical.
>
> I. Animal Cruelty
>   A. It is cruel to raise animals solely to harvest their organs.
>   B. We already raise animals for purposes such as food and clothing (leather).
>
> II. Risk of Disease Spreading from Animals to Humans
>   A. AIDS is thought to have spread to humans from monkeys.
>   B. Mad cow disease spread from sheep to cows.
>   C. Insulin from sheep has been used for over seventy-five years without presenting any immunological problems.
>
> III. Ethical Issues
>   A. We should not open a Pandora's box by introducing possible risks we do not understand.
>   B. It would be unethical to deny people who are suffering from medical problems such as diabetes or liver disease the possibility of improving their quality of life and in some cases saving their lives.

To generate a formal outline, do the following:

1. Begin your outline by writing your thesis statement at the top of the page.
2. Next, write the Roman numerals I, II, and III, spread apart, down the left side of the page.
3. Beside each Roman numeral, write one main idea that you have about your topic, or a main point that you want to make.
    a) If you are trying to persuade, you will want to write your best arguments.
    b) If you are trying to explain a process, you will want to write the steps to follow. (You will probably need to group these into categories. If you have trouble doing this, try using Beginning, Middle, and End.)
    c) If you are trying to inform, you may want to write the major categories into which your information can be divided. (For more detail on types of organization, see 1-3c.)
4. Under each Roman numeral, write A, B, and C down the left side of the page.
5. Next to each letter, write the fact or piece of information that relates to the main idea. Note that the information used may either support or refute the thesis, since the writer must manage all information, pro and con, related to the argument.

6. If you are adding more minor levels of ideas and information to the outline, under the alphabet letters, write numbers, and under these, lowercase letters.

   The traditional outline follows this pattern:

I. Introduction to classification of headaches
II. Kinds of headaches
    A. Vascular
        1. Migraines
        2. Cluster headaches
        3. High-blood-pressure headaches
    B. Myogenic
        1. Tension headaches
        2. Muscle aches of the neck or head
    C. Headaches from specific causes
        1. Ictal headaches
            a. seizure-related
            b. usually affect one side of the head
                (1) easily misdiagnosed
                (2) often mistaken as psychotic symptom
                    (a) detected with EEG
                    (b) treated with anticonvulsants

Here are a few guidelines.

- Each outline level should have more than one entry.
- Entries should be parallel grammatically if phrases are used.
- Outlines should remain flexible. Remember, you're still in the *planning* process, and often plans have to be adjusted. The outline does not have to be followed rigidly.

1-2: DRAFTING THE DOCUMENT: CREATING A STRUCTURE

The drafting stage is where all your planning pays off, because many of your critical writing decisions have been made, freeing you to think, write, and discover. **Drafting** is putting your ideas on paper in logically connected, coherent paragraphs composed of clear sentences.

But don't put too much pressure on yourself at this point. This part is called a **rough draft** for a reason. Once the rough draft is complete, you still have the revision stage to improve, edit, and proofread—in essence, to craft the rough draft into a finely polished piece of writing.

As you sit down to begin drafting (or stand, if you're Ernest Hemingway), ensure your writing resources are arranged meaningfully at your workstation. Resources might include these items:

- outlines
- index cards
- quotations with accompanying citations
- visuals such as diagrams and graphs

Writing quickly and maintaining a good momentum are important when drafting. And nothing can interrupt the flow of ideas more than having to stop to hunt for a scrap of paper on which you have noted a key supporting idea.

Generally, there are three major parts, or elements, to a piece of academic writing:

1. An **introduction** that engages the reader and introduces the controlling idea
2. A **body** that develops ideas logically and coherently and incorporates convincing supporting evidence
3. A **conclusion** that follows logically from the introduction and body and presents a summary or generalization

1-2A: DRAFTING AN INTRODUCTION

The introduction is your opening paragraph, which usually ranges between 100 and 150 words. The introduction should have these main goals:

1. To engage the reader, generating interest that will make him or her want to read further
2. To describe your topic, point of view, and the main points you will cover in the body of your document

To engage or hook the reader, you might consider using one of the following in your introduction:

- an anecdote, illustration, or incident
- background historical information
- a rhetorical question
- humour
- an analogy
- an apparent contradiction or ironic statement
- a shocking or unusual fact or statistic
- a quotation
- a description

Writers use a thesis statement to describe their topic, point of view, and the main points they will cover. Generally, a thesis statement is the last sentence in the introduction, though that is not a rigid rule.

In the following introductions, see if you can identify the hooks used by the writers. Ask yourself how well these hooks work to establish interest in what will follow. (The thesis statement of each introduction appears in italics.)

> A central feature of Alice Munro's literary technique is her use of paradox. Paradox may be understood as "an apparently self-contradictory statement which, on closer inspection, is found to contain a truth reconciling opposites."[1] In "Dulse" Munro contrasts romantic and empirical perspectives as embodied in Mr. Stanley and the telephone workers, respectively. Lydia moves to the realization that, exclusively, neither of these contradictory outlooks sufficiently defines the complexity of experience. *By examining in "Dulse" the relationship of style, point of view, structure, and imagery to paradox, one achieves an appreciation of how these technical features sustain Alice Munro's thematic insistence on the doubleness of reality.*
>
> —Carla Thorneloe, student

> A common criticism of the Internet is that it is dominated by the crude, the uninformed, the immature, the smug, the untalented, the repetitious, the pathetic, the hostile, the deluded, the self-righteous and the shrill. *This criticism overlooks the fact that the Internet also offers—to the savvy individual who knows where to look—the tasteless and the borderline insane.*
>
> —Dave Barry, *Dave Barry in Cyberspace*
> (New York: Crown Publishers, 1996).

QUALITIES OF A COMPELLING THESIS STATEMENT

Enough emphasis cannot be given to the importance of the thesis statement. In the thesis statement you should present a generalization about your topic. While it is a generalization, it should not be too broad, and the statement must be focused enough to avoid vagueness.

A weak thesis statement can play havoc with your drafting efforts, leaving you spinning your writing wheels without direction—

or worse, heading off futilely in too many directions. Keep your general aim in mind.

Avoid making thesis statements that are

- too factual or statistical
- too broad
- too vague

A thesis statement that is too factual cannot be argued, and it fails to give your reader an indication of the direction your content will take.

> ***Too Factual:*** At eighteen, Ty Tryon is the youngest full-time member in the history of the PGA tour.
>
> ***Improvement:*** Allowing teenagers to participate full-time in professional sports cannot be justified psychologically, educationally, and above all, morally.

Don't make your thesis or purpose statement too broad; otherwise, you will be expected to deliver on all your writing promises, and this will not be possible given deadline and assignment-length requirements.

> ***Too Broad:*** Recreational running has countless benefits.
>
> ***Improvement:*** Recent research indicates that regular recreational running has demonstrable physiological, psychological, and social benefits.

The thesis statement should have a clear and precise focus.

> ***Too Vague:*** Robertson Davies develops a universal human theme in his novel *Fifth Business*.
>
> ***Improvement:*** In Robertson Davies's *Fifth Business*, the opposition of imagination and "practicality" is dramatized through the worlds of the theatre and small-town Ontario. The paper will examine the tension between these two forces by examining the career of Paul Dempster/Magnus Eisengrim, the conflicts within the character of Dunstan Ramsay, and the narrator's description of the contrast between the theatre and the small town of Deptford.

The above thesis statement actually "blueprints" the essay content, informing the reader exactly what major points will be covered in the essay or report.

It's important to remember that generating a thesis statement is a recursive process: you must expect to go back and forth between the drafting and revising stages a number of times. For example, the writer of the last, improved thesis statement may have revised his thesis statement to reflect his content more accurately, or he may have shaped his content better to reflect the controlling idea of his thesis statement—or maybe he did both.

Once you've crafted a workable, focused thesis statement, there should be a seamless, logical transition into the body of your essay or report.

1-2B: DRAFTING THE BODY

As you draft the body, review your thesis statement and formal outline, if you are using one. Every body paragraph should be related either directly or indirectly to the intention outlined in your thesis statement.

If the document is very short, you might cover each lettered topic in one well-organized paragraph. Or, if you have the luxury of more space, you might break a main point down and cover it in a series of closely related paragraphs.

You might approach drafting the body in two stages:

1. First, concentrate on developing the paragraphs so they provide enough evidence and detail to support each key point. At this stage, follow the focus and direction of your outline, but be open to in-process writing discoveries that might lead to even better key points and hence different paragraphs.
2. After this initial rough drafting of the body, take a step back from your work and assess how well blocks of paragraphs work together as a unit and how well transitions between paragraphs are made. Then, make changes needed to achieve greater unity and balance. If this were a painting, it would mean sketching the broad figures and general composition of your work, then using a fine paintbrush to give better definition to the figures of your composition.

1-2C: DRAFTING THE CONCLUSION

Your final paragraph should be concise and echo what you have just told your readers, at the same time drawing a logical conclusion that relates to your thesis. Don't mechanically use the same words you used in your introduction. However, you may wish to pick up a few key words to create an "echo effect."

A good conclusion should have impact and be memorable. To achieve these goals, you might try one of the strategies on page 18.

Strategies for Creating a Strong Conclusion

- Indicate how all your main points strongly—even inevitably—point to your central thesis.
- Propose a solution to a problem.
- Offer a call to action.
- Refer to an anecdote or quotation you used in your introduction.
- Use a poetic turn of phrase.
- Provide a summary of the main arguments.
- Offer a commentary on the argument.
- Restate the thesis, usually in different words.

Never introduce new facts, ideas, and arguments in the conclusion. And avoid hesitancy and uncertainty about the ideas expressed in your conclusion. To make a musical analogy, you've structured your ideas and arguments to a crescendo and raised reader expectations, so don't let them down by ending with a barely audible peep. Rather, offer a conclusion that is confident, strong, and above all positive.

1-3: WRITING PARAGRAPHS

Let's focus on how to compose the very important paragraphs that make up the body of your document. They are different in purpose than the special-function paragraphs that introduce and conclude your essay or report. (See 1-2a and 1-2c on the functions of introductory and concluding paragraphs.) Paragraphs in the body contain arguments, ideas, and information to develop and support the main points of the essay or report. These paragraphs must

- have unity
- be fully and well developed
- have appropriate and logical organization
- be coherent
- have appropriate and easily digestible length (perhaps five to twelve sentences)

1-3A: KEEPING THE FOCUS OF THE ESSAY

You achieve unity within a paragraph by ensuring that all sentences within the paragraph relate to its central idea or main point.

STATING THE MAIN POINT IN THE TOPIC SENTENCE

Just as your entire essay is framed by a thesis statement or statement of purpose, each paragraph within the body should have a **topic sentence.** The topic sentence is usually the first sentence of the paragraph. It states the main point or controlling idea of the paragraph and prepares the reader for what follows in the rest of the paragraph. Here is a unified paragraph from a piece celebrating the life of the late Pierre Elliott Trudeau. The topic sentence appears in italics.

> *He was no neuter.* It is one of the grandest things we will say of his memory that, at times, he antagonized as much as he inspired; our affection for Pierre Trudeau was turbulent and always interesting. If citizens of this day lament that leadership is a game of polls and cozy focus groups there will always be the example of this man to remind us that convictions can be set in bedrock, and that adherence to principles is the most enduring charisma.
>
> —Rex Murphy, "Pierre Trudeau: He Has Gone to His Grace," http://www.cbc.ca/national/rex/rex20000928.html, September 28, 2000.

Topic sentences can be placed at other positions within the paragraph, such as the end, or they might even be implied. And sometimes they are not needed—for instance, when the unity of sentences within the paragraph is already so remarkable that a topic sentence would only state the obvious and interrupt the flow of ideas.

You might note that many accomplished professional writers do not always use topic sentences in their paragraphs. For them, the topic sentence can be an overly obvious signpost. Writing assignments in a school setting aim more at clarity than at subtlety, so err on the side of clarity, for best results.

For writers in an academic or a business setting, it is wise to use the topic sentence—especially when drafting—to ensure that paragraphs are unified and do not stray from your topic.

KEEPING TO THE MAIN POINT IN THE TOPIC SENTENCE

Any sentence within a paragraph that does not relate to the topic sentence undermines the paragraph's unity and focus, and should be deleted. The sentence may need to be shifted elsewhere, or it might become the basis of a new essential point and demand a separate paragraph. In the paragraph below, the sentence in italics clearly does not support the topic sentence, nor does it relate meaningfully to other sentences in the paragraph.

> While the Nanaimo Estuary is important to the forest industry, it is equally vital to the local fisheries. The estuary accounts for 25 percent of the catch in Georgia Strait fishing. It is one of the vital links in the life cycle of Nanaimo River salmon. *Recently, a firm selling bungee jumping experiences opened for business in a canyon along the Nanaimo River.* The estuary, then, is instrumental in the maintenance of fish which support commercial fishing, freshwater sport fishing, tidal sport fishing, and the Native food industry.

In a few instances, while drafting a paragraph, you may find your sentences naturally stray from the topic sentence to explain essential ideas relating to your topic. Writing is not always linear, slavish to a rigid plan. Don't censor yourself at this stage; go with the drafting flow. Once the paragraph is complete, you may have to revise the topic sentence to better reflect the true course of your paragraph's thoughts and sentences.

1-3B: MAKING YOUR POINT

Once you've drafted a paragraph, these writing questions arise:

- What is the optimum length?
- How much is too much?
- How much is not enough?

The common answer to these questions comes from the amount of development that your paragraph topic, or main point, requires. Paragraph development is the specific evidence and information needed to support successfully the generalization presented in your paragraph's topic sentence.

The length of your paragraph, and consequently the development that is required, may vary depending on these important considerations:

- ***Audience:*** A very young audience may require less supporting detail, whereas an older or unsympathetic audience may require a great deal of evidence to persuade it of the merit of your topic sentence's main point.
- ***Purpose:*** If your purpose is to persuade, an argument may need considerable development to convince your reader.

- ***Form:*** If you are writing for a newspaper, paragraphs are generally short; if you are writing for an academic or professional journal, paragraphs tend to be longer.

After drafting paragraphs, it's important to assess whether or not they are adequately developed. Let's consider a sample writing situation. In an issue of a Canadian fertility association journal, Dr. Janet Takefman writes about the psychological factors involved in the way men deal with infertility problems.

For such a topic, audience, purpose, and form, the following paragraph—which Dr. Takefman did not write—would be inadequately developed.

Lacks Adequate Paragraph Development

Generally, the way men react to fertility problems is taken a lot less seriously than the way women do. Men are not permitted to grieve, largely because society does not allow them the freedom to express their emotions openly.

The above paragraph is sketchy and underdeveloped, failing to clarify why men's reactions to fertility problems are taken less seriously than women's reactions. Now consider the following paragraph, which Dr. Takefman did write, and which reflects good paragraph development.

Good Paragraph Development

In general, the man's reaction to infertility has been viewed by mental health professionals as taking less of an emotional toll than his partner's. His reaction to his own infertility is often construed as interdependent with his partner's. Thus if she is coping well with it, he will follow accordingly. However, if she is having a difficult time, then his emotional stability will be compromised. His primary role is often relegated to that of a hand-holder, in charge of providing support for his partner during her grieving process. Little room is left for dealing with his own feelings of loss and sadness. This conforms with society's gender expectations in which men are not given permission to express deep feelings of loss; on the contrary, they are encouraged to suppress emotions. Thus, together society and the medical profession inadvertently conspire to ignore or underestimate the man's responsibility and role in the infertility process.

—Janet Takefman, "Psychological Issues in Male Factor Infertility," *Journal of the Infertility Awareness Association of Canada*, Volume 3 (October), 1996, p. 17.

A good way to test whether or not your paragraph is adequately developed is to have someone who fits the profile of the intended audience read the paragraph and provide feedback on how well it is developed. Another good strategy is to ask someone to read your work for you and let you know where what you have said does not make sense.

1-3C: SELECTING SUITABLE PARAGRAPH STRUCTURES

In addition to adequately developing each paragraph, you need to organize ideas within paragraphs appropriately. "Organize appropriately" means to organize ideas and information so they communicate your meaning the most effectively. Choosing a particular structure will help you keep your focus clear in your mind. The paragraph organization should be consistent with the overall purpose of your writing assignment. For example, if your assigned or chosen writing task is to create a piece in which you describe the landscape of Cape Breton, then paragraphs within your document should follow a *descriptive* pattern or **method of development.**

There are many patterns of paragraph organization and even more possible combinations. (Of course, authors often combine paragraph organization patterns to achieve their communication goals.) In the following pages, you will see some of the more common paragraph organization patterns:

- narration
- description
- definition
- classification and division
- process analysis
- comparison and contrast
- cause and effect
- examples and illustrations
- analogy
- argumentation or persuasion

NARRATION

Narration is storytelling. In a narrative paragraph, the writer tells all or part of a story, usually following the order in which events occurred (chronological order). In the following paragraph, an acclaimed Canadian poet narrates a story about her mother's working life.

> When I was eight Mom found a job at the outdoor swimming pool, lifting heavy baskets stuffed with shoes and clothing to their

numbered place on the four-tiered shelves, lifting them down again when the swimmers plunked their metal tags on the counter and claimed their belongings to get dressed. It was hard and menial work, but it was a paying job, and she finally had money of her own. She also did "day work," the name then given to cleaning other people's houses, and in the winter she sold tickets at the Bronco hockey games. After her first paycheck, I don't think she ever asked my father for grocery money again.

—Lorna Crozier, "What Stays in the Family"
in *Dropped Threads: An Anthology of Women's Writing,* edited by Marjorie Anderson and Carol Shields (Toronto: Vintage Canada, 2000).

DESCRIPTION

In a descriptive paragraph, the writer uses words evocatively to create a picture of a place, person, event, thing, or possibly a mood or idea. Details within the paragraph often appeal to the reader's senses. In the paragraph below, writer Andrew Ward describes the devastating effects of an oil spill on bird life along the North American west coast.

But even the hardiest birds were languishing. You can tell if a bird is dehydrated by the protrusion of its keel, and if it's anemic the inside of its beak turns bright orange. Some of the sickest birds lay apart from the huddled groups with their oily wings outstretched. You noticed them blinking their eyes more slowly, or holding their beaks open as if gulping for air. Some grasped feebly at the fish that was offered and then shook their heads, as if politely declining. They bunched together in the corners of the pens: some of them, I think, to keep warm, or maybe they had just followed the plane of a plywood wall, trying to escape.

—Andrew Ward, "Oil and Water"
in *Out Here: A Newcomer's Notes from the Great Northwest* (Harmondsworth, UK: Penguin, 1991).

DEFINITION

At certain points within an essay or report, you may need to define or clarify keywords or key terms in your composition. Often, this can be done in a few sentences, but occasionally it will require an entire paragraph. The paragraph below serves to define for the reader exactly how the writer will use a term within the context of her entire essay.

> The word "addiction" is often used loosely and wryly in conversation. People will refer to themselves as "mystery book addicts" or "cookie addicts." E.B. White writes of his annual surge of interest in gardening: "We are hooked and are making an attempt to kick the habit." Yet nobody really believes that reading mysteries or ordering seeds by catalogue is serious enough to be compared with addictions to heroin or alcohol. The word "addiction" is here used jokingly to denote a tendency to overindulge in some pleasurable activity.
>
> —Marie Winn, "Television Addiction" in *The Plug-in Drug: Television, Computers, and Family Life* (New York: Viking, 1977).

CLASSIFICATION AND DIVISION

Classification involves grouping items such as ideas, people, facts, or things according to some system of classification, known as the **basis of classification**. In the paragraph below, the basis for the classification is loneliness.

> Lonely Places are the places that don't fit in; the places that have no seat at our international dinner tables; the places that fall between the cracks on our tidy acronyms (EEC and OPEC, OAS and NATO). Cuba is the island that no one thinks of as West Indian; Iceland is the one that isn't really part of Europe.
>
> Australia is the odd place that no one knows whether to call an island or a continent; North Korea is the one that gives the lie to every generality about East Asian vitality and growth. Lonely Places are the exceptions that prove every rule: they are ascetics, castaways, and secessionists; prisoners, anchorites, and solipsists.
>
> —Pico Iyer, *Falling Off the Map: Some Lonely Places of the World* (New York: Vintage Departures, 1993).

In the division method of paragraph organization, the writer separates something into its elements to better understand the entity.

> Choral music is performed by groups of singers, called a choir or chorus, in which there is more than one voice to a part. A group with only one voice to a part is called an ensemble. A choir may consist of women only, men only (or boys and men) or may be

mixed, with both women and men. The voice parts in a mixed choir are usually soprano, alto, tenor, and bass. There is choral music for 8-part (or more) mixed choirs where the sections are subdivided into first and second soprano, first and second alto, first and second tenor, baritone and bass. The voices with the higher tessitura are designated by the term "first." Sometimes a descant (an ornamental line usually higher than the soprano) is added, most often to the harmony to enhance the sound but not to cover the voices.

—Isabelle Mills, "Choral Music"
in *The Canadian Encyclopedia: Year 2000 Edition* (Toronto: McClelland & Stewart, 2000).

PROCESS ANALYSIS

In a process analysis paragraph, the writer analyzes and explains how something works or how to do or make something. The paragraph pattern closely follows the chronological pattern in the process being described. Put one essential step out of sequence, or miss a step, and the reader can be in big trouble. In this paragraph, the writer describes how to cook spinach:

> The trick with spinach, I know, is to cook it as little as possible. Just grab a handful, chop off the heaviest stems, run cold water over what you have left and, without shaking it dry, pop it into a saucepan, jam the lid on and cook on high for *one minute*—Northern Dancer's time for five furlongs. Want to get fancy? Squeeze half a lemon over the spinach before you start to steam it. Want to get *really really* fancy? Plop a dash of sour cream on top as you bring your spinach to the table. With either or neither or both, it's wonderful.

—Peter Gzowski, "And the Best Damn Stew-Maker Too"
in *Selected Columns from* Canadian Living (Toronto: McClelland & Stewart, 1993).

COMPARISON AND CONTRAST

When you make comparisons, you usually examine similarities, although the dictionary meaning of compare also includes consideration of differences. When you contrast two entities, you focus exclusively on their differences. Juggling comparisons between two things you are writing about can be challenging.

There are two major approaches to organizing comparison and contrast paragraphs effectively. In the first method, sometimes called the block method, you deal first with one subject and then the other. In the following paragraph, the writer uses this method to present his response to changes in how we use phones.

> It's the cell phone, of course, that's putting the pay phone out of business. The pay phone is to the cell phone as the troubled and difficult older sibling is to the cherished newborn. People even treat their cell phones like babies, cradling them in their palms and beaming down upon them lovingly as they dial. You sometimes hear people yelling on their cell phones, but almost never yelling at them. Cell phones are toylike, nearly magic, and we get a huge kick out of them, as often happens with technological advances until the new wears off. Somehow I don't believe people had a similar honeymoon period with pay phones back in their early days, and they certainly have no such enthusiasm for them now. When I see the cell-phone user gently push the little antenna and fit the phone back into its brushed-vinyl carrying case and tuck the case inside his jacket beside his heart, I feel sorry for the beat-up pay phone standing in the rain.
>
> —Ian Frazier, "Dearly Disconnected,"
> *Mother Jones* (January–February 2000),
> http://www.motherjones.com/news/feature/2000/01/disconnected.html

In the point-by-point method, the elements of the two items being compared are dealt with at the same time, point by point, as can be seen in the following paragraph.

> If you drop a stone into the ocean the impact is as great as if you drop it into a farmer's pond. The difference is that the ocean doesn't seem to care. It swallows the stone and rolls on. But the pond, if the stone is large enough, breaks into waves and ripples that cover its surface and are audible in every cranny along its banks.
>
> So it is with life in a metropolis and life in a small town. It takes a colossal event to affect a city. After the bombing of Hamburg in which eighty thousand people were killed, the city was functioning within a few days. Grief did not paralyse it because, to the survivors, most of the casualties were people they had never met. But a single murder can convulse a small town for the reason that in

> such a community people care who lives and who dies. They care because they know each other. All knowledge is relative to our capacity to grasp its details, and no matter what the communists and industrial organizers may say, no man can think humanly if he thinks in terms of masses. In the small town, and not in the metropolis, human life is understood in fundamental terms.
>
> —Hugh MacLennan, "If You Drop a Stone . . ."
> in *The Other Side of Hugh MacLennan: Selected Essays Old and New*, edited by Elspeth Cameron (Toronto: Macmillan of Canada, 1978).

CAUSE AND EFFECT

In a cause-and-effect paragraph, the writer shows the relationship between ideas and events. The cause is often presented in the topic sentences, and the effect of that cause is explored in the rest of the paragraph. In the paragraph below, the author details the cause-and-effect relationship between the sinking of the *Titanic* and the development of radio. Although the sinking of the *Titanic* did not cause radio to develop, the disaster made it possible to showcase the power of radio and thus influenced its development.

> The *Titanic* disaster also had a profound influence on the rise to prominence of the medium of radio. It was the first occasion that news of the catastrophe reached the public over airwaves. Guglielmo Marconi, the Italian inventor who developed wireless and who had bought a ticket for the *Titanic*'s April 20th return voyage to England, was able to dramatically exploit the usefulness of the medium. Within a few years, radio would become the most powerful mass medium in the world, even supplanting film as the most pervasive of all media, a position usurped by television some 25 years later.
>
> —Derek Boles, "Titanic as Popular Culture"
> in *Deconstructing the Titanic: A Teaching Unit for Middle & Secondary Students* (Media Awareness Network, http://www.media-awareness.ca/english/resources/educational/teachable_moments/deconstructing_titanic_5.cfm).

EXAMPLES AND ILLUSTRATIONS

An example serves to support the generalization presented in the paragraph's topic sentence. In the paragraph below, the topic sentence generalization is this: "Many a successful magazine hoax plays on a local story." The remainder of the paragraph provides an example to support that generalization.

> Many a successful magazine hoax plays on a local story. This is clearly evident in a 1999 April/May issue hoax cooked up by editorial staff at *Ottawa City* magazine. In front of the British High Commission in Ottawa stood a group of sculptures, one nicknamed "Stump Girl" because it looked like a stump wearing red slippers. Regrettably (depending on your artistic taste), Stump Girl was stolen, so *Ottawa City* magazine editor Rosa Harris-Adler and her staff devised a "Find Stump Girl" contest. Within the same issue they published a hoax ad for "Ethel's Garden Ornaments & Landscaping." Superimposed amid the clutter of Ethel's merchandise was the unmistakable image of "statuenapped" Stump Girl.
>
> —Todd Mercer, "'April is the Cruelest [Magazine] Month': Hoaxes in Canadian Magazines."

In some instances, an example is extended to provide an illustration, as psychoanalyst Erich Fromm does in the following paragraph.

> Different from these "symbol dialects" is the fact that many symbols have more than one meaning in accordance with the various kinds of experiences which can be connected with one and the same natural phenomenon. Let us take the symbol fire again. If we watch fire in the fireplace, which is a source of pleasure and comfort, it is expressive of a mood of aliveness, warmth, and pleasure. But if we see a building or forest on fire, it conveys to us an experience of threat and terror, of the powerlessness of man against the elements of nature. Fire, then, can be the symbolic representation of inner aliveness and happiness as well as of fear, powerlessness, or of one's own destructive tendencies. The same holds true of the symbol of water. Water can be a most destructive force when it is whipped up by a storm or when a swollen river floods its banks. Therefore, it can be the symbolic expression of horror and chaos as well as of comfort and peace.
>
> —Erich Fromm, "Symbolic Language of Dreams" in *Language: An Inquiry into Meaning and Function*, edited by Ruth Nanda Anshen (New York: Harper & Row, 1957).

ANALOGY

Writers can use a type of comparison called an analogy to help the reader understand a difficult concept by relating that concept to something with which the reader is familiar. In the following paragraph, the author uses an analogy to a nation to explain the organization of exclusive clubs.

> Each of these modern pseudo-tribes sets up its own specialized kind of home base. In extreme cases non-members are totally excluded; in others they are allowed in as visitors with limited rights and under a control system of special rules. In many ways they are like miniature nations, with their own flags and emblems and their own border guards. The exclusive club has its own "customs barrier": the doorman who checks your "passport" (your membership card) and prevents strangers from passing in unchallenged. There is a government: the club committee; and often special displays of the tribal elders: photographs or portraits of previous officials on the walls. At the heart of the specialized territories, there is a powerful feeling of security and importance, a sense of shared defence against the outside world. Much of the club chatter, both serious and joking, directs itself against the rottenness of everything outside the club boundaries—in that "other world" beyond the protected portals.
>
> —Desmond Morris, "Territorial Behaviour"
> in *Manwatching: A Field-Guide to Human Behaviour* (London: Jonathan Cape, 1977).

ARGUMENTATION OR PERSUASION

Persuasive writing or argumentation needs to establish its point strongly and marshal the reasons for it.

> Volunteering one's time is an important part of education. Giving one's time to a cause—whether it be helping out at a homeless shelter, raising money for a good cause, reading to people who are visually impaired, or making visits at a local hospital—is a valuable way of developing altruism in one's character and ensuring that the future is better for everyone. The good effects work two ways: they improve conditions for others, and they leave us more satisfied with ourselves.

1-3D: MAKING PARAGRAPHS COHERENT

Coherence is the quality of writing by which the parts of a composition relate to each other closely, clearly, and logically. Good writing is coherent on the sentence and paragraph levels when ideas flow smoothly from one to the next. There are a number of thoughtful strategies for strengthening the connections, and hence the coherence, between paragraphs and within them.

LINKING IDEAS CLEARLY

While drafting a paragraph, you may find that ideas are occurring to you so quickly that you just want to get them down on paper. At this stage, ideas within the paragraph draft, as expressed in individual sentences, may not be strongly related or well linked.

ASSESSING COHERENCE AT THE PARAGRAPH LEVEL

Once an entire draft is complete, it is important to review each paragraph carefully, assuming the perspective of a highly critical reader who knows little or nothing about the subject. In the role of a discriminating reader, ask these questions:

- What is the main idea of this paragraph as communicated in its topic sentence?
- Does each paragraph sentence, either directly or indirectly, link to the main idea?
- Do paragraphs typically move from information that the reader already knows to new information, thus enabling understanding?

Then, as a writer, ask yourself these questions:

- Which sentences do not relate directly or indirectly to the main point of the paragraph (the topic sentence) and thus impair coherence?
- Can these poorly linked sentences be revised, or do they need to be moved elsewhere within the document or deleted to improve paragraph coherence?

Ask the questions listed above about the following paragraph written by naturalist Charles Darwin.

> Worms prepare the ground in an excellent manner for the growth of fibrous-rooted plants and for seedlings of all kinds. They periodically expose the mould to the air, and sift it so that no stone larger than the particles which they can swallow are left in it. They mingle the whole intimately together, like a gardener who prepares fine soil for his choicest plants. In this state it is well fitted to retain moisture and to absorb all soluble substances, as well as for the process of nitrification. The bones of dead animals, the harder parts of insects, the shells of land-molluscs, leaves, twigs, etc., are before long all buried beneath the accumulated castings of worms, and are thus brought in more or less decayed state within reach of the roots of plants. Worms likewise drag an infinite number of

dead leaves and other parts of plants into their burrows, partly for the sake of plugging them up and partly as food.

—Charles Darwin, "The Formation of Vegetable Mould through the Action of Worms" (London: John Murray, 1881).

You probably noted that in this very coherent paragraph, each sentence links to the main idea expressed in the topic sentence.

On occasion, you may sense that a paragraph lacks coherence but may not be able to pinpoint which sentence or sentences are creating problems. In such instances, you may need to perform a more in-depth analysis on paragraph content. One strategy is to rank each sentence within the paragraph according to how closely it links to the topic sentence. For example, suppose in an early draft of the previous paragraph, Darwin included sentences that related only weakly—or not at all—to the topic sentence. Each draft sentence could be classified as follows:

T	the *topic* sentence
D	*directly* related/linked to the topic sentence
I	*indirectly* related/linked to the topic sentence
W	*weakly* related/linked to the topic sentence
N	*not* related/linked to the topic sentence

If you are composing with a word processor, you might insert these designations at the end of each paragraph sentence. Once all sentences have been classified, ideas should flow in a logical hierarchy from T to D's to I's. Any sentences designated W or N should be revised or eliminated. So, for example, if Darwin's first paragraph had included a sentence such as "Gardeners often spread dung on the soil to improve its nutrient quality" (N), it would be eliminated from the paragraph because it is not linked to the topic sentence and it interrupts the flow of ideas. In short, the sentence detracts from the paragraph's coherence.

ASSESSING COHERENCE AT THE DOCUMENT LEVEL

You will also need to assess how well paragraphs are linked as a whole and how smoothly ideas flow from one paragraph to the next. Again, assume the role of an ultra-critical reader when evaluating your work for coherence. In most cases, the reader should be able to scan your thesis or purpose statement in the introduction and supporting topic sentences in each body paragraph and get a clear sense of how the paragraphs support the main point.

Examine the relationship between the following thesis statement and topic sentences that have been excerpted from an essay.

Thesis Statement
There is no doubt that the Web is reconnecting us with a civilization based on the written word.

Topic Sentence of First Body Paragraph
The Net is not a threat.

Topic Sentence of Second Body Paragraph
Never has so much been written in such a short period of time as since the introduction of the Internet.

Topic Sentence of Third Body Paragraph
And if you want to write well and acquire a functional vocabulary, you have to read, whether it's on-screen or on the printed page.

By reviewing these elements of the essay, you can obtain a clear sense of how information in the body paragraphs supports the argument presented in the thesis statement.

REPEATING KEY WORDS

By repeating key words, you can strengthen coherence in your paragraphs. However, too much repetition can create a highly undesirable mechanical "chiming" effect. Skilled writers achieve coherence and avoid exact repetition of keywords by using

- variations of keywords (*run, runner, running*)
- pronouns referring to the word (*the atom bomb . . . it*)
- synonyms for the keyword (*boat, craft, ship, liner*)

In the following paragraph, the author uses a synonym phrase, a pronoun, and direct keyword repetition to enhance paragraph coherence. These elements appear in italics.

> The *"third man in the ring,"* usually anonymous so far as the crowd is concerned, appears to many observers no more than an observer himself, even an intruder; a ghostly presence as fluid in motion and quick-footed as the boxers themselves (indeed, *he* is frequently an ex-boxer). But so central to the drama of boxing is *the referee* that the spectacle of two men fighting each other

unsupervised in an elevated ring would seem hellish, if not obscene—life rather than art. *The referee* makes boxing possible.

—Joyce Carol Oates, *On Boxing*
(New York: Doubleday, 1987).

USING RHETORICAL DEVICES

Think about the structures you use as you write. You can make a point more persuasively by presenting it with flourish. Below, in a paragraph by Nobel Peace Prize winner Elie Wiesel, two sentences begin with the "It is so much easier" structure. Parallel grammatical structures such as these help to link related ideas and information within paragraphs more strongly. Here Wiesel employs parallel structure to create a similar effect to that of refrains in poems; the "It is so much easier" repetition is like an echo of conscience. Use rhetorical devices judiciously. If you overuse them, your paragraph might sound mechanically repetitive, like a story from a Grade 2 reader.

> Of course, indifference can be tempting—more than that, seductive. It is so much easier to look away from victims. It is so much easier to avoid such rude interruptions to our work, our dreams, our hopes. It is, after all, awkward, troublesome, to be involved in another person's pain and despair. Yet, for the person who is indifferent, his or her neighbours are of no consequence. And, therefore, their lives are meaningless. Their hidden or even visible anguish is of no interest. Indifference reduces the other to an abstraction.

—Elie Wiesel, "The Perils of Indifference"
(speech given at the White House, April 12, 1999;
see http://www.historyplace.com/speeches/wiesel.htm).

MAINTAINING CONSISTENCY

Jolting and confusing shifts from one point of view to another, or one verb tense to another, can seriously impair paragraph consistency. (See 12-1.)

USING TRANSITIONS

Subtle and purposeful use of transitions can significantly improve coherence in paragraphs and in the document as a whole. Transitions are words or phrases that link ideas, sentences, or paragraphs, making it easier for the reader to perceive how these parts are related. Some of the more commonly used transitions are listed below. Use these words cautiously, and think about the directions they give the reader. They have a crucial effect on the logic of your writing.

Commonly Used Transitions

TO SHOW TIME

after, as, before, next, during, eventually, later, finally, meanwhile, then, when, while, immediately, soon, subsequently, next, today, tomorrow, yesterday

TO SHOW DIRECTION OR PLACE

above, around, below, beyond, beside, farther on, nearby, opposite to, close, to the right, elsewhere, here, there

TO SHOW ADDITION

additionally, and, again, also, too, at the same time, besides, equally important, finally, further, furthermore, in addition, lastly, moreover, next, first, second

TO COMPARE

also, similarly, likewise, compare, by way of comparison, in the same way

TO CONTRAST

but, however, at the same time, on the contrary, in contrast, yet, on the other hand, nevertheless, in spite of, conversely, still, although, even though, instead, though, despite

TO GIVE EXAMPLES

for instance, for example, specifically, to illustrate, in fact, indeed, that is, in particular, namely, thus

TO SHOW LOGICAL RELATIONSHIP

consequently, thus, as a result, if, so, therefore, hence, accordingly, because, otherwise, then, to this end

TO CONCEDE

of course, naturally, granted, although, certainly, even though, with the exception of

TO CONCLUDE OR SUMMARIZE

altogether, in brief, in conclusion, in other words, in short, in summary, to summarize, to sum up, therefore, that is, in general, finally

It is important to use transitional words precisely; for example, don't use *if* when *consequently* is more accurate. And it is important to use transitions that are consistent with the tone of your work; for instance, *namely* might be more appropriate in an informal piece of writing, while *thus* would be appropriate in formal, academic writing. This list is by no means exhaustive. As you read the works of other writers, it's a good idea to note which transitions they use and how they use them. Then, you can incorporate these transitions into your own writing. Sometimes, of course, coherence may be accomplished simply through careful sequencing. Transition words are not always a necessary component in creating coherence in written work.

Notice how well the author uses transitions in the following paragraph. The transitions appear in blue.

> We do a lot of complaining about the lack of "community" in modern societies, but few have noted the absence of public and participatory festivities can, however briefly, unite total strangers in ecstatic communion. Emile Durkheim calls this experience "collective effervescence," which he discerned in the ritual dance of Australian aborigines and postulated to be the emotional basis of all religion. A few religious denominations—Pentecostalism, for example—still offer a collective ecstatic experience, as did rock culture at its height. But the ecstatic religions tend to be marginal, and rock has been tamed for commercial consumption or driven into clubs and "raves." Hence, perhaps, the attempts by fans to transform sports events into an occasion for communal festivities—where else, in a culture of cubicles and class, can you lose yourself so completely in a transient community of a like-minded other?
>
> —Barbara Ehrenreich, "Where the Wild Things Are,"
> *Civilization,* June/July 2000.

1-3E: DECIDING ON PARAGRAPH LENGTH

How long should your paragraphs be? The answer, although it sounds evasive, is quite honestly this: as long as they need to be to make one coherent point. That said, there are a few considerations that will help you adjust your paragraphs to an appropriate length.

WRITING FORM: If you are writing for a newspaper or business report, your readers will be busy people who need to digest information in small, quick bites, so your paragraphs should be short, sometimes less than 100 words. The look on the page also may help determine the size of paragraphs. In the narrow columns of type used in newspapers and many reports, short paragraphs read more easily; in documents where type spans the page, paragraphs can be longer. Paragraphs in student essays or reports tend to be between 100 and 200 words, and instructors typically expect one or two paragraph breaks per page.

CONTENT: Paragraph length does not follow any hard and fast rules. Think about the content of your paragraph. If you are explaining a difficult idea, your paragraph may need to be longer to explain it adequately. Or, perhaps your paragraph has minimal content and only serves as a bridge between larger ideas within the document. Then, the paragraph might be fewer than 100 words.

AUDIENCE: Your audience can have a great deal to do with determining optimal paragraph length. A scholarly audience would probably feel very comfortable reading paragraphs of over 200 words.

FUNCTION: As a general rule, special-function paragraphs such as the introductory and concluding paragraphs are shorter than those in the body.

Often, after reading your draft silently or aloud, you will discover that you need to adjust paragraph length. In an assignment, it's always a good idea to consider paragraph length if you see that you have more than two breaks on a page, or if you have no breaks on a page. Much depends on how the page looks. Paragraphs might also seem short and choppy and thus interrupt the flow of your ideas. Or, they might be long and tedious. To remedy these problems, you might combine paragraphs or break very long paragraphs into shorter ones.

Combine paragraphs to

- eliminate the choppiness of too many short paragraphs
- link closely related ideas
- clarify structure

Break long paragraphs into shorter ones to

- indicate the shift to a new idea
- set off an idea, emphasizing its importance
- break up text that looks too intimidating
- signal a new speaker in story dialogues

- emphasize a contrast
- signal a place or time shift
- mark the end of your introduction or the beginning of your conclusion

---

1-4: REVISING

Revising is a crucial stage in the writing process. In fact, many experienced writers spend the greatest proportion of their time planning and revising. When revising, it is important to have a thought-provoking and efficient strategy. The best approach is to address large or prevalent problems first, then work your way down to the more minor ones. There's no point sweating over where to put a comma if in your next revision step you decide the paragraph in question has to go. Move from the whole to the parts. The best plan of attack for revising follows this sequence:

1. The broad view
   - *Focus:* Does the piece of writing suit its audience and fulfill its purpose?
   - *Structure:* Are paragraphs and ideas organized in the best possible way?
   - *Content:* Is the topic covered adequately?
2. Sentence problems
   - How can sentences be improved to make them as clear as possible?
3. Grammar, spelling, punctuation, and mechanics
   - How can you catch every other problem to make sure the work you submit is free of errors?

1-4A: MAKING STRUCTURAL REVISIONS

At the broad level of revision, your emphasis should be on the major writing concerns:

- focus
- structure
- content

Structural revisions, since they are often major, can be dramatic. They might entail any of these operations:

- **adding** material if you decide content coverage is incomplete or needs clarification or amplification

- **deleting** material that is off topic or redundant
- **replacing** material that doesn't work with a revised paragraph or paragraphs
- **reordering** paragraphs to improve the logical organization and flow of material

There are a number of useful strategies to help you decide whether or not structural revisions are needed in your draft.

- Budget time before the deadline so you can set the draft aside for a few days. By doing so, you can look at the draft from a fresh, objective perspective.
- Read your draft through once from beginning to end. As you read, in the margin make general impression notes relating to possible focus, structure, or content problems. Then, on subsequent readings, concentrate on any problems you flagged. Are they indeed problems? What causes the problems? How do you fix them?
- Have a neutral person read the draft. Make sure it is someone whose judgment you trust, who is honest and objective, and who you think will provide constructive, critical feedback.
- Use or generate a checklist that forces you to examine potential structural problems. Consult the following structural revision checklist for ideas. As with any writing checklist, remember that you can use a word-processing program to personalize the list for your particular writing needs.

Structural Revision Checklist

FOCUS

- My topic is sufficiently narrow for a document of this length.
- My thesis or purpose statement clearly states my topic, focus, and purpose.
- My document displays an awareness of my reading audience—their background knowledge, interests, and expectations.
- My document keeps to the controlling idea of my thesis statement or statement of purpose.

STRUCTURE

- My document is organized logically. The arrangement of ideas makes sense.
- Information within paragraphs is organized logically.
- Ideas are well linked between and within paragraphs.
- My conclusion follows naturally from the body and relates well to the thesis or purpose statement in my introduction.

CONTENT

- Enough information is provided to develop and support ideas adequately. All parts are well developed.
- Material that is not related to my topic has been cut.
- As a reader, I can say the author has answered all of my questions about the topic.
- No content needs to be revised or improved.
- I have given adequate emphasis to the really important ideas related to my topic.
- The material is interesting. My intended audience should find it engaging and compelling.

1-4B: REVISING AND EDITING SENTENCES

Many of the following pages in this handbook deal with

- writing clear, powerful sentences
- sentence grammar
- punctuating sentences correctly
- making sure your sentences are free of spelling and mechanical errors
- revising to improve conciseness

Information within these pages will be especially valuable when revising your sentences. Skim the table of contents and the index, and flip through the tabbed sections relating to sentences. You'll find a wealth of information at your fingertips.

When revising and editing, it's best to indicate your changes on hard-copy draft pages.

Before Sentence Revision

Raising public awareness will be undertaken through a variety of broad
comma splice
strategies and activities^, however, due to the extensive nature of this strategy, only the focused components encompassing public relations and communications will be detailed in this organizational consulting project. The emphasis of this project will be on understanding current
not a sentence
members. Also focusing on getting potential new members, marketing trends, and recruitment concepts. Once this research is distilled and
awkward pronoun use
analyzed, (it) will culminate in a broad strategy that will include repositioning, methods for attracting members and sponsors, and other methods for generating ongoing revenue streams. Research acquired
wordy
can ultimately be used as a template for best practices in the areas of non-profit management for public relations and communications management.

After Sentence Revision

An extensive variety of strategies and activities will be undertaken to raise public awareness; this project will detail only the public relations and communications components. The project emphasis will be on understanding current members, recruiting new members, and developing marketing trends. Drawing from project research analysis, the report will offer a strategy that includes repositioning, attracting members and sponsors, and generating continuous revenue streams. The research can also be used as a template of best practices for non-profit management in public relations and communications management.

Just from glancing at the revision, you can tell wording has been tightened. Generally, revision changes were made for these reasons:

- to follow the conventions (rules) of English
- to improve clarity
- to improve economy

Some of the changes are not open to debate; for instance, non-sentences must be turned into sentences or otherwise made grammatically correct. Other changes are optional, however, and more a matter of style, such as changing *ongoing* to *continuous*. In fact, as you will see in the remainder of this book, there are often several possibilities from which to choose when considering any revision or improvement.

1-4C: PROOFREADING THE FINAL MANUSCRIPT

Proofreading is the final stage of the writing process. It refers to correction of the following types of errors:

- grammar
- usage
- punctuation
- spelling
- capitalization
- typography
- missing words or letters
- layout problems
- any other mechanical or writing convention problems

As a fluent reader, you probably read text quickly, skipping over words and phrases because you know what they will be, based on your knowledge of language patterns. This problem is exacerbated when you are reading your own material, particularly if you haven't allowed it to get "cold" before checking it through. Proofreading is painstaking. It demands slow, careful, and methodical reading so you can identify any errors in the final draft.

PROOFREADING STRATEGIES

Here are a few proofreading strategies. Since proofreading requires checking and re-checking your work, you might consider combining strategies or experimenting with a series of strategies to reach your goal: an error-free manuscript.

- Read slowly, examining each word separately; consider proofreading using a ruler so that you focus on one line at a time.
- Make a list of your most common grammar, punctuation, spelling, and mechanical errors, then check your draft thoroughly for any occurrences of these errors.
- Use a proofreading checklist to check for errors systematically; better yet, create your own individualized checklist, or adapt an existing checklist to suit your particular writing needs.
- Proofread aloud, emphasizing each part of a word as you read.
- Proofread your sentences in reverse order (this will take your attention off meaning so you can focus on words, letters, and punctuation).

- Read "against copy"; this means comparing your final draft one sentence at a time against the edited draft to ensure that all editorial changes have been implemented.
- Use computer spell checkers and grammar checkers, but never rely on them exclusively. All such tools have limitations and should only be employed as part of your extensive proofreading repertoire.
- Have a classmate proofread your work (but never rely totally on this step).

Finally, don't underestimate the importance of proofreading. Submitting an error-free manuscript makes two clear statements about your relationship with the reader:

1. I care about my work.
2. I respect you as a reader.

Submitting a manuscript riddled with errors undermines a writer's credibility; it suggests that perhaps the writer didn't bother to check supporting facts either, or even think too rigorously about large ideas. In the working world, employers have been known to reject job applications containing a single spelling or punctuation error that should have been caught by careful proofreading.

1-5: WORKING ON A WORD PROCESSOR

As you've probably discovered, writing is a process of exploring, experimenting, changing, and improving. With its capabilities for easily adding, deleting, revising, replacing, reordering, and checking text, the computer is a dynamic tool to help you in the writing process.

Here is some advice to help you work with Word, the most popular word-processing program. There may, of course, be variations, depending on what version of Word you use:

Hints for Working with Word

To add page numbers	Insert menu > Page numbers
To avoid numbering your first page	File menu > Page Setup >Layout; select "Different first page"

To single-space	Control key + 1
To double-space	Control key + 2
To add a header for each page	View menu > Header and Footer; type your header in the box
To set a hanging indent (e.g., for a Works Cited page)	Format menu > Paragraph > Indents and Spacing > Special: select "Hanging"
To find and replace a word	Edit menu > Find; type the word; then select Replace and type the change you want to make
To prevent unwanted text colour (links to websites, for example)	Format menu > Font > Color; select black instead of automatic colour (alternatively, right-click on hyperlinked text and select Edit Hyperlink > Remove Hyperlink options)

However, it must be kept in mind that word-processing software is only a tool for writing; you are the ultimate writing decision-maker and must take complete responsibility for what appears on the page.

1-5A: PLANNING

The following are ways you can use a computer in the planning stage of the writing process.

BRAINSTORMING: The whole point of brainstorming is getting your ideas down quickly. If you are a proficient typist, you can probably input those ideas more quickly into a computer than you can write them out in longhand. To avoid being overly critical about brainstorming ideas, some writers dim the computer screen so they can't see what they've written, then brighten the screen after the brainstorming session is over. Similarly, you could select white as your font colour on a white background, then make the text visible at the end of the session by changing the font colour to black.

FREE-WRITING AND JOURNAL WRITING: Create a file in which to experiment with free-writing. Create another file in which to make regular entries about a topic. For example, if you know you're going to have to write a term paper on Margaret Atwood's *Alias Grace*, note your ideas and reflections about the novel as you read. These entries will provide a wealth of ideas.

CLUSTERING: Once you have your ideas in a computer file, you'll want to start looking for connections between ideas. Most word-processing programs will easily allow you to develop a coding system. For example, assign 1 to all ideas that relate to the theme of a poem, 2 for all ideas that relate to its mood, and so on. When you've classified all your ideas, activate the sort function so that all related ideas appear together. Repeat the process to refine your organization.

OUTLINING: It's not such a gargantuan organizational leap from clustering to informal, and then formal, outlining. Many word-processing programs have outlining features that provide proper outlining letters, Roman numerals, numbers, and indentations. More than a formatting tool, the outline feature in some word-processing programs enables you to move whole sections and to envision the structure of your entire document before you draft it. Experiment with this tool when you start composing your next piece of writing. You can also develop your own approach to the outline and save a template to use repeatedly.

QUESTIONING: Most academic disciplines have fairly standard questions that must be addressed or considered in papers. You might start a file of these questions for each course you are taking. The beauty of a word processor is that it allows you to add new questions or revise existing questions with ease.

SCHEDULING: Some word-processing programs, or other computer programs, have time- or project-management components. These tools can help you break the entire writing process down into manageable tasks and establish target dates for task completion so you meet the deadline on time. They will also allow you to flag specific tasks that you need to follow up on.

These are just some of the ways the word processor and other computer productivity programs can help you in the planning stage of writing. Remember to use the computer when and where it makes sense. There may be times when it's just more efficient to pull out a piece of scrap paper and sketch out a web to show the relationship between topic ideas.

1-5B: DRAFTING

Despite the wonders of modern technology, some established writers still prefer to write drafts in longhand, as it allows them to capture the rhythm of their thoughts on the page. However, there are undeniable advantages to using a computer when composing. Among them are these:

SPEED: Especially when creating a first draft, it's important to get ideas down quickly so you don't interrupt the flow of thoughts and aren't overly critical about the text you are generating. Once you at least have a rough draft, you can go back to revise, and revise, and ...

LEGIBILITY: Brilliant ideas can come to you at the strangest times. Beware: jotting down a paragraph on the back of a grocery receipt often yields unreadable results. Writing on a screen ensures your notes will be readable the next time you look at them.

FLEXIBILITY: Word-processing software affords you greater opportunity to try out ideas and move text around. Writers of any age and experience level can be incredibly inventive in how they apply word-processing features and functions to help them in the drafting stage.

CLARITY: Remember to make use of tools such as the thesaurus to avoid annoying repetition. Just make sure to use the thesaurus with the dictionary, so as to get exactly the meaning you want for a given word.

From time to time, it's not a bad idea to exchange writing strategies with fellow writers. In the meantime, here are a few useful strategies to consider:

CREATING A SCRAP FILE: As you start a writing project, create two separate files: one for your actual writing draft, and another in which you collect information that you're considering using, or possibly paragraphs that you've temporarily deleted from your draft but are not absolutely sure you're ready to get rid of. While writing, you might cut and paste from this scrap file.

SPLITTING THE SCREEN: PC and Macintosh systems allow you to view multiple files on your screen at the same time. This means you could draft a paragraph, then experiment with creating an alternate version in another file. By seeing the two paragraphs side by side, you can more easily judge which version is better.

ADDING NOTES: As you compose your draft, you may want to insert notes for yourself to help generate or improve the draft (e.g., *Last sentence doesn't work; revisit it and revise tonight* or *Need more information on Lester Pearson and the UN*). You can be creative in how you use word-processing functions and features to make notes. For instance, parentheses around text might indicate the material has to be deleted or moved; bold text could indicate it contains a crucial idea. Or you might devise a symbol such as "???" meaning "Needs reworking later." If you use such a symbol consistently throughout a document, it will be easy to revise later and strip out things you intend to change. Adding notes is a bit like "talking to yourself" about creating the draft.

TRACKING CHANGES: Note that many documents these days in group assignments or online may need a great deal of collaborative editing, something which may be done by tracking changes—that is, by inserting or deleting material or adding comments in another person's electronic document using different colours and/or fonts. This allows people to work together on a single document with ease.

Remember to regularly save and back up anything you create on a computer. And don't forget the computer's capability for printing. Often, it's beneficial to make a hard copy of the entire draft and spread it out on a table to obtain an overall picture of how ideas flow and are related. A serious limitation of using a computer to write is that you can see only what's on the screen. You can't see, for example, how well the wording of the thesis statement in the introduction relates to the concluding sentence of your twelfth paragraph.

1-5C: REVISING

Word-processing software offers many features and functions to help you revise. As when you revise on hard copy, revising on a computer must be done logically, systematically, and thoroughly. Do essential levels of revision in this order:

1. *Structural revisions:* First, do revisions that address concerns about focus, structure (overall organization and organization within paragraphs), and content.
2. *Sentence-level revisions:* Second, address concerns about sentence clarity, grammar, and variety, including word choice, spelling, punctuation, and mechanics.

STRUCTURAL REVISIONS

Here are a few ways you might employ word-processing software for revising in fairly common writing situations.

TO IMPROVE FOCUS

Your thesis statement does not truly reflect the major idea in a series of paragraphs or a longer paragraph within the document. On an electronic copy of your draft, revise the thesis statement so it reflects the content more accurately. Or, consider whether or not the paragraphs really do fit with your intended focus. On an electronic copy of the draft, try deleting paragraphs to see if the draft achieves better focus.

TO IMPROVE ORGANIZATION

In your draft of an opinion piece or persuasive essay, you decide that the most persuasive organization requires that you save your most compelling argument for the end; however, in the first draft, your best argument is somewhat lost in the third paragraph. Cut, move, and paste the paragraph containing your best argument so it appears just before the conclusion. Smooth the transitions and assess whether or not the new organization is indeed an improvement.

TO IMPROVE CONTENT

Once you've completed a draft explaining your position on cloning, you read a comprehensive piece in a national newspaper about cloning that contains an idea supporting your thesis, or a breakthrough scientific report is released. Draft a paragraph summarizing the new argument or scientific discovery (with appropriate acknowledgment), then insert it at the most important point in your essay or report.

SENTENCE-LEVEL REVISIONS

There are two major methods of using word-processing software to do sentence-level revisions:

1. Do the required revisions on screen, then save them.
2. Do the required revisions on hard copy, then input the changes and save them.

Here are just some of the ways word-processing software (e.g., Microsoft Word) can help you revise.

USING SPELLING AND GRAMMAR CHECKERS: These word-processing features can alert you to possible errors. However, these tools should never be trusted absolutely. Many spell checkers will recommend American spellings as the default, even though in some you can select Canadian English as an option from the Language menu. Grammar checkers often miss errors or offer misleading advice. For example, they will often highlight passive constructions, which usually should be avoided but in a few instances are required. You must decide which sentence construction is most useful for your communication purpose.

HIGHLIGHTING SENTENCE LENGTH AND REPETITION: In addition to using the word counting feature, which enables you easily to gauge your progress as you cut unnecessary words from a document, you may use other features to help you with sentence length and repetition. Make a copy of your draft file. On that copy, hit the return key after every sentence so that each looks like a separate paragraph. Then, examine the sentences and consider these questions:

- Are all sentences about the same length?
- Do they all begin the same way?
- How might you improve the variety of your sentences?

SPACING REVISION COPIES: Use the line-spacing function of the word-processing software to create large spaces between lines of your draft. Print out this working copy, and make needed sentence-level revisions using pencil in the gaps between lines.

SEARCHING FOR PARTICULAR PROBLEMS: Most word-processing programs have a search function. So, if you spell an author's name incorrectly or use a word incorrectly and discover your mistake when proofreading, you can use the search function to correct the error throughout the document. Often you can make needed changes through a global search and replace, though you must use such features with caution. Remember that the computer is not context-sensitive and cannot intuit your meaning.

Another way to guard against misspellings is to use the automatic correction feature in many programs, where common words are automatically corrected when mistyped. Again, you must be careful that the program doesn't introduce its own errors as it "corrects" your work.

MAINTAINING WRITING RESOURCE FILES: Consider setting up and maintaining computer files containing information to help you revise. For example, you might include in one file a list of strategic transition words and phrases you've encountered in your reading. When it comes time to revise a draft, you can draw from this list to improve writing unity.

GENERATING REVISION CHECKLISTS: Input a checklist that covers such revision concerns as sentence structure, word choice, grammar, punctuation, and mechanics. Boldface checklist items that have posed problems for you in previous writing assignments. Pay particular attention to these items when you revise and proofread. Add new checklist items as additional repeated problems emerge in your writing. Delete checklist items as you master writing skills. As a bonus, your checklist revisions become a measure of your personal writing growth.

When what you think is the final manuscript comes out of the printer, resist the temptation to believe that because it looks neat, it's perfect. Allow time to set the draft aside, and then check it again.

1-6: SAMPLE STUDENT ESSAY: THE PROCESS

PLANNING STAGE

Type: Persuasive

Topic: Why become a vegetarian?

Audience: General group of non-vegetarians who might respond to a number of different arguments

Thesis development: One should become a vegetarian for humanitarian reasons, for environmental reasons, and for health reasons.

OUTLINE STAGE

Title: Something catchy and persuasive

Introduction: What is vegetarianism? Why become a vegetarian? Why has it become popular recently?

Body:
Point 1 – Humanitarian reasons
- Use of land for cattle production is wasteful
- People die of malnutrition because of this waste

Point 2 – Environmental reasons
- Meat production causes global warming
- Meat production uses more fuel
- Rain forests are destroyed to allow for cattle grazing

Point 3 – Cruelty to animals
- North Americans do not think about where their food comes from

Point 4 – Health reasons
- Consumption of animal fat causes health problems
- Meat consumption can lead to exposure to pesticides
- Meat consumption can cause overexposure to antibiotics

Conclusion: Summarize the arguments and urge readers to reflect on their actions.

FIRST DRAFT

Never Eat Anything with a Face

Vegetarianism, the decision not to eat meat, is becoming increasingly common, particularly among young people whose principles with regard to world hunger, the environment, anti-cruelty issues, and health forbid it.

This is the thesis statement, including a preview of the arguments that follow.

For these reasons, especially, vegetarianism is often a preferred way of life that is seen as providing both personal and global benefits. While vegetarianism was once the choice of religious groups and rare health-conscious individuals, it is now embraced as a conscientious approach to life. It probably doesn't hurt the cause that vegetarianism is advocated by numerous celebrities, among them Paul McCartney, David Duchovny, Cindy Crawford, and Drew Barrymore.

The humanitarian reasons not to eat meat are overwhelming. Consider, for example, that the amount of land used for cattle production could much more efficiently be used to raise other kinds of food capable of feeding more people more economically. It is said that a meat-based diet requires seven times more land than a vegetarian diet (Eating for the Earth). World hunger could be sharply decreased if more of the corn and oats now grown in North America were eaten by humans and not by livestock intended for meat consumption. The horrifying statistic that a child dies of malnutrition somewhere in the world every five seconds ought to be enough to encourage people to rethink their position regarding wasteful meat consumption (Bread for the World).

Then there's the question of the environment. Meat production is one of the apparent causes of global warming, which threatens the survival of other species as well as humans. Three times more fuel is consumed in the production of a meat-centered diet compared with a meat-free diet. The destruction of tropical rain forests for cattle grazing leads to extinction at the rate of approximately one thousand species annually ("Beef exports fuel loss of Amazonian forest"). This meat industry exists in Central America largely to support North American meat-centered dietary habits. At the same time, however, about 75 percent of children in Central

America under the age of five are said to be malnourished (U.S. Agency for International Development). The wasteful and selfish eating habits of a wealthy few are clearly undermining others' chances for survival and quality of life.

Furthermore, natural resources are thrown away at a great rate in the service of meat production. More than half of all water used in North America alone is dedicated to livestock production, enough that it takes roughly 22,730 litres of water to produce half a kilogram of beef, compared with only 114 litres of water to produce half a kilogram of wheat. Roughly 30 percent of the withdrawal of water for cattle production is not returned, making it a serious loss (Agriculture and Agri-food Canada). Oil reserves and fossil fuels are similarly affected. If you are concerned about protecting natural resources for future generations, vegetarianism makes clear sense.

Global concerns aside, an abhorrence of cruelty to animals is, of course, a chief motivation to become vegetarian. For ethical reasons, many of us do not wish to kill animals for consumption. If people had to slaughter their own food, many would likely become vegetarians to avoid inflicting pain or taking lives. Chicken, eviscerated and wrapped in cellophane, as bought in grocery stores, doesn't present the horror of an animal's death. If hunting was essential to survival, a different argument might be possible, but among North Americans in the current economy, no such claim may reasonably be made.

Health issues are also part of the decision to become vegetarian. In societies where high consumption of animal fats has led to heart disease, widespread obesity, and attendant problems like diabetes, it may make sense to consider eating just plant sources and thus avoid a major health hazard. Opponents of vegetarianism who claim that some vitamins, like B12, are more readily available in meat-centered diets need to be reassured that a proper vegetarian diet with attention to complete plant proteins is easily and economically attainable, and that health benefits are actually to be expected. Partly this is due to the vegetarian's increased protection from pesticides and from unhealthy overexposure to antibiotics that can result from meat consumption. Levels of DDT in breast milk are significantly higher among meat-eating mothers than among vegetarians, an indication of the many dangers that accrue to meat consumption, even for infants (National Resources Defense Council).

For a number of reasons, not the least of which is revulsion at the suffering and death of animals, many of us choose to become vegetarian.

Consider the consequences of your meat-eating habits at your next meal, and become more conscious of the widespread, indeed global, effects of your routine behaviour. What are you willing to sacrifice for the supposed privilege of enjoying meat?

Note that the following is in accordance with MLA style.

Works Cited

Agriculture and Agri-food Canada. Water Use. 29 June 2006 <http://res2.agr.ca/publications/hw/03_e.htm>.

"Beef exports fuel loss of Amazonian forest." CIFOR News Online. No. 36. 29 June 2006 <http://www.cifor.cgiar.org/publications/corporate/newsonline/newsonline36/beef_exports.htm>.

Bread for the World. 28 June 2006 <http://www.bread.org/learn/hunger-basics/hunger-facts-international.html>.

Eating for the Earth. 16 June 2006 <http://www.veg.ca/issues/enintro.html#diet>.

Natural Resources Defense Council. "What Mothers Should Do." 1 June 2006 <http://www.nrdc.org/breastmilk/whattodo.asp>.

U.S. Agency for International Development Fact Sheet. "Food Crisis in Central America: USAID Response and Strategic Approach." 15 June 2006 <http://www.usaid.gov/press/releases/2002/fs021108.html>.

2

BUSINESS WRITING

Failure is ***not*** an option.
It comes bundled with the SOFTWARE
—*Anonymous*

2

Business Writing

2 Business Writing

While beginning to write involves making decisions that relate for the most part to subject matter and to audience, another important consideration is the kind of document you are writing. To a large extent, the quality of your writing depends on how well the writing conforms to the reader's expectations of its structure—and to the conventions it should follow. Typically, most of us find ourselves needing to master several different document forms. This chapter will reinforce your understanding of how to design a business letter, a memo, a résumé, and a report. It will also explore how document design can help you think through the purpose and audience of your business writing.

This chapter will focus on writing that you produce in career contexts, ranging from a résumé and covering letter for a job application to a formal business letter, memo (memorandum), and report for when you get the position. Each writing form has specific design, or **format,** requirements.

Although design conventions, by their very nature, are fairly standard, there can be some variation in preferred document design styles among—and even within—companies. This means it is incumbent upon you to ask your employer or supervisor which document design style applies for a particular task. He or she may refer you to a specific style.

When designing documents for business audiences, you may find style guides helpful, but the most effective guidelines will be those meeting the particular requirements and preferences of a specific company. If you know managers working in a field you are interested in or in an organization you'd like to work for, you might ask them what résumé style has proven successful for getting candidates a job interview.

Designing an effective document is very much about meeting expectations. It's also about ensuring that your document is highly readable and visually well organized. Even though designing documents in business contexts often means following rules or guidelines, sometimes there are opportunities for using creativity to make your document stand out. But even within these creative opportunities there are limits, so it is crucial to know what is acceptable or appropriate.

2-1: KEY QUESTIONS ABOUT DOCUMENT DESIGN

WHAT SHOULD EFFECTIVE DOCUMENT DESIGN DO?

Effective document design must satisfy the expectations of your particular writing audience and situation. For instance, if you are designing a résumé, you should follow the conventions of the modern résumé form and take into consideration any known format preferences of the person or company you plan to approach.

In a business context, effective design should increase document readability. *Readability* is a very broad term that could mean something as simple as choosing a large, clear font so that your message is easily legible. Or, if you are writing reports, readability could be increased by the use of headings that give the reader an overview of report organization and a means of locating needed information quickly.

WHY IS DOCUMENT DESIGN IMPORTANT?

In the Information Age, business people are overwhelmed with reading material, which demands a great amount of their time. Therefore, any writing you submit needs to be highly accessible. It must be presented correctly and clearly and be well organized visually.

You must also remember that business contexts are extremely competitive situations. To survive and succeed, your written work must stand out by following document design conventions and, where opportunities for creativity exist, by displaying effective innovation.

WHAT TEXT FEATURES CAN CONTRIBUTE TO EFFECTIVE DOCUMENT DESIGN?

There are many. Some apply exclusively to résumés, others to research reports, and still others to various forms of business communication. These design features are discussed in the following pages:

- paper choice, margins, line space, and justification
- fonts (typeface style and size)
- headings
- lists
- visuals (charts, graphs, tables, and diagrams)

WHAT TOOLS CAN ASSIST YOU IN CREATING EFFECTIVE DOCUMENT DESIGN?

A word-processing software program is an ideal tool for effective document design. For instance, it allows you easily to create and maintain a variety of heading styles using boldface or different fonts and sizes, thus clearly communicating the importance of the ideas presented under the headings. More specialized design and graphics programs allow you to create and insert visuals into a report to support the ideas set out in the text.

2-1A: SELECTING AN APPROPRIATE FORMAT

Ensure you have correctly set the following in your word-processing program:

- margins
- line spacing
- justification
- font—including typeface style and size

The following sections indicate which options are appropriate in *most* writing situations. Please note that for the instructional purposes of this text, sample document margins and page sizes throughout are not necessarily to scale.

PAPER, MARGINS, LINE SPACING, AND JUSTIFICATION

PAPER

Use letter-size (22 × 28 cm, or 8.5 × 11 in.) white bond paper that is of 16- or 20-pound (60 or 75 g/m^2) weight. Print on only one side of the paper and use the same type of paper for the entire document.

MARGINS

Leave a margin of 2.5 cm (1 in.) on the top, bottom, and both sides of the page. Check this requirement, as sometimes more space is preferred, up to 4 cm (roughly 1.5 in.) on at least one margin. This allows room for the reader or editor to make comments.

LINE SPACING

In most businesses, memos are single-spaced, so these communication documents, whenever possible, are kept to a single page. (By contrast, academic papers are usually double-spaced throughout.)

JUSTIFICATION

When type is **justified,** the lines of type are all the same length, and the right-hand margin is even. In the **ragged-right** style, the left margin is even (except for paragraph indentations) but all lines remain unjustified, so that the right margin is uneven. This textbook is set in ragged-right style.

Use ragged-right style in business writing. Justification often creates "rivers" of white space in the text and necessitates frequent use of hyphenation, which makes text difficult to read.

FONTS

You have two basic choices to make regarding fonts:

1. Font size
2. Font or typeface style

FONT SIZE

Normal font sizes for business writing range from 10 points to 12 points:

10-point font
11-point font
12-point font

FONT STYLE

Fonts may be serif or sans serif. Serif fonts have thin lines at the end of the main strokes of each letter. This usually makes the text easier to read, which is why serif fonts are most often used in the body of a document. For most business writing situations, a common serif font such as Times Roman is your best choice.

Sans-serif ("without serif") fonts, such as Arial or Helvetica, are simpler and more streamlined. In print documents, they are commonly used for headings and display text. Sans-serif fonts are also used extensively on websites, since many people find them easier to read on screen than serif fonts.

Don't use unusual font styles. These fonts are designed to be used on small amounts of text and are difficult to read for any long period.

Don't use all italics, script typeface, or all capitals in the main text of your document. These effects should be used only for documentation, headings, titles within the text where applicable, or

Serif font

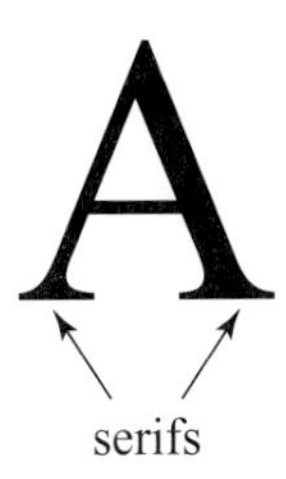

Example: Times New Roman

Sans-serif font

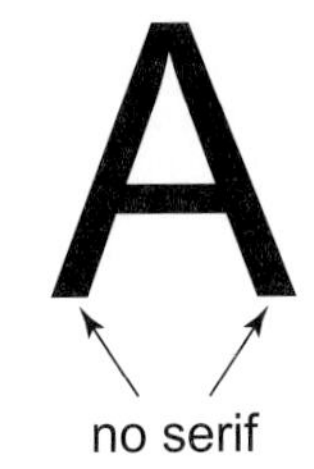

Example: Arial

emphasis of a word or phrase. Choose a readable font and stick with it throughout a document.

For the text body:

Times Roman
Garamond

For text headings:

Helvetica
Arial
Geneva

2-1B: USING HEADINGS

Headings can make some documents more readable and the ideas and information that fall under them more accessible. Here are some key questions and points to think about as you consider using headings.

WHEN ARE HEADINGS USED?

Headings are useful in complex documents that include different types of information, such as research reports, technical and scientific reports, and proposals.

WHEN ARE HEADINGS NOT USED?

Headings are not needed in shorter documents. Here, the structure of the document, its purpose, and the topic sentences in each paragraph should clearly outline the document's organization.

WHY ARE HEADINGS USED?

Headings provide readers with a quick, at-a-glance overview of a complex document's organization. Pick any longer section of this book. Examine how headings are used. What do the headings tell you about the organization of information within each section? Headings also help readers to locate information quickly.

HOW OFTEN SHOULD HEADINGS BE USED?

Headings are intended to emphasize information and signal where certain information can be found. As with any text feature, overusing headings detracts from the emphatic effect. Too many can make the flow of ideas within a text disjointed.

HOW SHOULD HEADINGS BE USED?

Headings must be appropriately phrased, placed, and highlighted. You'll find the information you need on these topics under appropriate headings in the following two sections.

PHRASING HEADINGS

Headings should be succinct, intriguing, and accurately describe or summarize the content of the document section they head. Some headings are single words or short sentences, but most are concise phrases. The following are the most common and acceptable heading styles:

- questions
- noun phrases
- *-ing* phrases
- imperative sentences

The heading style you choose will depend on your purpose, audience, and subject matter. For instance, if you are writing a sociological magazine article on dormitory dating for a young audience, you might use questions in your headings to attract your readers' attention (e.g., *How Does the Dormitory Dating Ritual Begin?*).

Whichever heading style you choose, it's crucial to follow the style consistently throughout your document. In other words, don't alternate questions and imperative sentences in the same level of headings.

QUESTIONS

Questions intrigue the reader. They can be used to good effect in a report, making it seem a bit like reading the transcript of an interview, in which the questions often frame what the responses will be.

Writers frequently have key questions that must be addressed in the body of the report. Using questions as headings is reader-friendly because it anticipates the questions that readers often ask. You might also see questions used in headings of informational brochures to help readers quickly locate needed information. This can be seen in the following headings used in a brochure about student loans for first-year students:

Where Can I Apply for a Loan?

What Documentation Is Required?

What Steps Are Involved in the Approval Process?

How Long Does Approval Take?

How Is Payment Made?

NOUN PHRASES

Noun phrases are useful as headings in research reports that provide a survey of people, places, or things. For instance, the following noun phrases might be useful in a survey report on types of economic systems:

Command Economies

Market Economies

Mixed Economies

In business documents, nouns and noun phrases identify key report parts and information, for example *Marketing Strategies*, *Implementation Problems*, *Solutions*, and *Market Projections*.

-ING PHRASES

These phrases, which include verb forms, communicate action and are useful as headings when you need to describe a process—that is, how to do or make something. For example, if you were to describe how to make a video, sections within your document might have these *-ing* phrases as headings: *Planning Shots*, *Taking Shots*, and *Editing Shots*.

For a report on developing students' critical analysis skills, which involves both actions and processes, the following *-ing* phrases are used in headings:

Distinguishing Fact from Opinion

Recognizing Deceptive Arguments

Evaluating Sources of Information

Detecting Ethnocentrism

Searching for Causal Relationships

Exploring Values

Taking a Stand

Notice the organization reflected in the headings. They progress from the more factual ideas to the more abstract and help the writer formulate his or her own position.

IMPERATIVE SENTENCES

An **imperative sentence** gives a command. Imperative sentences are useful as headings in a document when your purpose is to advise the reader. Often, imperative sentences begin with verbs, since it is assumed that the subject of the sentence is the reader. Here are imperative-sentence headings that might appear in a business book dealing with how to get a promotion:

Develop a positive attitude at work.

Surpass expectations.

Commit to develop your learning on the job.

Define specific goals for yourself and your future.

Be proactive.

PLACING AND HIGHLIGHTING HEADINGS

Once you determine the most appropriate heading style, you have two key questions to ask yourself.

1. Where do I most effectively place each heading?
2. How do I most effectively highlight each heading?

PLACING HEADINGS

In a typed document, main headings are usually centred, while sub-headings are placed flush against the left-hand margin. Because of the use of hyperlinks in electronic documents, underlining as a formatting device is less common than in the past. Most style guides don't elaborate on headings, except to demand that headings be used consistently.

Main Heading

Subheading

Important headings should have a lot of white space around them, while less important headings can be closer to the main text.

You may see variations of these heading placement guidelines in different types of documents. For instance, in some business reports, headings appear in a separate column to the left of the main body of text. Make sure the headings you use reflect the hierarchy of ideas in your report or essay. In a report on population distribution in Canadian cities, it wouldn't make sense to place "Suburbs" as a main heading and "Metropolitan Areas" as a subheading. Whichever heading placement approach you select, follow it consistently throughout the entire document.

HIGHLIGHTING HEADINGS

As the example above shows, main headings often appear in bold and/or a larger font size, while subheadings may be set in italics or a smaller font.

You can choose from the following options, or use combinations of these options, to highlight headings:

ALL CAPITAL LETTERS

colour

larger font

boldface

italics

underline

smaller font

Again, you must observe consistency when highlighting headings. If you use a particular highlighting option for one level of heading at the beginning of the document, use that option throughout the document. Guard against using too many headings or too many types of highlighting in your document—it can make text look busy and is distracting for readers.

Headings are usually capitalized according to title style (see 14-3c) but they may also be typed with just an initial capital. Use each style consistently.

2-1C: USING DISPLAYED LISTS

This section answers questions you might have about why to use a list and what kinds of information naturally fit a list.

WHY USE A LIST?

A list can do the following:

- allow the reader to skim or scan information quickly and easily
- break up long passages of narrative text, making documents less intimidating and more visually appealing
- draw the reader's eye to particular pieces of information

WHAT KINDS OF INFORMATION SUIT A LIST FORMAT?

Here are some list possibilities:

- checklist criteria
- steps in a process (e.g., how-to instructions)
- categories
- materials for an experiment
- parts of an object
- guidelines or recommendations
- items on a discussion agenda

As you've probably noticed, the above information is a sample list. Evaluate it using the following list of do's and don'ts.

Do's and Don'ts for Setting Up Lists

DO'S

- Introduce the list with an independent clause.
- Follow the independent clause with a colon.
- Indent items 1.25 cm (0.5 in.) from the left margin.
- Only use periods after list items if they are sentences.
- If you use no punctuation at the end of list items, follow this pattern throughout your document. Some writers use semi-colons or commas at the end of list items; if you use either of these punctuation patterns, place *and*, with a semicolon or comma before it, after the second-to-last list item. Then, after the final list item, use a period.
- Make list items grammatically parallel (e.g., items consistently begin with *-ing* or noun phrases)
- Use bullets, squares, dashes, and in some cases numbers to distinguish each list item.
- Above all, be consistent in list formatting and punctuation.

DON'TS

- Do not overuse displayed lists within your document. Too many lists make the text look cluttered and choppy to read.
- Do not include too many items in any one list. If the list is too long, by the time the reader gets to the end of it, he or she will have forgotten items from the beginning of it.

Many recent word-processing programs have automatic formatting features, which insert bullets, dashes, or numbers for each new item once you've started a list. Check that the automatic formatting complies with the style rules you need to follow for your particular document. Turn off any automatic formatting features that interfere with the layout you are using.

2-1D: ADDING VISUALS

Visuals include the following text features:

- charts
- graphs
- tables
- diagrams
- illustrations
- maps

Visuals can communicate ideas and information quickly and succinctly. They can add to, clarify, or enhance the meaning of the print text. In many instances visuals are the most efficient way to describe, explain, or compare concepts, patterns, and trends.

You can use visuals from other sources in your report as long as you correctly acknowledge where the information was obtained. (See 4-1.) You can also create your own visuals using such tools as graphics software programs. All visuals should have a title that clearly and concisely indicates what the visual is about.

There are two key decisions to make when considering visuals.

1. Which visuals are most appropriate for the ideas and information you want to communicate?
2. Where is the most effective place to position each visual within your document?

USING CHARTS, GRAPHS, TABLES, AND DIAGRAMS

Each type of visual serves a different purpose or purposes. You must decide which visual is most suitable for your communication purpose.

CHARTS

Charts are good for showing the relationships between ideas and data. A **flow chart** illustrates a process for the reader, showing how parts of the process are related. See Figure 2.1.

FIGURE 2.1
Example of a Flow Chart
Sources of Income

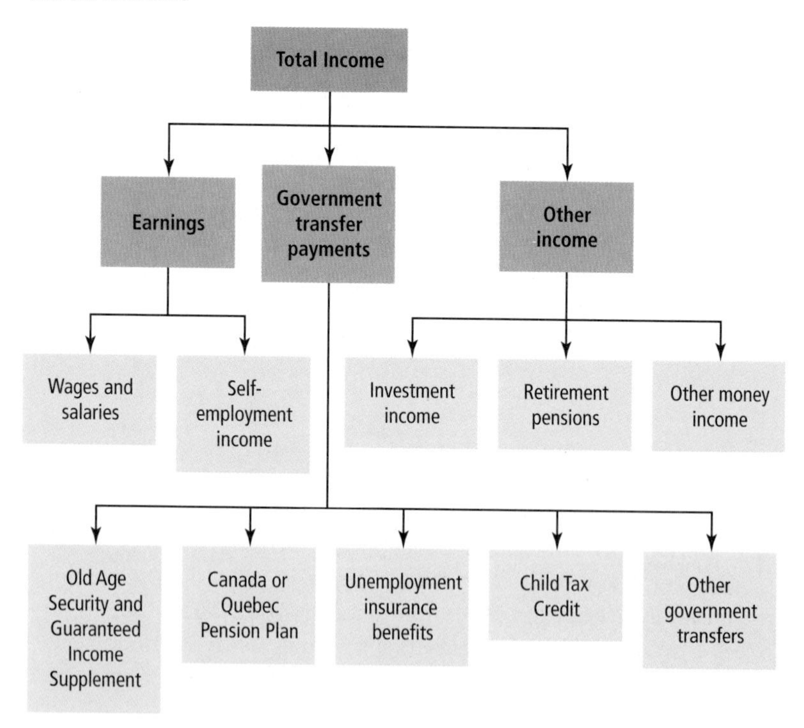

Source: Statistics Canada, 1997 Census Results Teacher's Kit, Activity 7, p. 6, at http://www.statcan.ca/english/kits/pdf/censu7.pdf

A **pie chart** is a circular graph that is appropriate for showing readers how a part of something relates to the whole. Information must be in percentages since the whole is represented as 100 percent. See Figure 2.2.

GRAPHS

Graphs are suitable for presenting statistical information in ways that make it easy to understand.

A **line graph** is useful when illustrating trends over time or comparing data for a relatively small number of entities. See Figure 2.3.

FIGURE 2.2
Example of a Pie Chart
Family Structure, 2001 Census

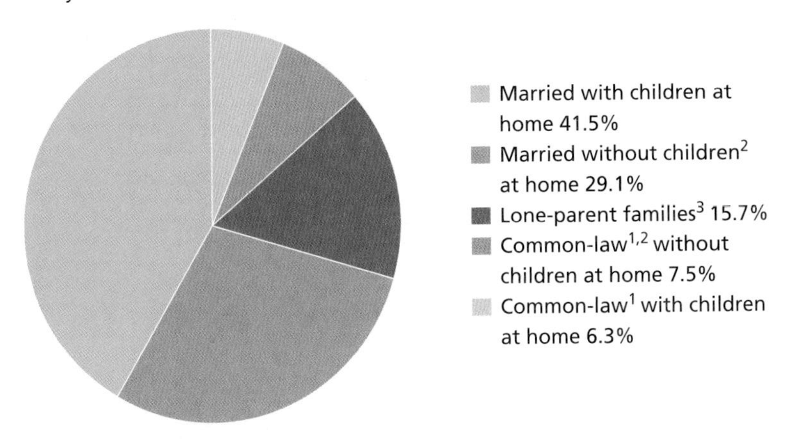

[1] Common-law couples are not legally married.

[2] Married and common-law couples without children at home are couples who have never had children, as well as "empty-nest" couples whose children have grown up and left home.

[3] A lone-parent family is headed by a single parent and has one or more children living at home.

Note that for all families with children at home, only children who have never been married are counted.

Source: Statistics Canada, 2001 Census Results Teacher's Kit—Activities, Activity Six, Handout 1: The Changing Canadian Family, http://www12.statcan.ca/english/census01/teacher's_kit/activity6_emptygraph.cfm

FIGURE 2.3
Example of a Line Graph
Number of Marriages and Divorces in Canada, 1921–2002

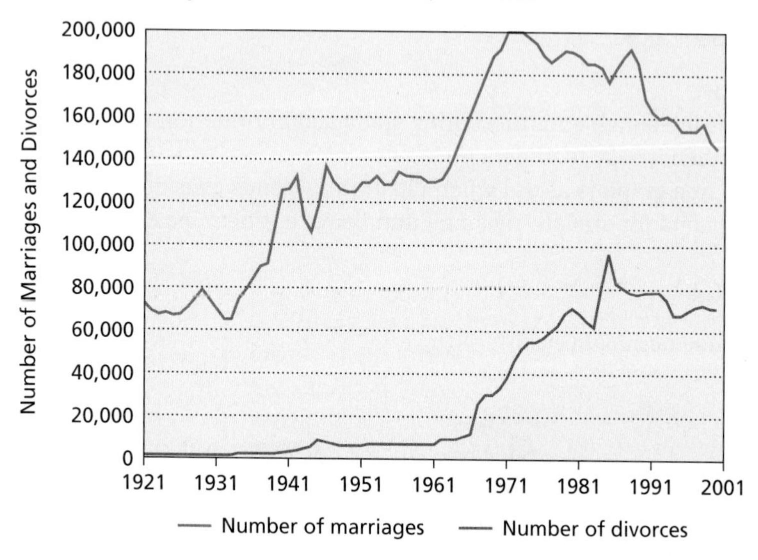

Source: Statistics Canada, "Divorces: 2001 and 2002," The Daily, May 4, 2004, http://www.statcan.ca/Daily/English/040504/d040504a.htm

A **bar graph** is suitable when you want to compare statistical information for a large number of entities. The reader can quickly see which variable is greatest, which is smallest, and how each entity compares with any other on the graph. See Figure 2.4.

TABLES

A **table** allows you to summarize large amounts of information, which is usually in statistical form. Since tables are set up in columns, they are also useful for comparing information. See Table 2.1.

DIAGRAMS

A **diagram** is a concise visual representation of an idea or object. It often allows you to explain a complex idea or describe an intricate object much more economically than you could with words. Sometimes diagrams are the only way to visualize and understand scientific phenomena, unless of course you have access to sophisticated technology such as electron microscopes.

FIGURE 2.4
Example of a Bar Graph
Immigrants, 1974–2002

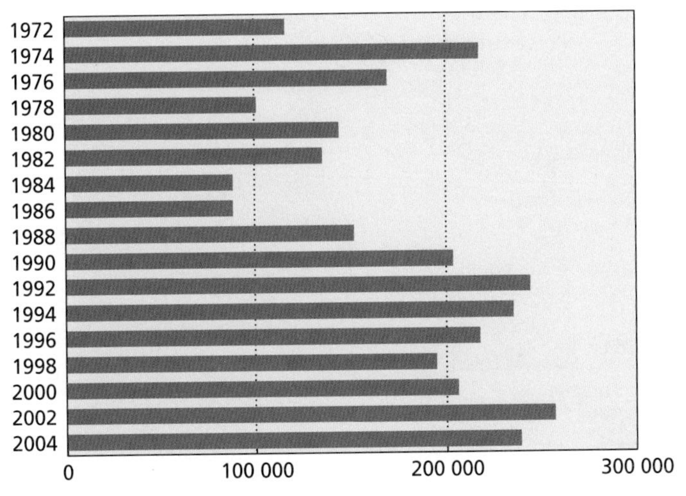

Note: Annual immigration numbers are for the period ending June 30 of each year.

Source: Statistics Canada, "Immigrants," Canada at a Glance 2006, http://www.statcan.ca/english/freepub/12-581-XIE/12-581-XIE2005001.pdf, p. 4.

TABLE 2.1
Example of a Table

TELEVISION VIEWING BY TYPE OF PROGRAM, FALL 2003

Total, all persons two years and older

	Total % of viewing time	Canadian programs	Foreign programs
All programs	100.0	40.2	59.8
News and public affairs	26.2	19.8	6.4
Drama	24.9	4.9	20.1
Variety and games	12.9	4.5	8.4
Comedy	11.3	1.3	10.1
Sports	8.2	5.1	3.1
Other television programs	16.3	4.8	11.6

Source: Statistics Canada, "Television viewing by type of program, Fall 2003," Canada at a Glance 2006, http://www.statcan.ca/english/freepub/12-581-XIE/12-581-XIE2005001.pdf, p. 8.

FIGURE 2.5
Example of a Diagram
Diagram of the Process of Hydroelectric Power Generation

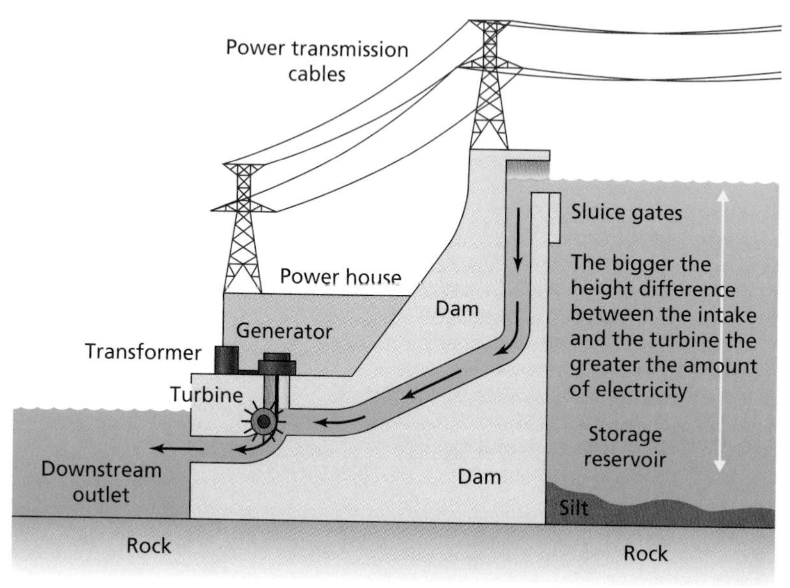

Source: Canada. Environment Canada. Freshwater: Instream uses – Hydroelectric power generation. Ottawa, 1999; reproduced in Natural Resources Canada, *The Atlas of Canada*, http://atlas.gc.ca/site.english/english/maps/freshwater/consumption/hydro_generation.jpg/image_view

PLACING VISUALS

A visual can be placed in one of two places within the document:

1. In or near the print text to which the visual relates
2. In an appendix to the document, where the visual should be labelled (the visual should be referenced within the text).

If you are placing a visual within the main text of the document, place the visual as near to the print text to which it relates as possible. Some software programs allow you to run text around the visual. You may need to position the visual later in the relevant print text discussion, or after it. Often it is easiest to place a visual at the bottom of the page, where space can be set aside. Put the title above the visual and place complete source information below it. Source information must include the name of the visual's creator and the place and date of publication. Ensure that any visual you use is readable and appropriately sized for the page. The visual should be large enough to understand but must still fit within the margins of the page. Of course, if a visual needs to be wider than a typical page, you could format it as a "landscape page" to be read horizontally rather than vertically.

2-2: FORMATTING BUSINESS DOCUMENTS: WHAT EMPLOYERS WANT

This section offers guidelines and useful models that will help you to write effective

- business letters
- résumés
- memos (memoranda)
- reports

All of these forms address a specific audience—the business community. The writing purposes vary among the models. For instance, the purpose might be to apply for a position and persuade a prospective employer of an applicant's suitability for a job. In another case, it could be to alert a superior about a problem and propose a solution.

There is a wide range of business documents you may be called upon to write. Among these forms are executive summaries, funding proposals, and progress reports. For guidance on how to write such documents, see a specialized business-writing textbook or resource book. To obtain a sense of a particular company's style and format preferences in business documents, locate and study models from that company's correspondence files or resource library.

2-2A: FORMAL BUSINESS LETTERS

Business letters must be clear, concise, and get to the point quickly since the recipients usually have high demands placed upon their time. Letters represent a person or a company and therefore must make a good impression. While composing a letter, devote some time to its purpose and its ultimate audience. Letters can deliver good news or bad news, serve as emissaries of goodwill for a company or individual, or persuade readers to act in a particular way. A good rule of thumb is to put yourself in the reader's shoes; that is, consider the reader's perspective, and take his or her feelings and attitudes into account. Moreover, remember your purpose in writing.

In the model business letter on page 72, notice that the writer clearly states her purpose—to find a position—in the first line of the body. While business letters need not be stiff and overly formal, they should still be polite and formal in tone. When composing a business letter, you should be aware of basic business-letter elements and the style options open to you.

STYLE

You may choose from the following three basic business-letter styles:

- the block style
- the modified block style
- the simplified style

The **block** style is used in the model on page 72. All body paragraphs are flush against the left margin. The **modified block** style is considered less formal. In this style, the date line, close, and signature begin at the centre of the page. Here, the first word of each paragraph in the body is indented (usually 1.25 cm or 0.5 in.). This style is often used when the letter is typed on company letterhead or the letterhead of the writer. **Simplified** style is least common. It looks like a block letter except that the salutation and closing are missing. The salutation is replaced by a subject line in all caps. Simplified style is useful when a letter is addressed to a company in general or a post office box number, rather than to a specific person. Select a style that is appropriate to your writing situation, purpose, and audience.

A NOTE ON PUNCTUATION IN BUSINESS LETTERS

Most commonly, punctuation is **mixed.** This means that a colon typically follows the salutation, and a comma follows the close. Sometimes, in **open** punctuation, both the colon after the salutation and the comma after the close are omitted.

ELEMENTS

It is important to know how to set up basic business-letter elements and what purpose each element serves.

RETURN ADDRESS AND DATE

Unless you are using company stationery or writing on behalf of a company, the return address is your own address. Include the date as well. In modified block style, the return address and date are placed at the top of the page and should be lined up just to the right of the centre of the page's width. The return address should be aligned with the close and signature at the bottom of the letter. In the more common block style, the return address and date are flush left.

INSIDE ADDRESS

The address of the person to whom you are writing is placed flush against the left margin in both modified block and block styles.

SALUTATION

The salutation is the word or phrase you use to greet the person to whom you are writing. Like the inside address, it is placed flush against the left margin. Usually you will address the person by their last name: for example, *Dear Mr. Deane.* If you are not writing to a particular person or can't find out the name of the person holding a position, you may use *Dear Sir* or *Dear Madam,* though some consider this too formal these days. Other options are to address the company—*Dear Miracle Air Conditioning*—or to use the person's title: *Dear Human Resources Manager.* If you are writing to a woman and you don't know her marital status or title, use Ms. Also use Ms. if you know the person prefers this form of address. If you do not know the gender of the person to whom you are writing, it is acceptable to write "Dear Lee Fiora," including both names with no title. You should make every effort to find out the name (check to be sure you have the correct spelling) and exact title of any person to whom you are writing. Follow the salutation with a colon.

BODY

Indent the first word of each paragraph (usually 1.25 cm or 0.5 in.) when using the modified block style. In the block style, the entire body begins at the left margin.

CLOSE

In a modified block style, the close is lined up just to the right of the centre of the page's width. (Block style, by contrast, begins the close flush left.) The first letter of the close is capitalized. In a business letter, *Sincerely* is the most common closing, although *Sincerely yours* and *Yours truly* (considered less formal) are also used.

SIGNATURE

Six line spaces below the close, type your name; then sign the letter above the typed name.

Sample Business Letter 1: Block Style with Mixed Punctuation

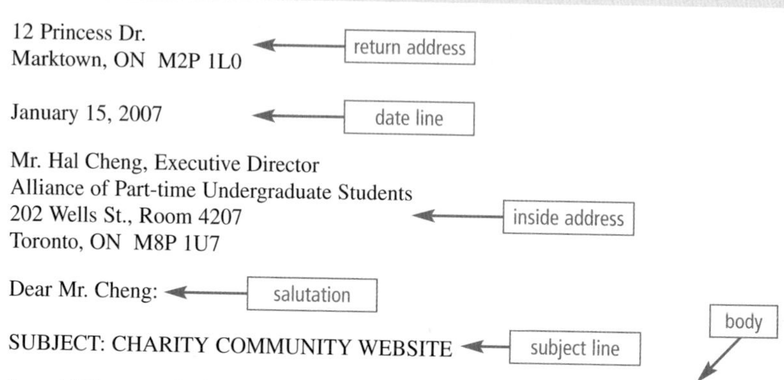

12 Princess Dr.
Marktown, ON M2P 1L0

January 15, 2007

Mr. Hal Cheng, Executive Director
Alliance of Part-time Undergraduate Students
202 Wells St., Room 4207
Toronto, ON M8P 1U7

Dear Mr. Cheng:

SUBJECT: CHARITY COMMUNITY WEBSITE

I would like to apply for the position of researcher in charge of educational opportunities for part-time students that you advertised in the *Globe and Mail* on January 10, 2007. I believe I would be an outstanding candidate for the position.

Over the past three years I have worked as a researcher for various instructors at the University of Waterloo. A significant part of my work involved assisting professors in their research to determine which teaching strategies and materials are used within the educational community. I was responsible for helping to administer research surveys and questionnaires by mail, telephone, and e-mail. As well, I proofread final analysis reports. My work often required contacting educational decision-makers at schools, school-board offices, colleges, universities, and departments of education.

I have also helped conduct market analysis research projects in the private sector. A recent project I worked on involved surveying telecommunications decision-makers to assess customer needs.

While a summer intern with the British Columbia Ministry of Education, I helped file in the Assessment Branch and gained organizational skills useful to researchers. I am sensitive to issues affecting part-time university students, having completed my second year on a part-time basis while working.

My writing skills are of a high standard. This past academic year, I won a prize for the best undergraduate essay, and I have published two short stories in the campus newspaper.

I would welcome the opportunity to meet with you to elaborate on my qualifications and discuss the advertised position.

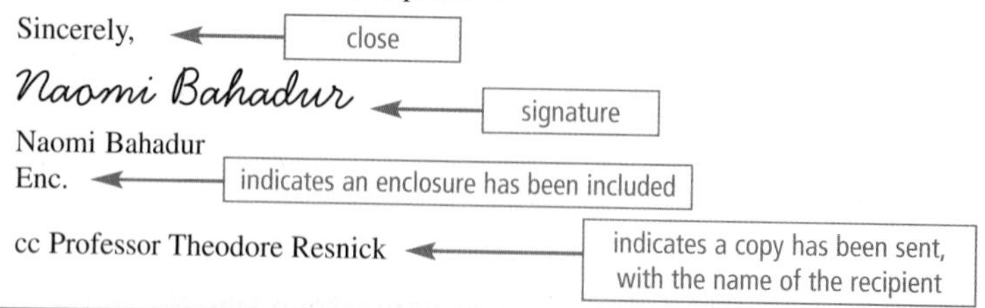

Sincerely,

Naomi Bahadur

Naomi Bahadur
Enc.

cc Professor Theodore Resnick

Sample Business Letter 2: Modified Block Style

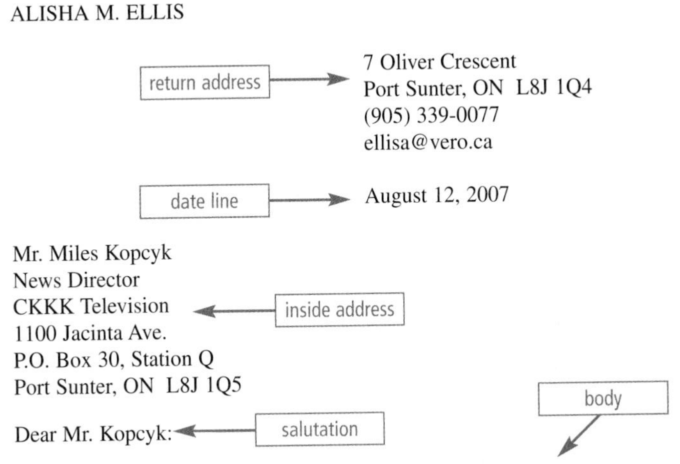

ALISHA M. ELLIS

7 Oliver Crescent
Port Sunter, ON L8J 1Q4
(905) 339-0077
ellisa@vero.ca

August 12, 2007

Mr. Miles Kopcyk
News Director
CKKK Television
1100 Jacinta Ave.
P.O. Box 30, Station Q
Port Sunter, ON L8J 1Q5

Dear Mr. Kopcyk:

Your advertisement for a News Videographer (CH 05-08-07), appearing on August 5 in the internal Career Opportunities for Global Television Network and CKKK Television, quickly grabbed my attention. I believe that my extensive education in television broadcasting and communications and my work experience at CKKK TV have provided me with the many skills required for the job.

When I first arrived at CKKK Television in the summer, my initial intentions were to job shadow for as long as the company would have me around! Every day that I showed up to follow a reporter, I learned something new about the process of television production. I was able to turn that experience into my current part-time position as a CKKK News Reporter. I believe that I am up for a new challenge, and the News Videographer position appears to be the perfect opportunity for me to use what I have already learned from my experiences on the CKKK team.

I hope that after you have examined my résumé and demo reel, you will allow me to continue contributing to your community-oriented vision, in the position of the CKKK News Videographer. I look forward to discussing this new opportunity in person at your earliest convenience.

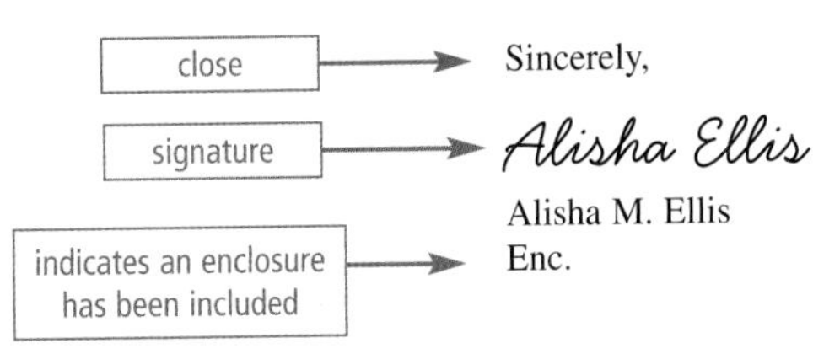

Sincerely,

Alisha Ellis

Alisha M. Ellis
Enc.

NOTATION

In certain business situations you may have to enclose material in the letter's envelope or have a copy of the letter sent to another person or persons. Use **Enc.** to indicate that something is enclosed. When another person is receiving a copy of the letter, use **cc** followed by a colon and the name of the person.

BUSINESS LETTER NOTATION

ABBREVIATION	STANDS FOR	PURPOSE
Enc.	enclosure	alerts the reader that there is material enclosed within the envelope in addition to the letter
cc	courtesy copy (or "carbon copy")	indicates that a copy of the letter has been sent to another person

In business letters, as with most other forms of business communication, you are often trying to make an impression, so it is vitally important that you carefully proofread your work to ensure that it is free of errors.

2-2B: RÉSUMÉS

Like the business letter, in consideration of your busy reading audience, the résumé must be clear and concise. Many employers prefer résumés that are two pages, or even a single page, in length. That means you will need to decide what about your work and education are most relevant to the position for which you are applying. As well, you are competing to make an impression. In part, a good impression can be created through effective résumé organization and attractive layout and document design. Do, however, avoid gimmicks and wild formats and fonts. Business readers tend to be quite conservative in their expectations about résumés.

There are several acceptable and highly effective résumé formats. A one-page model is provided on page 77, a two-page model on pages 78–79. You might consult a specialized career book that includes a range of résumé formats or check out résumé-related sites on the Internet.

A few elements are standard to most résumés. Here are some guidelines that you should consider as you compose and design an effective résumé.

HEADINGS

Your name and address should be centred at the top of the page. If possible, include alternative means of reaching you such as an e-mail address or fax number. For some positions, the preliminary application process is handled exclusively through e-mail.

OBJECTIVE/SKILLS

These elements are not found on all résumés. The objective shows that you are focused, ambitious, and have long-term goals. Indicate how the particular position you are applying for relates to your goals. Itemize skills and abilities you have that can be applied in the position.

WORK EXPERIENCE/EDUCATION

Arrange this information in reverse chronological order to emphasize your most recent accomplishments. If you have an extensive work and educational background, select only the information that most directly relates to the position for which you are applying.

ADDITIONAL EXPERIENCE

Information in this section might be specifically related to the position and/or varied to communicate that you are a well-rounded person. Related volunteer work, for example, may be usefully listed here.

RELATED INTERESTS

Some people like to mention other activities or interests—for example, particular sports, hobbies such as cooking or bridge, a love of travel, and so on. These can occasionally be helpful, but remember, your private enthusiasms may be off-putting to someone else, depending on her or his inclinations. Before you include such information, ask yourself, "Is this information relevant to my suitability for the position? Will it contribute to the impression that I would be a good addition to this company?"

REFERENCES

Always ask permission before using someone's name as a reference. Most often, two or three references are requested. Do not put the names of your references on your résumé unless they are specifically requested; an employer interested in hiring you will request references after your interview. On your résumé, as in the sample that follows, include the standard line "References available upon request."

Tips

- Have a computer copy of your résumé available. When you apply for a specific position, make an electronic copy of it, then customize the résumé to indicate how your background and abilities particularly relate to the position.
- Use headings to outline your résumé organization and help prospective employers find the information they need.
- Use bullets to draw the reader's eye to information you want to emphasize. Don't overuse them, however, as this defeats the purpose.

These days it is helpful to have a version of your résumé that is scannable. In this version, avoid enhancements such as bold, caps, italics, or underlining. Also use a sans-serif font style, such as Arial or Tahoma, and a font size of 10, 11, or 12. Avoid graphics or columns and print your résumé on a laser printer to make sure the print is clear. If a résumé is to be submitted electronically, keep formatting to a minimum: don't use tabs, bullets, parentheses, or brackets, though hyphens and asterisks are acceptable. Don't centre or justify text; use a ragged-right margin. Don't fold or staple your résumé when you send it through the mail, to facilitate scanning.

When submitting a résumé, always include a covering letter that indicates the position for which you are applying and where you heard about the job. Briefly summarize important and position-relevant information from your résumé, and state your availability for a meeting to discuss the position.

2-2C: MEMOS

Memos, short for memoranda, are internal company or organization communications. Memos are written for various purposes:

- to report information, such as progress or achievements
- to identify problems and possible solutions
- to make requests
- to ask questions and provide answers
- to announce meetings
- to serve as reminders
- to make recommendations

Sample Résumé 1: One Page

Naomi Bahadur
12 Princess Dr.
Marktown, ON M2P 1L0
(905) 995-9905
e-mail: nbahadur@posto.ca

OBJECTIVE: To become an investigative journalist specializing in educational issues.

SKILLS

- ability to research thoroughly and meticulously using a wide range of traditional and new media
- proficiency in analyzing information and statistical data
- excellent writing and editorial skills
- strong project management skills; ability to complete complex assignments on time
- high computer literacy; experience with many word-processing, graphics, and desktop design programs

WORK EXPERIENCE

Research Intern. University of Waterloo. April–September, 2003–2005. Assisted in educational research projects for three professors.

Administrative Assistant Intern. British Columbia Ministry of Education. April–September 2002. Helped administer and improve a computer records filing system in the Assessment Branch.

Market Research. Ed Delottenville Group. March–October 2001. Conducted telephone research to determine needs of decision-makers in the telecommunications industry.

ADDITIONAL EXPERIENCE

Adult Literacy volunteer tutor. Taught basic literacy skills to young adults with severe developmental problems.

EDUCATION

Carleton University, Ottawa. Bachelor of Arts (Journalism) expected in 2008.

References available upon request.

Sample Résumé 2: Two Pages

ALISHA M. ELLIS
7 Oliver Crescent • Port Sunter, Ontario L8J 1Q4 • (905) 339-0077 •
ellisa@vero.ca

Objective: Videographer Position with CKKK Television News Department

EDUCATION
Graduating April 2007 McMaster University, Hamilton, Ontario
Bachelor of Arts: Honours Communications
Areas of focus: Mass Communications and Performance Studies

1998–2001 Mohawk College, Hamilton, Ontario
Broadcast Journalism and Communications Diploma
Areas of focus: Newsgathering, Shooting, and Editing

TELEVISION EXPERIENCE
June 2005–Present CKKK Television, Hamilton, Ontario
Reporter
- Researched and developed original and creative news story ideas
- Arranged and conducted interviews
- Wrote and edited packages and voice-overs
- Presented live throws and tags for reports

Summer 2002 High School TV Network, Toronto, Ontario
Writer
- Produced scripts and storyboards for on-air hosts
- Selected and explored relevant topics for teenage audiences
- Established contacts and possible guests for future interviews

Summer 2001 CTV Newsnet, Scarborough, Ontario
Intern
- Monitored news and satellite feeds for corresponding information
- Wrote voice-over scripts for on-air anchors
- Selected, timed, and sequenced footage for voice-overs

PROFESSIONAL EXPERIENCE
2003–2004 Golden Martial Arts, Oakville, Ontario
Office Administrator
- Answered phones and provided potential clients with information
- Sold membership packages and helped establish new club in Oakville
- Organized filing system and established functional accounting systems

2002–2003 Dragon Health Fitness Club, Ancaster, Ontario
Certified Personal Trainer

- Administered physical fitness assessments for clientele
- Designed client-specific workout routines and diet plans
- Achieved 100% client renewal rate in personal training sales

1999–2002 Mohawk College, Hamilton, Ontario
Assistant Liquor Service Manager at "The Spot" Bar and Restaurant

- Hired, trained, and scheduled employees
- Supervised weekly "Pub Night" with capacity crowds of 800 people
- Ordered liquor, food products, and supplies to ensure proper inventory levels
- Prepared payroll and bank deposits

SKILLS
Computer

- Experienced with ENPS Newsgathering System
- Trained in Microsoft Word, Excel, and PowerPoint applications
- Skilled in Internet research and web design

Additional Skills

- Familiar with Hamilton and the surrounding area
- Valid "G" driver's license
- Proficient in speaking French and Jamaican patois

Demo reel enclosed.

References available upon request.

When producing written communications within any company or organization, it is important to identify and follow the particular format and style preferences of that company or organization. In most cases, memos should be brief—if possible, a single page in length. These days, memos are often electronic, most usually in the form of e-mail messages.

Memos must be written and designed so they can be read and understood quickly. Memos prompt action; thus, the last paragraph of a memo usually asks the reader to do something and includes contact and timing information. A memo's content, organization, and features should help a reader scan and skim the document for essential information. Most memos follow a fairly standard format and include three basic elements: heading, subject line, and body.

HEADING

The heading includes the following information:

To:	Tells to whom the memo is addressed
cc:	Indicates who, if anyone, will receive a copy of the memo
From:	Identifies the writer of the memo
Date:	States when the memo was written (information essential for filing purposes)

SUBJECT LINE

The subject line identifies clearly and concisely what the memo is about—its essential purpose.

BODY

Since the memo may not be read in its entirety, very important information should be summarized in the introductory paragraph. To help the reader scan and skim for important information, consider including the following text features:

- headings
- underlining
- displayed lists
- bullets

Do not overuse these features, however, as together they can contribute to visual clutter.

A sample memo is provided on page 81.

Sample Memo

Justintime Press
MEMORANDUM

To:	Company History Book Committee
cc:	Edward Laskins
From:	Shelly Entwistle
Date:	June 16, 2007
Subject:	Company history book progress

As you are aware, the official 50th anniversary of Justintime Press is January 15, 2008. Ms. McIroy, the Executive VP of our parent company, will be in attendance. It is imperative that the commemorative company history book be in our warehouse no later than January 13. I need to be brought up to speed on the project's progress.

Meeting
I'd like to have a meeting, at which time I'd like to hear short progress reports from each committee member. My schedule is extremely busy during July, as I will be going on the road for most of the month. However, I have the following dates and times open:

- July 17 4:00 p.m.–5:30 p.m.
- July 19 8:30 a.m.–10:30 a.m.
- July 21 11:00 a.m.–1:00 p.m.

Please let me know by e-mail no later than June 28 which dates are most convenient for each of you.

Budget
We have a very tight budget for this project, so please include in your reports an account of how much money you have spent to date in your respective areas, and how much you anticipate spending to complete this important project on time. Include in your estimates any overtime you foresee.

2-2D: REPORT WRITING

Reports aim to give information and, usually, make recommendations about a given course of action. They are often solicited from experts in a particular field, who research and study a problem and submit their response to it. Reports are not discussions written to consider ideas in the abstract; they are structured presentations designed to help someone act on a particular problem.

Reports may be formal or informal. Informal reports include an introduction, a problem statement or purpose, background, methodology (including schedule and budget), a statement of credentials, and perhaps an appendix. A formal report includes all of these items as well as a letter of transmittal or cover letter, an executive summary or abstract, a title page, a table of contents, and possibly a list of illustrations included in the report. This chapter will not deal with formal reports, but it will deal with the informal kind. Informal reports may appear in a variety of forms, from informal proposals to trip reports, incident reports, accident reports, sales reports, and progress reports.

When you write a report, you typically consider two rhetorical issues: audience and purpose.

AUDIENCE

Reports are generally written with multiple audiences in mind. In a company, for example, a report might be read not only by the president who requested it, but by the management teams who are to put its recommendations in place, and by the engineers who will be required to design and build certain equipment as a result.

When writing a report, ask yourself these questions:

- Who are the audiences you are writing for?
- What do they know already?
- What do they need to know?

PURPOSE

The purpose of a report is usually to solve a problem or make a recommendation for action. You need to decide what the issues are, gather information, analyze your findings, and then write up the final report.

CONTENT AND STRUCTURE

The body of the report usually comprises some or all of the following sections, as appropriate for the purpose and audience.

Depending on the context of the report, you may not need to include such sections as analysis and discussion, appendix, or bibliography.

- purpose and background
- methodology
- results
- analysis and discussion
- conclusions
- recommendations
- appendix
- bibliography
- credentials or qualifications

PURPOSE AND BACKGROUND

This section explains why the report was written and why it is important. It fills in gaps to explain the history of the problem and anything relevant to its investigation. Reports typically include a problem statement (or, less often, a thesis statement) that explains what led to the research and writing of the report. In addition, reports, like essays, avoid suspense, so if your research led to recommendations that are detailed later in the report, they should be summarized briefly here at the outset.

METHODOLOGY

Describe how the research was done and why you decided to approach the problem the way you did. You may include timelines and budgets in this section as well.

RESULTS

Clearly present what you found, showing essential data and calculations, and using visuals, where appropriate, to explain your findings.

ANALYSIS AND DISCUSSION

Here you may discuss your findings and offer various alternatives for action that you wish the reader to consider. (This section is more commonly found in a formal report.)

CONCLUSIONS

Summarize your main conclusions and compare them to your original purpose.

RECOMMENDATIONS

State your recommendations, if you have any to make. Make suggestions for action or further research.

APPENDIX

Include in this section any data or calculations that support your findings. These should be referred to in the body of the report.

BIBLIOGRAPHY

Cite any sources that you used to arrive at your final written work.

CREDENTIALS AND QUALIFICATIONS

List any credentials, qualifications, and experience that indicate your expertise in the subject area relevant to the report.

PROPOSALS

One of the most common types of report is the proposal, which outlines a project and asks for approval to go forward with it. In many respects, a proposal is like a job application, though in this case, you design your own job and show why you are the person who should be hired to do it.

Some proposals are formatted as a two- or three-page letter or memo. The letter format, of course, would be used when you are writing to a company for which you do not work. Memos are reserved for internal company correspondence.

A proposal that uses a letter or memo format must still contain the basic information sections discussed above:

- purpose and background
- methodology, including schedule and budget
- credentials: your (or your team's) qualifications

You should also include, if appropriate, a closing section that asks for approval or authorization. See Sample Informal Report 1 for an example of a proposal in letter format.

When proposals are produced internally at a company, they are often written in memo format. If you are working for a company and addressing someone in that company, a memo is the appropriate form of communication for an informal proposal. See Sample Informal Report 2 for a student example of a proposal in internal memo format.

Sample Informal Report 1: Proposal in Letter Format

Marnie Hamel
45 Ornaldo Ct.
Manfred, ON L9Q 1U7
(905) 555-1201
e-mail: mlhamel@togo.ca

November 28, 2007

Patricia O'Donohue
Public Affairs
KLQM Limited
1200 Meyer Pl.
Toronto, ON M2W 4Q5

Dear Patricia:

Time is extremely valuable with any learning experience. The more time you are given, the more chances you have to gain a deeper knowledge. This idea of a longer time span for an intern at KLQM Limited is one that you proposed to me. What I want to present to you is a concrete plan for increasing the length of the internship at KLQM. Specifically, this proposal hopes to enhance the programs already in place.

Problem Background

The short contract time of internships at KLQM Limited is not as useful and practical as it can be.

Currently, the internship program at KLQM runs for a period of four months. One of these appointments commences in September and the other in January. Once a student has earned an internship, he or she is scheduled for two to three days per week to work at KLQM. While this method ensures that at least two students are given a unique learning opportunity each year, a longer internship period would be helpful for both the student and the organization.

A prolonged contract with KLQM would allow an intern to become more intricately familiar with the workings of public affairs and result in more responsibilities and work for the intern to participate in. Also, a longer internship would give employees the chance to fully flex and exercise their knowledge and expertise in the working world.

KLQM invests resources, money, and efforts of employees into the internship program. Bettering the program can only benefit all parties involved: interns, KLQM Limited, and the employees in the public affairs department.

Proposed Idea

I would like you to consider the idea of lengthening the internship program. Rather than two positions in September and January, one continuous position from September until the end of April, merging two positions into one, would streamline operations and provide a more fulfilling experience. As well, it would be beneficial to introduce a summer internship position from May until the end of August.

Benefits to Idea
With internship positions, an employer is given the chance to consider a potential employee without having to make a long-term commitment. This allows the employer to train the potential employee to their working standards and practices. Lengthening the time would give KLQM a better period to achieve this. In the fast-paced working world of Canadian broadcasting, it is essential that potential employees have experience or adequate training. There is often not that much time to train new employees before throwing them into the action. An intern with a prolonged period of training can overcome this obstacle. It also reduces the risk an employer takes when hiring new employees. Familiarity with the working style of a person—that knowledge of what to expect—is an essential bonus to employers. Your time, resources, efforts, and financial investment will not be wasted on a bad hiring decision.

Creating an added summer internship position also places an extra person in the department to help in all areas and projects of the public affairs department. Summer months are very popular for vacations among employees. When an employee decides to go away for a few days, the work that he or she does will not have to halt with them. An intern can pitch in at this crucial time. Because the public affairs department at KLQM is small, the absence of even one person can greatly reduce the productivity of the work and increase the time it takes to accomplish a task. One needs only to examine the missed sponsorship and donations opportunities from previous summers to realize this. How many great causes and chances at positive, socially responsible publicity did KLQM Limited miss out on because the employee handling this work was away? That absence delayed KLQM's ability to examine and consider a donation request. It is another missed opportunity for KLQM to excel in fulfilling its social responsibility as a national corporation.

Merging two positions into one longer position does equal a loss of one intern through most of the year. However, it is a greater enhancement to the quality of education and experience provided to the selected internship candidate. Internships are highly competitive positions to begin with. KLQM received an excess of 100 applications for the September 2007 placement. From that mass volume of applications and the ones selected for interviews, it was then narrowed down to two candidates. A lot of time and effort was given to this process. This is then repeated when examining candidates for the January internship. This results in loss of time for the KLQM employees given the responsibility of recruiting and soliciting applicants. It is time away from their work and a distraction that can be reduced for a greater good. Selecting one candidate for one lengthier position would reduce the time and effort needed for the recruitment of potential interns. It would also enhance the quality of education and experience KLQM provides the successful candidate. This would give the intern a longer time to gain a broader amount of practical experience.

Budget
Presently, KLQM awards interns with a $1,000 honorarium at the completion of their contracted internship time. With this proposal, KLQM would award a $2,000 honorarium to the successful intern instead.

Because the summer position would last only about four months, an honorarium of $1,000 would be awarded to the intern upon completion.

Conclusion
KLQM takes pride in its internship program. It takes pride in the strong sense of community it nurtures throughout all aspects of KLQM Limited. KLQM has always strived to make the media and broadcasting industry accessible to a diverse public. Restructuring the internship program can only come with a gain in the investment of KLQM's resources, time, effort, people, and money.

Thank you for taking the time to read this proposal. I hope it has provided you with a critical look at what is currently in place. I would be happy to further discuss this matter with you. I have strongly benefited from my experience at KLQM and would like a chance to also pass on some of the perspective I am gaining from this experience to you.

Sincerely,

Marnie Hamel

Marnie Hamel

Sample Informal Report 2: Proposal in Internal Memo Format

Strewn Inc.
1339 Lakeshore Rd., R.R. #3
Niagara-on-the-Lake, ON LOS 1JO

DATE: June 29, 2007
TO: Jane Langdori, Owner/Coordinator of Wine Country Cooking School at Strewn Winery, and Joe Will, Winemaker
FROM: Caitlin P. Williams, Customer Service
SUBJECT: Proposal for December Winemaker's Dinners

Throughout the calendar year, Strewn Winery plays host to various events that draw tourism and buyers to the Niagara Region. However, every year, during the month of December, the winery does not offer a special event. That is why I wish to submit the following proposal outlining my plan for December Winemaker's Dinners that are designed to draw holiday buyers to Strewn Winery.

Background and Purpose

As you know, December is a quiet and slow month for Strewn Winery. Holiday buyers are rushing to local liquor stores and home decor stores to stock up on wine and wine accessories for holiday entertaining and gift-giving rather than visiting the wineries. Hours for staff are cut back and the lack of tours and customers can make the day drag on. Daily sales decrease significantly since the tourist season is "over." However, with the success of the Taste the Season Touring Passport in November and the Icewine Festival in January, it has been proven that "off-season" events can draw great business. That is why I have come up with the proposed plan for holding Winemaker's Dinners in the month of December. Such an event would continue to draw business to the winery over the holiday season.

Procedure

I propose that, starting in September 2007, planning for Winemaker's Dinners should begin. The dinners would be held over a three-weekend trial in December 2007 with the intention of becoming an annual event. The following outlines the organizational process that will be necessary, the execution of the event, and finally my intended results for Strewn Winery and the Wine Country Cooking School (WCCS) once the event is over.

Organization

Next September I would like to start brainstorming with you both, Jane and Joe. I have chosen you, Jane, because such an event needs a place where food can be prepared as well as a qualified staff to prepare it. The WCCS does not hold recreational classes over the month of December and therefore your facility and staff would be available over the designated Winemaker's Dinner weekends. I have chosen you, Joe, as the other member of this team since you are the winemaker and the event would be hosted by you. I believe there is great appeal in having the winemaker host the dinner because it makes people feel like honoured guests to have been invited to the winery for the evening and knowing you have hand-picked the appropriate wine to go with each course gives people an opportunity to ask you, a professional, about food and wine pairing.

Additionally, I like the idea of a husband-and-wife team working together in a "perfect marriage of food and wine," as you always say. The initial brainstorming session would primarily revolve around discussing food courses, the event layout, and any foreseeable problems that could arise.

The proposed event would take place on the Friday and Saturday of the first three weekends in December 2007 from 6:30 p.m. to approximately 9:30 p.m. I propose that the first two Saturdays and the entire final weekend of the event be reserved for any corporate or large private groups of between twenty and thirty people. For these dinners, the event would be marketed as a potential location for company staff parties. This leaves the first two Fridays open to the general public, providing an opportunity for single, rather than group, ticket sales for up to thirty people each night. Our guest list would target Strewn Barrel Club members, Futures members, and the corporate groups that you, Jane, have developed relationships with through the WCCS. These people are known high-end buyers and wine and food enthusiasts. We would use our website to post an advertisement for the Winemaker's Dinners as well as electronically send formal invitations through e-mail. Additionally, we may wish to set up a package deal for overnight accommodations with Harbour House. Tickets for the dinner would sell for $120, turning nearly a $60 profit for each ticket sold. This ticket price includes a four-course meal, wine, and winery tour. It does not include gratuities.

I have already worked out an approximate food and wine budget, as well as looked into pricing from Classic Party Rentals for tables, chairs, and linens. (This information can be found in the "Budget" section of this proposal.) The cutlery, dishes, and wine glasses would be provided from the WCCS's personal collection. I would like to continue our partnership with Vine Floral and purchase decorative wreaths and centrepieces that would last through all three weekends. Jane, at a later date, you and one of your staff members would get together to plan a four-course menu for the dinners. Then, two weeks later, you and that staff member would conduct trial runs of the decided menu to work out any hitches.

Execution

The Winemaker's Dinners would be held on the weekends of December 1–2, 8–9, and 15–16, 2007. I, as the event planner, would be overseeing each event, making sure everything runs smoothly and helping out where necessary. At 6:30 p.m. guests would arrive and congregate in the tasting bar for a wine and cheese course. At 7:00 Joe would officially greet and welcome everyone and then guests would be taken on a tour of the winery by a winery staff member. At 7:30 the guests would be escorted to the barrel cellar where the next three courses will be served. I believe the ambiance of the barrel cellar provides a unique setting for the dinner. Vine Floral does wonderful old-fashioned wreaths, garlands, and centrepieces that would help create a rustic but traditional holiday theme in the cellar. Additionally, I propose using small, white Christmas lights and candles for lighting the cellar. Joe would introduce each wine as it is served with each course. Our Terroir Reserve wines (the best of the best) would be poured and marketed as great holiday wines and/or gifts because of their aging potential and premium quality. At the end of the evening, guests would have an opportunity to visit our retail shop to browse for holiday wine and gift selections. From Strewn's previous experience, we know that after events like these, individuals will spend hundreds of dollars on wines they enjoyed and gift items they find intriguing.

Intended Results
Winemaker's Dinners are a solution to the uneventful, slow sales month of December. This event would draw high-end clientele away from the LCBO and toward the winery, where wider selections of Strewn wines are sold. Naturally, people spend more than usual in the month of December on entertaining and gifts. This event would provide a showcase for our high-end product which people would be inclined to buy in cases. It would also entice guests to buy gift certificates to the WCCS for 2008 classes and/or join the Barrel Club. In the end, the event would generate significantly higher sales and profit for the month of December and be excellent public relations for the winery. Additionally, since December is known for being a big spending month, these dinners would provide Strewn and WCCS staff members with desirable holiday hours to help plump up otherwise smaller paycheques.

Schedule
With your approval, the following 2007 schedule has been arranged for the planning and execution of the December Winemaker's Dinners:

Brainstorming session with Caitlin, Jane, and Joe	September 5
Devise list of high-end clients	September 25
Website advertisement set-up	September 29
E-mail high-end clientele	October 4
Booking groups	October 9–27
Menu decisions	October 30
Rental arrangements	October 30–31
Menu trials	November 13–14
Choose floral arrangements	November 14
Friday/Saturday Dinner Week 1	November 30–December 1
Friday/Saturday Dinner Week 2	December 7–8
Friday/Saturday Dinner Week 3	December 14–15

Credentials
As you know, I have been an employee of Strewn Winery for three years and will soon be graduating from McMaster University with the intention of pursuing a career in event planning or public relations. Already, I have experience helping co-coordinate Strewn events such as the spring White Release Party, the fall Red

Release Party, and last summer's Sobey's convention. Since I have had the opportunity to work alongside the cooking school for many of these events, I feel I have a thorough grasp of how all the inner workings of the winery operate. Additionally, I have been the event coordinator for the McMaster Theatre and Film Society semi-formal, which was a huge success. I feel I have proven myself as a qualified event planner who is organized, pays close attention to detail, and works well with others. I have a vested interest in Strewn Winery and am committed to seeing nothing but continued success in every aspect of our business.

Budget

Event Planning

	Estimated Hours	Rate	Total
Brainstorming session (3 people)	3	$20/hr	$180
Devise list of high-end clients	3	$20/hr	$ 60
Website advertisement set-up	3	$20/hr	$ 60
E-mail high-end clientele	2	$20/hr	$ 40
Booking groups	6	$20/hr	$120
Rental arrangements	3	$20/hr	$ 60
Menu decisions (2 people)	5	$18/hr	$180
Menu trials (2 people)	8	$18/hr	$288
Design			
Choosing floral arrangements	2	$20/hr	$ 40
Estimated floral/decorative costs			$300
Total Initial Costs			$1328

The following reflects one weekend (two nights) at the maximum of 30 attendees per night.

Staffing Costs

	Estimated Hours	Rate	Total
Set up (3 people)	4	$10/hr	$120
Cooking (4 people)	10	$20/hr	$800
Tour guide	2	$10/hr	$ 20
Serving staff/clean up (4 people)	8	$ 6/hr	$192
Event planner	12	$20/hr	$240
Food and Wine Costs			
Food			$600
Wine			$300
Event Rental Costs			
8" x 30" Banquet table x 3			$27
12' Table linen x 3			$45
Napkins x 30			$29
Chair rentals x 30			$240
Total Costs per Weekend			$2613

Authorization

I am convinced, Jane and Joe, that hosting December Winemaker's Dinners will be a huge financial and public relations success for Strewn Winery and the WCCS. Please let me know by August 1, 2007 if you decide that this is an event you would like to host at Strewn Winery. This way, we can work out the financial details before our first brainstorming session scheduled for September 5, 2007.

3

RESEARCH PAPERS

What is research but a **blind** date with knowledge?

–*Will Harvey*

3

Research Papers

3 Research Papers

Writing research papers is an essential part of your postsecondary education and, quite possibly, of your occupation. Many of the skills and techniques you apply in writing a paper draw heavily on what you learned about writing essays in Chapter 1, "Composing a Document." However, an essential difference between the short essay and the research paper is that, in the latter, the majority of the information you present comes from other sources. Often you will need to use other people's information and ideas to formulate your own conclusions. This does not mean that you can blithely reproduce verbatim what others have said and written. Rather you must analyze, evaluate, and synthesize your research findings and organize them to develop and support your own views and positions.

Before even entering a library or going online to start your research, you will need to do considerable planning to ensure that your research time is spent efficiently and productively. Any research project you choose will demand a research strategy, a careful and systematic assessment of your findings, and the ability to write down your findings in a way that will enable others to learn from and benefit from your work.

With computer-based research capabilities that allow quick and convenient access to a world of accurate information, you can write an outstanding research paper using brilliant sources that are at your fingertips. You need, however, to take charge of the schedule and the research process to break down the overall assignment into manageable tasks.

KEY TASKS IN THE RESEARCH PROCESS

Before entering a library or going online to conduct research:

- identify a worthwhile research-paper topic from good research questions
- focus the topic to make it manageable in scope
- identify good potential information sources about that topic
- generate workable research strategies

At the research library and online:

- locate sources
- evaluate sources to ensure that the information they provide is credible, is reliable, and meets research-topic needs
- read to gather information

- take useful research notes
- ethically, completely, and correctly document and acknowledge all sources consulted and used in the paper

The last point is crucial to academic researching and research-paper writing. Since you will need to draw from other sources, it is important to know what, when, and how to acknowledge these research sources properly. In this way, you can avoid plagiarism (see Chapter 4 for a detailed discussion of what plagiarism is and how to avoid it.) One of the best ways to avoid plagiarism problems is to use an accepted style of documentation to cite the sources for any phrases or ideas not completely your own.

3-1: RESEARCHING A TOPIC

In most academic disciplines, certain questions or types of questions appear again and again. For instance, in discussions or readings in political history courses, you will frequently hear or see variations of questions such as these:

- How does (such and such contemporary source) account for the causes of the conflict/war?
- What factors might explain the success/failure of the treaty/policy decision?

As you plan your research for a paper, keep in mind those questions central to your discipline. The goal of most academic research is to answer a question. This question may be stated explicitly in your research paper, or it may be implicit. Often a definitive answer cannot be found, but new light can be shed on important and complex issues and ideas.

A manageable research question is the fundamental starting point of the research process. A good question provides a solid framework and a clear direction for your research.

3-1A: FORMULATING RESEARCH QUESTIONS

As with writing a short essay, the first challenge in writing a research paper is getting ideas—here research questions—on paper. Your instructor may have given you a specific research question or topic. Often, however, you will be given the freedom to frame your own research question.

There are a number of sources you might call on for help in developing ideas for research questions in any subject:

- *Your own interests:* Jot down questions that have sparked your interest and aroused curiosity during your studies.
- *Core questions in your discipline:* Good research questions can come from your recollections of class discussions or lectures, or from your course notes.
- *Course materials:* Reviewing your textbooks can help give you a sense of important questions and issues. These might even be suggested by section or chapter headings.
- *Print or broadcast media:* Reliable and credible media can offer leads to research questions on more current topics. Sources can include popular magazines or academic journals, depending on the subject.
- *Discussion with experts:* From this source you can often get leads on what sources to consult next, such as books or other experts who could answer questions.
- *The Web:* Enter a general topic related to your discipline in an Internet search engine, then review article annotations. Sometimes posted research papers suggest issues and questions for further study.

You may also find it helpful to apply some of the idea-generating techniques outlined in 1-1b, such as brainstorming and free-writing.

An overall consideration of potential research topics might yield very general potential research questions such as the following:

> What would be the major consequences of Canada's becoming a republic?
>
> Are monitoring devices a suitable alternative to incarceration for certain types of crimes?
>
> What are the pros and cons of solar-powered transportation in Canada?
>
> What are the ethical and medical issues associated with stem cell research?

By consulting general and course resources and opening your mind to free association, you can generate research questions that can either frame your research or lead you to other questions that could serve as the starting point for your research paper. This kind of research question gives your search and the work you finally produce a focus. This focus will usually become your thesis statement, but you need to work toward finding a specific direction for your thinking. Seek questions that are open to discussion, provocative, and unlikely to be answered definitively. Your work is thus intended to persuade the reader of the best possible answer, given the evidence you uncover.

3-1B: NARROWING YOUR RESEARCH FOCUS

Initial ideas for research questions will probably be based on your existing knowledge of the topic and reflect your own particular interests. Next, you will need to explore general resources to obtain a better understanding of the topic. As you become more knowledgeable, you will want to focus your guiding research question more precisely.

Time invested in narrowing your focus will make your research task ultimately much more manageable and less frustrating. At this stage of your research, take a realistic look at

- the time you can afford to spend on researching and writing
- the research resources available on your topic

It's a good idea to make an exploratory trip to the library, then limit your research question based on available library resources. Among the techniques you might apply and the resources you might explore to do this are the following:

- Check the library's website to see if subject research guides have been set up. Some libraries list subject headings (e.g., Art) followed by the major encyclopedias, dictionaries, bibliographies, and online databases on that subject, plus any major reference works (online and printed materials). For an example, see http://main.library.utoronto.ca/eir/articlesbytopic.cfm?subject=10.
- Visit the library and ask for any printed material the library has produced for research guides.
- Visit or e-mail the subject librarian.
- Attend information sessions by librarians on the reference tools for a particular subject.
- Scan headings of online university catalogues to get a sense of topics and sub-topics related to your general research question.
- Browse online or hard-copy periodical listings to obtain a sense of important research questions.
- Look up keywords in the indexes of subject encyclopedias such as the *Encyclopedia of Psychology* or the *Encyclopedia of Science and Technology*. These keywords may lead to more specific sub-topics

related to a general topic. Online encyclopedias, while not always indexed, may offer subject groups that can lead to sub-topics.
- Read articles in a general information source such as the current edition of *The Canadian Encyclopedia*. Ideas and information in a general article might spark ideas for more focused questions that will frame a precise context for further research.
- Note any relevant encyclopedia articles or further readings at the end of general articles. These resources could lead you to a more refined research question.

3-1C: FINDING SOURCES

A research strategy is an organized, systematic plan for tracking down and assembling sources of information for your research. By creating such a plan, you give direction to the research process, and you will find that you locate the information you need more efficiently.

A successful plan will take into consideration the requirements of the topic, your own background knowledge about the topic, the library resources available, and the time available to conduct the research. Research work requires that you locate and evaluate many more sources than you eventually use in your paper.

While an intelligent research strategy must be systematic, it should not be treated as lock step. Once the strategy is created, you do not need to follow it blindly. Research should be a process of discovery, so you must be open to ideas and information that will take you in directions you did not anticipate. As well, any research process can be recursive; this means that once you think you've completed one stage, you could find ideas or information that require you to revisit and repeat steps.

Here are some general questions you might consider as you formulate your research strategy.

- What do I already know about the topic?
- What kinds of information will I need for a research paper of this nature?
- What kinds of sources should I consult to find this needed information?
- In what order should I find and evaluate these sources?
- Where can I obtain these sources of information (e.g., at a university or reference library, at a community library, in a personal library, on the Web)?

- What skills, resources, technologies, and research resource people will help me tap into the information I need?

Generally, the type of information you need for the assignment will affect your research strategy and scheduling. For instance, if you need to base your research on primary sources, such as interviews and surveys, it will take longer to collect the required information. And if you use secondary sources, or work from other investigators and researchers, you will need to be systematic and meticulous in recording and ethically acknowledging the work of others.

The best way to structure your strategy is from the general to the specific. For example, when working on a humanities research paper, in the early stages of research, you should read very general articles about the topic, such as those found in encyclopedias. As you become more knowledgeable about the topic, locate and read more specialized articles, such those found in journals. Often you will find that by reading article abstracts, you can decide if it is worth your time and effort to read an entire article.

As you articulate your search strategy on paper, you will probably find that sources start to cluster. For instance, some sources are general and available at the university or college library, so these libraries will be a logical place to start your research. Other sources might be more highly specialized and stored in special collections, so you would pursue this information later in the research process.

KEEPING A RESEARCH LOG

Keep a list of the sources you examine, both physical and virtual, either in a notebook or in an electronic file.

- Mark down titles and location of materials according to the documentation system you intend to use (APA, MLA, Chicago, or otherwise). These will constitute your working bibliography.
- Summarize briefly in your own words what you found that was useful in a given resource, and keep track of details and quotations that might be pertinent later.
- Keep notes about your thinking as you peruse these resources.

FINDING RESEARCH MATERIALS

Many people find libraries intimidating, but they are very helpful resources, either in person or electronically. There are many online resources published by colleges and universities that provide step-by-step guides to using the resources available, regardless of your discipline. An example of one such guide (from York University) can be found at http://www.library.yorku.ca/roadmap/index.html. Your college or university likely has similar helpful online resources, all aimed at making the process easier. You may feel that your questions might seem stupid, but in fact, because resources change daily, your questions will often make good sense. Ask a librarian how to go about gaining access—both in person and online—to library materials.

These days, a great many resources are available online. With a user name and password from the educational institution in which you are enrolled, you will find you have instant access, even when you are at home, to thousands of resources, often in full-text form. Publicly available resources on the Internet are only a small part of the story. The online resources available in your school library allow you access to many authoritative resources that have been purchased for your use—up-to-date and across all disciplines. That said, the library is a great place to start, in person as well as online.

With this initial survey of key topic ideas and available resources completed, it's time to look more critically for specific subquestions that naturally grow out of general research questions. One approach is shown in the cluster diagram below.

The diagram illustrates how one student focused a very general and unmanageable research question about the consequences of

FIGURE 3.1
Sample Cluster Diagram

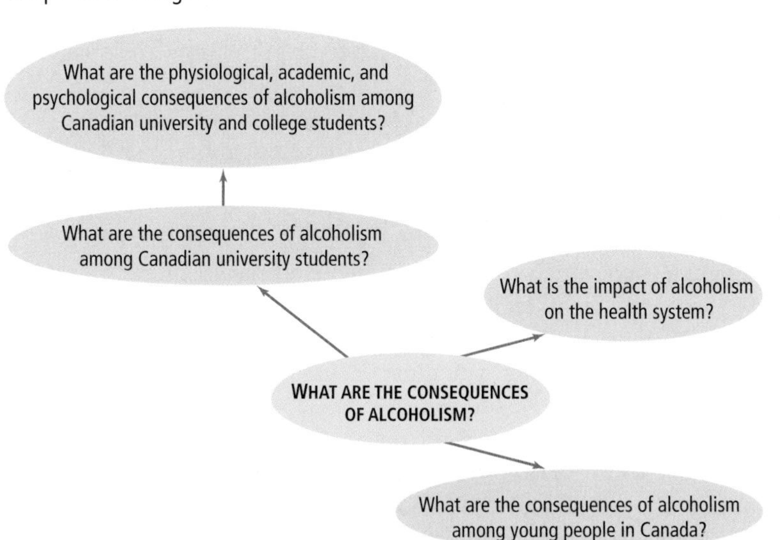

alcoholism. Depending on assignment requirements, the student might want to narrow his or her research even more precisely, for example, by focusing exclusively on physiological or psychological consequences.

Eventually, as you move into the writing stage, you will need to develop your research question into a good thesis statement. A thesis statement is a sentence that explicitly identifies the main point of the paper and perhaps previews its main ideas. (See 1-1c.)

TESTING YOUR RESEARCH QUESTION: TOO BROAD OR TOO NARROW?

You can test whether your overriding research question is too narrow or too broad by using keywords within the question as search terms on a library's catalogue system, periodical indexes, or Internet search engines. Generally, if you are finding too much material, it may indicate that your research question is too broad. If you are finding too little material, it may indicate that you need to broaden the scope of your research question.

In most cases, avoid research questions that are too current, as a significant body of research information may not yet be available. As well, avoid topics that are too obscure—say, nightlife on the Falkland Islands—as it may be highly frustrating trying to find good information on a very specialized topic.

When you have a research question that you think is a good one, review it by asking these questions:

- Can I research and write about this topic in the time and space allowed?
- Does the topic satisfy all the research assignment criteria?
- Am I interested enough in the topic to spend my time and energy researching it and writing about it?

If you answered yes to all three questions, you're ready to formulate a good search strategy and then start researching.

Because a great deal of information is available in electronic format or must be located through computerized catalogues, databases, or search engines, you must ensure that your online research skills are up-to-date. When you go to the library at the institution where you work or go to school, make sure you know how to find materials by title, by author, and by subject keyword. Can you quickly find out about resources and technology tools to help you efficiently locate needed information? Also, keep your library skills current: make sure you can find shelf numbers that you need; investigate databases you may use for a project; and make sure you can find and use an index or other general reference work when you need to. Don't overlook the actual (as opposed to virtual) library—books and other printed materials are good sources of information. And if you get stuck at any stage of your research strategy, don't forget that one of your most reliable resources is "non–technology based": in other words, ask the librarian.

RESEARCHING: INSIDE AND OUTSIDE THE LIBRARY

College or university libraries offer storehouses of information. The library will probably be the focus of most of your search efforts. What resources you use will depend on your specific assignment, and the resources available at your particular college or university will vary. As well, what is available in libraries and how information is presented and accessed have changed dramatically in recent years: what used to be offered only in hard-copy format now appears in electronic, often online, formats. Becoming familiar with the library's website is also key to knowing where access tools such as the catalogue and the research databases are and how they are organized. The information provided below focuses on key strategies.

Learning how to find and retrieve needed information efficiently is a key part of your postsecondary education. Early in the academic year, you should thoroughly familiarize yourself with the college or university's library or libraries. It is your responsibility to find out what is available in the library, where that information is located, and whom to ask if you need help. Many universities provide free handouts on research skills; this information may be on their website as well. These resources can be as specific as "How to Research and Write a History Paper." Since so many university and college libraries allow you to access information through the computer, it is a good idea to learn how to use information-location technology before you need to use it for a particular research assignment. By doing so, you will avoid frustration and save precious research time.

The types of information you will probably use can be grouped into five broad categories.

1. Reference resources
2. Periodicals
3. Books from the library's general collection
4. Other sources within the library
5. Information outside the library

REFERENCE RESOURCES

Reference resources are good sources for factual information such as quick facts, subject overviews, and definitions. Many (e.g., *The Canadian Encyclopedia*) are available in both print and electronic form. Some library websites have a page for reference resources by subject.

Reference resources in print form are usually found in a specific reference section of the library. Most often, you should use them only for preliminary research, to obtain an overall understanding of your topic. Never rely exclusively on general reference resources; you will need to investigate further by exploring sources offering more specific information. Usually printed reference resources do not circulate; that is, they must be used within the library. Good resources for finding out about the various general reference books available are *Guide to Reference Books* by Eugene P. Sheehy and *Introduction to Reference Work*, 8th edition, by William A. Katz. A library website may also offer a brief introduction to reference works both in print and online, and librarians are good resources for finding the reference works related to a project.

Make sure to look at reference books independent of the Internet. These books provide a touchstone for the reader, a place to start. They give a basis of common, accepted knowledge in a particular discipline and often provide you with respected secondary sources that you should be aware of. Reference books, when up-to-date, are a guaranteed source of agreed-upon expert knowledge in any given field, whereas the Internet may give a basic common knowledge. Go to the field experts first, and get a good grounding in the subject before you let yourself loose on the Internet, where things are more disorganized and some contributors are self-appointed experts.

Reference resources can be located through the library's computer cataloguing system. Often they are labelled REF, for reference books. The following are some major types of reference resources and examples of each type.

ENCYCLOPEDIAS: Note that encyclopedias give information on a breadth of topics, and they usually provide extensive bibliographies that can serve as the basis for your own research. Whether online or in the library, encyclopedias are a wealth of general, if not absolutely current, information. If an entry on your topic is not available, try other keywords.

Reference Resources

TYPE	EXAMPLE
General Encyclopedias	*The Canadian Encyclopedia*
Word or Phrase Dictionaries	*ITP Nelson Canadian Dictionary*
Biographical Dictionaries	*Dictionary of Current Biography*
Almanacs and Yearbooks	*The World Almanac and Book of Facts*
Atlases	*Historical Atlas of Canada*
Gazetteers	*Columbia Lippincott Gazetteer of the World*
Directories	*Encyclopedia of Associations*
Books of Quotations	*Bartlett's Familiar Quotations*

Do not overlook special reference works for subject areas, such as the following:

History	*Cambridge Ancient History*
Literature	*Literary History of Canada*
Drama	*The Oxford Companion to the Theatre*
Philosophy	*The Encyclopedia of Philosophy*
Mythology	*Larousse World Mythology*
Music	*Grove's Dictionary of Music and Musicians*
Science	*The Encyclopedia of the Biological Sciences*
Technology	*McGraw-Hill Encyclopedia of Science and Technology*

WORD OR PHRASE DICTIONARIES: These works define words or terms. Use abridged dictionaries to limit the number of words, and use unabridged to find the wealth of words in a given language or discipline. Besides general dictionaries, remember that there are dictionaries that address individual disciplines.

BIOGRAPHICAL DICTIONARIES: These dictionaries tell you basic information about the lives of people that may help you to trace important events in a particular person's life. Ask for the volume appropriate to your research. Common examples include *The Dictionary of Canadian Biography* and *The Dictionary of National*

Biography (for British biographies); there are also volumes that have a narrower focus, such as *The Biographical Dictionary of American Sports*.

ALMANACS AND YEARBOOKS: These are compendiums of facts in a variety of subject areas, published both in print and online. They often provide good summaries of a year's events in areas as diverse as technology, sports, government, and science. Works such as *Canadian News Facts*, *Canada Year Book*, or *Demographic Yearbook* may contain information suitable for your topic.

ATLASES: These works compile maps of our planet and even of other planets. Depending on your topic, you might consult *The Atlas of Canada* or *The Times Atlas of the World*.

GAZETTEERS: These volumes contain geographical information, such as climate, population, resources, and topographical features. Examples include *Gazetteer of Canada*, *Canada Gazetteer Atlas*, and *The Columbia Gazetteer of the World*.

PERIODICALS AND NEWSPAPERS

Periodicals are publications, such as magazines and academic journals, that are issued on a regular basis but less frequently than daily. They can differ widely in content, readership, and frequency of publication. An example of a daily newspaper is *The Globe and Mail*; of a magazine, *Canadian Geographic*; and of an academic journal, *English Studies in Canada*. A periodical's audience can be as general as that of *Maclean's* or as specialized as that of *Dermatology Times*. Newspapers and periodicals can offer good sources of opinion and current information.

Within libraries, current or recent issues are often displayed in separate areas or rooms, while back issues are available from storage, or bound and placed in the general stacks. Some back issues of newspapers and magazines may be accessible online or on microfiche. Some are not published in print form at all but are available only as e-journals.

Periodicals and newspapers, as well as books, may be found in electronic databases as well as in the physical library. Note that databases may be convenient, but they also have their limitations, one of which is their focus on recent events. Often a periodical online will not include early references, so print sources are still a must. Coverage of online journals may go back only to the 1990s. If you need to refer to things less current, print is the only answer.

A database is a collection of information on a particular subject, usually acquired by a college or a university to allow users to search for information in a particular field. User fees may apply, so your registration in a particular institution may grant you access to materials not readily available to the general public. Databases may be accessed online or by CD-ROM, and there are two major types:

1. *Reference* databases indicate books or other print sources of information. Examples of popular source databases include Canadian Business and Current Affairs (CBCA) and PAIS International. These provide bibliographical material, such as title, author, date of publication, and publisher or periodical, depending on whether the material is a book or an article. You may also find an abstract, or summary, of the article, to help you ascertain whether it will be useful to you.
2. *Source* databases provide the information itself, which may include complete articles, statistics, and surveys. Some like ERIC (Educational Resources Information Center) give full text of articles or allow you to look up the article in microfiche. Depending on your subject matter, you may find EBSCOhost, Proquest, or a specialized medical database like OVID useful for your purposes. Sometimes these databases allow you to purchase articles in full. Ask a librarian for advice on which electronic databases pertinent to your topic are available in your library and how to access them.

LOCATING A PARTICULAR PERIODICAL ARTICLE: The best resource to use for locating particular periodical articles is a periodicals index. *The Readers' Guide to Periodical Literature* covers most American and some Canadian magazines, while the *Canadian Periodicals Index* focuses on Canadian magazines. Indexes can be available online or in print form. Sometime they are a combination, with more recent references indexed online and earlier references available in print form indexes. Often these indexes are available in print form in the reference section of a library, but increasingly libraries are offering these indexes in electronic databases. Computer databases make searching for particular entries easier, but you must know how to search the database using author, title, subject, or keyword search terms.

Other more specialized periodicals indexes include the following, many of which can be found online:

Art Index
Business Periodicals Index
Education Index
General Science Abstracts

Humanities Index
MLA International Bibliography of Books and Articles in the Modern Languages and Literatures
Music Index Online
PsychINFO
Social Sciences Abstracts

Many journal and newspaper articles are now accessible through electronic indexes and abstracts such as CBCA Current Events and Canadian Newsstand, or services such as Factiva. Generally these are organized by subject matter. Article sources may also be found under "reference databases" or "article databases" on a library website; finding a journal title will involve using the library's catalogue. For specific instruction on how to find articles and journals relevant to your topic through the library website, ask your librarian.

BOOKS

Books within the library's main collection will probably be one of the principal sources of information for your research report. At the majority of modern college and university libraries, books can be accessed through a computer catalogue system. As illustrated in the screen capture in Figure 3.2, you can search for a particular book through four major routes:

- by subject
- by title
- by author
- by a combination of keywords

Use whatever is most suitable in your circumstances.

Note that many books are now available electronically; a library catalogue will indicate whether a specific title is available in both hard-copy and electronic formats. The library catalogue may also direct you to publications that exist only in electronic format on the Web, as is the case with some Canadian government publications.

Suppose you were creating a research paper on regulating drinking water quality in Canada. You might enter the search term *drinking water quality*, and the computer might provide the entries found in Figure 3.3.

If your keyword search terms called up too many entries, you could narrow the search down by entering *drinking water quality* AND *Canadian* AND *regulations* (see Figure 3.4).

FIGURE 3.2
Sample Library Catalogue Web Page

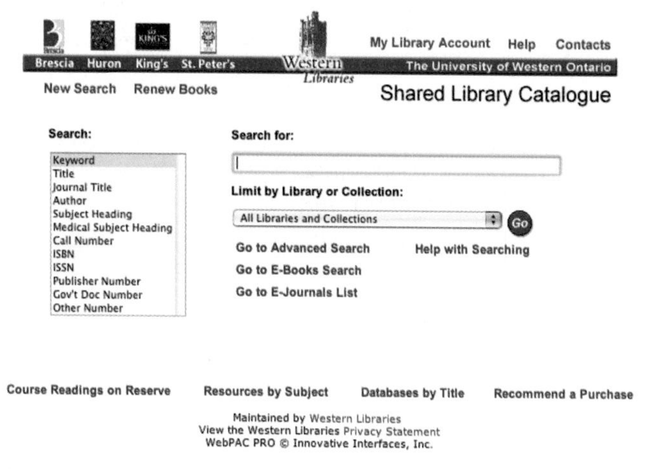

Source: University of Western Ontario, Shared Library Catalogue, http://alpha.lib.uwo.ca/

From the list of possible entries, you would select one that looked promising. The entry shown in Figure 3.5 appears most relevant to the research topic.

Finally, you would record the information you need to locate the book in the stacks, such as its call number, title, and author. Some libraries allow you to print out this display page.

OTHER SOURCES WITHIN THE LIBRARY

Any college or university library may include a host of other types of resources that are extremely useful for a wide range of research purposes.

SPECIAL COLLECTIONS: These could include rare books, unpublished manuscripts, or the papers of writers or other people who have made contributions in their field.

INFORMATION OR VERTICAL FILES: Information stored in library filing cabinets could include newspaper or magazine clippings, visuals, and pamphlets from governments, companies, professional groups, universities, or special-interest groups.

MEDIA: Audio-visual materials might include records, tapes, CDs, DVDs, films, videos, visuals, and multimedia. Usually this material cannot be borrowed, so you will have to use it at the library.

FIGURE 3.3
Sample Online Catalogue Search Results

Save Marked Items | Mark All Items

KEYWORDS (1-50 of 681)

Most Relevant: entries 1-46

1 Mark	1983 Regina/Moose Jaw drinking water quality [microform]. **Author:** Saskatchewan. Water Pollution Control Branch. **Location:** Weldon	1984
2 Mark	Annual drinking water quality reports across America [electronic resource]. **Author:** **Location:** Online	2005-
3 Mark	Assessment of drinking water quality in the Northern River Basins Study area [microform] : synthesis **Author:** Armstrong, Tanya F. **Location:** Weldon	1996
4 Mark	An Assessment of drinking water quality for Alberta communities in the Peace, Athabasca and Slave Ri **Author:** Prince, Dennis S. **Location:** Weldon	1997
5 Mark	Drinking water quality : problems and solutions / N.F. Gray. **Author:** Gray, N. F. **Location:** Weldon	1994
6 Mark	Drinking water quality improvement plan. **Author:** **Location:** Weldon	1993
7 Mark	Drinking Water Quality Improvement Plan [microform] : final summary report. **Author:** Economic and Engineering Services, Inc. **Location:** Weldon	1990
8 Mark	Drinking water quality in Indian country [electronic resource] : protecting your sources. **Author:** **Location:** Online	2000

Source: University of Western Ontario, Shared Library Catalogue, http://alpha.lib.uwo.ca/search/?searchtype=X&searcharg=drinking+water+quality&searchscope=20&search.x=22&search.y=21&SORT=A

SOURCES BEYOND YOUR COLLEGE OR UNIVERSITY LIBRARY

INTER-LIBRARY LOAN: Occasionally a book that you need will not be available at your college or university, but could be available through inter-library loan. Check with your reference librarian about lending procedures for this service. Also ask how long it will take to obtain the needed resources. This could be crucial if your research paper has a very tight deadline.

GOVERNMENT DEPARTMENTS: Many federal, provincial, and local government departments provide a wealth of useful research information that could be relevant for reports in a range of college and university disciplines. The main federal government directory is at http://www.gc.ca/depts/major/depind_e.html. Your library website

FIGURE 3.4
Sample Search Results with Narrowed Search

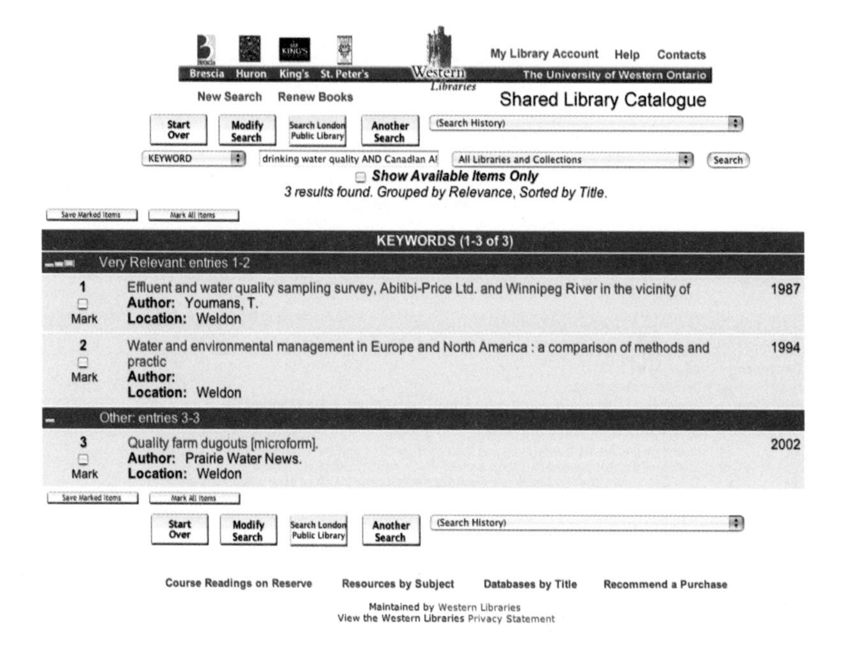

Source: University of Western Ontario, shared Library Catalogue, http://alpha.lib.uwo.ca/search/X?SEARCH=drinking+water+quality+AND+Canadlan+AND+regulations&startLimit=&searchscope=20&m=&l=&SORT=A&Da=&Db=&j=

may have created a pathfinder document on various federal and international government access points. Government department numbers are listed in the blue pages of the telephone book. A very useful research number for the federal government is 1-800-OCANADA. Often, operators will connect you with the specific department and possibly the person you need to speak with to obtain certain information. If you require statistical information, a good first step is to visit the Statistics Canada website (www.statcan.ca).

PRIMARY SOURCES

Research can include information generated from your own interviews, surveys, and experiments. Communication technology such as e-mail allows you to interview a person who may live a great distance away. Other primary source information can be obtained from attending a play or concert, or visiting a museum. If you use this

FIGURE 3.5
Sample Online Catalogue Search: Selection of Entry

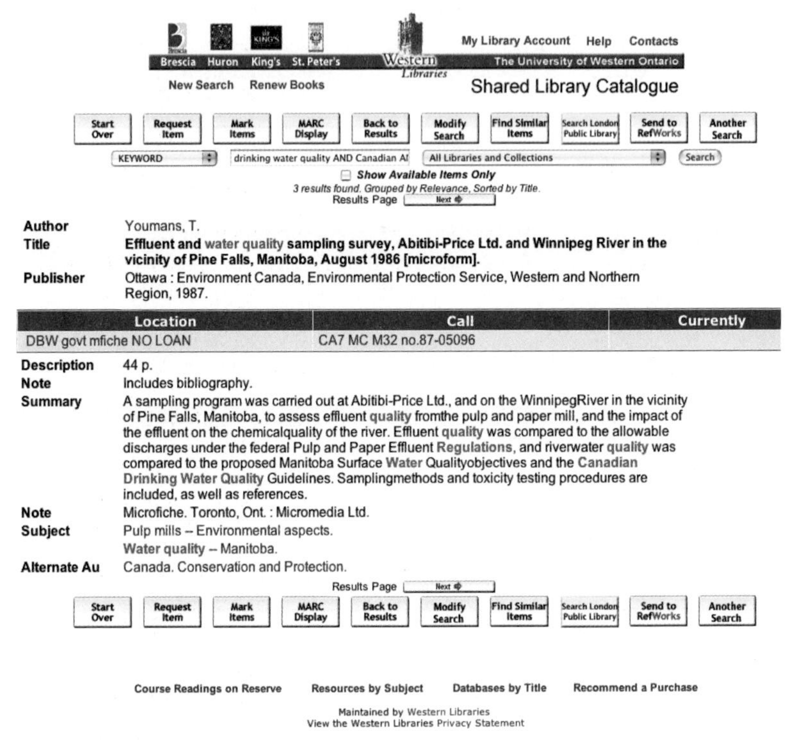

Source: University of Western Ontario, shared Library Catalogue http://alpha.lib.uwo.ca/search/Xdrinking+water+quality+AND+Canadlan+AND+regulations&startLimit=&search-scope=20&m=&l=&SORT=A&Da=&Db=&j=/Xdrinking+water+quality+AND+Canadlan+AND+regulations&startLimit=&searchscope=20&m=&l=&SORT=A&Da=&Db=&j=&SUBKEY=drinking%20water%20quality%20AND%20Canadlan%20AND%20regulations/1%2C3%2C3%2CB/frameset&FF=Xdrinking+water+quality+AND+Canadlan+AND+regulations&SORT=A&1%2C1%2C

kind of information in a research report, allow adequate time to prepare and collect information.

THE INTERNET, WORLD WIDE WEB, AND OTHER ELECTRONIC SOURCES

The Internet and the World Wide Web allow you 24-hour-a-day access to research information. However, there is not a research librarian available to assist you, and all information obtained from these sources must be carefully evaluated for reliability and credibility. Publicly accessible websites, such as those you find through Google, may not always be authoritative; don't restrict yourself to the Web alone.

Make sure to use library-based resources too. Libraries provide access to a wealth of peer-reviewed full-text articles and information without your needing to leave your house. Although there are a profusion of resources on the Internet, such as websites from the United Nations and Statistics Canada, many sites are not easy to search. Library resources are apt to be searchable and hence more readily accessible and organized.

LEARNING TO SEARCH THE WEB

The Web can provide researchers with a feast of information or meagre pickings, depending on what they are looking for. Research on controversial topics can be very successful, since the Web, by its very nature, is a democratic and fluid medium. The Web is often the best source for current news and material on popular culture. No matter what you are looking for, however, it is best to have a grounding in typical library sources before you turn to the Web. That way, you will have a better understanding of the value of what you find. Some good websites to start with are Internet Public Library (http://www.ipl.org/div/subject/browse/ref32.00.00/), Librarians' Internet Index (http://lii.org/), and Alcove 9 (www.loc.gov/rr/ main/alcove9/). Also useful is Voice of the Shuttle, found at http://vos.ucsb.edu/; this site is a good compendium of up-to-date materials, particularly those with a technological bent. Librarians have been studious in their attempts to create organized, easy access to the Web.

Go to the search engine of your choice by opening your browser and clicking on *Search*. Note that some search engines (like *AltaVista* and *HotBot*) use a robot and an indexer to seek information and provide keyword searches. Others, like *Yahoo!* and *WebCrawler*, are directories with professional editors who decide to index sites. These will allow you to search by subject as well. Experience and experiment will show you which engines give you the best results. Here are some URLs for possible search engines:

- www.google.ca
- www.yahoo.ca
- www.altavista.com
- www.excite.com
- www.webcrawler.com
- www.go.com
- www.hotbot.com

A comprehensive list of search engines can be found at http://www.allsearchengines.com.

USING SEARCH TECHNIQUES IN DATABASES OR ON THE WEB

Often you will need to tailor your search by using options such as "all the words" or "the exact phrase." Although search engines vary (both in what they find and in their exact instructions for searching), all of them have *Help* files that may be accessed to narrow down a search to a manageable size. Be aware that some search engines can do Boolean searches, which use certain standard commands to narrow the search criteria:

- If you type Internet AND copyright, you get materials with both terms in that order.
- If you type Internet OR copyright, you get a broader search of either term separately.
- If you type Internet AND copyright NOT Napster, you get a search that eliminates documents with the word *Napster* in them.
- If you type "Internet copyright" the search will be confined to those words grouped together. The words will be found in that order in the documents selected.
- If you type Internet NEAR copyright, you will get (on some engines, like AltaVista) documents where the two words are within 10 words of each other.
- If you type parentheses ( ) to group words together, you will find Internet articles that include both terms, as with quotation marks. (Internet copyright) AND (intellectual property) will find articles about both issues together.

Here are some other general search tips:

- Use a number of nouns as keywords to narrow your search to specifics and weed out irrelevant results (e.g., sleep disturbance apnea).
- Think of alternative terms if your keywords are not getting results: skin cancer/melanoma; cat/feline; moon/lunar; gun/firearm/weapon.
- Use an asterisk (*) as a "wild card" to stand in for letters at the end of a word. This is a good way to broaden a search if you aren't getting results. For example, account* will find articles that contain the words accounts, accounting, accountancy, accountant, etc. The wild card is also effective in searching for words that have variable spellings or variable numbers. For example, colo*r will retrieve materials that include color and colour, and 199* will retrieve materials from 1990 to 1999.

- Use "stop words" (small words, like prepositions and articles) in quotation marks *only* if they need to be included; otherwise they are commonly ignored (e.g., "To Have and Have Not").
- Remember that AND or NOT will narrow a search (e.g., politics AND Lithuania; pollution NOT water) whereas OR will broaden a search (e.g., cancer OR oncology).

Use Boolean logic to combine different fields in a catalogue or database to produce more accurate results. Remember, you can go beyond using simple keywords by combining or excluding catalogue and database fields (e.g., enter hobbit in the Title field and Tolkien in the Author field).

KEEPING TRACK OF VALUABLE INFORMATION

Keep track of reference sites that may be important to you in your writing. Record the following websites in your *Bookmarks* or *Favourites* (or on your personal website, if you have one) for easy reference:

Roget's Thesaurus
http://www.thesaurus.com

Encyclopedia Britannica
http://www.britannica.com

The Voice of the Shuttle
"Web Site for Humanities Research"
http://vos.ucsb.edu/

Bartleby Library
http://www.bartleby.com

These sites (and many associated links) provide invaluable resource materials—without charge.

SAVING MATERIALS YOU FIND

It is often a good idea to download material from a website onto a CD or memory stick. You can do this with a simple right click of the mouse. Websites often change from day to day, and the material you find today may not be accessible tomorrow. Keep a log to tell you when you accessed the websites you use.

USING ANOTHER FONT FOR MATERIALS FROM WEBSITES

To avoid charges of plagiarism, it is often a good idea to use another font when taking "notes" by copying and pasting from a website you visit. That way, it is easy to tell where your words stop and another's words begin.

DOCUMENTING WEB SOURCES

This is often a difficult matter, but the same rules apply as for written sources. List websites as follows:

1. Author's name, last name first (if there is an author's name listed)
2. The title of the website
3. The date you accessed the site, in case the material has changed since then
4. The URL, enclosed in angle brackets (<>), so that the reader can easily find your source (this is the style used in the MLA system of documentation; other styles vary)

For more details, go to http://www.mla.org and click on the section "MLA Style." Then, click on "Frequently Asked Questions" and finally on "How Do I Document Sources from the World Wide Web in My Works Cited List?" This will give you more detailed information if you need it.

ASSESSING WEBSITES FOR CREDIBILITY

It is absolutely essential to evaluate your sources, especially when they are taken from the Internet. While the Internet is often the most up-to-date and reliable source imaginable, it is hampered by the fact that it is possible (indeed, easy) to publish something on the Internet that is inaccurate, misleading, or biased. You must make sure that the sources you have chosen for evidence are impeccable.

Here are some guidelines for evaluating websites:

- ***Consider the source.*** Note the extension on the address: a site that ends in **.gc.ca** comes from the Canadian government; one that ends in **.gov** comes from the American government; one that ends in **.com** may well be a commercial site which, while informative, may also be trying to sell you something; **.edu** is an extension that denotes an educational institution. Can you trust the authority of the source?
- ***Consider the authorship.*** Who wrote the material on the website, if an author is named? Is that person a recognized authority on the subject?

- ***Consider the date of posting.*** Has the site been recently updated? (This information is often at the bottom of the main webpage.) Is it current?
- ***Consider the evidence.*** What kind of support is included for the information? Are there facts, interviews, and statistics that may be verified? Is the evidence convincing to you? Is it accurate? Can it be checked? Does it cover issues responsibly?
- ***Consider bias and motivation.*** Can you trace bias in the author's point of view? Does the site aim to sell you something instead of just provide information? Is it objective, and does it cover all sides of the story?
- ***Consider commercial influences.*** Do banners and ads clutter up the website? Do they affect the objectivity of the research?
- ***Consider readability and ease of navigation.*** Like books, webpages are visual as well as textual. A webpage should be aesthetically appealing and easy to read. In a professional (and thus likely more credible) website, information will be presented in a satisfactory way appropriate to the subject matter. Does the visual quality help or hinder your sense of the site's authority?
- ***Consider Web resources for assessment.*** Investigate these websites for guidelines on how to assess online materials:

  Five Criteria for Evaluating Web Pages
  http://www.library.cornell.edu/olinuris/ref/research/webcrit.html

  Judging Quality on the Web
  http://www.library.ucla.edu/libraries/url/referenc/judging.htm

  Assessing Website Quality
  http://depts.washington.edu/trio/center/howto/design/site/assess/index.html

To summarize, a good website for research material will possess these qualities:

- accuracy
- authority
- objectivity
- currency
- coverage

Ask yourself if the material fits these criteria. Checking out websites' sources, motives, and links should help you decide whether you trust the findings or not.

RADIO AND TELEVISION

Radio and television programs, especially those produced by the CBC or PBS, can provide worthwhile research information. You will need to check print or Internet broadcasting schedules to identify programs that relate to your research needs.

3-1D: CREATING A WORKING BIBLIOGRAPHY

BE DISCRIMINATING

As you work toward meeting your research paper deadline, you will probably find that your research yields more sources than you can possibly read. Often, when looking at a computer entry on a library's catalogue screen, you will have to decide whether the source is worth locating and reading. Then, once you locate the source, you will need to skim or scan the content to assess whether or not it is worth investigating further. Criteria you might use to evaluate a potential research source include the following:

- Is the information relevant to my research question?
- Is the information current, if it needs to be (e.g., the latest development in water-testing technology)?
- Does the material come from a credible, reliable author?
- Does the material reflect any bias?

MAINTAIN A WORKING BIBLIOGRAPHY

The working bibliography is the information you record about your research sources. It should include all the information you will later need to create a list of works cited or a complete bibliography.

As you locate and consider sources through the library's computer catalogue or via the Internet, it is important that you accurately record documentation information for potentially useful books, periodicals, websites, or other materials.

Although such detailed recording may seem time consuming at this stage of the research process, it will save time later. The consequence of not recording complete source information will be that you will need to make several trips to the library to obtain missing bibliographic details. Accurately recording each resource's call number will allow you to find the resource easily if you need to do any fact-checking or obtain more information.

CHECK YOUR INSTRUCTOR'S PREFERRED DOCUMENTATION STYLE

Before you start locating research resources, check with your instructor about the documentation style he or she prefers. Then, look at this handbook's examples of bibliographical entries following that documentation style (Chapters 5 through 8).

Scan the relevant documentation style to identify the details required to write a complete bibliographic citation for

- a book
- a periodical (journal or magazine) or newspaper
- an online source, such as a website
- any other type of source you plan to use in your research report

Now you can be sure you are recording all the information needed to create a complete entry for a list of works cited or a bibliography.

WHAT TO RECORD AND HOW TO RECORD IT

There are a number of ways to record entries and maintain your working research bibliography. Traditionally, researchers have often recorded entries on 7.5 × 13 cm (3 × 5 in.) note cards. A separate card is used for each source. The advantage of cards is that they allow you to manipulate entries. For example, as your collection of cards grows, you could alphabetize cards by authors' last names, organize the cards by source type (e.g., books, periodicals), or separate out any sources you consulted but did not cite within your paper.

Do not throw away cards. In a complete bibliography, you will list all resources you consulted in your research, while in a list of works cited, you will only list the works you referred to in your paper. Other options for maintaining a working bibliography include keeping a journal of resources or compiling a computer file of bibliographic information. Some researchers no longer keep cards because their library's computer can print out bibliographic information. You can also highlight, copy, and paste copies of electronic information and store the data yourself. Use the working-bibliography strategy that works best for you.

Here is the information you will need to complete a working-bibliography entry for a book, a periodical, or an online source.

BOOK

Record the following information for a book:

- all authors, and any editors or translators
- title and subtitle

- edition (if not the first edition)
- publication information, including the city, country, publisher, and date of publication
- call number

PERIODICAL

Record the following information for a periodical article, such as one from an academic journal or a magazine:

- all authors of the article
- title and subtitle of the article
- title of the magazine or journal

FIGURE 3.6
Card with Book Information

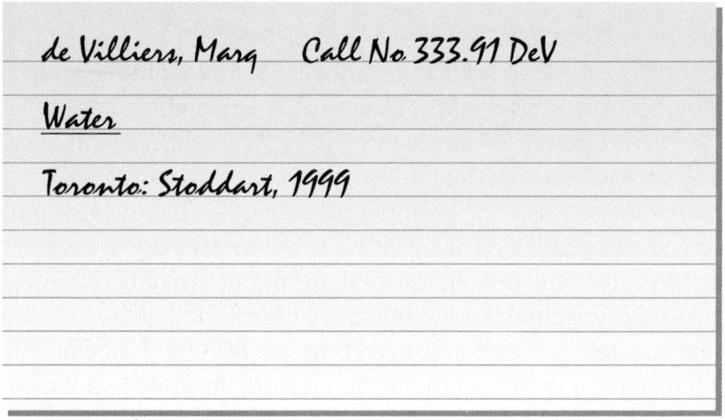

de Villiers, Marq Call No. 333.91 DeV
Water
Toronto: Stoddart, 1999

FIGURE 3.7
Card with Periodical Information

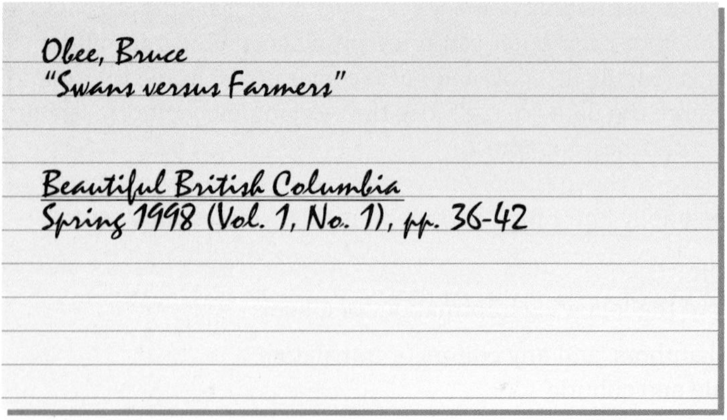

Obee, Bruce
"Swans versus Farmers"
Beautiful British Columbia
Spring 1998 (Vol. 1, No. 1), pp. 36-42

- date and page numbers (inclusive)
- volume and issue number, if relevant

NEWSPAPER

Record the same information as for periodicals, plus the following:

- the section of the newspaper in which the article appears
- all article page numbers, especially if the article does not appear on consecutive pages
- the edition, if any (e.g., *western ed.*, *nat'l. ed.*, *afternoon ed.*, etc.)

If the information is from an editorial, letter, or review, you should make a note of this as well.

ONLINE SOURCE

Record the following information for any website you use in your research:

- any authors or site sponsors
- title and subtitle of the document
- title of longer works to which the document belongs
- document date (or date last modified)
- date you accessed the site
- address of the site or its network path

3-1E: TAKING NOTES

Taking notes is essential for using source material in a research paper. Note-taking should never be merely collecting and copying information; rather, it should involve active thinking as you select,

FIGURE 3.8
Card with Online Source Information

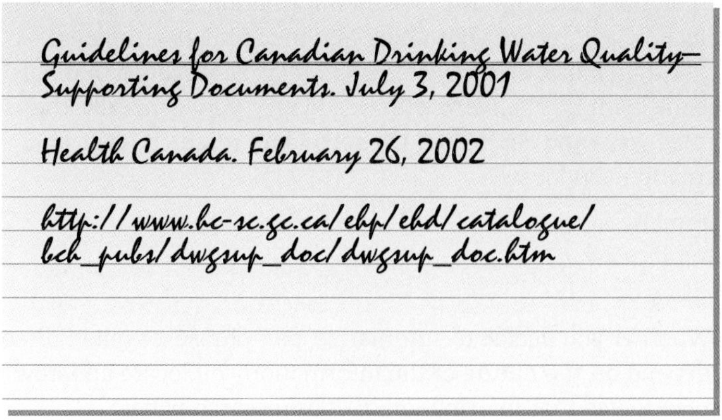

organize, analyze, and synthesize information and ideas to develop and support your thesis. Slavish copying of material will not make your case for you. The point of good note-taking is that it helps you get ready for your first draft by helping you find your own words and form your own educated opinions in light of the evidence you uncover. Efficient note-taking does not depend on the quantity of your notes but on their quality. Indeed, gathering too many notes without discriminating between what is essential to your research purpose and what is not can make organizing your secondary source material completely overwhelming.

USING NOTE CARDS

Many researchers find that recording research information on cards is a handy and systematic way of taking notes. Note cards can be the same size as those used for compiling a working bibliography (7.5 × 13 cm, or 3 × 5 in.). When you locate a piece of information that you consider important, record it on a separate card. In the upper right-hand corner, place the author's name and the title of the work. In the upper left-hand corner, record the subject. You might do this in pencil, since you may later wish to reclassify information as you organize ideas. Sample note cards appear throughout this section.

There are several advantages to using cards for note-taking, such as their portability—you can take the cards wherever you must work. But perhaps most importantly, cards allow you to manipulate the information you locate. For instance, you can sort information into important and less important ideas, then organize the information into an overall report or even a paragraph structure. This makes essay-writing much easier.

RECORDING NOTES

The materials you employ to record information are not as important as how you record your notes. You may find electronic notes handier than paper and just as easy to take, especially if you have a notebook computer to work with in a library. Very generally, there are three ways you can record the secondary research ideas and information you locate:

- summarizing
- paraphrasing
- quoting directly

Whether you decide to summarize, paraphrase, or quote directly will depend on the nature of the information you locate and how you plan to use that information in your research paper.

The remainder of this section explores how a piece of original source information can be appropriately summarized, paraphrased, and directly quoted on note cards.

Original Source

More than $2-billion worth of products and agricultural commodities from Canada's farms and fisheries is exported to developing countries each year. The developing countries, for most of the 1980s, purchased more manufactured goods from Canada than did either Japan or all members of the European Community combined.

Canadian diplomatic, trade, and consular representatives are resident in developing countries in every region of the world. Ottawa is host to one of the world's largest resident foreign diplomatic corps: 105 embassies and high commissions, of which 73 are from developing countries. Canada's political independence and territorial integrity depend heavily upon the juridical recognition that these countries extend to Canada, as well as their adherence to the United Nations Charter.

SUMMARIZING

A summary of source material captures in your own words, and in a highly condensed form, the very essential ideas of a passage. Since the summary contains only major points, it is much shorter than the original text.

To create a summary, first identify the main points of the source information, then express them very economically in your own

FIGURE 3.9
Card Showing Summarized Material

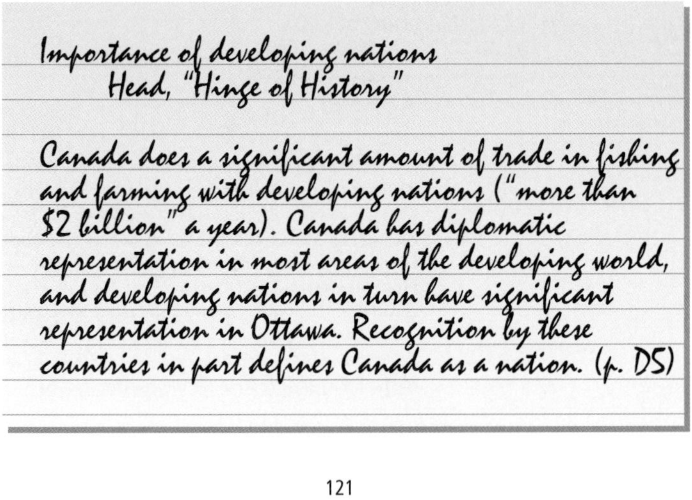

Importance of developing nations
Head, "Hinge of History"

Canada does a significant amount of trade in fishing and farming with developing nations ("more than $2 billion" a year). Canada has diplomatic representation in most areas of the developing world, and developing nations in turn have significant representation in Ottawa. Recognition by these countries in part defines Canada as a nation. (p. D5)

words without losing the essential meaning of the original. If you must use any words or phrases from the original, place this material within quotation marks. Within the summary itself, do not attempt to interpret the author's work. If you wish to record your thoughts, use a pencil and write in any white space on the note card.

Generally it is best to use a summary when you want to record the central idea of a longer passage. This record could be a longer explanation, argument, or background information.

PARAPHRASING

In a paraphrase, you restate information in your own words instead of quoting the source directly. Unlike a summary, which is a short version containing only essential information from the original source, the paraphrase is often the same length as the original, and it may be longer. A paraphrase should closely parallel the presentation of ideas in the original, including particular points of emphasis. However, the paraphrase should not use the same words, phrases, or sentence structure as the original, since this would constitute plagiarism.

FIGURE 3.10
Cards Showing Paraphrased Material

Importance of developing nations
Head, "Hinge of History"

Canada does a great deal of yearly trade with developing nations. Ivan Head, the former president of the International Development Centre, says the figure is "more than $2-billion worth" in sectors such as fisheries and farming. From 1980 to 1989, our trade with developing nations exceeded that with Japan and all the countries of the European Community.

Canada has diplomatic and trade representatives stationed in most developing nations, or at least in the regions where these countries are located. Many developing countries have representatives stationed in Ottawa. According to Head, of the 105 embassies and high commissions in Ottawa, 73 are from developing countries. Developing countries also play a significant role in defining Canada's unique identity. This is done through their legal recognition of Canada, and the fact that they follow the UN charter. (p.D5)

Paraphrasing demands that you think about the ideas in an original source and clearly understand them. Use your own words, phrasing, and sentence structure to restate the message of the original. If you need to quote directly, make sure this material is framed within quotation marks. Reproduce the order of ideas in the original and retain any points of emphasis.

It is very easy to slip inadvertently into plagiarism when paraphrasing. To avoid doing this, refrain from looking at the original source when you paraphrase. Then, when you complete the paraphrase, check to ensure you have kept the general meaning of the original but not the author's exact words.

Use paraphrasing when you find important information or ideas relevant to your research topic that you want to restate. Since a paraphrase is often as long as the original source material, do not try to paraphrase whole pages or chapters. Paraphrases are most useful when you want to present an author's general line of thought.

QUOTING DIRECTLY

When quoting a source directly, you copy the author's words exactly.

If you locate a passage that you think would make an interesting quotation, copy it down word for word, and enclose the material within quotation marks. When copying, make sure that you take down the exact wording, spelling, capitalization, and punctuation of the original. Proofread the quotation a number of times to ensure that it is accurate. If you need to add words for explanation or

FIGURE 3.11
Card Recording Direct Quotation and Related Information

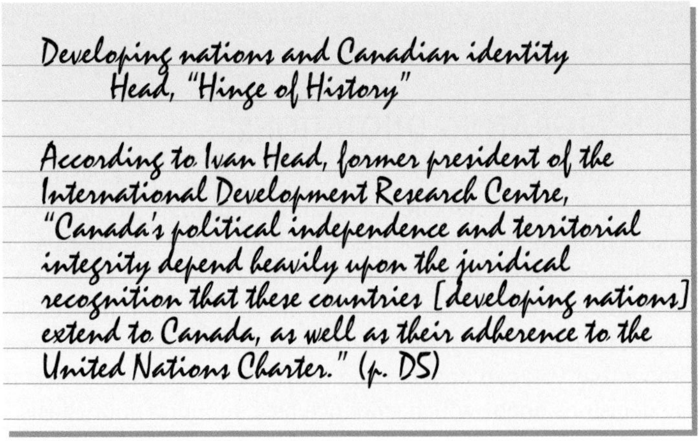

clarity, do so within square brackets. Whenever you leave anything out, indicate this with an ellipsis mark.

In literary essays, when you analyze stories, novels, poems, or plays, it is often necessary to quote extensively to provide evidence for your ideas. However, be selective when you use direct quotations in research papers. Here, direct quotations might be best employed to present an especially clear explanation from an expert, a colourfully or passionately stated idea, or another writer's key arguments.

OTHER WAYS OF TAKING NOTES

COMPUTER

As an alternative to using note cards, some researchers prefer to input notes using a computer. Taking notes in this way allows you to easily rearrange ideas, print out material, and incorporate notes into research report drafts. On the downside, sometimes it is not possible to have a computer handy at all times, although the growing popularity of laptops is eliminating this argument. Guard against typos when using a computer to record direct quotations.

PHOTOCOPIES

Making photocopies of source material ensures that it is accurate. While useful when writing shorter papers, it is not practical for longer papers because of the cost. As well, the high volume of photocopies could make it exceedingly difficult to organize secondary source material when it comes time to generate an outline. Further, photocopying sometimes discourages writers from thinking deeply enough about the information they are using.

As with any learning strategy, use the note-taking system that works best for you.

3-2: INTEGRATING QUOTATIONS

When drafting your research paper, avoid using too many quotations. Just because you collect a significant number of direct quotations on note cards does not mean that you must use them all in your research paper. Having too many quotations can interrupt the flow of ideas and give readers the impression you cannot think independently. A central purpose of the academic research paper is to show that you can analyze and synthesize information and make wise decisions about which evidence best supports your thesis.

When used appropriately and judiciously, though, direct quotations can be an extremely powerful way to make or reinforce a point. However, you must integrate quotations into your papers so that there is a smooth transition between your own ideas and any quoted materials.

Following are guidelines and techniques for integrating quotations smoothly and clearly into the text of your research paper.

3-2A: USING SIGNAL PHRASES

Signal phrases are excellent for introducing direct quotations and integrating them into a research paper. A signal phrase alerts the reader that a quotation is about to begin. It can indicate who spoke or wrote the words and from what source the material comes. An example of a signal phrase is, "According to Mordecai Richler in *Oh Canada! Oh Quebec!*, . . ."

NEVER INCLUDE A QUOTATION WITHOUT A CLEAR SIGNAL PHRASE

Without a signal phrase to integrate the quotation into the flow of your paper, quoted information can appear disjointed and confusing to the reader.

> ***Quotation without a Clear Signal Phrase***
> Some think Canada has an inferiority complex. "Sometimes it appears to me that Canada, even intact Canada, is not so much a country as a continental suburb, where Little Leaguers govern ineffectually, desperate for American approval" (Richler 147).

> ***Quotation with a Clear Signal Phrase***
> Some think Canada has an inferiority complex. According to Mordecai Richler in *Oh Canada! Oh Quebec!*, "Sometimes it appears to me that Canada, even intact Canada, is not so much a country as a continental suburb, where Little Leaguers govern ineffectually, desperate for American approval" (147).

VARY YOUR SIGNAL PHRASES

Just as you should use sentence variety in your general writing, so too should you employ variety in your use of signal phrases. If you require a number of direct quotations, don't use similar wording or structure in the signal phrases. For instance, using a phrase such as, "According to Mordecai Richler . . ." or "Richler says . . ." again and again makes the writing seem mechanical. A few ideas for varied constructions include the following:

In *Amusing Ourselves to Death,* Postman argues . . .

Jung describes the fire jumper's role graphically . . .

. . . argues Naomi Wolf in *The Beauty Myth.*

By including the author's name and the title of the work or the author's credentials in the signal phrase, you can introduce the quotation and at the same time emphasize the credibility of the source.

USE APPROPRIATE VERBS IN SIGNAL PHRASES

A key element of the signal phrase is the verb. Avoid using the same verbs, such as *says, notes, writes,* or *states,* again and again.

Through the judicious choice of verbs in your signal phrases, you can communicate the quoted writer's tone or intent and how the quotation relates to the flow of your own ideas. For example, the verb can indicate whether the quotation offers an observation, explanation, or argument.

See the box below for a list of verbs that can be used in signal phrases to indicate a speaker or writer's intention.

WEAVE QUOTED FRAGMENTS OR PHRASES INTO YOUR TEXT

As an alternative to using a full-sentence quotation, you might quote only a fragment or fragments, which may be easier to integrate into your text and will often make a point just as convincingly. When using a phrase or fragment, make sure that it retains the source's original meaning.

Orwell contends that the English language "becomes ugly and inaccurate" for the simple reason that people's thoughts can be foolish (370).

Effective Verbs to Use in Signal Phrases

acknowledges	admits	agrees	argues	asserts
believes	claims	complains	concedes	concludes
concurs	confirms	contends	declares	disagrees
denies	disputes	emphasizes	grants	holds
implies	insists	laments	maintains	observes
points out	predicts	proposes	reasons	refutes
rejects	speculates	suggests	warns	

To evaluate how well you have integrated quotations within your paper, try reading the text aloud. As well, you might focus on the integration of quotations at the editing stage of your writing process.

3-2B: SETTING OFF LONG QUOTATIONS

A long quotation in poetry is considered more than three lines, while in prose it is more than four lines. Indent the quoted material 2.5 cm (1 in.) from the left-hand margin. (See 11-5b.) The right-hand margin does not change. Double-space the quoted material. You do not need to use quotation marks with a longer quotation because the convention of indenting indicates to the reader that the material comes from another source.

Direct quotations should be as succinct as possible. However, in some instances, such as to illustrate a writer's evocative description, a long quotation may be needed. When quoting material of more than two paragraphs in length, indent the first line of each new paragraph an additional 1.25 cm (0.5 in.).

Introduce the long quotation with a complete sentence that usually ends with a colon. The colon indicates that the introduction is closely related to the quotation that follows it.

> E.D. Hirsch Jr. clearly defines in his preface what it means to be culturally literate:
>
> > To be culturally literate is to possess the basic information needed to thrive in the modern world. The breadth of that information is great, extending over the major domains of human activity from sports to science. It is by no means confined to "culture" narrowly understood as an acquaintance with the arts. Nor is it confined to one social class. (xiii)

The parenthetical citation for a longer quotation appears outside the punctuation of the last sentence.

3-2C: USING THE ELLIPSIS MARK AND BRACKETS

Two useful types of punctuation for working with quotations are the ellipsis mark and brackets. The ellipsis is commonly used to shorten quotations, while brackets allow you to add words to quotations. Use both where appropriate to integrate quotations smoothly into your text.

ELLIPSIS MARK

The ellipsis mark indicates that you have omitted a word, phrase, sentence, or more from a quoted passage. This punctuation form communicates to the reader that a quotation does not completely reproduce the original. An ellipsis mark normally consists of three spaced periods. Leave a space before them and after them as well. However, when you have deleted something at the end of a sentence, use four spaced periods, thus. . . . In this case, there is no space before the first period because it is seen to be the period marking the end of the previous sentence.

Ellipsis marks can be employed to keep a long quotation as short and to the point as possible. When using ellipsis marks to shorten quotations, follow two guiding principles:

1. Maintain the meaning of the original source in your shortened version.
2. Ensure that the briefer version is grammatically correct and consistent with the surrounding text.

To distinguish between your ellipses and those of the author of the quotation, MLA documentation guidelines formerly required that you place square brackets around any ellipses you add. Though the MLA, with the sixth edition of its handbook, abandoned the practice, many instructors feel that the use of brackets was a good idea, since brackets enabled readers to tell at a glance that an ellipsis did not appear in the original quotation.

> Ivan Head, the man behind the Earth Clock and nonstop generator of ideas about the realities behind the Doomsday equation, is leaving the research centre on an angry note after thirteen years as president. Mr. Head [. . .] cannot accept the indifference of the planet's North, the world's industrialized nations, to the Third World South. (D2)

The writer omitted the words "diplomat, lawyer, and foreign policy adviser"—perhaps because, in the context of the paper or the point being made, these roles were not relevant.

The use of the ellipsis mark with quotations is quite refined:

- Use [. . .] for any omission from the middle of a single sentence.
- Use , [. . .] to show a jump from the middle of one sentence to the middle of another.
- In all other cases, use a period with the ellipsis mark, positioned to show if text is missing before [. . .]. or after .[. . .] the period.

If you are using other documentation guidelines, do not use brackets around your ellipsis marks. APA Style uses . . . for omissions within sentences and . . . . whenever the omitted text contains a period.

> Pheromones influence the onset of puberty in males and females. . . . They can act as an aphrodisiac and, by stimulating the sex hormones, augment the sex drive. (Smith, 2005, p. 61)

Usually you do not use an ellipsis mark at the beginning or end of a quotation. Include one at the end of the quotation only if you have omitted words at the end of the final quoted sentence and it is important to indicate that the quotation ends mid-sentence.

BRACKETS

Brackets are sometimes called "square parentheses"; they allow you to insert words in quoted material. For instance, you might use square brackets within a quotation to enclose information clarifying a pronoun or to change the tense of a verb so that it fits grammatically with the surrounding text. As with the ellipsis mark, your use of brackets should never distort the meaning of the original quotation.

> Full light showed her [Marilyn Bell] haggard and gaunt. Pain probed her arms and legs, her stomach throbbed. Her breathing and her stroke had lost their coordination, and she gulped unwanted water from the lake. She began to cry. Ryder extended liniment on the stick for her dragging legs. (363)

4 PLAGIARISM AND DOCUMENTATION OVERVIEW

THE PROBLEM ISN'T THAT THERE ARE CASES THAT FALL OUTSIDE THE RULES. THE PROBLEM IS THAT THERE IS A RULE FOR EVERY CASE, AND NO STYLE MANUAL CAN HOPE TO LIST THEM ALL. BUT WE WANT THE RULES ANYWAY. WHAT WE DON'T WANT TO BE TOLD IS "BE FLEXIBLE," OR "YOU HAVE CHOICES."

—LOUIS MENAND, "THE END MATTER"

Plagiarism and Documentation Overview

4 Plagiarism and Documentation Overview

In research writing, whenever you summarize, paraphrase, or directly quote another person's words, ideas, or thoughts, or use facts and statistics that are not commonly known, you must ethically acknowledge your source to avoid plagiarism (see 4-1) and properly document your source in accordance with one of the special documentation styles scholars require in their academic journals (see 4-2).

4-1: PLAGIARISM

Plagiarism occurs when you use facts, words, or opinions that you obtained from someone else without identifying your source or acknowledging that they weren't originally yours. Plagiarism occurs when an author appropriates—steals—and passes off the ideas or words of another as her or his own without crediting the original author. Plagiarism can be a deliberate act, such as copying longer passages without proper acknowledgment, or an unintentional offence, such as neglecting to credit direct quotations and frame them in quotation marks.

Since the purpose of a research essay is research, you shouldn't be put off by the fact that something is not original. Just make sure to give credit where credit is due.

Things to Do to Avoid Plagiarism

- Credit any ideas you found, whether in person or on the TV, radio, or Internet.
- Use quotation marks whenever you use exact wording.
- Learn to paraphrase. Write your papers without borrowing wording from other sources, at least in the first draft. Your wording and your understanding of ideas are what count.
- Don't just copy and paste. Reword it or quote it exactly, remembering in both cases to include sources.
- Don't hand over the essay to your sources. You are the writer; use the sources to make your own case. The sources provide the evidence and support for your opinions.

When researching, it is vital to keep accurate notes in which you document where you obtained information and exactly what ideas and words came directly from another author. Be systematic. Careless note-taking can easily result in inadvertent plagiarism—using someone else's ideas or wording without proper acknowledgment. Plagiarism carries severe academic consequences, and it is penalized by academic institutions whether it is intentional or unintentional. You, the writer, are responsible for the integrity of anything that appears on the page under your name.

Don't take words or ideas from a website without noting where you found them. Highlight or use a different font to make sure that information you glean from online sources is attributed correctly to its source. Whenever you gather material, get into the habit of acknowledging where it comes from immediately, so that you don't lose track and face embarrassment or accusation later. These days it is simple for an instructor to find your online sources, either through Google or a similar search engine or by using software like Turnitin (http://www.turnitin.com/static/home.html). Don't run the risk of severe academic penalties by putting off source acknowledgment.

One of the best ways to avoid plagiarism problems is to use an accepted style of documentation to cite the sources for any phrases or ideas not completely your own.

4-1A: USING A CONSISTENT SYSTEM FOR CITING SOURCES

When are in-text citations appropriate?

- when you are using the exact words of others, making sure to place those words within quotation marks
- when you are using facts or ideas obtained from other sources
- when you are expressing the words or ideas of others in your own words, as in summaries and paraphrases

When are citations not required?

- when you are using your own ideas
- when you are presenting common knowledge (e.g., the Magna Carta was signed in 1215)

There are a number of acceptable academic styles for citing sources in your paper. Always ask your instructor which documentation style he or she prefers. One of the most common documentation styles is that of the Modern Language Association (MLA); see 4-2a and Chapter 5.

In MLA style, you acknowledge your sources with brief parenthetical citations in your text; these correspond to an alphabetical list of works cited, which appears at the end of the paper. The citations follow these rules:

1. If you have introduced the information from another source with a signal phrase clearly identifying the author, then only the page reference is needed in parentheses, so long as the reference clearly refers to the work of the author you mention.

According to James Joyce biographer Richard Ellmann, the great Irish writer "sometimes used *Ulysses* to demonstrate that even English, that best of languages, was inadequate" (397).

2. Otherwise, the citation should include the author's last name and a page reference for the source work.

It may be true that Joyce "sometimes used *Ulysses* to demonstrate that even English, that best of languages, was inadequate" (Ellmann 397).

3. In a list of works cited, at the end of the research paper, the name of the author, title of the work, and other publishing information about the source are provided.

Ellmann, Richard. *James Joyce*. New York: Oxford UP, 1983.

For more details on MLA documentation style, see 4-2a, where you will also find guidelines on APA style for in-text citations and instructions on using footnotes.

4-1B: QUOTING SOURCES ACCURATELY

In academic research writing, whenever a writer draws on another's work, he or she must acknowledge that intellectual indebtedness by precisely specifying what was borrowed (a fact, an opinion, the writer's own words) and from where it was borrowed.

It is possible to commit plagiarism inadvertently, either by not clearly distinguishing between your own thoughts and material you gathered from others, or through ignorance of what constitutes unethical use of another writer's work. To avoid unintentional plagiarism, be aware of these common errors:

1. Failing to cite quotations and borrowed ideas
2. Failing to enclose borrowed language within quotation marks
3. Failing to write summaries and paraphrases completely in your own words

All of the above may be accidental, but each qualifies as academic plagiarism.

FAILING TO CITE QUOTATIONS AND BORROWED IDEAS

You should have a good idea of what to cite and what not to cite. Here are a few guidelines.

WHAT YOU MUST CITE

1. Any direct quotation
2. Any idea, opinion, fact, or resource borrowed from another source, including the following:
   a) paraphrases of sentences
   b) summaries of sentences or chapters
   c) statistics and little-known facts
   d) visual information such as tables, graphs, diagrams, and illustrations, including photographs and screen shots from the Internet

WHAT YOU DO NOT NEED TO CITE

- proverbs like "A stitch in time saves nine" or "Money doesn't grow on trees"
- common knowledge, such as the knowledge that Shakespeare wrote *Hamlet* or that the Bible is Christianity's holy book
- things you discover in conversation or in a classroom setting

Sometimes it can be a challenge to decide whether factual information is common knowledge or not. Generally, if you see the information in a number of sources, treat it as common knowledge in your paper. If you are not sure, you might ask an expert. Cite any factual information that is controversial. If you are still in doubt, it is wise to be cautious and cite the source.

FAILING TO ENCLOSE BORROWED LANGUAGE WITHIN QUOTATION MARKS

If, in the text of your research paper, you are using the exact words of another author, you must clearly indicate this to the reader by enclosing the borrowed material within quotation marks. It is not adequate to use the author's words and merely provide a citation at the end of the quoted sentence. Failure to use quotation marks qualifies as plagiarism. The only exception to this rule is if you are quoting a longer passage and using indentation, as opposed to quotation marks, to indicate that the quoted material contains the exact words of the author. (See 3-2b.)

The following examples indicate how a researcher could commit and correct plagiarism.

Original Source Material

In India, which invented family planning, but has made a mockery of it, it seems unlikely that the government will be able to fix the population crisis without first fixing itself.

—John Stackhouse, "Okay, You Can Take Her," p. A1

Plagiarism

According to John Stackhouse, in India, which invented family planning, but has made a mockery of it, it seems unlikely that the government will be able to fix the population crisis without first fixing itself (A1).

The researcher has not used quotation marks to set off exact words from John Stackhouse's article. The impression is given that the researcher generated the content and structure of the comment on India, which is not true.

Correcting Plagiarism with Quotation Marks

According to John Stackhouse, "In India, which invented family planning, but has made a mockery of it, it seems unlikely that the government will be able to fix the population crisis without first fixing itself" (A1).

It is now abundantly clear that the opinion as well as the words and sentence structure used to express that opinion are exclusively attributable to John Stackhouse.

FAILING TO WRITE SUMMARIES AND PARAPHRASES COMPLETELY IN YOUR OWN WORDS

It is very easy to lapse into plagiarism when summarizing or paraphrasing the work of others. You must acknowledge not only another writer's ideas and facts, but also the writer's language and form—the exact words and sentence structures he or she uses to present those ideas and facts. Therefore, anything directly borrowed must appear within quotation marks. A borrowed sentence structure must be recast so it is truly your own.

To avoid any accusation of plagiarism, ensure that when summarizing and paraphrasing you use your own words and sentence structures. Then, of course, cite the source.

Original Source Material

The mass of men serve the state thus, not as men mainly, but as machines, with their bodies.

—Henry David Thoreau, *Civil Disobedience*, p. 361

Plagiarism due to Borrowing Phrases

Rather than working for their country as men, the mass of men work for it as machines, with their bodies (Thoreau 361).

Plagiarism due to Borrowing Sentence Structure

The preponderance of men serve the country, not as men mainly, rather as machines, using their physical labour (Thoreau 361).

Acceptable Paraphrase

During Thoreau's time, workers were not considered individuals; instead, they were only valued for the physical work they could provide (Thoreau 361).

Neither words, phrases, nor sentence structure are used in the acceptable paraphrase. The information from Thoreau illustrates a fundamental research choice you may have to make: is it better to use a paraphrase or, because the thought is so succinctly and eloquently expressed by the author, quote the original directly and place the author's exact words within quotation marks?

To avoid inadvertent plagiarism when summarizing or paraphrasing, close the book containing the original source material. Since you must rely on your own understanding and memory of the original content, this should prevent copying. Once you have completed the summary or paraphrase, check it against the original to ensure that you are not indebted to the author for any word, phrase, or sentence structure.

4-2: DOCUMENTATION OVERVIEW

You must also think about your final product—the research paper. There are a number of acceptable report presentation and documentation styles. The most common ones are covered in this handbook. One of your first tasks should be to ask your instructor which style he or she wants you to follow.

Once you identify the style you are to follow, review the relevant section. Then, as you conduct your research, you will know the source information needed.

4-2A: STYLES OF DOCUMENTATION

There are numerous academic style guides, and each discipline tends to follow a particular documentation style. The documentation styles differ in the way they cite sources and format citations.

If you read the following sections carefully, you'll notice that "often" is an operative word. Just because you are writing a sociology research paper does not necessarily mean that you follow APA style. Don't assume anything. You may be required to follow MLA style guidelines in some of your courses and APA guidelines in others. It is always best to check with your instructor to find out exactly which manuscript and documentation style he or she wants you to follow.

The rest of this chapter provides a brief overview of the major academic manuscript and documentation styles as well as some alternatives you may encounter. For detailed descriptions of the major styles, see Chapters 5 (MLA), 6 (APA), 7 (Chicago Style), and 8 (CSE and Columbia Online Style).

MODERN LANGUAGE ASSOCIATION (MLA) STYLE

Manuscript format and documentation guidelines presented in the *MLA Handbook for Writers of Research Papers* are often followed in English and humanities courses. Chapter 5 outlines essential style guidelines from the *MLA Handbook* (6th ed., 2003) and concludes with a model research paper following the MLA format and documentation style.

AMERICAN PSYCHOLOGICAL ASSOCIATION (APA) STYLE

Manuscript format and documentation guidelines presented in the *Publication Manual of the American Psychological Association* are often followed in social science courses such as psychology, anthropology, business, economics, and sociology. Chapter 6 outlines essential style guidelines from the *APA Manual* (5th ed., 2001) and concludes with a model research paper following the APA format and documentation style.

UNIVERSITY OF CHICAGO (CHICAGO) STYLE

Manuscript format and documentation guidelines presented in *The Chicago Manual of Style* are often followed in history and other humanities courses. Chapter 7 outlines the basic style guidelines from *The Chicago Manual of Style* (15th ed., 2003) and concludes with a partial model research paper following Chicago format and documentation style.

COUNCIL OF SCIENCE EDITORS (CSE) STYLE

The style guidelines of the Council of Science Editors are followed in many branches of science. Documentation guidelines presented in *Scientific Style and Format: The CSE Manual for Authors, Editors, and Publishers* (7th ed., 2006) are outlined in 8-1.

COLUMBIA ONLINE STYLE

COS style, which has been endorsed by the Alliance for Computers and Writing, has variations for humanities and scientific disciplines and can be useful for citing electronic sources no matter which specific style of documentation you are required to use. Documentation guidelines presented in *The Columbia Guide to Online Style* (2nd ed., 2006) are outlined in 8-2.

OTHER STYLES AND STYLE GUIDES

INSTITUTE OF ELECTRICAL AND ELECTRONICS ENGINEERS

IEEE provides a comprehensive website for research and documentation that allows access to thousands of articles in abstract or in full text and makes standards of documentation clear on its website at http://www.ieee.org/portal/cms_docs_iportals/iportals/publications/journmag/transactions/eic-guide.pdf.

ALTERNATIVE STYLE GUIDES

In some disciplines, such as physics and geology, you may be asked to follow documentation guidelines produced by an association related to the discipline. A list of specialized style guides, organized by discipline, is provided below.

As well, many academic institutions—and departments—produce style guides. These published guidelines are often available at your college or university library.

BIOLOGY AND OTHER SCIENCES

Huth, Edward J. *Scientific Style and Format: The CSE Manual for Authors, Editors, and Publishers.* 7th ed. New York: Cambridge UP, 2006, http://www.councilscienceeditors.org.

CHEMISTRY

Coghill, Anne M., and Lorrin R. Garson, eds. *The ACS Style Guide: Effective Communication of Scientific Information*. 3rd ed. Washington, DC: American Chemical Society, 2006, http://pubs.acs.org.

ENGLISH AND THE HUMANITIES

The Canadian Style: A Guide to Writing and Editing. Rev. ed. Toronto: Dundurn Press and Public Works and Government Services Canada Translation Bureau, 1996.

The Chicago Manual of Style. 15th ed. Chicago: U of Chicago P, 2003, http://www.chicagomanualofstyle.org.

Dodds, Jack, and Judi Jewinski. *The Ready Reference Handbook: Writing, Revising, Editing*. 2nd Canadian ed. Scarborough: Allyn and Bacon Canada, 2001.

Gibaldi, Joseph. *MLA Handbook for Writers of Research Papers*. 6th ed. New York: MLA, 2003, http://www.mla.org.

Gibaldi, Joseph. *MLA Style Manual and Guide to Scholarly Publishing*. 2nd ed. New York: MLA, 1999.

Strunk, William Jr., and E.B. White. *The Elements of Style*. 4th ed. Boston: Allyn and Bacon, 1999.

Turabian, Kate L. *A Manual for Writers of Term Papers, Theses, and Dissertations*. 6th ed. Chicago: U of Chicago P, 1996.

JOURNALISM

Goldstein, Norm, ed. *The Associated Press Stylebook and Libel Manual*. New York: Perseus Books, 2000.

Buckley, Peter, ed. *CP Stylebook: A Guide for Writers and Editors*. 12th ed. Toronto: Canadian Press, 2002.

McFarlane, J.A., and Warren Clements. *The Globe and Mail Style Book*. 9th ed. Toronto: McClelland & Stewart, 2003.

LAW

Yogis, John A., et al. *Legal Writing and Research Manual*. 5th ed. Toronto: Butterworths Canada, 2000.

LINGUISTICS

Linguistic Society of America. "Language Style Sheet." Published each year in the December issue of the *LSA Bulletin* and available online at http://www.lsadc.org/info/pubs-lang-style.cfm.

MATHEMATICS

Swanson, Ellen. *Mathematics into Type.* Updated ed. Providence, RI: American Mathematical Society, 1999, http://www.ams.org.

MEDICINE

American Medical Association. *American Medical Association Manual of Style*. 9th ed. Baltimore: Williams and Wilkins, 1997.

MUSIC

Holoman, D. Kern. *Writing about Music: A Style Sheet from the Editors of Nineteenth-Century Music*. Berkeley: U of California P, 1988.

PHYSICS

American Institute of Physics. *AIP Style Manual.* 4th ed. New York: AIP, 1990. Available online at http://www.aip.org/pubservs/style.html.

POLITICAL SCIENCE

Sigleman, Lee, ed. *Style Manual for Political Science*. Rev. ed. Washington, DC: American Political Science Association, 2001, http://www.apsanet.org.

PSYCHOLOGY AND THE SOCIAL SCIENCES

American Psychological Association. *Publication Manual of the American Psychological Association*. 5th ed. Washington: APA, 2001, http://www.apastyle.org.

SCIENCE AND TECHNICAL WRITING

Rubens, Philip, ed. *Science and Technical Writing: A Manual of Style*. 2nd ed. New York: Routledge, 2000.

5

MLA STYLE OF DOCUMENTATION

If I had enough time, I could write less.

—Blaise Pascal

MLA Style of Documentation

5 MLA Style of Documentation

Writers in the arts and humanities generally follow the Modern Language Association (MLA) guidelines for formatting research papers and documenting sources. This chapter summarizes MLA style guidelines published in the MLA *Handbook for Writers of Research Papers*, 6th ed. (New York: MLA, 2003) and concludes with a model research paper following MLA format and documentation style.

If a reader, such as your instructor, wants to check any source you used for words, facts, or ideas, he or she needs complete information about your sources. When following MLA style, you document your sources in two ways:

1. within the body of the paper, using **in-text citations**
2. at the end of the paper, in a **list of works cited** (see 5-2)

The citation briefly cites the author and page in parentheses within the essay, and each of these parenthetical citations has a matching entry giving complete publication information in the Works Cited list on a separate page at the end of the essay.

5-1: IN-TEXT CITATIONS

An in-text citation consists of a **parenthetical reference** that gives the minimum information necessary to identify a source and locate the relevant material within it. Most often, this is the author's last name (unless the signal phrase mentions the author's name) and a page number or numbers. Full information on the source is supplied in the list of works cited. The goal is to be as brief as possible while enabling the reader to locate the source in the Works Cited list accurately.

The following sample references illustrate how to document many different kinds of sources.

5-1A: IN-TEXT REFERENCES TO AUTHORS

AUTHOR MENTIONED IN A SIGNAL PHRASE

A signal phrase indicates that something taken from a source—for example, a quotation, summary, or paraphrase—is about to be used. When you mention the author's name in a signal phrase, give only the page reference within the parentheses. Note that the parentheses are inside the end punctuation.

Peter Schrag observes that America is "divided between affluence and poverty, between slums and suburbs" (118).

AUTHOR NOT MENTIONED IN A SIGNAL PHRASE

If the author's name is not mentioned in a signal phrase, it must appear in parentheses along with the page reference. No punctuation is required between the author's name and the page reference.

One commentator notes that America is "divided between affluence and poverty, between slums and suburbs" (Schrag 118).

TWO OR MORE WORKS BY THE SAME AUTHOR

When you use two or more works by the same author in a research paper, you will have multiple entries for that author in your list of works cited. Your in-text citation must direct the reader to the correct entry in the Works Cited list. You can do this in one of three ways.

1. If you have provided the author's name and the title of the work in the signal phrase, include only the page number(s) in parentheses.

In Lament for a Nation, George Grant claims that "modern civilization makes all local cultures anachronistic" (54).

2. If only the author's name is given in the signal phrase, include the title of the work (abbreviated if the title is long) within the parenthetical reference.

George Grant claims that "modern civilization makes all local cultures anachronistic" (Lament 54).

3. If there is no signal phrase, the parenthetical reference should include the author's last name, the title or a shortened version of it, and the page number(s). Use a comma to separate the author's name and the title.

Some propose that "modern civilization makes all local cultures anachronistic" (Grant, Lament 54).

TWO OR THREE AUTHORS

You can include the names of the authors in the signal phrase or place them within the parenthetical reference.

According to Clarkson and McCall, even late in the decade of the Quiet Revolution, "Trudeau saw the constitutional question as only one facet of his general mandate for the Justice Department" (258).

Even late in the decade of the Quiet Revolution, "Trudeau saw the constitutional question as only one facet of his general mandate for the Justice Department" (Clarkson and McCall 258).

With three authors, use a serial comma in the reference:

(Wynkin, Blynkin, and Nodd viii)

MORE THAN THREE AUTHORS

If the work you are citing has more than three authors, you have two options:

1. Name only the first author and use et al. (Latin abbreviation for "and others").
2. Give all names in full.

The method you choose should match the one you use in the Works Cited list.

One position is that "in cultures whose religion, unlike Christianity, offers no promise of an afterlife, a name that will live on after one's death serves as the closest substitute for immortality" (Abrams et al. 3).

Note that al. takes a period (it is an abbreviation), but et does not.

CORPORATE AUTHOR

A corporate author is a company, an agency, or an institution that is credited with authorship of a work and is treated like an individual author. Since long references tend to be disruptive, put long names in a signal phrase if possible. For long names in parentheses, shorten terms that are commonly abbreviated.

The former Council of Biology Editors states in the previous edition of the style manual that "any coordinate system must be based upon a known reference point" (241).

The previous edition of the manual states that "any coordinate system must be based upon a known reference point" (Council 241).

NO AUTHOR

If there is no author named, the parenthetical citation should give the full title (if brief) or a shortened version, unless the title appears in a signal phrase. The following example illustrates a reference to a magazine article, with the shortened title enclosed in quotation marks.

The incidence of deep vein thrombosis, the so-called Economy Class Syndrome, has been associated with a genetic predisposition to this type of blood clotting ("Flying" 8).

AUTHORS WITH THE SAME LAST NAME

In a parenthetical citation, add the first initial. If the initial is also shared, give the full first name.

> Some have claimed that "the terms 'black' and 'white' ultimately acquire meaning only in opposition to each other" (L. Hill 208).

In a signal phrase, give the full name.

> When considering mixed-race issues in Canada, Lawrence Hill contends "the terms 'black' and 'white' ultimately acquire meaning only in opposition to each other" (208).

5-1B: IN-TEXT REFERENCES TO PRINT SOURCES

MULTI-VOLUME WORK

If you cite specific material from a multi-volume work, in the parenthetical reference include the volume number followed by a colon, a space, and then the page reference. Do not include the words volume or page or their abbreviations.

> Abram et al. state that "the period of more than four hundred years that followed the Norman Conquest presents a much more diversified picture than the Old English period" (1: 5).

If you are referring to an entire volume of a multi-volume work, however, it is not necessary to cite the page(s). The author's name is followed by a comma and the abbreviation vol. (Abram et al., vol. 1). Note that if such a reference is included in a signal phrase, volume should be spelled out.

LITERARY WORK

Since literary works are often available in different editions and therefore have different page numbering, you should refer to a particular chapter, act, scene, or line using appropriate abbreviations.

NOVEL

When citing a passage from a novel, the parenthetical reference should give the page number followed by a semicolon and other identifying information.

> In Atwood's <u>The Robber Bride</u>, Tony reveals a distorted picture of Zenia: "She has thought of Zenia as tearless, more tearless even than herself. And now there are not only tears but many tears, rolling fluently down Zenia's strangely immobile face, which always looks made-up even when it isn't" (190; ch. 25).

POETRY

When citing lines from poems and verse plays, omit page numbers and cite the division (e.g., act, scene, book, or part), and then the line, using periods (without spaces) to separate the numbers.

> In Civil Elegies, Lee describes Canadians' relationship with the rugged land:
>
> > We lie on occupied soil.
> > Across the barren Shield, immortal scrubland and our own,
> > where near the beginning the spasm of lava
> > settled to bedrock schist,
> > barbaric land, initial, our
> > own, scoured bare under
> > crush of glacial recessions (3.40-46)

DRAMA

Include the act, scene, and line numbers in the parenthetical citation. Use Arabic numerals unless instructed otherwise.

> Shakespeare establishes the dark mood of Macbeth in the second witch's response to the first witch's query on when they should meet again: "When the battle's lost and won" (1.1.3).

THE BIBLE

When citing a passage from the Bible, include—either in the signal phrase or the parenthetical reference—the book, chapter, and verse. Books of the Bible may be abbreviated in a parenthetical reference if you wish (e.g., 1 Chron. 13.4, Rev. 20.2).

WORK IN AN ANTHOLOGY

If you are referencing a particular part of an anthology—for example, an essay or a story—name the author of that piece rather than the editor of the anthology. The Works Cited list gives additional information about the anthology and the editor (see 5-2).

INDIRECT SOURCE

Although you should try to use original sources, if your only option is an indirect source, begin the citation in the parenthetical reference with the abbreviation qtd. in ("quoted in").

> To Woody Allen, the successful monologue is a matter of attitude: "I can only surmise that you have to give the material a fair shake at the time and you have to deliver it with confidence" (qtd. in Lax 134).

ENTIRE WORK

When citing an entire work, it is preferable to provide the author's name in a signal phrase rather than a parenthetical reference. No page reference is required. The corresponding entry in the Works Cited list provides publication information. This also applies to works with no page numbers, such as a film or television program.

> In The Second Sex, Simone de Beauvoir brilliantly argues her position on women's inequality.

MORE THAN ONE WORK IN A SINGLE CITATION

Cite each work as you normally would, using semicolons to separate the citations.

> An understanding of the business cycle is fundamental to successful investing (Gardner 69; Lasch 125).

5-1C: ELECTRONIC SOURCES

The MLA guidelines for in-text citations of electronic sources are the same as those for print sources. However, many online sources do not include a page numbering system. You should not take page numbers from a printout, as pagination may vary in different printouts. Some electronic sources use alternate systems, numbering text by paragraph, section, or screen, but others do not. Here are some guidelines for situations you may encounter when citing electronic sources.

THE ELECTRONIC SOURCE HAS AN AUTHOR AND FIXED PAGE NUMBERS

Give both the author's name and the page numbers, with the author's name either in the signal phrase or the parenthetical reference.

> According to Caroline Spurgeon, "The main image in Othello is that of animals in action, preying upon one another, mischievous, lascivious, cruel or suffering, and throughout the general sense of pain and unpleasantness is much increased and kept constantly before us" (2).

THE ELECTRONIC SOURCE HAS AN AUTHOR BUT NO PAGE NUMBER

If the electronic source uses an alternate numbering system, use it to cite a specific location in the source, abbreviating "paragraph(s)" as par. or pars. and "section" as sec., or using the full word screen(s).

Fackrell asserts the accommodation for animals is adequate: "We have lodgings for up to 12 dogs at a time in our indoor/outdoor runs" (par. 9).

THE ELECTRONIC SOURCE HAS NO NUMBERING SYSTEM

Give the author's name where possible and cite the entire work in the Works Cited list.

Human rights violations are said to be decreasing as a result of foreign aid initiatives in the region (Danko).

THE ELECTRONIC SOURCE HAS NO AUTHOR

If the author of the electronic source is not known, either use the complete title in the signal phrase or use a shortened form of the title in the parenthetical reference.

According to the webpage sponsored by Children Now, an American organization that provides support for children and families, "52% of girls and 53% of boys say there are enough good role models for girls in television, although more girls (44%) than boys (36%) say there are too few" ("Reflections in Media").

5-2: LIST OF WORKS CITED

When you are following the MLA documentation style, a list of works cited should appear on a separate page at the end of your paper. The list provides essential publication information for each of the sources cited in your paper and simplifies documentation by allowing you to make only brief references to these works in the text. Include in your list of works cited only the sources from which you quoted, paraphrased, or summarized information. Do not include sources that you consulted but did not refer to in your paper. (Some instructors may require an additional listing of works consulted.)

5-2A: FORMAT OF A LIST OF WORKS CITED

TITLE AND PLACEMENT

Start the list of works cited on a new page at the end of your research paper. Title the listing Works Cited, and centre the title at the top of the page. The title word *Works* allows you to include books and articles, as well as films, recordings, websites, television programs, and other non-print sources.

PAGINATION

Continue the page numbering of the text throughout the Works Cited list; for example, if the last page of your research paper is 15, the first page of Works Cited would be 16. Position page numbers in the upper right-hand corner.

SPACING

Double-space within and between entries.

INDENTATION

Begin each entry at the left margin; if an entry runs more than one line, indent the subsequent line or lines 1.25 cm (0.5 inches) from the left margin.

ARRANGEMENT OF ENTRIES

Alphabetize entries in the Works Cited list by the last name of the author. For entries with more than one author that begin with the same author name, alphabetize according to the last names of the second authors listed. If a source has no author or editor, alphabetize by the title, ignoring any initial articles (*A*, *An*, or *The*).

For a sample Works Cited list, refer to the model essay provided at the end of this chapter (5-5).

Examples of Works Cited entries are shown below. If you encounter sources that are not covered here, consult *MLA Handbook for Writers of Research Papers*, 6th ed. (New York: MLA, 2003).

5-2B: BOOKS

There are three main units of information in a book entry. They are (1) author's name, (2) book title, and (3) publication information.

Author's name — Book title

Seabrook, John. Nobrow: The Culture of Marketing—The Marketing of Culture. New York: Knopf, 2000.

Publication information

The publication details for a book are found on the **title page** and on the reverse side of the title page, which is known as the **copyright page.** A very few books have publication information at the back of the book. When writing an entry, use information from the source itself as opposed to information from a bibliography or library catalogue. This will reduce the chance of errors in your entry.

AUTHOR'S NAME

Put the last name first, followed by a comma and a space, and then the first name and initials, if any are included on the title page. Leave a space between two initials. Put a period after the complete name.

BOOK TITLE

Provide the full name of the book, including any subtitles. The entire title, but not the period following it, should be underlined (or italicized, although MLA prefers underlining). Capitalize important words within the title (see 14-3c). If there is a subtitle, separate it from the main title with a colon and one space. Always capitalize the first and last words in any subtitle. End the title with a period and leave one space before the publication information.

TITLE WITHIN A TITLE:

- If a title within an underlined title would normally be underlined, neither underline it nor place it in quotation marks.

  White, E. B. Writings from The New Yorker 1927-1976. Ed. Rebecca M. Dale. New York: HarperPerennial, 1991.

- If a title within an underlined title would normally be in quotation marks, keep them. Note that the period is inside the quotation marks.

  Card, James Van Dyck. An Anatomy of "Penelope." Rutherford: Farleigh Dickinson UP, 1984.

- For a title within a title in quotation marks, underline if that is what you would normally do. If you would normally use quotation marks, use single quotation marks.

For information on whether to underline or use quotation marks for titles, see 14-6a.

PUBLICATION INFORMATION

PLACE OF PUBLICATION: If several cities are listed on title or copyright pages, use only the first. Place a colon and one space between the place of publication and the name of the publisher. For cities outside the United States that may be unfamiliar or ambiguous, add a comma and the province or country in abbreviated form. For example, if London, Ontario is meant rather than London, England, write London, ON. For a foreign city, you may substitute the English name or add a translation in brackets.

PUBLISHER: You do not need to use the complete name of the publisher; simply give enough information to enable your reader to find the source easily. Omit any articles (*A*, *An*, *The*), common abbreviations (*Inc.*, *Co.*, and *Ltd.*), and descriptive words (*Books*, *House*, *Press*, and *Publishers*). However, for university presses always include the abbreviations *U* and *P* or *UP* as the case may be (e.g. *Oxford UP* or *U of Chicago P*) because the university itself may publish independently of its press. If the publishing company includes the name of one person, cite the surname alone (*Norton* rather than *W. W. Norton*). If it includes two names, cite the first surname only (*McGraw* rather than *McGraw-Hill*). Place a comma between the name of the publisher and the year of publication.

YEAR OF PUBLICATION: If no date appears on the title page, use the latest copyright date.

SINGLE AUTHOR

A book by a single author is likely to be one of the items you will most frequently include in your Works Cited list. Follow the guidelines regarding the author's name, book title, and publication information as described above.

> Cameron, Julia. The Sound of Paper: Starting from Scratch. New York: Penguin, 2004.

TWO OR THREE AUTHORS

Give the authors' names in the same order as they appear on the title page, which may not be in alphabetical order. Reverse the name of the first author only, add a comma, and give the other name(s) in normal order. Use and rather than an ampersand (&) before the last name in the list. Place a period after the last name.

> McKercher, Catherine, and Carman Cumming. The Canadian Reporter: News Writing and Reporting. Toronto: Harcourt, 1998.

> Petty, Walter T., Dorothy C. Petty, and Marjorie F. Becking. Experiences in Language: Tools and Techniques for Language Arts Methods. Boston: Allyn and Bacon, 1973.

MORE THAN THREE AUTHORS

For more than three authors, either list all names as described above or give the first name followed by a comma and the abbreviation et al.

> Newman, Garfield, et al. Canada: A Nation Unfolding. Toronto: McGraw, 2000.

EDITOR(S)

If you are citing an edited collection, follow the same guidelines as for authors, adding a comma and the lower-case abbreviation ed. or eds.

> Richler, Mordecai, ed. The Best of Modern Humour. Toronto: McClelland & Stewart, 1983.

EDITION (AUTHOR WITH AN EDITOR)

If a work was prepared for publication by an editor, start the entry with the name of the author and the title; then use the abbreviation Ed. followed by the name(s) of the editor(s), with no comma in between.

> Brontë, Charlotte. Jane Eyre. Ed. Susan Cockcroft. Cambridge: Cambridge UP, 1996.

TRANSLATION

The translator of a work is listed after the title of the work. Use the abbreviation Trans.

> Apuleius. The Golden Ass. Trans. Jack Lindsay. Bloomington: Indiana UP, 1962.

CORPORATE AUTHOR

A corporate author could be a company, institution, association, or agency that is credited with authorship of a publication. This name should begin the entry. Omit any initial article (*A*, *An*, *The*).

> PriceWaterhouseCoopers Inc. Technology Forecast: 2000. Menlo Park: PriceWaterhouseCoopers Technology Center, 2000.

ANONYMOUS WORK

Begin the entry with the title and alphabetize it by the title, ignoring any initial article (*A*, *An*, *The*). In the example below, *Second* would be the word used to alphabetize.

> "The Second Shepherds' Pageant." Everyman and Medieval Miracle Plays. Ed. A. C. Cawley. New York: Dutton, 1959.

TWO OR MORE WORKS BY THE SAME AUTHOR

Give the name of the author in the first entry only. In succeeding entries, type three hyphens followed by a period in place of the author's name. Then provide the title and publication information. If the author served as an editor, translator, or compiler on a work cited, follow the hyphens with a comma followed by ed. or trans. or comp. Alphabetize by title.

Roth, Philip. The Human Stain. Boston: Houghton, 2000.

---. Patrimony: A True Story. New York: Simon, 1991.

If an author is the coauthor of a second entry, do not use three hyphens; begin the second entry with the author's full name.

SECOND OR SUBSEQUENT EDITION

The edition number or name is shown on the title page. If there is none, the work is probably a first edition. Identify later editions by placing the number or name and the abbreviation ed. after the title, for example, 2nd ed., Rev. ed. for "Revised edition," Abr. ed. for "Abridged edition," or 1994 ed.

Strunk, William, Jr., and E. B. White. The Elements of Style. 3rd ed. New York: Macmillan, 1979.

MULTI-VOLUME WORK

Cite the number of volumes after the title (and editor or edition, if any) and before the publication information, using the abbreviation *vols*. Do not indicate any specific volume or page number(s) here; rather, supply these in the parenthetical reference in the text.

Daymond, Douglas, and Leslie Monkman, eds. Literature in Canada. 2 vols. Toronto: Gage, 1978.

If you used only one of the volumes, give the volume number and publication information for that volume alone. In this case, give only page numbers in the parenthetical citation. You may add the total number of volumes at the end of the entry.

Daymond, Douglas, and Leslie Monkman, eds. Literature in Canada. Vol. 2. Toronto: Gage, 1978. 2 vols.

ENCYCLOPEDIA, DICTIONARY, OR OTHER REFERENCE WORK

If the articles in the source are arranged alphabetically, you do not need to provide the volume and page numbers. If the reference is familiar, you may also omit publication information. These sources may be listed in a shortened form as follows:

1. Author of the article (if known)
2. Title of the article, in quotation marks
3. Title of the source, underlined

4. Edition (if stated)
5. Year of publication

Boles, Glen. "Mount Assiniboine." The Canadian Encyclopedia. 2000 ed. 1999.

If the articles are not alphabetically arranged, provide the page number. If the resource is not well known, provide complete publication information.

WORK IN AN ANTHOLOGY

If you cite a short story, poem, essay, or other work that is published in an anthology, provide the following information, placing a period after each major unit of information as shown in the example below.

1. For the selection:
   a) author's name, reversed
   b) title, enclosed in quotation marks (unless the work was previously published as a single work, in which case the title is underlined)
   c) translator (if any)
2. For the anthology:
   a) title, underlined
   b) editor, translator, or compiler (if any)
   c) publication information (place of publication, publisher, and publication date)
3. Inclusive page numbers for the selection (not just the material you used); do not use the abbreviations *p.* or *pp.*

Fitzgerald, Penelope. "At Hiruharama." New Writing. Ed. Malcolm Bradbury and Judy Cooke. London: Minerva, 1992. 33-39.

If you wish to indicate that a work other than a scholarly article was previously published, give the year of original publication after the title, followed by a period.

For a previously published scholarly article, give all information for the earlier publication immediately after the selection title (or after the selection translator, if any). Add Rpt. in (for "Reprinted in") followed by the title of the collection, the new publication facts, and inclusive page numbers.

Fuller, Lon L. "Positivism and Fidelity to Law—A Reply to Professor Hart." Harvard Law Review 71 (1958): 98-106. Rpt. in Classic Readings and Canadian Cases in the Philosophy of Law. Ed. Susan Dimock. Toronto: Prentice-Hall, 2002. 211-12.

If the article was first published under another title, give the new title and publication facts first, followed by Rpt. of and the original title and publication information.

For two or more works published in a single anthology, you may create a complete entry for the anthology and cross-reference individual pieces to the entry.

1. Create a complete entry for the anthology.

Remnick, David, and Henry Finder, eds. Fierce Pajamas: An Anthology of Humor Writing from The New Yorker. New York: Random, 2001.

2. Create a separate entry for each piece in the anthology, giving the author and title. Then cross-reference to the anthology by giving the last name(s) of the anthology editor(s) and the inclusive page numbers for the piece. The following are examples of cross-references to the anthology entry shown above.

Brickman, Marshall. "The Analytic Napkin." Remnick and Finder 25-28.

Geng, Veronica. "My Mao." Remnick and Finder 95-99.

INTRODUCTION, PREFACE, FOREWORD, OR AFTERWORD

Include the following:

1. Author of the element
2. Name of the element
3. Book title
4. Author of the book preceded by By. If the book author is different from the element author, cite the full name in normal order. If there is only one author, give only the last name.
5. Book editor or translator (if any)
6. Publication information
7. Inclusive page numbers for the element

Green, Richard. Introduction. The Consolation of Philosophy. By Boethius. Trans. Richard Green. Indianapolis: Bobbs-Merrill, 1962. ix-xxiii.

BOOK IN A SERIES

Give the author name(s) and the title of the work followed by the series name and number, followed by a period and the publication information. The series name has neither underlining nor quotation marks and uses common abbreviations.

Lecker, Robert, Jack David, and Ellen Quigley. Bissoondath, Clarke, Kogawa, Mistry, Skvorecky. Can. Writers and Their Works 11. Toronto: ECW Press, 1996.

REPUBLISHED BOOK

Place the original publication date after the title and then give the republishing information. When the republication includes new material, such as an afterword, include the information after the original publication date.

> Moodie, Susanna. Roughing It in the Bush. 1852. Afterword Susan Glickman. Toronto: McClelland & Stewart, 1989.

PUBLISHER'S IMPRINT

If a publisher groups some of its books under imprints, this information appears on the title page along with the publisher's name. After the place of publication, give the name of the imprint followed by a hyphen and then the name of the publisher.

> Munro, Alice. Friend of My Youth. Toronto: A Douglas Gibson Book-McClelland & Stewart, 1990.

5-2C: ARTICLES

ARTICLE IN A MONTHLY MAGAZINE

Give the author name followed by a period, the name of the article in quotation marks with a period inside, and the name of the magazine, underlined and followed by the month and year and then a colon and space. With the exception of May, June, and July, abbreviate the months. Volume and issue number should not be included. Lastly, give the inclusive page numbers for the entire article, followed by a period. If the article is not printed on consecutive pages, give only the first page number and a plus sign.

> Bass, George F. "Golden Age Treasures." National Geographic Mar. 2002: 102-17.

ARTICLE IN A WEEKLY MAGAZINE

Follow the same general pattern as for a monthly magazine, but add the day of publication before the month.

> Begley, Sharon. "The Schizophrenic Mind." Newsweek 11 Mar. 2002: 44-51.

ARTICLE IN A JOURNAL PAGINATED BY VOLUME

Some journals use continuous pagination, with all issues published in a single year composing one volume. The pages in these volumes are usually numbered in continuous sequence, with the numbering beginning at 1 in the next volume. To cite an article in a volume with continuous pagination, give the journal title, volume number, year of publication in parentheses followed by a colon, a space, and inclusive page numbers.

Strain, Laurel A. "Seniors' Centres: Who Cares?" Canadian Journal of Aging 20 (2001): 471-91.

ARTICLE IN A JOURNAL PAGINATED BY ISSUE

If the journal begins each issue as page 1, you must give the issue number to locate the source. Give the volume number followed by a period and no space and then the issue number, followed by the year and inclusive page numbers.

Frickle, Michele. "In This Pure Land." Surface Design Journal 25.3 (2002): 26-29.

ARTICLE IN A DAILY NEWSPAPER

Give the author's name followed by the title of the article in quotation marks and then the name of the newspaper. Omit any introductory article (*the*). If the city is not included in the newspaper's name, add it in square brackets after the name, unless it is a nationally published newspaper (for example, *The Globe and Mail*).

Then, give the full date (day, month, and year), abbreviating the names of all months except May, June, and July. This information is followed by a colon, a space, and the page number preceded by the section in which the article appears. Use a plus sign (+) after the initial page number if the article is not printed on consecutive pages.

Conlogue, Ray. "All the News of 1752." Globe and Mail 4 Mar. 2002: R1+.

If the section is identified not by letter but by number, follow the pattern of the example below.

Smith, David. "Britain Leads the Way as Markets Start to Recover." Sunday Times 3 Mar. 2002, sec. 3: 1.

Some newspapers produce multiple editions of the same issue, and these contain different material. If the edition is specified on the newspaper masthead, add a comma after the date and then give the edition (e.g., *western ed., natl. ed., afternoon ed.*) followed by a colon and the page numbers.

ANONYMOUS ARTICLE

If no author is given, begin the citation with the title. Include any initial article (*A*, *An*, or *The*), but alphabetize by the following word.

"Northern Rockies Whopper." Beautiful British Columbia Spring 1998: 46.

EDITORIAL

Add the word Editorial after the title, followed by a period. For unsigned editorials, begin with the title.

"Where Justice Stumbled." Editorial. Globe and Mail 4 March 2001: A10.

LETTER TO THE EDITOR

Give the writer's name followed by a period; then add the word Letter followed by a period and the publication information.

Kennedy, Paul. Letter. Harper's Sept. 2002: 4.

REVIEW

When citing a book review, start with the reviewer's name and the title of the review, if there is one, followed by Rev. of (for "Review of") and the title of the work reviewed. The title is followed by a comma and the word by and the name of the author. Then include publication information for the source containing the review.

Gartner, Zsuzsi. "In Search of a Vanished Zeitgeist." Rev. of The Doctor's House, by Ann Beattie. Globe and Mail 2 March 2002: D3.

For a film review, instead of *by* use dir. (for *director* or *directed by*).

Ansen, David. "Brave Heart of Darkness." Rev. of We Were Soldiers, dir. Randall Wallace. Newsweek 11 March 2002: 63.

For a review of a performance such as theatre, dance, or music, add any significant details about the production.

Walker, Susan. "Spanish Dance Troupe Goes Wild in the Garden." Rev. of Senza Tempo dance/theatre troupe. Power of Place. Harbourfront Centre, Toronto. Toronto Star 29 June 2006: G6.

5-2D: ELECTRONIC SOURCES

Citations for electronic sources serve the same purposes as do citations for print sources, and there are similarities in their formats. However, because standards for electronic media are less well established, a reader requires optimal information to locate many electronic sources.

The documentation style described below reflects that found in the most recent MLA guidelines. To learn more about particular citation content and formats or to learn about electronic sources not covered in the following pages, consult these authoritative sources:

- *MLA Handbook for Writers of Research Papers* (6th ed., 2003)
- *MLA Style Manual and Guide to Scholarly Publishing* (2nd ed., 1998)

Bear in mind that documentation styles for electronic sources are still evolving and updates are sometimes posted online. For articles on documenting electronic sources, visit the MLA website at www.mla.org and follow the link to the Frequently Asked Questions page.

The list below indicates the information to include in a Works Cited entry for an online source. No source will require all items on the list. Choose those which are relevant and available, following the order shown below.

1. *Author:* Name of the author (or editor, compiler, or translator), last name first, using appropriate abbreviations (for example, *ed.*)
2. *Title A:* Title of a poem, short story, article, or similar short work, placed in quotation marks and followed by a period. If the source is a posting to a discussion list or forum, take the title from the subject line and follow it with Online posting (not underlined) and a period.
3. *Title B:* Title of a book, underlined or italicized
4. *Editor:* Name(s) of the editor, compiler, or translator cited earlier, preceded by Ed., Comp., or Trans.
5. *Print version:* Publication details about any print version of the source, including date of original print publication
6. *Title C:* Title of the Internet site, underlined; if there is no title, a description such as Home page, not underlined
7. *Site editor:* Name(s) of the editor or director of the scholarly project or database, if given, preceded by Ed., Eds., or Dir.
8. *Version:* Version number, if not part of the title; for a journal, the volume number, issue number, or other identifying number
9. *Date 1:* Date of electronic publication, update, or posting
10. *Subscription service:* Name of the service, and, if a library is the subscriber, the library name and city (and province or state abbreviation, if needed), separated by commas.

11. *List or Forum:* Name of the discussion list or forum, if applicable
12. *Pages:* Number range (for example, 16-27) or total number of pages (pp.), paragraphs (pars.), or other sections (secs.), if they are numbered
13. *Sponsor:* Name of any institution or organization sponsoring or associated with the website
14. *Date 2:* Date when you accessed the source
15. *URL:* Complete electronic address of the source (in angle brackets); or, for a subscription service, the URL of the service's home page (if known) or the keyword assigned by the service, preceded by keyword. Include the access-mode identifier (*http, flp, gopher, telnet, news*) and any relevant path and file names. If a URL runs over a line, break it only after a slash and make sure no hyphens are inadvertently added at line breaks. A final period appears after the closing angle bracket containing the URL.

SOURCE IN SCHOLARLY PROJECT OR REFERENCE DATABASE

"Charles George Douglas Roberts." The Electronic Text Centre. Dir. Alan Burk. 1996. U of New Brunswick Libraries. 5 Mar. 2002 <http://www.lib.unb.ca/Texts/research.htm>.

Frost, Robert. "Mowing." A Boy's Will. New York: Henry Holt, 1915. Project Bartleby Archive. Ed. Steven van Leeuwen. Dec. 1995. Columbia U. 6 Mar. 2002 <http://www.bartleby.com/117/19.html>.

ENTIRE ONLINE SCHOLARLY PROJECT

The Complete Writings and Pictures of Dante Gabriel Rossetti: A Hypermedia Archive. Ed. Jerome McCann. 1993-2008 (projected). Institute for Advanced Technology in the Humanities, U of Virginia. 10 Sept. 2006 <http://www.rossettiarchive.org/>.

PERSONAL WEBSITE

Rockwell, Geoffrey. Home page. 2004. 10 Sept. 2006 <http:// www. humanities.mcmaster.ca/~grockwel/personal/index.htm>.

PROFESSIONAL WEBSITE

Epic Records. 2001. Sony Music Inc. 18 Mar. 2006 <http:// www.epicrecords.com>.

ONLINE BOOK

Keats, John. Poetical Works. London, 1884. Bartleby.com: Great Books Online. Ed. Steven van Leeuwen. 2002. 4 July 2006 <http://www.bartleby.com/126/>

ONLINE BOOK IN SCHOLARLY PROJECT OR REFERENCE DATABASE

Dickens, Charles. A Tale of Two Cities. 1859. Literature.org. Ed. Peter Galbavy. 23 May 2005. 3 July 2006 <http://www.literature.org/authors/dickens-charles/two-cities/>.

ARTICLE IN ONLINE SCHOLARLY JOURNAL

Rist, Thomas. "Religion, Politics, Revenge: The Dead in Renaissance Drama." Early Modern Literary Studies 9.1 (2003): 20 pars. 3 July 2006 <http://www.shu.ac.uk/emls/09-1/ristdead.html>.

ARTICLE IN ONLINE MAGAZINE

Nyhan, Brendan. "Bully Brigade." Salon.com. 5 Mar. 2002. 4 July 2006 <http://www.salon.com/politics/col/spinsanity/2002/03/05/dissent/index.html>.

ARTICLE IN ONLINE NEWSPAPER

Barzak, Ibrahim. "Israel Rejects Militants' Ultimatum." globeandmail.com. 3 July 2006. 3 July 2006 <http://www.theglobeandmail.com/servlet/story/RTGAM.20060703.wisrael0703/BNStory/International/home>.

INTERNET SOURCE WITH NO AUTHOR

"Everything Postmodern." Ebbflux. Oct. 2004. 3 July 2006. <http://www.ebbflux.com/postmodern/>.

E-MAIL

Chamberlain, Tim. "Re: Credibility in Magazines." E-mail to the author. 12 Nov. 2006.

5-2E: MISCELLANEOUS SOURCES

GOVERNMENT PUBLICATION

If you do not know the author of the work, give the name of the government followed by the name of the agency.

Ontario. Ontario Human Rights Commission. Human Rights: Employment Application Forms and Interview. Toronto: Ontario Human Rights Commission, 1991.

If you know the author's name, you may put it either at the beginning of the entry or after the title, preceded by By or an abbreviation such as Ed. or Comp.

PAMPHLET

Use the same format as that of a book entry.

Canada. Revenue Canada. Customs, Excise and Taxation. Basics for Self-Employed Craftspeople. Ottawa: Revenue Canada, 1993.

DISSERTATION

For a published dissertation, give the name of the author, the name of the dissertation (underlined and followed by a period), the abbreviation Diss., the name of the institution that accepted the dissertation, the year it was accepted, and publishing information.

Haas, Arthur G. Metternich, Reorganization and Nationality, 1813-1818. Diss. U of Chicago, 1963. Knoxville: U of Tennessee P, 1964.

For an unpublished dissertation, the title appears in quotation marks rather than underlined.

Mercer, Todd. "Perspective, Point of View, and Perception: James Joyce and Fredric Jameson." Diss. U of Victoria, 1987.

PUBLISHED PROCEEDINGS OF A CONFERENCE

Treat as you would a book. Give any information about the conference after the title.

Cassidy, Frank, ed. Reaching Just Settlements. Proc. of Land Claims in British Columbia Conf., Feb. 21-22, 1990. Lantzville and Halifax: Oolichan and Inst. for Research on Public Policy, 1991.

LECTURE OR PUBLIC ADDRESS

Give the speaker's name, the title of the presentation in quotation marks, the name of the sponsoring organization, the location, and the date.

Hill, Larry. "Navigating the Void and Developing a Sense of Identity." Traill College, Trent University, Peterborough. 30 Jan. 2002.

CD-ROM

Citations are similar to those for print sources, but state the publication medium.

The Rosetta Stone. CD-ROM. Harrisburg, VA: Fairfield Language Technologies, 1995.

"Einstein, Albert." The 1995 Grolier Multimedia Encyclopedia. CD-ROM. Danbury, CT: Grolier, 1997.

MUSICAL COMPOSITION

Give the composer's name, then the title of the work. Underline the title unless the form, number, and key are used to identify the composition; in that case, do not underline or use quotation marks. You may add the date of composition after the title.

Mozart, Wolfgang Amadeus. The Marriage of Figaro. 1786.

Mozart, Wolfgang Amadeus. Piano Concerto in B Flat.

Published scores are treated like books.

Beethoven, Ludwig van. Symphony No. 7 in A, Op. 92. New York: Dover, 1998.

SOUND RECORDING

Which person you list first (composer, conductor, or performer) depends on what aspect of the recording you wish to emphasize. Give the title of a specific song in quotation marks and the title of the recording underlined. Next give the names of other artists. End with the manufacturer and year of issue, separated by a comma. Periods follow all other items. Note any medium other than a CD.

Verdi, Guiseppe. Arias. Perf. Simon Estes. New Philharmonic Orchestra. Cond. Gaetano Delogu. Philips, 1987.

The Band. "It Makes No Difference." The Best of the Band. Audiocassette. Capitol, 1976.

PERFORMANCE

Give the title, underlined, followed by the names of contributors such as the playwright, choreographer, director, or performers, preceded by By, Chor., Dir., or Perf. as appropriate. Then give the site of the performance: usually the theatre name, followed by a comma, then the city, followed by a period. Conclude with the date of the performance.

Indian Ink. By Tom Stoppard. Dir. Richard Cottrell. Perf. Fiona Reid. Bluma Appel Theatre, Toronto. 1 Apr. 2002.

FILM OR VIDEO

Give the title, underlined, followed by the name of the director, preceded by Dir. You may also name the writer, performers, narrator, or producer, preceded by the appropriate abbreviation. Then give the distributor and year of release.

Othello. Dir. Stuart Burge. Perf. Laurence Olivier, Maggie Smith, Joyce Redman, and Frank Finlay. Warner Bros., 1965.

For a video recording, include the original release date if applicable. Add the appropriate label or abbreviation, for example Videocassette or DVD, then give the distributor's name and the year the video was released.

The Big Snit. Dir. Richard Condie. Videocassette. National Film Board of Canada, 1985.

Suspicion. Dir. Alfred Hitchcock. Perf. Cary Grant and Joan Fontaine. 1941. Laser disc. Turner, 1995.

RADIO OR TELEVISION PROGRAM

Give the title of the episode in quotation marks, then the title of the program, underlined. If applicable and relevant, give the name of the writer, narrator, producer, and/or performer(s) preceded by By, Narr., Prod., or Perf. Give the series (if any) and the network; then list the call letters of the station and the city, separated by a comma. Finish with the date of the broadcast.

"A Hail of Bullets." The Fifth Estate. CBC Newsworld. 7 July 2006.

"Second City: First Family of Comedy." Life and Times. CBC Newsworld. 25 Aug 2006.

"Ravel's Brain." Dir. Larry Weinstein. Sunday Encore. CBC. 9 July, 2006.

INTERVIEW

Give the name of the person interviewed followed by the title of the interview, if any, usually in quotation marks but underlined if it was published independently. If there is no title, use the label Interview after the name of the person interviewed, followed by with and the name of the interviewer, if relevant. Then give publication or broadcast information.

Bellow, Saul. "Treading on the Toes of Brahmans." Endangered Species. Cambridge, MA: De Capo, 2001: 1-60.

Brumlik, Micha. Interview with Rick MacInnes-Rae. The Current. CBC Radio One. 5 July 2006.

If you cite information from an interview you have conducted, give the name of the person interviewed followed by a description such as Personal interview, Telephone interview, or E-mail interview and the date.

Robertson, Robbie. Personal interview. 5 July 2006.

FINE ART

Give the artist's full name, then the title of the work, underlined. Then name the institution (or owner) and the city.

Weiland, Joyce. Defendez la Terre. National Science Library, Ottawa.

You may add the date of origin immediately after the title.

For a photograph of a work of art, follow the example above and add the publication information for the source containing the photograph.

CARTOON

Give the artist's name, the title of the cartoon or comic (if any) in quotation marks, the descriptive label Cartoon or Comic strip, and the publication information.

Moudakis, Theo. Cartoon. Toronto Star 4 July 2006: A14.

PERSONAL LETTER

Give the letter writer's name followed by Letter to the author and the date.

Helm, Levon. Letter to the author. 5 July 2006.

MAP OR CHART

Treat as you would an anonymous book, adding the label Map or Chart as appropriate.

Great Britain/Scotland. Map. Paris: Michelin, 2001/2002.

Common Abbreviations in MLA Style

abr.	abridgment, abridged
Acad.	Academy
adapt.	adaptation, adapter, adapted by
Amer.	America, American
anon.	anonymous
app.	appendix
Assn.	Association
Can.	Canadian
ch. (chap.)	chapter
chor.	choreographer, choreographed by
Coll.	College
comp.	compiler, compiled by
cond.	conductor, conducted by
Conf.	Conference
Dept.	Department
dir.	director, directed by
diss.	dissertation
distr.	distributor, distributed by
ed.	edition, editor, edited by
Educ.	Education, Educational
et al.	and others
fig.	figure
front.	frontispiece
fwd.	foreword, foreword by
gen.	general (as in *gen. ed.*)
hist.	historian
illus.	illustration, illustrator, illustrated by
Inst.	Institute, Institution
Intl.	International
introd.	introduction, introduced by
Lib.	Library
narr.	narrator, narrated by

n.d.	no date of publication
n. pag.	no pagination
orch.	orchestra, orchestrated by
P	Press (used in documentation)
par.	paragraph
perf.	performer, performed by
proc.	proceedings
prod.	producer, produced by
pt.	part
pub. (publ.)	publisher, published by
qtd.	quoted
rev.	revised, revision, reviewed by, revised by (spell out if ambiguous)
rpt.	reprint, reprinted by
sc.	scene (omitted when act and scene numbers are used together)
sec. (sect.)	section
ser.	series
Soc.	Society
trans. (tr.)	translation, translator, translated by
U	University (used in documentation)
Univ.	University (used outside documentation)
vol.	volume
writ.	writer, written by

Note: Capitalize abbreviations in documentation only when they represent proper nouns or when they appear immediately after a period.

5-3: INFORMATION NOTES

Two types of optional information notes may be used with parenthetical documentation.

1. **Content notes** give the reader additional information that would have interrupted the flow of ideas in the text. They should be brief.

2. **Bibliographic notes** provide evaluative commentary on sources and may be used for references containing numerous citations.

To create an information note, place a superscript Arabic number at the appropriate place in the text and insert a matching numeral either at the bottom of the page (footnote) or on a separate page at the end of the paper before the Works Cited page (endnote).

Try to organize your sentence so the need for an information note falls at the end of the sentence. Give the end-of-sentence punctuation followed by the raised (superscript) note number. Information notes should be numbered consecutively throughout the paper.

When writing a footnote or endnote, indent the first line, then put the number in superscript, followed by a space. Do not indent any line after the first one. Double-space within and between notes.

> Circumnavigation of any large land body in a kayak requires significant, time-consuming preparation.[1] The catastrophic effects of inadequate equipment or ill-prepared participants have been well documented in recent testimonials.[2]
>
> [1] For a full discussion of the preparation required, see Fenger 32.
>
> [2] Foremost among these are the stories of Smith and Patterson, the Ontario Kayak Club, and Michael Summers.

5-4: MANUSCRIPT FORMAT

The following sections detail the current MLA specifications for formatting a research paper. Check with your instructor to find out if there are any additional or alternative requirements for a particular assignment.

5-4A: MATERIALS AND TYPEFACE

For academic writing, use good-quality, white, letter-size (22 × 28 cm or 8.5 × 11 in.) paper. If possible, use a high-quality printer. Make sure your printer cartridge is new enough to create distinct and—above all—readable text. Print on one side of the paper only. Many instructors prefer that you use a paper clip rather than a folder or binder; some may want the paper stapled. Keep a spare copy of any paper you submit (ideally, both a hard copy and an electronic backup).

Ensure that your paper is easy to read by using one of the standard book typefaces, such as Times Roman, and use 12-point font. Do not justify the text; it should be ragged right.

5-4B: TITLE

MLA requires no title page. Your name, your instructor's name, the course number, and the date appear at the top of the first page, flush with the left margin, and double-spaced. The title is centred two lines below the date. In the title, capitalize the first word, the last word, and all principal words including those that follow hyphens, but not articles, prepositions, coordinating conjunctions, and the *to* in infinitives. (See 14-3c.) The title is not underlined or in quotation marks and is not followed by a period. Double-space after the title and indent 1.25 cm (0.5 in.) at the beginning of the first line of the text.

For an example of the heading and title, see the sample essay on page 173.

If your instructor requires a title page, centre the title of your research paper approximately one-third of the way down the page. In the middle of the page, centre your name. Centred near the bottom of the title page are the course name and section number, the instructor's name, and the date. Begin your paper on page 2, starting with the title. An example of a title page appears on page 171.

5-4C: MARGINS AND SPACING

Leave margins of 2.5 cm (1 in.) on the top, bottom, and both sides of the page unless your instructor requires a larger margin for marking purposes.

Double-space everything in the paper, including quotations, notes, and the Works Cited list. Leave one space after a period or other punctuation mark, but do not space before or after a dash or between the two hyphens that compose a dash.

Indent the first line of each paragraph 1.25 cm (0.5 in.) from the left margin.

For quotations of more than four lines of prose and more than three lines of poetry, indent 2.5 cm (1 in.) from the left margin without adding quotation marks. Introduce the quotation with a colon. (See page 178 and 11-5b for examples.)

5-4D: PAGE NUMBERS

Number all pages consecutively in the upper right-hand corner, 1.25 cm (0.5 in.) from the top of the page and flush with the right margin.

Use only Arabic numerals and place your last name before every page number. Your can use your word processing program to create a header with your name and page number that will automatically appear on every page. Do not use the abbreviation *p.* or include hyphens or parentheses.

5-4E: HEADINGS

MLA does not provide guidelines for headings and subheadings. In papers for English and the humanities, headings are not used as frequently as they are in business reports or research papers for social science disciplines. If you wish to use headings, first check with your instructor to determine if they are acceptable for a specific writing assignment. If they are, follow the APA guidelines for headings described in 6-3g.

5-4F: VISUALS

Visuals should be positioned as close as possible to the relevant text unless your instructor wants visuals placed together in an appendix at the end of the paper. MLA identifies two major types of visuals:

1. Tables
2. Figures (photographs, maps, drawings, graphs, and charts)

TABLES

A table should be given a label consisting of the word Table and an Arabic numeral (for example, *Table 1*). It should also have a caption, a brief description such as *Production Data for All Branches in 2006*. Both should be flush left above the table, double-spaced, and capitalized in title style. The source and any information notes appear below the table, double-spaced.

FIGURES

Any illustration other than a table should be labelled Fig. with an Arabic numeral and should also be captioned. Both the label and caption appear below the illustration, double-spaced.

5-4G: OUTLINE

Some instructors may request that you include an outline along with the final draft of your paper. For information on creating and formatting a formal outline, see 1-1d.

5-5: SAMPLE PAPER

The formatting of the sample research paper—an actual student paper—presented in this section is consistent with the recommendations provided in the *MLA Handbook for Writers of Research Papers* (6th ed., 2003).

Another source you might consult for more detailed information about MLA format and documentation style is the *MLA Style Manual and Guide to Scholarly Publishing* (2nd ed., 1998).

Sample MLA Essay

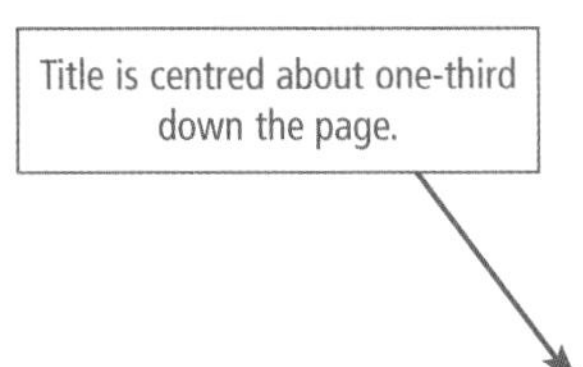

"The White Man's Burden" and Characterization in

E. M. Forster's A Passage to India

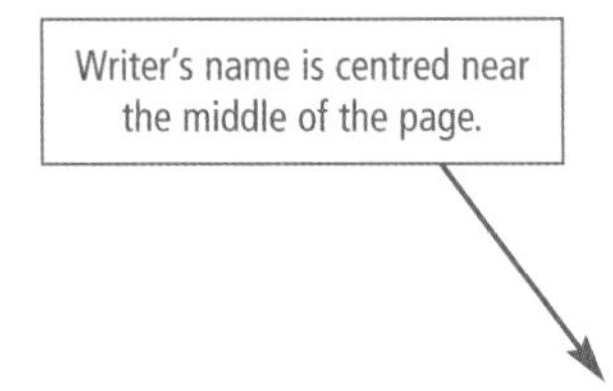

Dan McKeown

Course name and section number, professor's name, and date are centred near the bottom of the page.

English 4W03

Dr. S. O'Brien

26 February 2007

NOTE: A title page is not required in MLA style; however, some instructors may ask that you include one.

Outline pages are numbered with small roman numerals.

McKeown i

Outline

Thesis: Forster uses the British and Indian characters of Chandrapore in A Passage to India to demonstrate the impossibility of engaging Orientalist "truths" about Indians and shows the inherent flaws in the philosophy of "the white man's burden."

Outline begins with thesis and uses standard format.

I. "The white man's burden" was the unspoken philosophy of the League of Nations Covenant in 1919 and became the underlying principle of British Imperialism in the 1920s.

Sentences are parallel throughout.

1. A novelist of conscience, Forster shows the British intent to interact with the Indians rather than force rule upon them.
2. Liberal humanism, as Forster refers to it, depends on Indian assimilation of laws imposed on Indians by British Imperialists.
3. The trial in A Passage to India tests the ideology of "the white man's burden" as a means of justifying racial subordination.
4. Said's notion of Orientalism is shown in the polarization between the British and the Indians in the novel.

II. The novel shows the "burden" will be a permanent superior role for the British and not the enlightened "civilizing" force originally intended.

1. All the British characters feel superiority to the Indians.
2. Mrs. Moore and Fielding, though sympathetic, see the Empire as essential.
3. Adela's relationship to Indians shows some change, but not progress.
4. Forster shows through the trial the failure of this "civilizing force" ideologically and legally.

NOTE: An outline is not required in MLA style; however, some instructors may ask that you include one.

Dan McKeown

Dr. S. O'Brien

English 4W03

26 February 2007

"The White Man's Burden" and Characterization in
E. M. Forster's A Passage to India

Nobel Prize winner V. S. Naipaul claims that E. M. Forster knew hardly anything about India: "He just knew a few middle-class Indians and the garden boys whom he wished to seduce." (E. M. Forster). Yet Forster demonstrates that he knows a great deal about the cultural divide between the races in A Passage to India. Indeed, Forster uses his characters to show the impossibility of understanding Indians when one is limited to Victorian conceptions such as the "white man's burden."

The most fundamental way to describe "the white man's burden," especially in a historical-literary context, is to understand it as an extension of Edward Said's principle of Orientalism. As Said explains, Orientalism is a way of organizing and understanding "truths" about the East. The British, for example, establish and understand a system of knowledge about India by opposing the racial "truths" of "us" and "them" (Said 1279-80).

Citation includes author's name and page numbers in parentheses.

Author is named in signal phrase; page number is given in parentheses at end of paraphrase.

When the British physically enter India, however, this knowledge must somehow be transferred from the British imagination and, in a sense, "re-projected" onto India so that it can be actualized in the operation of the Empire. As Said explains, the Westerner creates "a whole series of possible relationships with the Orient" without ever relinquishing his or her hegemony (1281). "The white man's burden" was one such relationship. Between the late nineteenth

McKeown 2

century and World War II, "the white man's burden" was the underlying ideology of Britain's Imperial relationship with India. Straightforward and relatively uniform in Britain, the "burden" was to "civilize" India. In India itself, however, the relationship was conflicted and certainly not uniform. As E. M. Forster demonstrates in A Passage to India, the main characters (British and Indian) of Chandrapore have highly conflicted views about the role of the white man in India. Ultimately, Forster uses his characters to demonstrate the impossibility of engaging Orientalist "truths" about Indians via "the white man's burden."

One imperative for understanding "the white man's burden" in its literary-historical context as well as in Forster's novel is to note that it is seldom mentioned explicitly as "the white man's burden." This is because the "burden" is an implied ideology and was never an official doctrine or canon. International treaties and agreements do not make explicit claims of racial superiority. Imperial political figures and public opinion interpret the written doctrines to accord with their Orientalist and, often, racist views. As Said explains, racial representation by the public or in literature is one such "code of understanding" and means for making sense of the Orient (1290). The Berlin Conference of 1885, for example, declared that it was the "burden" of every European nation to "civilize" their "uncivilized colonies." British ambassador to the conference Cecil Rhodes declared aside that it was their duty to "civilize . . . races who were considered unfit to manage their own affairs" (Lawrence 46). Referring to Britain's Imperial mission, Rudyard Kipling coined the term in a literary context in his 1887 poem, "The White Man's Burden." The League of Nations Covenant in 1919 dedicated an article to assign mandates to nations acting for protectorates. The mandate principle has been considered by some historians to be a direct descendant of Kipling's racial "burden" (Van Creveld 321). Historically, "the white man's burden" was indeed the underlying principle of British Imperialism by the 1920s. Britain had come to rely much more heavily on the ideological "truth" that the Orient was inferior and uncivilized. Violent forms of racial subordination were no longer acceptable in international circles.

Reflected in the literature of the time period is a similar movement away from violent subordination to "justified" racial subordination. Literary historians like Kurt Loeb and Jeffrey Meyers classify Imperial writers of Forster's time (roughly 1900-39) as novelists of conscience. They differ from their earlier Imperial counterparts, known as adventure novelists (roughly 1850-1900) in their marked absence of violence. Rudyard Kipling was seen as a writer in transition between adventure and conscience (Meyers 29). Indeed, his poem "The White Man's Burden" retains elements of the desire to use force to uphold the "burden." At the same time, acknowledging a "burden" to "civilize" at least demonstrates a conscience in interaction with the Indians, something absent in Imperial writing before Kipling (Meyers vii). According to Said, this is one positive aspect of Orientalism: at least by engaging and attempting to understand the East, even if manipulation and oppression are required, progress is being made by the mere fact of cross-cultural interaction (1284).

For Lidan Lin, this is the exact irony that Forster's "liberal humanism" demonstrates. Liberal humanism simply refers to the spread of civilization and humanity through "liberal" British institutions such as the court. The irony is in the fact that the British must still employ racial subordination to achieve the civilization sought (Lin 133). Thus, the Imperial authorities in Chandrapore attempt to employ their "burden" in sociopolitical institutions such as the court. There is significant room to argue that the Indians could receive the practical benefits of these civilizing institutions. Recall that the attempt to regain hegemony can come from a whole series of possible relationships (Said 1281). The law is one example in Chandrapore. Mahmoud Ali and Das are inclined to follow the rule of British law to the letter. However, this is where Forster demonstrates that the British authorities' "re-projection" of the "burden" begins to fail. In order for the "burden" to succeed, an Indian mind must receive and assimilate the projected ideology. Of course, the Indians do not accept the white man's interpretation that these civil institutions are characteristic of a superior race. Although hesitant at times, they do ultimately stand against imposed racial subordination as Das does

McKeown 4

during Aziz's trial (Forster 224). Mahmoud Ali does what he can to resist by storming out of the trial, calling it a farce, and bringing to Das's attention the attempted racial subordination: "I am not defending a case, nor are you trying one. We are both of us slaves" (227).

In a reference to a novel that has appeared in many editions, it is wise to include chapter numbers as well as page numbers, for ease of reference. Because this edition is a class text, only page numbers are needed.

The trial reveals the most fundamental truth about Forster's notion of the "burden." It demonstrates just how dependent the contemporary "burden" is on the rule of law to justify racial subordination. On the part of the characters of Chandrapore, there is a noticeable absence of interest in traditional Imperial goals, such as economic profit and conquest of living space. Nor is there any indication in Chandrapore of armed conflict. The main British characters in A Passage to India are entirely guided, instead, by a desire to subordinate the Indians legally. The Indians are equally guided by this desire in the sense that they must respond to the British. If the required acceptance on the part of the Indians were not available, then the racial subordination would have to be explicitly stated by the Imperial authorities. This is not so simple, however. This difficulty is perhaps why Ronny "really can't explain everything" (55). As Meyer notes, this is an example of the colonial novel where the villain or antagonist is portrayed as unable to "make clear distinctions between good and evil" (x). The racial subordination of the "burden" must be implied because it cannot be justified outright as the truth. In the actual operation of the sociopolitical and legal systems, much of the racial justification, therefore, comes in the form of perverted rationalization. Logic is formed out of tangible "evidence," such as the "newly broken" strap on Adela's field glasses, which logically says that Aziz is guilty (176). It also comes in abstract forms. Mr. McBryde claims to know how the "psychology here is different" as does Mr. Turton who can claim "twenty-five years experience of this country" (177, 173). Drawing on the assumed psychological knowledge of the Indians, Ronny likewise rationalizes that the Indians even welcome the British rule: "'Your sentiments are those of a god,' [Mrs. Moore] said. [. . . Ronny] said, 'India likes gods. And Englishmen like posing as gods.'" (69). This is an extreme rationalization and an assertion of British superiority. It makes the claim that the British are acting as no less than a deus ex machina in India.

The writer interprets his findings for readers and does not leave them to draw their own conclusions.

The trial itself is a definitive test for determining how successfully the "burden" has been "re-projected" into India. A guilty verdict will mean that the Imperial authorities' twisted logic and evidence have achieved the hegemony Britain desires over the legal system. As Forster demonstrates, the British are so convinced of their superiority and of the righteousness of their "burden" that the narration places the entire weight of Imperial legitimacy on one climactic moment. The British are absolutely convinced of Aziz's guilt simply because he is Indian. Ronny is convinced even in light of Adela claiming she wrongfully accused him (208-11). Major Callendar comments, "cut the cackle and let's have the verdict" as though a guilty verdict is pending (224). The only way the British could get their desired conviction is if Adela were to believe the racial subordination the authorities have pressed on her. The desired outcome of the trial is entirely dependent on how far their idea of racial subordination has permeated Adela's imagination. Evidently, however, it has not been completely assimilated in Adela's mind, nor in the minds of the Indians. Das dismisses the idea of racial subordination when he orders the English group to come down from their elevated position (224). In doing so, Das also foreshadows the trial's outcome by hinting at the disappointment the British are about to face when they realize that their idea of racial superiority does not overcome. Indeed, throughout the rest of the novel, the narrative makes only scattered references to any of the Imperial authorities.

McKeown 6

Thus, another truth is revealed about the "burden" in accordance with Said's Orientalism. At the trial, a massive movement in the novel occurs as every character must choose between two polarities. You are either British (us) or Indian (them). The polarization is so severe, in fact, that it culminates by resting on Das's shoulders. He is saved from having to choose sides by Adela. Das is perfectly symbolic of exactly how far "the white man's burden" has permeated India. He is an Indian judge in a British legal system. His decision will determine whether or not the British have successfully subordinated the Indians to a point where they can use faulty evidence and twisted logic to support their sense of racial superiority. Ironically, and to the misfortune of the Imperial authorities, the twisted legal logic works only as compensation for the lack of truth behind the racist and Orientalist views. Adela's testimony exposes the lack of truth in racial generalizations, and in doing so, she unravels the entire chain of twisted logic on which the operation of the Empire's "burden" rests.

These irrational justifications reveal another important aspect of Forster's notion of how the "burden" works. The "burden" does not maintain its original goal. The ideal situation would entail only temporary British occupation. Indeed, the League of Nations Covenant intended a mandate to be employed only as needed to help another nation to establish a democratic self-government. Kipling's poem "The White Man's Burden" makes no reference to temporary occupation, but it certainly does suggest an end purpose to the "burden":

Long quotation is clearly introduced.

> And when your goal is nearest
> The end for other sought . . .
> The cry of hosts ye humour
> (Ah slowly!) toward the light:—
> Why brought ye us from bondage,
> Our loved Egyptian night? (21:78)

Indent quotations of longer than four lines 2.5 cm (1 in.) from the left margin. Do not enclose them in quotation marks. Use no period after the citation's parentheses.

McKeown 7

Ellipsis indicates words removed from the original source for the sake of clarity.

The ideal civilization process would see an end to the occupation (Lin 135). Lin describes another irony of Forster's liberal humanism: Britain can never leave India because Britain itself is constantly becoming more civilized (134). "The white man's burden" to civilize India is a permanent responsibility. This aspect of the "burden" is not troublesome to the British, however. In Kipling's Imperialism, the British "take up the burden" with "fidelity . . . discipline . . . and honour" (Meyers 7). The permanence of the "burden" is actually fuelled by the British sense of dignity and goodwill to the fellow humans. It would be a significant honour to England to know that other people are being "civilized" with the good manners and reserved behaviour of the British. Doubly ironic, therefore, as Mrs. Moore notes, that all goodwill and manners are lost in India once the white man takes up his "burden" and its unjust methods (70). Therefore, the Imperial authorities, namely Ronny, Mr. Turton, and Mr. McBryde, are one grouping of characters who demonstrate a unique response to the Empire's "burden." They essentially "take up the white man's burden," as Kipling implores, and attempt to make it a reality by engaging in sociopolitical and legal interaction with the Indians (78). They cannot, and thus, Foster demonstrates the impossibility of bringing into India an Orientalist approach to civilizing anyone.

The non-official British characters in Chandrapore may not deal with the "burden" on a daily basis; nevertheless, they play an important role in bringing the idea of the white man's racial superiority into India. As civilians in the British Empire, they are believers in Britain's duty to civilize. Said discusses the "us" and "them" principle as all-inclusive (1280). In other words, notions of European superiority infect all of Europe, not just select people who are part of the Imperialist administration. As noted earlier, there is a complete lack of interest in Chandrapore in traditional Imperial goals such as economic profit. The "burden" is the superstructure that guides the conduct of the British characters. Nor are the women excluded, though they are involved only in an unofficial manner. Just as

McKeown 8

the authorities professionally subordinate the Indians, these characters reinforce the subordination. This is how Aziz understands "the inevitable snub." He sees it as an instinctive reaction of British ladies who are "full of their own affairs" (39). These characters have no responsibility toward or desire to acknowledge the Indian. It is instead Imperial authorities like Major Callendar who have the professional conscience to chastise Aziz openly (40). To Aziz, however, the professional subordination he suffers at the hands of authorities and the ideological subordination from non-officials are both part of the same ignorance. Aziz responds in kind. Instead of assimilating notions of inferiority, Aziz assimilates the "us" and "them" mentality. Aziz sees this subordination from all the British; this ultimate answer to the question "Why can't we be friends now?" is "No, not yet" (316). Indeed, as Paul Armstrong explains, the racial subordination in the novel is enforced by a greater range of British characters than it may at first seem. Ultimately, all the British feel themselves superior to all the Indians. To Forster, the conflict between race and culture is very real, and is demarcated along very distinct racial lines. This is emphasized by the fact that Aziz re-dignifies himself after the "gross snub" by turning to his religion (Armstrong 368).

The research paper uses a variety of different sources. Note that the citation appears in parentheses before the period.

All the British characters subordinate the Indians. Even Mrs. Moore is a product of the Empire's "burden" ideology. As Jeffrey Heath argues, she envisions some kind of loving big-brotherly Empire, but it is an Empire nevertheless: "One touch of regret . . . would have made [Ronny] a different man, and the British Empire a different institution" (70). She is restricted by the limits of the British imagination and cannot imagine India without an Empire (Heath 288). Moreover, her Imperially ordered universe is still burdened: "To be one with the universe! So dignified and simple. But there was always some little duty to be

Use square brackets to indicate words you have added that are not in the original.

performed first" (212). She is similar to the other women of Chandrapore in the sense that she is detached from the professional duty of the Imperial authorities. This is why her attacks on Imperial practices are so idealistic. She cannot comment on Ronny's professional duty, so she attacks his emotions, rather than the actual Imperial ideology he embodies.

Fielding, a school teacher, is much more involved with the public sphere, owing also to his gender role in relation to the "burden." Unlike Mrs. Moore, he is much more practical and direct in his attacks on Imperial practices. When Mr. McBryde challenges his attacks ("Well, she tells her own story, doesn't she?"), Fielding counters by highlighting exactly how the "burden" is racially manipulated: "Yes but she tells it to you" (179). Again, it is manipulated by Imperial authorities who need to justify racial prejudice to support the "burden." Fielding's direct attacks on Imperial practice make him much more anti-Imperial than Mrs. Moore. Nevertheless, he also associates the Empire with a romanticized India. At the Club he is involved in an argument over an issue of Imperial procedure: the etiquette of rising when a magistrate walks into the room. Immediately after Fielding leaves, "to cool himself and regain mental balance he went onto the upper veranda for a moment, where the first object he saw was the Marabar Hills. At this distance and hour they leapt into beauty" (197). His role is significant to the novel because it demonstrates how even someone so critical of Imperial practice still believes there is a purpose for Britain in India. True, Fielding may not necessarily believe in British superiority. Forster is ambiguous on this point; as Fielding remarks, "I cannot tell you why England is here or whether she ought to be here. It's beyond me." Nevertheless, he believes in an Imperial purpose: "England holds India for her own good" (124). Like Mrs. Moore, he is a product of British ideology and cannot escape the British imagination: "He experienced nothing himself; it was as if someone had told him there was such a moment, and he was obliged to believe" (197). Thus, another significant truth about the "burden" is revealed. For at least three characters, the "burden" ideology is not necessarily racial. For Mrs. Moore, Fielding, and Adela, the "white" requirement is incidentally applicable; it just so happens that a white race must "civilize" an Oriental race.

Use clear transitions between main points of your paper.

Recall that one of the characteristics of Imperial writing prior to Kipling was a complete absence of Anglo-Indian interaction (Meyers vii). Adela's desire for "seeing the real India" marks another definite truth about how far the "burden" has progressed from Kipling's expression of it (52). Someone like Adela can come to India with an adventurous desire because the Imperial authorities have "tamed" India for British civilians. She can actively mingle with the Indians, and she still maintains a distinct awareness of Britain's purpose in India. Adela directly associates her sense of the "burden" with her romantic adventure: "'Yes, Ron is always hard-worked,' she replied, contemplating the hills. How lovely they suddenly were!" (66). Her sense of Britain's "burden" in India is certainly not as pronounced as that of other characters. However, she does understand it and does not question the British claim on civilization until after her epiphany at the Marabar Caves (221). Without a doubt, this instance in the novel is Forster's greatest insistence that no outside ideology can ever be brought into India, let alone "re-projected" onto an Indian. As Heath argues, Adela is warned that "nothing embraces the whole of India" and that it is impossible for the human mind to grasp India (156; Heath 289).

Thus, through a limited range of responses from different characters, Forster shows the impossibility of imposing the notion of "the white man's burden" on India. The "burden" groups the characters according to their function in the Empire. The non-official British characters function in India as extensions of British society at home. They congregate in mock British societies, such as the Club, and only enter the public sphere of India when necessity requires them to assert their "whiteness" in times of Imperial crisis. In the meantime, they ideologically reinforce the racial superiority that British Orientalism asserts over the Indian. It is the Imperial authorities who actively engage this racial assertion on a daily basis. Legally, they claim that it is the "burden" of the white man to "civilize" and maintain order in a disorderly country. However, both ideologically and legally, the racial assertion is denied by India. The former is illustrated at its fullest through Adela's failure in the cave. The latter is illustrated at its fullest through the failure of Aziz's prosecution.

McKeown 12

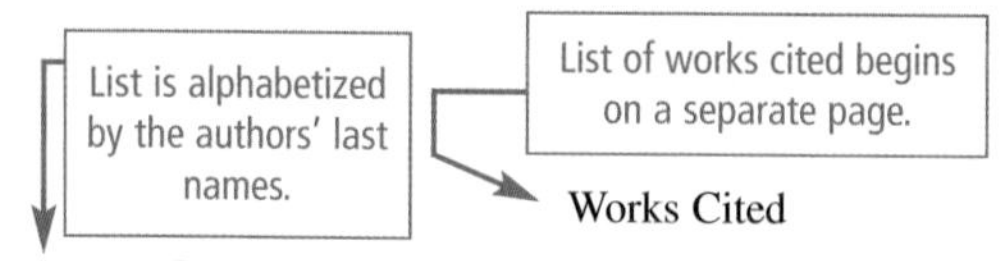

Works Cited

Armstrong, Paul. “Reading India: E. M. Forster and the Politics of Interpretation.” Twentieth-Century Literature: A Scholarly and Critical Journal 18.4 (1992): 365-85.

Edward Morgan Forster (1879-1970). 30 Jan. 2007 <http://www.kirjasto.sci.fi/forster.htm>.

Forster, E. M. A Passage to India. London: Penguin, 1979.

Heath, Jeffrey. “A Voluntary Surrender: Imperialism and Imagination in A Passage to India.” U of Toronto Quarterly 59 (1998-99): 287-309.

Kipling, Rudyard. “The White Man’s Burden.” The Writings in Prose and Verse of Rudyard Kipling. Vol. 21. New York: Scribner’s, 1903. 36 vols.

Lawrence, James. “The White Man’s Burden? Imperial Wars in the 1890s.” History Today 42 (1992): 45-51.

Lin, Lidan. “The Irony of Colonial Humanism.” Review of International English Literature 28 (1997): 133-53.

Loeb, Kurt. White Man’s Burden. Toronto: Lugus, 1992.

Meyers, Jeffrey. Fiction and the Colonial Experience. New Jersey: Rowman and Littlefield, 1973.

Said, Edward. “From the Introduction to Orientalism.” The Critical Tradition. Ed. David Richter. Boston: Bedford, 1998. 1278-92.

Van Creveld, Martin. The Rise and Decline of the State. Cambridge: Cambridge UP, 1999.

Each entry is a hanging indent, where the first line is typed flush left.

6

APA STYLE OF DOCUMENTATION

The *best* way to have a *good idea* is to have *lots of ideas.*

-Linus Pauling

6

APA Style of Documentation

6 APA Style of Documentation

Writers in the social sciences generally follow the American Psychological Association guidelines for formatting and documenting sources. APA style is used in disciplines such as psychology, sociology, business, and economics, and may be used in other areas such as political science, nursing, and history. Check with your instructor regarding the preferred style for a particular course.

This chapter summarizes the APA guidelines in the *Publication Manual of the American Psychological Association*, 5th ed. (Washington: APA, 2001) and concludes with a model research paper following APA format and documentation style. The APA website at www.apastyle.org also provides regularly updated documentation guidelines.

If readers want to check any source you used for words, facts, or ideas, they need complete information about your sources. When following APA style, you document your sources in two ways:

1. Within the body of the paper, using **in-text citations**
2. At the end of the paper, in a **list of references** (see 6-2)

6-1: IN-TEXT CITATIONS

APA style uses the author-date method of citation, giving the author and date of publication in parentheses within the essay. Each of these parenthetical citations has a matching entry giving complete publication information in the References list on a separate page at the end of the essay. If a specific part of a source is paraphrased or quoted, the citation also includes the page number (or chapter, figure, table, or equation), as detailed below.

6-1A: FORMAT OF CITATIONS FOR PRINT SOURCES

ONE AUTHOR

Give the name and the year of publication in parentheses, separated by a comma.

> One study (Woods, 2006) cast some doubt on the efficacy of the procedure.

If the name of the author is given in a signal phrase, cite only the year of publication in parentheses.

> As Bayly clearly demonstrates (2006), the technical excellence of the procedure resulted in long wait times for patients.

If both the author and the year are given in a signal phrase, do not add parenthetical information.

> Fawcett's seminal 2006 study showed that the data had been doctored to illustrate the desired result.

SPECIFIC PART OF A SOURCE

To cite quotations or paraphrased information taken from a precise location in a work, follow the guidelines above but also give a location reference such as the page number or the chapter, figure, table, or equation. Abbreviate *page* (p.), *pages* (pp.), and *chapter* (chap.).

> Peter Newman (1995, p. 183) observes, "As the institutional touchstones that had once been the nation's Pole Star fell away, Canadians began automatically to distrust anyone who exercised authority over their lives."

> One observer notes, "As the institutional touchstones that had once been the nation's Pole Star fell away, Canadians began automatically to distrust anyone who exercised authority over their lives" (Newman, 1995, p. 183).

TWO AUTHORS

Cite both names along with the year of publication. If the names appear in a signal phrase, join them with and; in a parenthetical reference, use the ampersand (&).

> Clarkson and McCall (1990) agree that Trudeau's writings during the early 1960s revealed him at the height of his powers as a writer and Quebec theoretician on federalism.

> During the early 1960s, Trudeau was at the height of his powers as a writer and was viewed as the preeminent Quebec theoretician on federalism (Clarkson & McCall, 1990).

THREE TO FIVE AUTHORS

Give the names of all the authors only in the first citation; remember to use the ampersand (&) instead of *and*. In subsequent citations, give only the first author's last name and the abbreviation et al. (not italicized and with a period only after "al").

First Citation of the Source

> Effective class groups do not happen randomly; however, an instructor can encourage their development by employing effective teaching

methods and monitoring group performance (Lang, McBeath, & Hebert, 1995).

Subsequent Citation of the Source

Classroom management approaches can be classified according to the degree of teacher intervention and the control each approach needs (Lang et al., 1995).

SIX OR MORE AUTHORS

For all citations of a work with six or more authors, use the first author's last name followed by et al.

Many assert that Canada's involvement in World War I was characterized by racism in some instances and by greed and corruption in others (Newman et al., 2000).

NO AUTHOR

Cite the first few words of the title along with the year. Underline titles of books, magazines, journals, and reports. Use quotation marks around titles of articles or chapters.

One recent report ("UN Guns," 2006) suggests that the UN conference on the illicit gun trade ended in disarray, with weaker results than in 2001.

CORPORATE AUTHOR

The name of a group author such as a corporation, organization, or agency is usually given in full. However, if the name is long and the abbreviation is readily understandable, you may first cite the source using the full name followed by the abbreviation in square brackets and then give subsequent citations using the abbreviation and year.

Entry in Reference List: Assembly of First Nations. (2006).

First Citation: (Assembly of First Nations [AFN], 2006)

Subsequent Citations: (AFN, 2006)

AUTHORS WITH THE SAME SURNAME

Include the initials in all text citations, even if the year of publication differs.

A study by R. J. Jones (2006) indicates that . . .

TWO OR MORE WORKS IN A SINGLE CITATION

Give the sources in alphabetical order by the authors' last names. Separate the citations with a semicolon.

Researchers have concluded that there is no point in searching for a single creativity score comparable to an IQ score (Halpern, 1984; Rothstein, 1990).

Two or more works by the same author(s) are arranged by year of publication with commas separating the years. If two or more works by the same author(s) have the same publication date, distinguish the works by adding a, b, c, and so on after the year.

(Nichol, 1984, 1986, 1987a, 1987b)

TRANSLATION

Cite both the original publication date and the date of the translation, separated by a virgule, also known as a forward slash (/).

(Barthes, 1957/1987)

PERSONAL COMMUNICATION

For letters, memos, e-mails, interviews, and telephone conversations, give the initials and last name of the communicator and the date on which the communication took place. Because they are not verifiable, personal communications are not included in the References list.

J. Nadler (personal communication, November 12, 2006) indicated that the Russian mafia played a significant role in supplying protection for Budapest nightclub owners.

6-1B: FORMAT OF CITATIONS FOR ELECTRONIC SOURCES

Follow the guidelines for print sources but add location information to direct the reader to a specific part of the source. For an electronic source with no page numbers, use the paragraph number if it is available, preceded by the paragraph symbol (¶) or the abbreviation para. and a space.

As Myers (2000, ¶ 7) aptly phrased it, "positive emotions are both an end—better to live fulfilled, with joy [and other positive emotions]—and a means to a more caring and healthy society."

If neither paragraph nor page numbers are available, cite the heading and the number of the paragraph following it.

Panic disorder currently affects six million American adults (NIMH, 2006, Panic Disorder, ¶ 6).

If no page numbers, paragraph numbers, or headings are provided, it may be necessary to omit a location reference.

6-2: LIST OF REFERENCES

For every citation in the text of your paper, there must be a matching entry in a list of references at the end of the paper. Only sources used in the research and preparation of the paper are included in the References list.

The following section presents guidelines for setting up a list of references and model entries for common types of sources. If the source you have used in your research paper is not described in this section, consult the *Publication Manual of the American Psychological Association*, 5th ed. (Washington: APA, 2001). Some tips and guidelines are also available on the APA website at www.apastyle.org.

6-2A: FORMAT OF A REFERENCES LIST

TITLE AND PLACEMENT

Begin the list of references at the end of your paper on a separate page. Centre the title, References. Do not italicize (or underline) the title or put it within quotation marks. Use an initial capital only, not all caps. See the References list in the sample APA-style essay at the end of this chapter (page 210).

PAGINATION

Number the page or pages of your References list sequentially with the rest of the research paper.

SPACING

Double-space all entries in your References list.

INDENTATION

Use a "hanging indent" format, with the first line of each reference flush left and subsequent lines indented 1.25 cm (0.5 in.).

Sale, K. (1991). *The conquests of paradise: Christopher Columbus and the Columbian legacy*. New York: Plume.

ARRANGEMENT OF ENTRIES

All sources that you used for your research paper and cited in the text must be listed alphabetically in your References list.

Alphabetize entries by the authors' surnames.

If you need to list two or more works by the same author or authors in your list of references, give the author name(s) each time and organize the works chronologically by their year of publication.

Jameson, F. (1972). *The prison-house of language: A critical account of structuralism and Russian formalism*. Princeton, NJ: Princeton University Press.

Jameson, F. (1979). *Fables of aggression: Wyndham Lewis, the modernist fascist*. Berkeley: University of California Press.

When the author is the sole author of one or more works and the leading coauthor of others, put the entry or entries for the single-author works first.

For references with the same first author and different second or third authors, arrange entries alphabetically by the surname of the second author.

For two or more works by the same author with the same publication date, arrange entries alphabetically by title, and add lowercase letters—a, b, c, and so on—immediately after the year within the parentheses.

Berndt, T. J. (1981a). Age changes and changes over time in prosocial intentions and behavior between friends. *Developmental Psychology, 17*, 408–416.

Berndt, T. J. (1981b). Effects of friendship on prosocial intentions and behavior. *Child Development, 52*, 636–643.

If no author is given of if there is a group author such as an agency, association, or institution, alphabetize by the first significant word of the name. Do not consider initial articles—*A*, *An*, or *The*—when you alphabetize. Use full official names rather than abbreviations.

6-2B: ELEMENTS OF ENTRIES

AUTHOR

Invert all author names. Give the last name, followed by a comma, and then the initial(s)—do not use the full first name.

When there are two or more authors, use the ampersand (&) rather than the word *and*. Separate author names with commas, including before an ampersand.

For an edited book, place the name of the editor or editors in the author position, followed by the abbreviation Ed. or Eds. in parentheses.

If the reference has no author, move the title to the author position.

For references with more than six authors, replace the seventh and subsequent authors with et al. (not italicized and with a period only after *al.*).

The author element of the entry should end with a period; if it closes with a parenthesis—for example, with (Ed.)—add a period after the closing parenthesis. If an author's initial with a period ends the element, do not add an extra period.

PUBLICATION DATE

Place the publication date in parentheses after the last author's (or editor's) name.

For a published work, give the year the work was copyrighted; for an unpublished work, give the year it was produced.

For magazines, newsletters, or newspapers, give the year followed by the exact date of publication as it appears on the issue: the month or months, the season, or the month and day. Spell the names of months in full.

If no date is given, place n.d. in parentheses. For articles accepted for publication but not yet published, write in press in parentheses.

Finish the date element of the entry with a period after the closing parenthesis.

TITLE OF ARTICLE OR CHAPTER

Do not italicize or underline article or chapter titles or place them within quotation marks.

Capitalize only the first word of the title and of the subtitle and any proper nouns.

After the article title, other identifying information may be included in brackets, for example, [Letter to the editor] or [Abstract].

Finish the element with a period.

TITLE OF WORK AND PUBLICATION INFORMATION

NON-PERIODICALS

For a non-periodical such as a book, after the author name(s) and date give the following information: title of work; additional information such as edition; a description of the form of the work if applicable; place of publication; publisher.

TITLE: Italicize book titles and subtitles. Capitalize only the first word of the title and of the subtitle as well as any proper nouns. End the title with a period, unless you will be adding additional information (see next item).

ADDITIONAL INFORMATION: Give edition, report number, or volume number, if applicable, in parentheses immediately after the title. Do not use a period between the title and the parenthetical information and do not italicize.

Following any parenthetical information, give a description of the form of the work if necessary, enclosed in brackets—for example, [Brochure] or [Videotape]. End with a period.

PLACE OF PUBLICATION: Give the city where the work was published. If the city could be confused with another location, also give the state or province and, if necessary, the country. Use two-letter postal abbreviations for states and provinces. Use a colon to separate the place of publication from the publisher's name.

PUBLISHER: Give the publisher's name as briefly as possible, omitting words and abbreviations such as *Publishers, Co.,* and *Inc.,* but retaining the words *Books* and *Press*. End with a period.

PART OF A NON-PERIODICAL: When referencing part of a non-periodical, such as a book chapter, give the author, date, and chapter title as described above, and then add the following elements:

1. The word In followed by the editor's name, not inverted, followed by the abbreviation Ed. in parentheses. If there is no editor, simply include the word In followed by the title of the work.
2. The title of the work in italics
3. Inclusive page numbers for the chapter, in parentheses and preceded by the abbreviation pp.
4. The publication information as outlined above

PERIODICALS

After the author(s), date, and title of article, additional information appears in the following order: periodical name, volume number (if applicable), issue number (if applicable), and inclusive page numbers.

PERIODICAL NAME: Give the complete name, in italics, followed by a comma. Capitalize the first letter of all significant words (see 14-3c).

VOLUME NUMBER: Give the volume number, if any, in italics. Do not use *Vol.* before the volume number. Place a comma after the volume number unless it is followed by an issue number. If there is no volume number, include the month or season with the year, for example, (2006, September).

ISSUE NUMBER: If each issue of the periodical begins on page 1, give the issue number in parentheses immediately after the volume number, leaving no space, followed by a comma.

PAGE NUMBERS: Give inclusive page numbers after the volume (or issue) number. Use the abbreviations p. or pp. for newspaper articles but not for magazine or journal articles.

6-2C: EXAMPLES OF REFERENCES ENTRIES

BOOKS

ONE AUTHOR

McConnell, J. (1974). *Understanding human behavior: An introduction to psychology*. New York: Holt, Rinehart.

TWO OR MORE AUTHORS

Krebs, D., & Blackman, R. (1988). *Psychology: A first encounter*. San Diego: Harcourt.

Griffin, R. W., Ebert, R. J., & Starke, F. A. (1999). *Business* (3rd Canadian ed.). Scarborough, ON: Prentice Hall.

EDITED BOOK

Fraser, K. (Ed.). (1991). *Bad Trips*. Toronto: Random.

TRANSLATION

Barthes, R. (1987). *Mythologies* (A. Lavers, Trans.). London: Paladin Grafton Books. (Original work published 1957)

CORPORATE AUTHOR

Ministry of Education and Training. (1990). *Ministry of Education and Training style guide for editors and writers*. Toronto: Author.

NO AUTHOR OR EDITOR

German for travellers. (1986). Lausanne: Editions Berlitz.

SUBSEQUENT EDITIONS

Gifford, D. (1982). *Joyce annotated* (2nd ed.). Berkeley: University of California Press.

MULTI-VOLUME WORK

Mansion, J. E. (1974). *Harrap's new standard French and English dictionary* (Vols. 1–2). London: Harrap.

ARTICLE IN AN EDITED BOOK

Bruce, H. (1988). Portugal. In K. Dobbs (Ed.), *Away from home: Canadian writers in exotic places* (pp. 297–301). Toronto: Deneau.

ARTICLE IN A REFERENCE BOOK

Watkins, C. (1998). Indo-European and the Indo-Europeans. In *Canadian Dictionary of the English Language* (pp. 1631–1637). Toronto: ITP Nelson.

PERIODICALS

ARTICLE IN A JOURNAL PAGINATED BY VOLUME

Dodd, D. (2001). Helen MacMurchy, MD: Gender and professional conflict in the medical inspection of Toronto schools, 1910–1911. *Ontario History, 93*, 127–149.

ARTICLE IN A JOURNAL PAGINATED BY ISSUE

Martin, R. (2002). The virtue matrix: Calculating the return on corporate responsibility. *Harvard Business Review, 80*(3), 69–75.

ARTICLE IN A MAGAZINE

Tarry, C. (2002, March). The Danube: Europe's river of harmony and discord. *National Geographic, 201*, 62–79.

ARTICLE IN A NEWSPAPER

MacGregor, K. (2002, March 12). Zimbabwe voting ends in confusion. *The Globe and Mail*, p. A14.

ANONYMOUS ARTICLE

Newsmakers. (2006, February 6). *Maclean's, 119*(1), 44–45.

LETTER TO THE EDITOR

Marajh, T. (2002, March 12). Father was following natural love [Letter to the editor]. *The Toronto Star*, p. A27.

REVIEW

Chodoff, P. (2002). Redeeming Frieda [Review of the book *To redeem one person is to redeem the world: The life of Frieda Fromm-Reichmann*]. *Psychology Today, 35*, 76.

6-2D: ELECTRONIC SOURCES

As with any reference, the goals of referencing electronic sources are to give credit to the author and to allow the reader to find the source material with a minimum of effort.

At a minimum, a reference for an Internet source should include the author name(s) if possible, the title or a description of the document, a publication date and/or date of retrieval, and an exact address (URL).

The date should indicate the year of publication or, if the source undergoes regular revision, the most recent update. If the document has no date, put n.d. in parentheses after the first element (author or title) and provide the date of retrieval before the URL (for example, *Retrieved July 12, 2006, from http://www.apa.org*).

The retrieval statement containing an exact address replaces the publication information typically provided for print references. Help readers to locate information by being as specific as possible. As well as the host name, include the protocol *(http, ftp, gopher, telnet, news)* and any relevant path and file names. If a URL runs over a line, break it only after a slash or before a period and make sure no hyphens are inadvertently added at line breaks. No final period appears after the end of the URL, and the URL is not placed in angle brackets.

Since electronic media change rapidly, check the APA website (http://www.apastyle.org/elecref.html) for regularly updated information about documenting electronic sources.

ARTICLE BASED ON A PRINT SOURCE

Often articles retrieved from online publications are exact duplicates of print versions. In these cases, follow the format of the print form. However, if you have viewed the article only in electronic form, add [Electronic version] after the article title and before the name of the periodical.

Strain, L. A. (2000). Seniors' centres: Who cares? [Electronic version]. *Canadian Journal of Aging, 20,* 471–491.

If the online article and the print article differ (for example, if page numbers are not included or additional information is given), add the retrieval date and the URL.

Sands, P. (2003, Fall). Pushing and pulling toward the middle. *Kairos, 7*(3). Retrieved May 2, 2003, from http://english.ttu.edu/kairos/7.3/binder2.html?coverweb.html#gender

INTERNET-ONLY JOURNAL

Reference as in the preceding example. However, if no volume or issue numbers are used, simply provide the name of the periodical, the retrieval date, and the URL.

Smith, J. (2003, January 16). Journalism fails its sobriety test. *Salon.* Retrieved January 19, 2003, from http://www.salon.com/news/feature/2003/01/16/dui/index_np.html

STAND-ALONE DOCUMENT, NO AUTHOR IDENTIFIED, NO DATE

Begin the reference with the title of the document.

Erikson's development stages. (n.d.). Retrieved July 12, 2006, from http://www.hcc.hawaii.edu/intranet/committees/FacDevCom/guidebk/teachtip/erikson

ONLINE DISCUSSION SOURCES

Often newsgroups, forums, discussion groups, and electronic mailing lists are not referenced because they are not peer reviewed and posts are not retrievable. If the source is archived, cite the author's name and the exact date of online posting. Follow this with the subject line of the message and the address of the message group or forum beginning with Message posted to.

Nivalainen, M. (2002, December 17). The key and stupid web moments of 2002 [Msg 3]. Message posted to Cybermind@listserv.aol.com

ARTICLE RETRIEVED FROM A DATABASE

Use the appropriate format for the source, adding the retrieval date and the name of the database.

Lindblad, F., Lindberg, L., & Hjern, A. (2006, July 6). Anorexia nervosa in young men: A cohort study. *International Journal of Eating Disorders.* Retrieved July 12, 2006, from PubMed database.

DOCUMENT ON A UNIVERSITY WEBSITE

For a document on a large and complex website (for example, a university or government site), identify the host organization and the relevant program or department before giving the URL for the document itself. Precede the URL with a colon.

Megginson, D. (1996). *Noun and pronoun characteristics.* Retrieved July 12, 2006, from University of Ottawa, The Writing Centre website: http://www.uottawa.ca/academic/arts/writcent/hypergrammar/nounchar.html

E-MAIL

Since e-mail messages are not retrievable by the reader, they should not be included in a reference list. They may be cited in the text as a personal communication (see 6-1a).

6-2E: MISCELLANEOUS SOURCES

MUSIC RECORDING

Manuel, R. (1968). Lonesome Suzie. [Recorded by The Band].On *Music from Big Pink* [CD]. Hollywood, CA: Capitol. (2003)

TELEVISION BROADCAST

Burman, T. (Executive Producer). (2003, October 5). *The national* [Television broadcast]. Toronto: Canadian Broadcasting Corporation.

SINGLE EPISODE FROM A TELEVISION SERIES

Ferrand, C. (Director). (2006, February 11). People of the ice. [Television series episode]. In M. Allder (Executive Producer), *The nature of things with David Suzuki.* Toronto: Canadian Broadcasting Corporation.

MOTION PICTURE

Anderson, W., Mendel, B., & Rudin, S. (Producers), & Anderson, W. (Director). (2001). *The Royal Tenenbaums* [Motion picture]. United States: Touchstone Pictures.

DISSERTATION ABSTRACT

Karim, Y. (1999). Arab political dispute mediations (Doctoral dissertation, Wayne State University, 1999). *Dissertation Abstracts International, 61*, 350.

GOVERNMENT DOCUMENT

Solicitor General of Canada. (1995). *Annual report on the use of electronic surveillance.* Ottawa: Author.

CONFERENCE PROCEEDINGS PUBLISHED IN A BOOK

Chorney, H. (1991). A regional approach to monetary and fiscal policy. In J. N. McCrorie & M. L. MacDonald (Eds.), *The constitutional future of the prairie and Atlantic regions of Canada* (pp. 107–121). Regina, SK: Canadian Plains Research Center Press.

Note that regularly published conference proceedings are treated as periodicals.

6-3: MANUSCRIPT FORMAT

6-3A: MATERIALS AND TYPEFACE

Use letter-size (22 × 28 cm, 8.5 × 11 in.), heavy (20-lb.) white bond paper. Type on only one side of the paper.

Use a standard serif typeface, such as Times Roman, in 12-point size. Avoid typefaces that are unusual or too small. Serif typeface is preferable since it enhances readability and reduces eyestrain. The type on the paper must be dark, clear, and easy to photocopy.

6-3B: TITLE AND IDENTIFICATION

Although APA style does not give specific guidelines for formatting a title page for college and university papers, the example on page 202 and the following guidelines are typical of the format most instructors require. Check with your instructor for the format you should use.

In a manuscript intended for publication, APA suggests that, in the upper half of the title page, you type the title in uppercase and lowercase letters, centred between the left and right margins. If the title is more than two lines, double-space it.

About half-way down the page, provide your name.

Centred in the bottom third of the title page are the course name and section number, your instructor's name, and the date you submitted the paper. Double-space throughout.

6-3C: MARGINS, SPACING, AND INDENTATION

Leave margins of at least 2.5 cm (1 in.) at the top, bottom, left, and right sides of every page.

Double-space the text throughout, including the title, headings, quotations, footnotes, figure captions, and all parts of tables. Text should be ragged right rather than right justified. Do not divide words at the end of a line or use the hyphenation feature of your word-processing software.

Indent the first line of every paragraph 1.25 cm (0.5 in.). APA style specifies that quotations of forty or more words should be further indented by 1.25 cm and double-spaced, without an opening paragraph indent and without quotation marks.

6-3D: PAGE NUMBERS AND SHORT TITLES

Number all pages consecutively, beginning with the title page, placing Arabic numerals in the upper right-hand corner at least 2.5 cm (1 in.) from the right side of the page, in the space between the top of the page and the first line of text.

Directly above or 1.25 cm (0.5 in.) to the left of the page number, include an abbreviated title—the first two or three words of the full title. This shortened title will identify pages should they become separated. APA, in its guidelines for manuscript preparation, does not recommend putting your name on each page.

6-3E: PUNCTUATION

APA guidelines call for one space after a period or any other punctuation mark. To create a dash, type two hyphens (--) with no spaces before or after. You may also use your word-processing program to create a dash (—).

6-3F: ABSTRACT

Your instructor may ask you to include an abstract—a brief summary of your research paper. An abstract appears separately on page 2 and is one paragraph, double-spaced, and typed as a block without indentation. The maximum length for an abstract is 120 words, and it can be considerably less. It is meant to provide a summary of your paper, including your thesis and the main points of your research. It should also suggest what your research implies and how it might be applied. Centre the heading Abstract over the paragraph.

6-3G: HEADINGS

Headings are encouraged in APA style. They define the hierarchy of ideas and help the reader understand the structure and organization of the paper.

The APA guidelines for formatting headings are as follows:

Main Headings: centred, uppercase and lowercase (first letter of important words capitalized)
Second-Level Headings: flush left, italicized, uppercase and lowercase

Third-Level Headings: indented, italicized, lowercase paragraph heading (with initial capital) ending with a period

See 14-3c for information on capitalizing titles.

6-3H: VISUALS

In APA style, any type of illustration other than a table is called a figure, including charts, graphs, drawings, and photographs. While tables are preferred for the presentation of quantitative data, figures are used to convey structural or pictorial concepts. Use the following guidelines to identify illustrations.

TABLES

Above the table, number consecutively with Arabic numerals. Give the title of the table in italics, double-spaced.

Table 1

Univariate Analyses of Continuous Non-Academic Variables

FIGURES

Below the figure, number consecutively with Arabic numerals, in italics, followed by a caption (no italics). The caption acts as both the title and an explanation of the figure.

Figure 1. Desired service response and links for young people with mental health issues.

If you include a visual, make sure that it is mentioned and discussed in the body of your paper so that the reader is alerted to its presence and its significance to your argument.

Tables and figures may appear in the body of a student paper rather than at the end. Ask your instructor for guidelines regarding the preferred placement.

6-3I: DOCUMENTATION

Any sources you have used in the research and writing of your paper must be correctly documented according to APA guidelines. For information about APA documentation style see 6-1 and 6-2, as well as the sample paper in 6-4.

6-4: SAMPLE PAPER

Daniel Rosenfield, a university student, wrote the research paper on pages 202–210 as part of his requirements for a humanities course. Rosenfield's assignment was to review recent, credible, and reliable sources documenting stem cell research policies and regulations, then evaluate the effectiveness of those policies and regulations.

Rosenfield used the APA guidelines for manuscript formatting and documentation of sources that are presented in this handbook. His in-text citations follow APA style, as does his list of references. Rosenfield's instructor required that students provide a title page with their papers but not an abstract, since the paper was to be fairly short.

Sample APA Essay

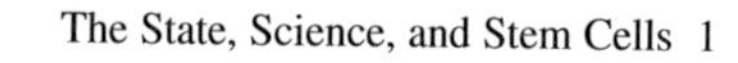

Abbreviated title appears half an inch to the left of the page number, which is flush against the right margin. Page numbering begins on the title page.

The State, Science, and Stem Cells:

An Analysis of the American Stance on Stem Cell Research

The full title of the paper is typed in upper- and lowercase, double-spaced, and centred in the upper half of the title page.

Daniel Rosenfield

The author's name should be centred, and appears approximately midway down the page.

Health Sciences 3A03

Professor Gildiner

November 18, 2006

Centred in the bottom third of the page are the course number and section number, the instructor's name, and the date the paper was submitted.

Include full title, centred, at the beginning of the essay.

The State, Science, and Stem Cells:

An Analysis of the American Stance on Stem Cell Research

Headings are commonly used in APA style. Because this essay is short, it uses a Level 2 heading throughout. You may need a more elaborate hierarchy of headings if your work is long or complex.

Introduction

In the United States and around the world, a growing debate is emerging surrounding the regulation of new biotechnologies. With cloning, gene manipulation and stem cell research all blossoming, the need for government intervention and regulation is becoming increasingly clear. In this paper, I will focus on the regulation of stem cell research in the United States, and the debates surrounding policy. Specifically, I will highlight the debate around whether or not stem cells should be regulated, and if so, to what degree. I will also draw attention to the role of the state and various civil groups in determining stem cell research policies.

Paraphrases demand the author's name, if it is not mentioned in the text in a signal phrase, and the date.

A Brief History

The debate surrounding stem cells is a relatively recent one, as the first isolation of embryonic stem cells was announced at the University of Wisconsin in 1998 (Knowles, 2004). However, after stem cells were identified, a flurry of controversy arose due to various ideologies presenting their views on the nature of embryos, and the sanctity of life. This was contrasted with the optimism of many scientists, who saw seemingly endless healing possibilities with stem cells.[1] Policy makers in the United States recognized the need to develop guidelines for the utilization and creation of stem cells, as well as their regulation. In addition, rules regarding the use of federal funds for stem cell research would have to be created and/or altered.

Superscript is used to indicate explanatory endnotes, listed at the end of the paper for simplicity of formatting.

Today, the regulation of stem cell research in the United States is accomplished by the stipulation that no federal funds can be used to develop new stem cells. Before 1996, rules regarding stem cells came from the ethical principles established in the wake of the Tuskegee Syphilis Trials (Fischbach & Fischbach, 2004).[2] These guidelines regulate the treatment of human subjects in medicine; however, with regard to embryos, they only apply once the embryo is implanted in the uterus. Since stem cell research and utilization occur before implantation, manipulation of stem cells is legal according to Tuskegee rules. However, in 1996, two senate representatives included an amendment stipulating regulation for stem cells, which said that research to create new lines of these cells would receive no federal funding (Childress, 2004). This rule was solidified in 2001, when President Bush prohibited federal funding from anyone researching stem cells deriving from a batch other than a specified 62 germ lines already in existence (Childress, 2004).[3]

Note the use of the ampersand instead of "and" in APA style.

Polar Extremes: Pure, Objective Science versus Religion, Ethics, and Morals

Biotechnology, with specific reference to stem cells, presents an extremely complex argument around regulation, due to the ethical concerns associated with it. There are numerous sides to this debate, and I will begin with the first extreme—that of the "pure," objective scientists. A purely scientific viewpoint views research in all domains (not just stem cells) as one for scientists exclusively. To these scientists, politics and science are on opposite ends of the spectrum—science is entirely objective—and scientific research is for the betterment of humanity. With reference to stem cells, these researchers believe they should not be impeded by government intervention into their research. Scientists are generally held in higher regard than politicians, philosophers, and legislators, and thus non-scientists should be removed from making decisions about controlling stem cell research (Fukuyama, 2003b). Fukuyama disagrees

Note that the author's name is not repeated here because it is used in the sentence as a signal phrase.

with notion, saying that "science by itself cannot establish the ends to which it [science] is put" (2003b, p. 185). He highlights the multiple usages of science; scientists can discover vaccines, or they can create highly infectious agents. He argues that science is inherently political, and that while scientists should be involved in establishing moral regulations for the development of new technologies, control over these technologies ultimately resides with democratically elected officials. This perspective allows for civil groups to be directly involved, as evidenced by the many religious groups who oppose stem cell research in the United States (Fukuyama, 2003b).

On the opposite side of the pure scientists are those who argue that embryonic stem cells should never be used for research since they are living beings (or have the potential to be). The extreme view from this perspective says that all stem cell related research should be banned, and many believe researchers who delve into this area should be imprisoned or fined. Those who ascribe to these views are typically religious, and believe in a Judeo-Christian set of values (Childress, 2004).

At the heart of the stem cell debate is the moral discussion of when human life truly begins. While I will not discuss this issue in the paper, I agree with Fukuyama, who says that human embryos have an "intermediate moral status: they are not the moral equivalents of infants, nor are they simply clumps of cells like any other tissue sample that can be used and discarded at will" (2005, p. 195). Evidently, stem cells occupy a unique regulatory challenge. Many view today's legislation as inadequate, and thus I will examine what may occur in the future regarding stem cell regulation.

Note that quoted words require a page number.

Future Regulation & Analysis

Despite a recent trend towards self regulation or deregulation of biotechnologies, Fukuyama and Wagner have identified that in the late 20th century, attitudes have changed dramatically around regulation (2000). Distrust in the scientific community, as well technologies with distinctly ethical concerns have fueled the move towards creating regulations for many information and biotechnologies. Researchers have agreed that a traditional "top down" approach "to the governance of these technologies would not be practical" (Fukuyama & Wagner, 2000, ix). One model suggested would involve numerous councils that would examine and establish the "norms of use, regulation and governance of technology" (Fukuyama & Wagner, 2000, xi). This model would be able to combat the idea of regulatory capture, something Fukuyama warns vehemently against. Regulatory capture occurs when the group overseeing something becomes an agent for it (Fukuyama, 2003a). To combat this, the aforementioned councils, as well as independent research could be used to regulate stem cell research, as opposed to one legislative body (Fukuyama & Wagner).

Fukuyama believes "as a general rule, we should not invite more regulation than is absolutely necessary so as not to hold back important scientific inquiry" (2005, p. 198). In addition, Fukuyama believes that there must be a broad social consensus surrounding the policy. This idea is something that troubles me, especially with an issue as contentious as stem cell research. Due to the religious and moral nature of stem cells, I highly doubt there will ever be the broad social consensus that Fukuyama desires; however, this does not exempt stem cell technologies from being regulated. This is a clear inconsistency in Fukuyama's work, since he is a proponent of both broad social consensus and small independent councils, which, by their very nature, will not achieve a broad social consensus.

Although most of Fukuyama's arguments apply to an international arena, many are applicable in a national sphere. In the United States, since current regulation says nothing about what can be done with outside funding, many researchers have looked to private corporations for money to research new lines of stem cells. As a result, legislators have proposed strict laws that would prohibit the formation of embryos for stem cell research. Breaking these laws could result in up to 10 years in prison and a fine of up to a million dollars (Childress, 2004). This illustrates the struggle between civil groups (i.e., researchers) and the state (legislators), and highlights the need for more elaborate and concrete regulation of stem cell research. On the one hand, state legislators with specific interests in mind want to pass legislation banning stem cell research entirely, with strict penalties to those who do not follow. Civil groups (i.e., scientists, researchers, and private industries) would prefer laxer rules, or no regulation at all. Thus, many policy debates are "widening gulf between those in public office and the scientific community" (Towns & Jones, 2004, p. 1369).

It is worth noting that the debate between stem cell research and traditional biotechnologies (i.e., agricultural technologies, gene manipulation, etc.) are significantly different in one respect: stem cell research will not result in harm for anyone except the embryo. Traditional approaches to regulating biotechnology have often erred on the side of caution (especially in the European Union) due to potentially dangerous outcomes, but these same dangers are not inherent with stem cell research. The crux of the issue lies with the moral determination of the status of the embryo; however, these issues are inextricably linked to concerns around abortion and cloning. As Fukuyama says, the politics of stem cell research are inherently complex and do not fall into political categories. For example, "if one is a conservative Republic or a left-wing Social Democrat, it is not immediately obvious how one should vote on a bill to permit so called therapeutic cloning or stem cell research" (Fukuyama, 2003a, p. 211). As a result, many legislators ignore the issue, hoping it will be resolved. I agree with other authors (Baylis, 2002, p. 11; Brainard, 2005, p. 51; Frist, 2001, p. 2) that this laissez-faire attitude will ultimately be detrimental to stem cell research and regulation as a whole, since an issue so inexorably linked with deep moral and religious implications must be dealt with on a legislative level. The American people must have faith that their legislators (and judiciary) will create appropriate guidelines. Despite the fact that scientists may agree or disagree with whatever guidelines are created, the nature of international scientific regulation today is that it is highly variable; in other words, if an American scientist is unhappy with American rules, he can move to a country more accepting of his religious or political views.

Conclusion

The regulation of stem cell research in the United States is still in its fledgling stages. Currently, research can be conducted on existing stem cells, but no new lines can be generated with federal funds. However, this allows for those with outside funding (via private civil groups such as pharmaceutical companies) to fund further research on new lines. At the heart of the regulation issue is the moral debate over the status of an embryo, and this debate encompasses religious, ethical, and political arguments. Most researchers agree that further regulation regarding stem cell research should be enacted, although they have not come to a consensus about how. Creating councils and task forces should be the first step, but ultimately, American legislators have the only legitimate power to create proper regulation of stem cell research—not scientists, religious groups, or lobbyists. Despite the fact that legislation vis à vis state involvement may be slow, this will be the only truly equitable source for stem cell regulation, and it is to be hoped that meaningful policy will be enacted in the years to come.

If you include explanatory notes, you must list them on a separate page.

Endnotes

[1] For a full discussion of how stem cells work, and what researchers think stem cell research may be able to accomplish, see Fischbach and Fischbach's "Stem Cells: Science, Policy, and Ethics," 2004.

[2] These guidelines were discussed in class and refer to regulations put in place after a large number of African Americans were deliberately denied penicillin so doctors could see the symptoms of syphilis.

[3] The scientific complexity of stem cell research is beyond the scope of this paper (see note 1 for a better understanding of stem cells) but, simply stated, no federal money can go to researching new sources of stem cells other than ones currently in existence in the United States.

References begin on a new page with this heading.

The State, Science, and Stem Cells 9

References

Baylis, F. (2002). Betwixt and between human stem cell guidelines and legislation. *Health Law Review*, *11*(1), 44–50.

Brainard, J. (2005). National academies report recommends tighter rules for stem-cell research. *Chronicle of Higher Education*, *51*(35), A25.

Childress, J. F. (2004). Human stem cell research: Some controversies in bioethics and public policy. *Blood Cells, Molecules and Diseases*, *32*(1), 100–105.

Fischbach, G. D., & Fischbach, R. L. (2004). Stem cells: Science, policy, and ethics. *Journal of Clinical Investigation*, *114*(10), 1364–1370.

Frist, B. (2001). The promise and peril of embryonic stem cell research: A call for vigilant oversight. *Yale Journal of Health Policy, Law, and Ethics*, *2*(1), 109, 167–176.

Fukuyama, F. (2003a). Policies for the future. In *Our posthuman future: Consequences of the biotechnology revolution*. London: MacMillan.

Fukuyama, F. (2003b). The political control of biotechnology. In *Our posthuman future: Consequences of the biotechnology revolution*. London: MacMillan.

For two entries by the same author, list the author's name for each entry. If they are published in the same year, add the suffix a, b, c, and so on to the year of publication.

Fukuyama, F. (2005). Human biomedicine and the problem of governance. *Perspectives in Biology and Medicine*, *48*(2), 195–200.

Fukuyama, F., & Wagner, C. (2000). Information and biological revolutions: Global governance challenges—Summary of a study group. Washington: RAND.

Knowles, L. P. (2004). A regulatory patchwork—human ES cell research oversight. *Nature and Biotechnology*, *22*(2), 157–163.

Towns, C. R., & Jones, D. G. (2004). Stem cells: Public policy and ethics. *New Zealand Bioethics Journal*, *5*(1), 22–28.

References are listed alphabetically by author's last name. First names are reduced to initials. Each entry appears as a hanging indent.

7 CHICAGO STYLE OF DOCUMENTATION

THE (CHICAGO) "MANUAL" IS NOT TOO LONG.
IT IS NOT LONG ENOUGH.
IT WILL NEVER BE LONG ENOUGH.
THE PERFECT MANUAL OF STYLE WOULD BE LIKE THE PERFECT MAP OF THE WORLD: EXACTLY COTERMINOUS WITH ITS SUBJECT, CONTAINING A RULE FOR EVERY WORD OF EVERY SENTENCE.
WE WOULD NEED AN EXTRA UNIVERSE TO ACCOMMODATE IT.
IT WOULD BE WORTH IT.
–LOUIS MENAND

7

Chicago Style of Documentation

7 Chicago Style of Documentation

This chapter outlines the basic style guidelines published in *The Chicago Manual of Style*, 15th ed. (Chicago: University of Chicago Press, 2003) and concludes with sample pages that follow Chicago format and documentation style.

The Chicago Manual of Style website (found at http://www.chicagomanualofstyle.org/cmosfaq.html) also provides information on documentation style and format. For examples of cited materials, follow the "Tools" link. The "Q & A" page allows you to submit questions and the "Search the Manual" link gives a list of relevant numbers and subheadings in the print edition. You may also access *The Chicago Manual of Style Online*, which offers the fully searchable text of the 15th edition.

Chicago recommends two basic systems of documentation: (1) the author–date system and (2) the notes and bibliography system.

AUTHOR–DATE SYSTEM

This system is recommended for writers in the physical, natural, and social sciences. Sources are given in brief in-text citations in parentheses, with full details supplied in a complete list of sources cited, usually called a references list. This system is recommended if all or most of the sources are easily convertible to author–date references. The author–date system follows the same principle as APA style with only minor differences. See Chapter 6 for detailed guidelines and examples.

NOTES AND BIBLIOGRAPHY SYSTEM

Also called "humanities style," this system is favoured by many writers in literature, history, and the arts. Notes (either endnotes or footnotes) are used instead of in-text citations. If the notes give full bibliographical information, the bibliography may be omitted. It is preferable, however, to give complete details in the bibliography, in which case the notes may be shortened to avoid unnecessary duplication. Check with your instructor to determine which approach is preferred and whether to format notes as footnotes or endnotes.

WITH A BIBLIOGRAPHY

All notes, including the first reference to a particular source, are shortened, giving the author's last name, a shortened version of the title, and the page number(s). Readers wanting additional information about the source will find it in the bibliography. Chicago recommends this practice since it minimizes duplication and is user-friendly and economical.

WITHOUT A BIBLIOGRAPHY

In a work without a full bibliography, the first citation of a particular source gives complete bibliographical information, and subsequent references to that source are shortened.

See section 7-3 for discussion and examples of both types of documentation.

7-1: NOTES

Notes can appear either together at the end of your research paper, as **endnotes**, or at the foot of the page on which the citation appears, as **footnotes**. Use the footnote or endnote function of your word processor to create notes. Note numbers should be placed at the end of a sentence or at the end of a clause, indicating that the information in that sentence or clause is from another source. When readers wish to locate specific source information, they can do so by locating the note with the corresponding number.

> "The possibility of a Marxist literary theory," in the words of Frow, "is given in the promise and the ambiguity of the central Marxist metaphors relating the symbolic order to the social process."[1]

The note will be formatted in one of two ways, depending on whether or not the paper includes a bibliography. Here is the key used to identify the type of example shown in the following sections:

SN	=	shortened note
FN	=	full note
B	=	bibliography entry

7-1A: IN A WORK WITH A BIBLIOGRAPHY

Complete information about the source is given in the bibliography. (For guidelines on formatting bibliography entries, see 7-3.)

B Frow, John. *Marxism and Literary History*. Cambridge, MA: Harvard University Press, 1986.

Note citations (even the first citation of a work) are shortened to avoid duplication of information given in the bibliography entry. Shortened notes typically include the author's last name, a condensed version of the title, and the page number.

SN 1. Frow, *Marxism*, 7.

7-1B: IN A WORK WITHOUT A BIBLIOGRAPHY

The first note gives complete bibliographical information. (For guidelines on formatting full notes, see 7-3.)

FN 1. John Frow, *Marxism and Literary History* (Cambridge, MA: Harvard University Press, 1986), 7.

Subsequent notes can be shortened.

SN 7. Frow, *Marxism*, 156.

If a work cited is identical in two successive notes, the abbreviation ibid. (from *ibidem*, "in the same place") may be used in place of the author/editor name, the title, and other identical information.

1. Frow, *Marxism*, 112–13.
2. Ibid.
3. Ibid., 132.

7-2: BIBLIOGRAPHY

Although not always necessary provided that full bibliographic details are given in notes, an alphabetical bibliography is a convenience for the reader since it provides an overview of all sources and an easy reference to individual sources cited.

A bibliography is placed at the end of the paper and should list any sources you have cited in your notes. Some bibliographies also include entries for works consulted but not cited. Check with your instructor to determine if a bibliography is required and which sources should be included.

For guidelines on formatting a bibliography see 7-3. A sample bibliography is also included in 7-5.

7-3: EXAMPLES OF NOTES AND BIBLIOGRAPHY ENTRIES

Entries in the following pages provide model notes and bibliographic entries for most of the types of resources you will use in your research. The following key identifies the example shown:

SN	=	shortened note
FN	=	full note
B	=	bibliographical entry

7-3A: BOOKS

ONE AUTHOR

SN 1. Roberts, *Empire of the Soul*, 85.

FN 1. Paul William Roberts, *Empire of the Soul: Some Journeys in India* (Toronto: Stoddart, 1994), 85.

B Roberts, Paul William. *Empire of the Soul: Some Journeys in India*. Toronto: Stoddard, 1994.

TWO OR THREE AUTHORS

SN 2. Johnson and Blair, *Logical Self-Defence*, 17.

FN 2. Ralph H. Johnson and J. Anthony Blair, *Logical Self-Defence*, 2nd ed. (Toronto: McGraw-Hill Ryerson, 1983), 17.

B Johnson, Ralph H., and J. Anthony Blair. *Logical Self-Defence*, 2nd ed. Toronto: McGraw-Hill Ryerson, 1983.

Note that in the bibliographic entry only the name of the first author is reversed and a comma precedes the *and*. Do not use an ampersand.

FOUR OR MORE AUTHORS

SN 3. Newman et al., *Echoes from the Past*, 168.

FN 3. Garfield Newman et al., *Echoes from the Past: World History to the Sixteenth Century* (Toronto: McGraw-Hill Ryerson, 2001), 168.

B Newman, Garfield, Elizabeth Graham, Osman Y. Mohamed, Gerry Schaus, Narinder Wagle, Rick Guisso, David Pendergast. *Echoes from the Past: World History to the Sixteenth Century*. Toronto: McGraw-Hill Ryerson, 2001.

This work has eleven authors. Chicago recommends that for ten authors or fewer, all should be listed in the bibliography. For eleven authors or more, only the first seven should be listed.

EDITED WORK WITHOUT AN AUTHOR

SN 5. Lamb and Arnold, *Reading*, 29.

FN 5. Pose Lamb and Richard Arnold, eds., *Reading: Foundations and Instructional Strategies* (Belmont, CA: Wadsworth, 1976), 29.

B Lamb, Pose, and Richard Arnold, eds. *Reading: Foundations and Instructional Strategies*. Belmont, CA: Wadsworth, 1976.

Note that the abbreviation *ed.* or *eds.* is omitted in shortened notes.

EDITED WORK WITH AN AUTHOR

SN 6. Mill, *On Liberty*, 45–46.

FN 6. John Stuart Mill, *On Liberty*, ed. Currin V. Shields (New York: Macmillan, 1956), 45–46.

B Mill, John Stuart. *On Liberty*. Edited by Currin V. Shields. New York: Macmillan, 1956.

Note that *Edited by* is spelled out in a bibliography but abbreviated in notes.

TRANSLATED WORK

SN 7. Sartre, *Iron in the Soul*, 58.

FN 7. Jean-Paul Sartre, *Iron in the Soul*, trans. Gerard Hopkins (Harmondsworth, UK: Penguin Books, 1978), 58.

B Sartre, Jean-Paul. *Iron in the Soul*. Translated by Gerard Hopkins. Harmondsworth, UK: Penguin Books, 1978.

Note that *Translated by* is spelled out in a bibliography but abbreviated in notes.

EDITIONS OTHER THAN THE FIRST

SN 8. Abrams, *Norton Anthology*, 117–48.

FN 8. M. H. Abrams, ed., *The Norton Anthology of English Literature*, 5th ed. (New York: W. W. Norton, 1987), 117–48.

B Abrams, M. H., ed. *The Norton Anthology of English Literature*. 5th ed. New York: W. W. Norton, 1987.

PARTICULAR VOLUME IN A MULTI-VOLUME WORK

SN 10. Kallen, *The 1400s*, 50–55.

FN 10. Stuart A. Kallen, ed., *The 1400s*. (San Diego, CA: Greenhaven Press, 2001), 5:50–55.

B Kallen, Stuart A., ed. *The 1400s*. Vol. 5, *Headlines in History*. San Diego, CA: Greenhaven Press, 2001.

The full note shown above indicates that all volumes of the Kallen work appeared in 2001. If only volume 5 had been published in 2001, the note would be formatted as follows:

FN 10. Stuart A. Kallen, ed., *The 1400s*, vol. 5, *Headlines in History* (San Diego, CA: Greenhaven Press, 2001), 50–55.

WORK IN AN ANTHOLOGY

SN 11. Morrison, "The Site of Memory," 185–206.

FN 11. Toni Morrison, "The Site of Memory," in *Inventing the Truth: The Art and Craft of Memoir*, ed. William Zinsser, 185–206 (Boston: Houghton Mifflin, 1998).

B Morrison, Toni. "The Site of Memory." In *Inventing the Truth: The Art and Craft of Memoir*, edited by William Zinsser, 185–206. Boston: Houghton Mifflin, 1998.

WORK IN A SERIES

SN 12. Lecker, David, and Quigley, *Bissoondath*, 29.

FN 2. Robert Lecker, Jack David, and Ellen Quigley, *Bissoondath, Clarke, Kogawa, Mistry, Skvorecky*, Canadian Writers and Their Works 11 (Toronto: ECW Press, 1996), 29.

B Lecker, Robert, Jack David, and Ellen Quigley. *Bissoondath, Clarke, Kogawa, Mistry, Skvorecky*. Canadian Writers and Their Works 11. Toronto: ECW Press, 1996.

DICTIONARY OR ENCYCLOPEDIA

SN 13. *ITP Nelson Canadian Dictionary*, s.v. "saltire."

FN 13. *ITP Nelson Canadian Dictionary of the English Language*, (Toronto: ITP Nelson, 1998), s.v. "saltire."

B *ITP Nelson Canadian Dictionary of the English Language*. Toronto: ITP Nelson, 1998.

Well-known reference books are normally cited in notes rather than in bibliographies, with the facts of publication often omitted, but with the edition specified. Certain reference works, however, may be listed with publication details, as shown above. For an alphabetically arranged work, cite the item preceded by s.v. (for the Latin *sub verbo*, which means "under the word").

7-3B: PERIODICALS

In the entries below, note that, while specific page references are given in the notes, inclusive pages for the article are given in the bibliographic entries.

ARTICLE IN A JOURNAL

SN 14. Beattie, "Real Place," 11.

FN 14. Ann Beattie, "Real Place, Imagined Life," *Literary Imagination: The Review of the Association of Literary Scholars and Critics* 4, no. 1 (2002): 11.

B Beattie, Ann. "Real Place, Imagined Life." *Literary Imagination: The Review of the Association of Literary Scholars and Critics* 4, no. 1 (2002): 10–16.

Most journal citations include both volume and issue numbers, although the issue number may be omitted if pagination is continuous throughout a volume or when a month or season precedes the year.

ARTICLE IN A MAGAZINE

SN 15. Lazare, "False Testament," 40.

FN 15. Daniel Lazare, "False Testament: Archeology Refutes the Bible Claim to History," *Harper's*, March 2002, 40.

B Lazare, Daniel. "False Testament: Archeology Refutes the Bible Claim to History." *Harper's*, March 2002, 39–47.

ARTICLE IN A NEWSPAPER

SN 16. Reynolds, "UN to Add 'Nazi' Stamp," A2.

FN 16. Matt Reynolds, "UN to Add 'Nazi' Stamp to Auschwitz Camp Site," *Toronto Star*, July 13, 2006, A2.

B Reynolds, Matt. "UN to Add 'Nazi' Stamp to Auschwitz Camp Site." *Toronto Star*, July 13, 2006, A2.

An initial *The* is omitted from a newspaper name. Except for well-known national papers, if the city is not part of the name, it should be added in italics, along with the abbreviated form for the province in parentheses if necessary. For example, *National Post* needs no clarification, but *Daily Gleaner* becomes *Fredericton (NB) Daily Gleaner*.

For unsigned articles, the name of the newspaper stands in place of the author.

7-3C: ELECTRONIC SOURCES

Many of the rules for citing print sources apply to electronic sources. In addition to the information discussed above, it is important to indicate the medium from which the source was retrieved. A URL is added to the citation to indicate that a source was retrieved from the Internet. If the material is time-sensitive or if the discipline demands it, the retrieval date should be recorded in parentheses as part of the citation.

If a URL has to be broken at the end of a line, do not add a hyphen to denote a line break and do not break a line after a hyphen that is part of the URL. The line break should occur *after* a slash or double slash or *before* a period, comma, hyphen, tilde (~), or underscore.

ONLINE BOOK

SN 17. Jameson, The History of Historical Writing.

FN 17. John Franklin Jameson, *The History of Historical Writing in America* (Boston: Houghton Mifflin, 1891; Electronic Library of Historiography, 1996), http://www.eliohs.unifi.it/testi/800/jameson/jameson.html (accessed July 17, 2006).

B Jameson, John Franklin. *The History of Historical Writing in America*. Boston: Houghton Mifflin, 1891; Electronic Library of

Historiography, 1996. http://www.eliohs.unifi.it/testi/800/ jameson/ jameson.html (accessed July 17, 2006).

Wherever possible, include the original facts of publication when citing electronic editions of older works, as in the preceding example.

ONLINE JOURNAL

SN 18. Green, "Poisoned Ears."

FN 18. Reina Green. "Poisoned Ears and Parental Advice in *Hamlet*," *Early Modern Literary Studies* 11, no. 3 (2006), para. 23, http://www.shu.ac.uk/emls/11-3/greeham2.htm (accessed July 17, 2006).

B Green, Reina. "Poisoned Ears and Parental Advice in *Hamlet*." *Early Modern Literary Studies* 11, no. 3 (2006). http://www.shu.ac.uk/emls/11-3/greeham2.htm (accessed May 19, 2006).

Note the descriptive locator, *para. 23*, in the full note above, directing readers to a specific location in the article. If it is available, also include the page range in the bibliography.

WEBSITE

SN 19. Giblin, "Introduction: Diffusion and Other Problems."

FN 19. James Giblin, "Introduction: Diffusion and Other Problems in the History of African States," *Arts and Life in Africa Online*, http://www.uiowa.edu/~africart/toc/history/giblistat.html (accessed March 15, 2006; site now discontinued).

B Giblin, James. "Introduction: Diffusion and Other Problems in the History of African States." *Arts and Life in Africa Online*. http://www.uiowa.edu/~africart/toc/history/giblistat.html (accessed March 15, 2006; site now discontinued).

If a site ceases to exist, as in the above example, state this parenthetically at the end of the citation, separated from the access information by a semicolon.

E-MAIL MESSAGE

References to personal communications such as e-mail messages, letters, and conversations are usually run into the text or given a brief note.

IN TEXT

In an e-mail on July 17, 2006, Damian Collom indicated his displeasure with the new strategic plan.

IN A NOTE

N 20. Damian Collom, e-mail message to author, July 17, 2006.

Personal communications are rarely listed in a bibliography. Be aware, too, that a personal e-mail address may be cited only with the permission of its owner.

ELECTRONIC MAILING LIST

N 21. Molly Millar, e-mail to The Design Café mailing list, July 17, 2006, http://lists.graphic-design.net/mailman/listinfo/cafe.

Citations to mailing lists are generally limited to text and notes.

DATABASE

SN 22. Lagapa, "Something from Nothing," 54.

FN 22. Jason Lagapa, "Something from Nothing: Disontological Poetics of Leslie Scalapino," *Contemporary Literature* 47, no. 1 (Spring 2006): 54, http://muse.jhu.edu.ezproxy.library.yorku.ca/journals/ (accessed July 18, 2006).

B Lagapa, Jason. "Something from Nothing: Disontological Poetics of Leslie Scalapino." *Contemporary Literature* 47, no. 1 (Spring 2006): 30–61. http://muse.jhu.edu.ezproxy.library.yorku.ca/journals/ (accessed July 18, 2006).

7-3D: MISCELLANEOUS SOURCES

GOVERNMENT DOCUMENT

Follow these general guidelines for the order of citation elements when citing government documents:

1. division of government issuing the document
2. legislative body, department, court, committee, and so forth
3. subsidiary divisions, regional offices, and so forth
4. document title
5. author or editor (if given)
6. report number or other identifying information
7. publisher, if different from the issuing body
8. date
9. page (if relevant)

SN 23. Treasury Board of Canada, *Canada's Performance*, 8.

FN 23. Treasury Board of Canada, *Canada's Performance: The Government of Canada's Contribution*, 2005, 8.

B Treasury Board of Canada. *Canada's Performance: The Government of Canada's Contribution*. 2005.

The order of these items may vary to suit the subject matter. If the government body issuing the document is not obvious from the context, begin the citation with "Canada," followed by the provincial or territorial legislature.

UNPUBLISHED DISSERTATION

SN 24. Warbey, "The Acquisition of Modal Notions," 90.

FN 24. Margaretta Warbey, "The Acquisition of Modal Notions by Advanced-Level Adult English as a Second Language Learners" (PhD diss., University of Victoria, 1986), 90.

B Warbey, Margaretta. "The Acquisition of Modal Notions by Advanced-Level Adult English as a Second Language Learners." PhD diss., University of Victoria, 1986.

PERSONAL COMMUNICATION

See "E-Mail Message" under "Electronic Sources" above.

INTERVIEW

SN 25. Diski, interview.

FN 25. Jenny Diski, interview by Eleanor Wachtel, *Writers & Company*, CBC Radio, July 23, 2006.

B Diski, Jenny. Interview by Eleanor Wachtel. *Writers & Company*. CBC Radio. July 23, 2006.

SOUND RECORDING

SN 26. Gould, *The Goldberg Variations*.

LN 26. Glenn Gould, *The Goldberg Variations*, by Johann Sebastian Bach, Sony Music compact disc SMK 52594.

B Gould, Glenn. *The Goldberg Variations*, by Johann Sebastian Bach. Sony Music compact disc SMK 53594.

DVD

SN 27. Young, "When God Made Me."

LN 27. Neil Young, "When God Made Me," *Neil Young: Heart of Gold*, DVD, directed by Jonathan Demme (Hollywood, CA: Paramount, 2005).

B Young, Neil. "When God Made Me." *Neil Young: Heart of Gold*, DVD. Directed by Jonathan Demme. Hollywood, CA: Paramount, 2005.

7-4: MANUSCRIPT FORMAT

7-4A: MATERIALS AND TYPEFACE

Use letter-size (22 × 28 cm, 8.5 × 11 in.), good-quality white paper. Type on only one side of the paper.

Use the same typeface throughout and avoid sans-serif fonts, since these do not clearly distinguish between 1, l, and I (Arabic numeral one, lowercase letter *L*, and Roman numeral one).

7-4B: TITLE AND IDENTIFICATION

The Chicago Manual of Style does not give guidelines for title pages in student papers. Check with your instructor to determine the preferred format.

7-4C: MARGINS, SPACING, AND INDENTATION

Use margins of at least 2.5 cm (1 in.) on all four sides of the page.

Double-space the entire text, including notes and bibliography. Leave one space after periods and colons.

Text should be flush left and ragged right. Do not use full justification.

Indent the first line of a paragraph. Indent block quotations (100 words or 8 lines or more) and leave extra space above and below them.

7-4D: PAGE NUMBERS

The Chicago Manual of Style does not give guidelines specifically for student papers. Check with your instructor to determine the preferred numbering system.

7-4E: ENDNOTES PAGE

Use the footnote or endnote function of your word-processing software to create notes. If you use endnotes, they should follow the last text page or any appendixes and precede the bibliography. Use the title Notes and double-space throughout. The endnotes page or pages should be numbered consecutively with the rest of the research paper and have the same margins.

7-4F: BIBLIOGRAPHY PAGE

PLACEMENT

The bibliography is placed at the end of the paper.

INDENTATION

Use a hanging indent, with the first line of the entry flush left and subsequent lines indented.

AUTHOR NAME

Invert names to put the surname first. For multiple authors, only the first name is inverted.

ARRANGEMENT OF ENTRIES

All sources are arranged alphabetically by the last name of the author or editor.

If a source has no author or editor, alphabetize by the first main word of the title. Do not consider articles—*A*, *An*, or *The*—when alphabetizing.

A single-author entry precedes a multi-author entry beginning with the same name.

For successive entries by the same author, a 3-em dash (———) followed by a period replaces the name after the first appearance.

PUBLICATION INFORMATION

Do not place publication information within parentheses.

PAGE NUMBERS

Give inclusive page numbers for an article or specific chapter. Otherwise, do not provide page numbers in the bibliography.

For an example of a correctly formatted bibliography, see page 226 in 7-5.

7-5: SAMPLE PAGES

In the sample on pages 223–226, you will find these model elements of a Chicago-style research paper:

- title page
- text page
- notes page
- bibliography page

Sample Chicago-Style Essay

A page number is not placed on the title page. Note, however, that this page is counted as the first page of the paper.

Historical Criticism and the Work of James Joyce

Carla Thorneloe

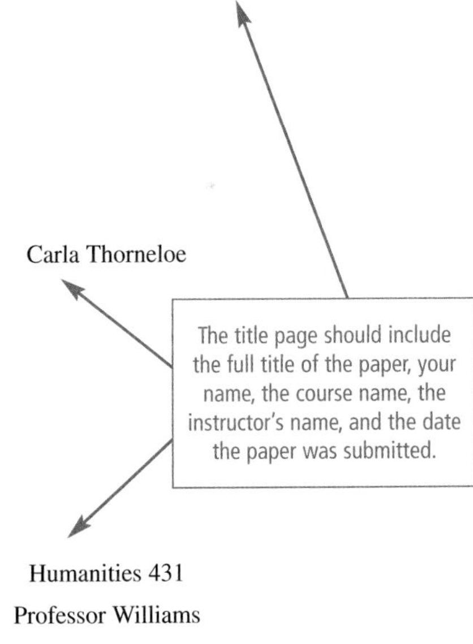

Humanities 431

Professor Williams

March 23, 2007

NOTE: The *Chicago Manual of Style* does not address the subject of title pages with research papers, so the guidelines on this page are offered to students whose instructors prefer to see title pages with essays.

The page number appears in the upper right-hand corner. Numbering starts on the first page after the title page. Many instructors ask that you use your last name as a header.

Thorneloe 2

The Marxist critic Georg Lukács, in rejecting modernist writers like James Joyce, suggests that their exaggerated concern for formal considerations—"experimental gimmicks" of style and literary technique—reflects a "tendency towards disintegration . . . [the] loss of artistic unity."[1] Fredric Jameson, a later Marxist critic, also observes fragmentation in literature of the Modernist period, which he identifies as exhibiting reifications. Jameson defines reification as

> a disease of that mapping function whereby the individual subject projects and models his or her own insertion into the collectivity. . . . The reification of late capitalism—the transformation of relations into an appearance of relationships between things—renders society opaque; it is the lived source of mystification on which ideology is based and by which domination and exploitation are legitimized.[2]

With the market exchange-value economy, people are commodified—they become depersonalized, reduced to mere things. We see evidence of this in Ulysses when Buck Mulligan remarks, "Redheaded women buck like goats," and when, through Father Conmee's intelligence, we learn "a tiny yawn opened the mouth of the wife of the gentleman with the glasses."[3] In both instances people are described in terms of things. Jameson suggests that capitalism is

The note number signals an acknowledgment. The number 2 corresponds to the second entry in the "Notes" section of the paper.

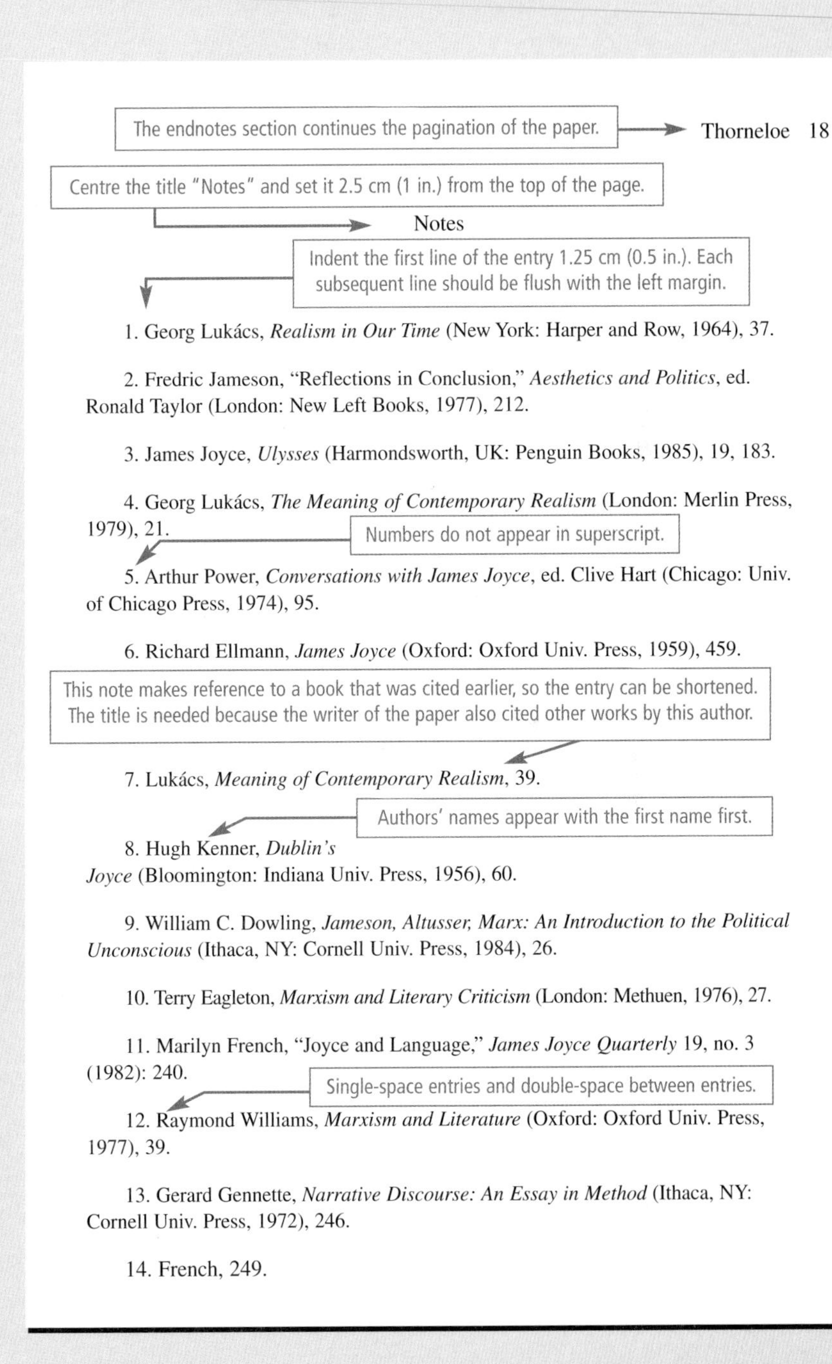

Thorneloe 18

Notes

1. Georg Lukács, *Realism in Our Time* (New York: Harper and Row, 1964), 37.

2. Fredric Jameson, "Reflections in Conclusion," *Aesthetics and Politics*, ed. Ronald Taylor (London: New Left Books, 1977), 212.

3. James Joyce, *Ulysses* (Harmondsworth, UK: Penguin Books, 1985), 19, 183.

4. Georg Lukács, *The Meaning of Contemporary Realism* (London: Merlin Press, 1979), 21.

5. Arthur Power, *Conversations with James Joyce*, ed. Clive Hart (Chicago: Univ. of Chicago Press, 1974), 95.

6. Richard Ellmann, *James Joyce* (Oxford: Oxford Univ. Press, 1959), 459.

7. Lukács, *Meaning of Contemporary Realism*, 39.

8. Hugh Kenner, *Dublin's Joyce* (Bloomington: Indiana Univ. Press, 1956), 60.

9. William C. Dowling, *Jameson, Altusser, Marx: An Introduction to the Political Unconscious* (Ithaca, NY: Cornell Univ. Press, 1984), 26.

10. Terry Eagleton, *Marxism and Literary Criticism* (London: Methuen, 1976), 27.

11. Marilyn French, "Joyce and Language," *James Joyce Quarterly* 19, no. 3 (1982): 240.

12. Raymond Williams, *Marxism and Literature* (Oxford: Oxford Univ. Press, 1977), 39.

13. Gerard Gennette, *Narrative Discourse: An Essay in Method* (Ithaca, NY: Cornell Univ. Press, 1972), 246.

14. French, 249.

Centre the title "Bibliography" and set it 2.5 cm (1 in.) from the top of the page.

Thorneloe 19

The bibliography continues the pagination of the paper.

Bibliography

The first line of an entry is flush with the left margin. Indent subsequent lines 1.25 cm (0.5 in.).

Dowling, William C. *Jameson, Althusser, Marx: An Introduction to the Political Unconscious*. Ithaca, NY: Cornell Univ. Press, 1984.

Eagleton, Terry. *Marxism and Literary Criticism*. London: Methuen, 1976.

Ellmann, Richard. *James Joyce*. Oxford: Oxford Univ. Press, 1959.

French, Marilyn. "Joyce and Language." *James Joyce Quarterly* 19, no. 3 (1982): 227–50.

Authors' names are reversed so the last name appears first. Entries are arranged in alphabetical order according to authors' last names.

Gennette, Gerard. *Narrative Discourse: An Essay in Method*. Ithaca, NY: Cornell Univ. Press, 1972.

Single-space entries and double-space between entries.

Jameson, Fredric. "Reflections in Conclusion." *Aesthetics and Politics*. Edited by Ronald Taylor. London: New Left Books, 1977.

Joyce, James. *Ulysses*. Harmondsworth, UK: Penguin Books, 1985.

Kenner, Hugh. *Dublin's Joyce*. Bloomington: Indiana Univ. Press, 1956.

Lukács, Georg. *Realism in Our Time*. New York: Harper and Row, 1964.

———. *The Meaning of Contemporary Realism*. London: Merlin Press, 1979.

Power, Arthur. *Conversations with James Joyce*. Edited by Clive Hart. Chicago: Univ. of Chicago Press, 1974.

Williams, Raymond. *Marxism and Literature*. Oxford: Oxford Univ. Press, 1977.

When more than one work by an author is cited, you may use a 3-em dash in place of the author's name for entries after the first. Arrange such entries in either chronological or alphabetical order.

CSE STYLE AND COLUMBIA ONLINE STYLE

My spelling is Wobbly.
It's good spelling
but it Wobbles,
and the letters get in
the wrong places.

-A.A. Milne

8

CSE Style and Columbia Online Style

8 CSE Style and Columbia Online Style

The Council of Science Editors (CSE) is the recognized authority on documentation style in all areas of science and related fields. Documentation guidelines presented in *Scientific Style and Format: The CSE Manual for Authors, Editors, and Publishers* (7th ed., 2006) are outlined in 8-1.

Columbia Online Style (COS) has variations for humanities and scientific disciplines and can be useful for citing electronic sources no matter which specific style of documentation you are required to use. Documentation guidelines presented in *The Columbia Guide to Online Style* (2nd ed., 2006) are outlined in 8-2.

8-1: CSE STYLE OF DOCUMENTATION

8-1A: DOCUMENTATION STYLES

The *CSE Manual* outlines three styles of documentation: name-year, citation-sequence, and citation-name.

NAME-YEAR

This system is very similar to APA style (see Chapter 6). Sources are identified in the text in parenthetical name-year references with complete bibliographical information given at the end of the paper in a reference list organized alphabetically by author surname. As the following examples illustrate, CSE style emphasizes simplicity, avoiding effects such as italics and reducing punctuation to a minimum.

In-text reference:

Dietary soy intake in man is proposed to provide cardiovascular protection, but it is not established whether this property is attributable to the soy protein per se or to associated dietary isoflavones (Douglas et al. 2006).

End reference:

Douglas G, Armitage JA, Taylor PD, Lawson JR, Mann GE, Poston L. 2006. Cardiovascular consequences of life-long exposure to dietary isoflavones in the rat. J Physiol. 571(2):477-487.

In CSE style, names are given for up to ten authors with *et al.* used only after the tenth. Notice that journal names are abbreviated and use of spaces and punctuation is minimal.

CITATION-SEQUENCE

In this system, superscript numbers in the text correspond to numbered references in a list at the end of the document. References are numbered in the order in which they appear within the text, with the number placed immediately after the reference in the text and before any punctuation. If the sentence uses the authority's name, the number is inserted after the name. If a single reference points to more than one source, numbers are given in a series, with commas and no spaces separating discontinuous numbers and a hyphen inserted to show more than two inclusive source numbers.

...the incidence of T cells was seen [2,9,23-17,22,23] to decrease...

Once a source has been assigned a number, it is referred to by that number throughout.

In the reference list, entries are ordered in the sequence in which they first appear in the text, with numbers placed on the line followed by a period and a space. For example, if the first reference in the text is to a work by Zeleny, number 1 in the reference list at the end of the paper will be Zeleny.

In-text reference:

Savage-Rumbaugh and Lewin's[1] work on Kanzi describes a chimpanzee who understands a good deal of spoken English, and the text expands our notions of what constitutes animal intelligence. McCarthy and Masson[2] wrote a book that not only touched on a subject not much examined before—animals' emotions—but became a popular nonfiction work as well.

End reference:

1. Savage-Rumbaugh ES, Lewin R. The ape at the brink of the human mind. New York: Wiley; 1994. 299 p.

2. McCarthy S, Masson JM. When elephants weep: the emotional lives of animals. New York: Delacorte; 1995. 291 p.

Note that the last element of these entries indicates the total number of pages in a book. This is an optional component of a book reference, but it can be useful for the reader.

CITATION-NAME

In this system, the list of end references is compiled alphabetically by author surname. The references are then numbered in that sequence, with Aaba number 1, Backnell number 2, and so on. These numbers are used for in-text references regardless of the sequence in which they appear in the text. If Mobbitt is number 38 in the reference list, the in-text reference is number 38, and the same number is used for subsequent in-text references.

When several in-text references occur at the same point, place their corresponding reference list numbers in numeric order. In-text reference numbers not in a continuous sequence are separated by commas with no spaces. For more than two numbers in a continuous sequence, connect the first and last by a hyphen.

...in several research projects [2,7-11,16,25] that had shown...

Formats for end references are similar to those used in the citation-sequence style, as shown above and in 8-1b.

8-1B: END REFERENCES

PAGE LAYOUT

Begin your reference list on a separate page with the centred title References or Cited References at the top. Single-space with a blank line between entries. Use a flush-left style for entries (no hanging indent).

SEQUENCE OF REFERENCES

Give the reference number in regular type followed by a period and a space. For the name-year system, place references in alphabetical order by author. For citation-sequence, list and number end references in the order in which they are cited in the text. For citation-name, place references in alphabetical order by author and then number the in-text references in the same sequence.

AUTHOR NAME(S)

Names are inverted, with surnames followed by initials with no punctuation and no space between initials. Names of multiple authors are separated with a comma, with no *and* before the last author's name and a period following.

TITLE

In both citation-sequence and citation-name styles, the title follows the author name. In the name-year system, the title follows the year of publication. If no author is given, the title always begins the reference. Titles of books should not be italicized and titles of articles should not be placed in quotation marks. Only the first word and proper nouns are capitalized. Subtitles are preceded by a colon and space; note that the first word in a subtitle is not capitalized. End the title with a period.

PUBLICATION INFORMATION

BOOKS

CITY OF PUBLICATION: If clarification is needed, include the abbreviation for the state/province or country in parentheses. Use postal abbreviations, for example, *UK*, *US*, or *ON*, with no periods or spaces. Place a colon and a space after the place of publication.

PUBLISHER'S NAME: Omit an initial *The*. Well-known publisher names may be abbreviated, so that, for example, *J. B. Lippincott Company* becomes *Lippincott*, although such abbreviations should be used with caution to avoid confusion. If no publisher can be determined, put publisher unknown in square brackets. When using the citation-name and citation-sequence systems, use a semicolon and a space after the publisher's name; with the name-year system, use a period.

YEAR OF PUBLICATION: If no year of publication can be determined, use the year of copyright preceded by c; if neither a year of publication nor the copyright date can be found, use the words date unknown in square brackets. The exception to this is with electronic references, in which case the dates of update/revision or citation (or both) are used instead.

ARTICLES

JOURNAL OR NEWSPAPER NAME: Put the name in title case, using standard abbreviations for journal names unless the name is only one word. No periods are used with abbreviated journal names. Newspaper names are never abbreviated, although an initial *The* may be dropped. If it is not part of the title, add the city either within or after the title. If the city is not well known, give the two-letter postal abbreviation for the U.S. state or Canadian province; for other countries, give the country name. All location information is in parentheses. End with a period.

DATE: The year of publication is required for all journal references. In the name-year system, the year follows the author name; in the citation-sequence and citation-name systems, it follows the journal title. Give the month and day only for a journal that has no volume or issue number, abbreviating the month to the first three letters with no period—for example, *2006 Aug 20*. In the citation-sequence and citation-name systems, the date is followed by a semicolon; in the name-year system, it is followed by a period.

VOLUME AND ISSUE INFORMATION: The volume number must be included, followed by the issue number, if there is one, in parentheses. No other punctuation is used. For citation-sequence and citation-name systems, include this information immediately after the semicolon following the date, with no space. Conclude with a colon.

PAGE NUMBERS

Location within a work, for example, a journal article or a chapter of a book, is a required part of an end reference. For a chapter or other part of a book, give inclusive pages preceded by the abbreviation p. (note the period). For a journal article, list inclusive page numbers but do not precede them with *p.* and do not leave any space between the preceding colon and the first digit.

The extent of a work—for example, the length of an entire book—is an optional part of a reference. Extent is expressed as the total number of pages followed by a space, as in *672 p*.

EXAMPLES OF CSE STYLE

The following examples illustrate the correct formatting for end references as they would occur in either the citation-sequence or citation-name system. For the name-year system, the date is moved up to follow the author name. Refer to Chapter 6 for detailed information about the name-year system.

BOOK WITH ONE AUTHOR

1. Hawking SW. The universe in a nutshell. New York: Bantam; 2001. 216 p.

BOOK WITH MORE THAN ONE AUTHOR

2. McCarthy S, Masson JM. When elephants weep: the emotional lives of animals. New York: Delacorte; 1995. 291 p.

EDITED BOOK

3. Bowling AT, Ruvinsky A, editors. The genetics of the horse. New York: Oxford University Press; 2000. 527 p.

CHAPTER FROM AN EDITED BOOK

4. Polanyi JC. The transition state. In: Zewail AH, editor. The chemical bond: structure and dynamics. Boston: Academic Press; 1992. p. 201-227.

EDITION OTHER THAN THE FIRST

5. Lyon MF, Searle AG, editors. Genetic variants and strains of the laboratory mouse. 3rd ed. New York: Oxford University Press; 1989. 896 p.

JOURNAL ARTICLE WITH VOLUME AND ISSUE NUMBERS

6. Reimann N, Barnitzeke S, Nolte I, Bullerdick J. Working with canine chromosomes: current recommendations for karyotype description. J Hered. 1999;90(1):31-34.

JOURNAL ARTICLE WITH DISCONTINUOUS PAGINATION

7. Crews D, Gartska WR. The ecological physiology of the garter snake. Sci Am. 1981;245:158-164,166-168.

NEWSPAPER ARTICLE

8. Vincent D. 1st West Nile case reported. Toronto Star. 2006 Aug 20;Sect. A3 (col. 5).

WEBSITE

9. Canadian Science Writers' Association [homepage on the Internet]. Toronto (ON): Canadian Science Writers' Association; c2006 [updated 2006 Aug 15; cited 2006 Aug 22]. Available from: http://www.sciencewriters.ca/index.html

ONLINE BOOK

10. Farabee MJ. The online biology book [Internet]. Avondale (AZ): Estrella Mountain Community College; c1992-2002 [updated 2001 Sep 17; cited 2006 Aug 22]. Available from: http://www.emc.maricopa.edu/faculty/farabee/BIOBK/BioBookTOC.html

ONLINE ARTICLE

11. Brown VW. Neurofeedback and Lyme's disease: a clinical application of the five phase model of CNS functional transformation and integration. JNT [Internet]. 1995 Fall [cited 2006 Aug 22]; 1(2):[about 32 screens]. Available from: http://www.snr-jnt.org/journalnt/jnt(1-2)6.html

ONLINE DATABASE

12. Alcohol and Alcohol Problems Science Database (ETOH) [Internet]. Bethesda (MD): National Institute on Alcohol Abuse and Alcoholism. 1972-2003 [cited 2006 Aug 22]. Available from: http://etoh.niaaa.nih.gov/Archive.htm

8-2: COLUMBIA ONLINE STYLE OF DOCUMENTATION

The following material is based on Janice R. Walker and Todd Taylor's *The Columbia Online Style*, 2nd ed. (New York: Columbia UP, 2006). You will also find guidelines and examples of Columbia Online Style at the Columbia University Press website (http://www.columbia.edu/cu/cup/cgos2006/basic.html).

Citing information from online sources can be difficult. For one thing, sites often move or disappear; for another, websites often fail to supply the detailed information necessary to cite them properly. To date, no single standard exists for documenting online sources, but Columbia Online Style offers practical guidelines for citing electronic sources in both the humanities and the sciences. In both cases, COS advocates a citation style that includes as much information as necessary stated as briefly as possible.

8-2A: HUMANITIES STYLE

COS uses a humanities style based on MLA criteria but modified for online sources. As with other styles, citations include a note in the text and a matching entry in a list of works cited that gives complete bibliographic information.

IN-TEXT REFERENCES

Although page numbers are usually given in the case of print documents, they rarely appear within an electronic document or file. In-text references therefore usually include only the author's last name, either in the body of the text or in parentheses next to quoted or paraphrased material:

Cohen states that North American audiences responded negatively.

North American audiences responded negatively (Cohen).

If no author is named, cite the name of the corporation or organization:

In the 2001 census, it was found that both divorce and marriage were on the rise (Statistics Canada).

When no author or organization is listed, use the document title or a shortened version of the title:

("Jazz Beat")

(*cbc.ca*)

For citations with no author or title, use the file name:

(18165.html)

For multiple works by the same author, include the author's last name followed by a comma and a shortened version of the title. This information can be given either in a parenthetical note or in the text.

BIBLIOGRAPHIC ENTRIES

The list of works cited should begin on a separate page and should be double-spaced throughout. When citing electronic sources, attempt to include in bibliographic citations as many of the following key information elements as you can:

1. **Author's last name**, followed by a comma and the first name and initial(s) (if known). Sometimes the only designation of authorship is an e-mail address, login name, or alias. Use a comma after the last name and end with a period.
2. **Title of document**, usually a webpage or article, in quotation marks with the first word and all major words capitalized. For untitled files, give a designation (for example, *Home Page*), with no quotation marks or italics. End with a period.
3. **Title of complete work**, such as a website or online book or journal, in italics. Capitalize the first word and all major words. End with a period.
4. **Version or edition**, if applicable, followed by a period.
5. **Date of publication or last revision**, if available, in international date format (day, month, year), followed by a period.
6. **Protocol and address**, or name of database (in italics) and publisher.
7. **Access path**, directories, keywords, or file numbers, if applicable, in parentheses.
8. **Date of access**, in parentheses, in day-month-year format, followed by a period.

Following are some examples of citations for electronic sources in the humanities. Other examples can be found in the COS manual or at the COS website.

WEBPAGE

Macklem, Katherine. "A 'Devastated' Leonard Cohen." 17 Aug. 2005. *Macleans.ca.* http://www.macleans.ca/topstories/finance/article.jsp?content=20050822_110877_110877 (8 Nov. 2006).

WEBSITE

National Association of Photoshop Professionals. NAPP. 2006. http://www.photoshopuser.com/ (6 Nov. 2006).

FULL-TEXT ARTICLE FROM LIBRARY DATABASE

Goldie, Terry. "The Canadian homosexual." Journal of Canadian Studies 33.4 (Winter 1998/1999): 132-143. Research Library. ProQuest. ISSN 00219495 (8 Nov. 2006).

ABSTRACT FROM LIBRARY DATABASE

Cohen, Mark. Abstract. "Just Judgment: Censorship of and in Canadian Literature." Diss. McGill University, 1999. ProQuest Dissertations and Theses. ProQuest. AAT NQ50133 (8 Nov. 2006).

ONLINE REFERENCE WORK

"Philistine." Merriam-Webster OnlineDictionary. Merriam-Webster OnLine. 2006. http://www.m-w.com/dictionary/Philistine (6 Nov. 2006).

MAILING LIST

Long, Tom. "Re: Certification." 6 Nov. 2006. Editors' Association of Canada members' discussion list. eac-acr-l@list.web.net (6 Nov. 2006).

8-2B: SCIENTIFIC STYLE

For scientific sources, COS style is designed to complement APA guidelines for citing print sources while providing more complete suggestions for citing electronic sources. As with other styles, citations include a note in the text and a matching entry in the list of references, which gives complete bibliographic information.

IN-TEXT REFERENCES

Since most electronic sources are not paginated, in-text references include only the author's last name followed by a comma and the year of publication:

> The glycerol produced during transesterification contains a very high percentage of excess methanol (Kemp, 2006).

Subsequent references may omit the date, giving only the author's name.

If there is no publication date, use the date of access (day-month-year):

There is no concrete evidence to suggest that the drug is effective in controlling performance anxiety (Millar, 8 Nov. 2006).

If the author's name is given in the text, include the date in parentheses immediately after the author's name:

Fenton (2006) claims that many events are either silent or clinically unrecognized.

Two or more references in the same note are separated with a semicolon:

(Peters & Collom, 2005; Stendall, 2006)

If no author is given, use the document or webpage title and the date:

("Quirks & Quarks," 2006)

(CBC.ca, 2006)

BIBLIOGRAPHIC ENTRIES

The list of works cited should begin on a separate page and should be double-spaced throughout. When citing electronic sources, attempt to include in bibliographic citations as many of the following key information elements as you can:

1. **Author's last name and initial(s)**, or the author's e-mail, login name, or alias. Use a comma after the last name and end with a period.
2. **Date of document**, in parentheses, followed by a period.
3. **Title of document**, capitalizing only the first word, any proper nouns, and the first word following a colon, if applicable. End with a period.
4. **Title of complete work**, in italics, capitalizing only the first word and any proper nouns. End with a period.
5. **Edition or revision**, if applicable, enclosed in parentheses and followed by a period.
6. **Protocol and address**, or name of database (in italics) and database publisher.
7. **Access path**, or directories or document or file number, in parentheses.
8. **Date of access**, in parentheses, followed by a period.

Following are some examples of citations for electronic sources in the sciences. Other examples can be found in the COS manual or at the COS website.

WEBPAGE

Nobel Foundation. (2006). The Nobel Prize in Chemistry. Nobelprize.org. http://nobelprize.org/nobel_prizes/chemistry/ (8 Nov. 2006).

WEBSITE

National Biodiesel Board (2006). Biodiesel. http://www.biodiesel.org/ (8 Nov. 2006).

FULL-TEXT ARTICLE FROM LIBRARY DATABASE

Maviglia, M.A. (2006). Alcohol and drug abuse intervention in the emergency department. Psychiatric Times, 23(1), 40. ProQuest Nursing & Allied Health. ProQuest. (ISSN 08932905). (8 Nov. 2006).

ABSTRACT FROM LIBRARY DATABASE

Kuhlen, M. (2006). Adventures in numerical cosmology [Abstract]. ProQuest Dissertations and Theses. ProQuest. (9780542705502). (8 Nov. 2006).

ONLINE REFERENCE WORK

Maquiladora. (2006). In Encyclopaedia Britannica online. http://www.britannica.com/eb/article-9050713/maquiladora (8 Nov. 2006).

MAILING LIST

Fennel, R. (2006, November 8). Re: Editing science texts. Editors' Association of Canada members' discussion list. eac-acr-l @list.web.net (8 Nov. 2006).

9

GRAMMAR

Every English poet should master the *rules* of grammar before he attempts to

bend

or

break

them.

-Robert Graves

9

Grammar

9 Grammar

This section will teach you the basic concepts of grammar you will need in order to understand how your sentences are put together. This knowledge can be used to explain or to justify what you have written and why. When in doubt about a grammatical issue, whether in your first or subsequent drafts, consult this section.

9-1: PARTS OF SPEECH

Every word in a sentence can be classified as a part of speech. Which part a word plays depends on how it functions in the sentence it is in. Words can be classified as one or more of the following parts of speech:

- nouns
- articles, or determiners
- pronouns
- verbs
- adjectives
- adverbs
- prepositions
- conjunctions
- interjections

A word can play more than one part.

Verb
When she attempts to dance, she is often embarrassed by her lack of grace.

Noun
My attempts to dance are sometimes met with ridicule.

Some words are **singular**, which means they denote a single person or thing (*I*, *cat*); some are **plural**, designating more than one person or thing (*we*, *cats*). Some words may function as the **subject**, or doer of the action, in a sentence (<u>*Math*</u> *is fun*), or as the **object** affected by the action (*I like* <u>*math*</u>), or as a **complement** (*Math is* <u>*fun*</u>).

A group of words may form a **sentence**, which has two main parts, a subject and a **predicate** (which includes the verb, object, and phrases governed by the verb), and can stand alone; a **clause**, which has a subject and predicate but is a part of a larger sentence; or a **phrase**, which does not have a subject or verb and cannot stand alone. A word, phrase, or clause may be a **modifier**, meaning that it describes or limits another word, phrase, or clause within a sentence.

To distinguish parts of speech, follow the guidelines below.

9-1A: NOUNS

A **noun** names a person, place, or thing. Whenever an **article** (*a*, *an*, *the*) could precede a word without destroying the logic of a sentence, that word is a noun. Nouns can be classified by type:

WWW

Types of Nouns

NOUN TYPE	THESE NOUNS NAME	EXAMPLES	SEE ALSO
proper	specific people, places, and things (always with an initial capital)	*Buckminster Fuller, Moose Jaw, Honda*	14-3a
common	general people, places, or things	*architect, town, car*	14-3a
concrete	things you experience through your senses	*gravel, ice cream, storm*	13-3b
abstract	things you do not experience through your senses	*knowledge, liberation, fear*	13-3b
collective	groups	*jury, police*	10-3e, 10-3a
noncount	things that cannot be counted	*snow, porridge*	15-1a, 15-1b, 15-1d
count	things that can be counted	*snowflakes, cornflakes*	15-1a, 15-1b, 15-1d
possessive	things that are owned by someone	*Nathan's, Maria's, Daddy's*	11-4a

Watch out for certain common suffixes (or endings) on nouns. These endings are often a clue that the word in question is a noun. These endings include *ance, ence, ness, ion*, and *ty.*

9-1B: ARTICLES

Articles, or determiners, come before nouns. The **indefinite** articles are *a* and *an*, and the **definite** article is *the*.

9-1C: PRONOUNS

A **pronoun** can replace a noun. The word (or words) replaced by a pronoun is called the **antecedent.**

Antecedent
Homer lives in Springfield.

Pronouns
He is married to Marge.

His children, Bart, Lisa, and Maggie, also live with him.

TYPES OF PRONOUNS

PERSONAL

Personal pronouns refer to people, places, or things. When **subjective** (*I, you he, she, it, we, they*), personal pronouns refer to people or things who are performing actions or that are the subject being described.

We asked Hermione, but she wouldn't tell.

Objective personal pronouns (*me, you, him, her, it, us, them*) refer to people or things that are acted on. They often follow a preposition.

Don't look at me; look at him.

The audience hated us and loved her.

POSSESSIVE

Possessive pronouns (*my, your, his, her, its, our, their*) indicate ownership, or possession. They function like adjectives in front of a noun.

Every dog has its day.

Absolute possessive pronouns (*mine, yours, his, hers, its, ours, theirs*) also indicate ownership. They stand in for both the owner and the thing owned.

The bank account is mine, the property is yours, and the debt is ours.

RELATIVE

Relative pronouns (*who, which, that*) introduce subordinate clauses (see 9-3e) that operate as adjectives, describing the noun or pronoun in the main clause.

People who live in glass houses shouldn't throw stones.

DEMONSTRATIVE

Demonstrative pronouns (*this, these, that, those*) point to nouns. They may function as adjectives modifying a noun, or they may replace the noun entirely.

Those who ignore history are condemned to repeat it.

INTERROGATIVE

Interrogative pronouns (*who, whose, what, which,* and others) begin questions.

Who wants to be a millionaire?

REFLEXIVE AND INTENSIVE

Reflexive pronouns (*myself, yourself, himself, herself, itself, ourselves, yourselves, themselves*) name the receiver of an action who is identical to the performer of an action.

Cats keep themselves very clean.

Intensive pronouns look like reflexive pronouns, but are used to emphasize a noun or pronoun.

You yourself scorn a daily bath.

RECIPROCAL

Reciprocal pronouns (*each other, one another*) refer to the separate parts of a plural antecedent.

Kathleen and Aitken despise each other.

INDEFINITE

Indefinite pronouns *(all, anybody, anyone, anything, each, either, everybody, everyone, everything, neither, no one, nobody, none, nothing, one, some, somebody, someone, something)* refer to general (not specific) people or things. Many are always singular, some are always plural, and some may be either singular or plural.

Everyone should have someone to love.

9-1D: VERBS

The **verb** in a sentence usually expresses an action (*work, climb*), an occurrence (*became*) or a state of being (*is, seemed*). It may be one verb or a phrase made up of a main verb and an auxiliary verb. In English, the verb frequently appears as the second element of a sentence.

Verb Expressing Action
Cupid shot his arrow.

Verb Expressing Occurrence
It happened one night.

Verb Expressing State of Being
Blondie and Dagwood have been married for decades.

Verbs may be **regular** *(I/you/we/they love; he/she/it loves)* or **irregular** *(I am; you/we/they are; he/she/it is)*.

KINDS OF VERBS

TRANSITIVE AND INTRANSITIVE

Transitive verbs always take an object.

Ken hates math.

The verb *hates* is transitive because it is followed by the object *math*.

Intransitive verbs do not take an object.

Barbie giggled.

The verb *giggled* is intransitive because it does not take an object.

LINKING AND ACTION

Linking verbs (e.g., forms of *to be, to feel, to seem,* etc.) join the subject to the complement.

I feel pretty.

The linking verb, *feel,* joins the subject, *I,* to the complement, the adjective *pretty.*

Action verbs are verbs that involve some activity, movement, or action, rather than expressing a state of being, like linking verbs.

The bomb exploded.

MAIN AND AUXILIARY

A **main** verb describes a simple action or state of being.

Byron mocked Keats.

Auxiliary verbs are helping verbs. *Be, do,* and *have* operate as auxiliary verbs in English.

He *had* scorned other poets for years.

MODAL

Modal verbs (like *can, could, may, might, should, would, must,* and *ought to,* or the most common modals, *do, have, and be*) are used with the present tense form of the verb to express doubt or certainty, necessity or obligation, probability or possibility. They are also often used to make polite requests.

You *might* have called before barging in.

"*May* I suggest the duck confit salad?" asked the waiter.

Betting on the stock market *could* be dangerous.

FORMS OF VERBS

Verb forms vary according to

- tense
- person
- number
- mood
- voice

TENSE

The **tense** of a verb refers to when an action occurs, in the **past**, in the **present**, or in the **future**. Tense expresses the time of an action. To show changes in time, verbs change form and combine with auxiliary verbs.

The **simple** tenses describe a one-time or regular occurrence; the **progressive** form refers to an ongoing event. The **perfect** tenses express completed actions. (See 10-4f.)

SIMPLE TENSES

TYPE	EXAMPLE	PROGRESSIVE FORM
Present	I laugh	I am laughing
Past	I laughed	I was laughing
Future	I will laugh	I will be laughing

PERFECT TENSES

TYPE	EXAMPLE	PROGRESSIVE FORM
Present Perfect	I have laughed	I have been laughing
Past Perfect	I had laughed	I had been laughing
Future Perfect	I will have laughed	I will have been laughing

PERSON AND NUMBER

Depending on the **person** the verb is attached to, its form may change. Look at the conjugation of a regular verb in English, below; note that, in the present tense, regular verbs take an s in the third person singular (with *he, she,* or *it*):

First Person Singular: I work
Second Person Singular: you work
Third Person Singular: he/she/it works
First Person Plural: we work
Second Person Plural: you work
Third Person Plural: they work

The **number** of a verb tells you whether the verb refers to a singular subject or a plural subject. *She works* is singular, but *they work* is plural, and the form of the verb changes to reflect the change in number of the subject.

For more information on the person and number of verbs, see 10-3.

MOOD

The **mood** of a verb refers to whether it is indicative, imperative, or subjunctive.

The **indicative** mood is used for events that are real or that commonly recur.

He who laughs last laughs best.

The **imperative** mood is used for commands. The subject in these cases is left out, but is understood to be *you*.

Don't laugh at me.

The **subjunctive** mood is used to express hypothetical situations, things contrary to fact, wishes, requirements, and speculations.

If I were you, I would learn to laugh at myself.

VOICE

The **voice** of a verb refers to whether the subject *performs* the action or whether it *receives* the action.

In the **active** voice, the subject performs the action.

Customers found the wait staff to be inattentive, careless, and rude.

The subject (*customers*) performs the action (*found*).

In the **passive** voice, the subject is acted upon.

The wait staff was found to be inattentive, careless, and rude.

The subject (*the wait staff*) receives the action of an implied but unstated performer (*the customers*).

Because the active voice emphasizes the performer of an action, it is more direct and less wordy than the passive voice. On the other hand, because the passive voice stresses the receiver of an action, it is especially useful when the performer of an action is unknown or unimportant.

For more information on active and passive voice, see 10-4h.

9-1E: ADJECTIVES

Adjectives modify or describe nouns or pronouns. They give information about *which one, what kind,* or *how many.*

Common Adjective
Life is beautiful.

Proper Adjective
The play was set in Edwardian times.

Words with the suffixes *-ful, -ish, -less,* and *-like* are usually adjectives.

9-1F: ADVERBS

An **adverb** can modify a verb, an adjective, another adverb, or a complete sentence. Adverbs give information about *when, where, how,* and *how much.*

Adverb Modifying Verb
Buffy screamed loudly.

Adverb Modifying Adjective
Computers are a very significant cause of a sedentary lifestyle.

Adverb Modifying Adverb
I cannot swim now because I have eaten too recently.

Adverb Modifying Sentence
Mercifully, the lost children were reunited with their frightened parents.

Many adverbs, though not all adverbs, end in -ly; however, it is important to realize that many adjectives do as well (e.g., *jolly, silly,* and *smelly*).

Note that adjectives and adverbs may also be **comparative** or **superlative**.

Comparative Adjective
I prefer you in redder lipstick.

Superlative Adjective
The reddest lipstick is my favourite.

Comparative Adverb
The younger child came more willingly.

Superlative Adverb
I will share my sandwich with you most willingly.

9-1G: PREPOSITIONS

Prepositions are words that often express position. They form phrases with nouns and pronouns, and together they often provide information about time and space.

After the party, they had lots of bottles to throw out.

In summer, they eat on the patio.

The use of prepositions in English is complex. For more discussion of prepositions, see 15-3g.

Common Prepositions

about	between	next	through
above	beyond	of	throughout
across	by	off	till
after	concerning	on	to
against	considering	onto	toward
along	despite	opposite	under
among	down	out	underneath
around	during	outside	unlike
as	except	over	until
at	for	past	unto
before	from	plus	up
behind	in	regarding	upon
below	inside	respecting	with
beneath	into	round	within
beside	like	since	without
besides	near	than	

9-1H: CONJUNCTIONS

Conjunctions are words that connect.

COORDINATING CONJUNCTIONS

and	or	nor
but	yet	so
for (meaning because)		

When one of these seven words joins two complete sentences, it is working as a **coordinating** conjunction. Coordinating conjunctions join two coordinate or balanced structures.

On holidays, we go to theatres, and we eat in expensive restaurants.

SUBORDINATE CONJUNCTIONS

Subordinate conjunctions connect main clauses with subordinate clauses. (See 9-3e.)

Because he had gained fifty pounds, the doctor put him on a diet.

Common Subordinate Conjunctions

after	even if	rather than	until
although	even though	since	when
as	if	so that	whenever
as if	if only	than	where
as long as	in order that	that	wherever
as though	now that	though	whereas
because	once	till	while
before		unless	

CORRELATIVE CONJUNCTIONS

Correlative conjunctions work in pairs to balance sentence structures. (See 9-4a.)

Either that wall paper goes, or I do.

—Oscar Wilde, on his deathbed

Correlative Conjunctions

both . . . and	not only . . . but also
either . . . or	whether . . . or
neither . . . nor	and not . . . so much as

CONJUNCTIVE ADVERBS

Conjunctive adverbs are used to indicate a connection between main clauses. (See 10-2b and 11-2b.)

I have a headache; therefore, I'm going to bed.

Many adverbs can function as conjunctive adverbs. Learning to distinguish between conjunctive adverbs and coordinating conjunctions is essential to avoid comma splice errors and to punctuate correctly. (See 10-2, 11-1a, and 11-2b.)

9-1I: INTERJECTIONS

An **interjection** is a word that expresses strong feeling. These words are seldom used in formal writing.

Ouch! I hate going to the dentist.

9-2: PARTS OF SENTENCES

English sentences are usually composed of (a) subjects and (b) verbs, often completed with (c) objects or complements.

A sentence is composed of a subject and a predicate. The latter is the name for the verb, its modifiers, and the object or complement in the sentence.

9-2A: SUBJECTS

The subject (S) of a sentence is what the sentence is about. To find the **complete** subject, ask *who* or *what* of the verb.

S
My professor writes grammar textbooks.

S
Grammar books that are genuinely useful are hard to come by.

Who writes grammar textbooks? My *professor.* What are hard to come by? *Grammar books that are genuinely useful.*

The **simple** subject (SS) is the one-word subject that is left after all modifiers, phrases, and clauses are stripped away. A simple subject is always either a noun or a pronoun.

SS
My professor writes grammar textbooks.

SS
Grammar books that are genuinely useful are hard to come by.

Remember, though, that some subjects can be **compound** if they are joined by a coordinating conjunction such as *and* or *or.*

S S
Time and tide wait for no man.

In commands (or **imperatives**), *you* is understood to be the subject.

S
[You] Use it or lose it.

Sometimes subjects do not appear before the verb in English sentences. If a sentence begins with an **expletive,** such as *there is* or *there are* (or *there was* or *there were*), then the subject follows the verb. Expletives function as placeholders to begin the sentence.

S
There is an owl sitting on that branch.

Subjects sometimes appear at the ends of sentences for dramatic effect.

S
In the doorway stood her father.

In questions, the subject often appears between parts of the verb.

S
Do you *know* the answer?

Note: Being able to identify the subject of a sentence is crucial to understanding many common errors in your editing. Look, for example, at Sentence Fragments (10-1), Subject–Verb Agreement (10-3), and Pronoun Case (10-5c).

See the Note above. If your first language is not English, check out 15-3a and 15-3b.

9-2B: VERBS, OBJECTS, AND COMPLEMENTS

As you saw in 9-1d, verbs may be categorized as linking, if followed by a complement; transitive, if followed by an object; or intransitive, if the verb cannot take an object.

LINKING VERBS AND COMPLEMENTS

A linking verb (LV) must take a complement, or **subjective completion** (SC), which is a word (or words) that completes the meaning of the subject (S) by renaming or describing that subject.

Recess *is* the part of school we enjoy most.

Life *is* what you make it.

The lake *was* calm.

When a subjective completion, or complement, renames the subject, it is a noun or pronoun, or a phrase beginning with a noun or pronoun, such as *the part of school we enjoy most* or *what you make it*. When it describes the subject, it is an adjective, such as *calm*.

Linking verbs are often forms of the verb *to be: be, am, is, are, was, were, being, been*. Verbs that have no action, such as *appear, become, feel, grow, look, make, prove, remain, stay, seem, smell, sound,* and *taste* are also linking verbs when they are followed by a word or word group that names or describes the subject of the sentence.

TRANSITIVE VERBS THAT TAKE DIRECT OBJECTS

Remember, transitive verbs (TV) always take an object. They may take a **direct object** (DO). Direct objects name the receiver of an action. A simple direct object must be a noun or pronoun.

You *will pay* the price.

Transitive verbs are often in the active voice, with the subject (or performer of the action) at the beginning of the sentence and the direct object (the receiver of the action) following the verb. Transitive verbs are the only verbs that may appear in the passive voice, where the receiver of the action becomes the subject and the performer of the action is moved to the end of the sentence.

Active Voice: The Stratford Festival *presented* the play.

Passive Voice: The play *was presented* by the Stratford Festival.

Passive Voice: The play *was presented.*

The direct object (*the play*) becomes the subject when the sentence is made passive; the original subject is relegated to the end of the sentence, in a prepositional phrase beginning with *by*. Sometimes these *by* phrases are left out in passive constructions, leaving the performer of the action unstated.

TRANSITIVE VERBS WITH BOTH INDIRECT AND DIRECT OBJECTS

Sometimes transitive verbs take both direct and **indirect objects** (IO). In this case, the indirect object comes first.

> You *catch* [for] me a fish, and I *will cook* [for] you dinner.

TRANSITIVE VERBS, DIRECT OBJECTS, AND OBJECT COMPLEMENTS

A transitive verb and a direct object are sometimes followed by an **object complement** (OC), a word or group of words that completes the direct object's meaning by describing it or renaming it. If the object complement is used to rename the direct object, it is a noun (or noun phrase) or a pronoun.

> Some people *find* stamp collecting a dull hobby.

The object complement renames the direct object, *stamp collecting, a dull hobby.*

If the object complement describes the direct object, it is an adjective or adjective phrase.

> The passage of time *makes* antiques more valuable.

The object complement describes the direct object, *antiques,* as *more valuable.*

INTRANSITIVE VERBS

An intransitive verb (IV) cannot take either an object or a complement.

S IV
The soccer team *succeeds*.

There is no receiver for the action in this sentence because *succeed* is an intransitive verb.

Intransitive verbs may, however, be followed by adverbs or **adverbial phrases** that modify them. An adverbial phrase is a group of words that modifies a verb, an adverb, or an adjective; for example, *slowly but surely* is an adverbial phrase in the sentence *He walked, slowly but surely, to the closet door.*

S IV
Tarzan and Jane *exercise* every day.

The intransitive verb *exercise* takes no object, but it is followed by an adverbial phrase that modifies it: *every day.*

Check a dictionary to determine if a verb is transitive or intransitive. Sometimes a verb can be both, depending on its context.

S TV DO
Transitive: The coach *swam* the Australian crawl.

S IV
Intransitive: The coach *swam* every morning.

In the first sentence, the verb *swam* takes a direct object (*the Australian crawl* answers the question *swam what?*). In the next sentence, *swam* takes no object and is followed by an adverbial phrase (*every morning* answers the question *swam when?*).

9-3: PHRASES AND CLAUSES

Each sentence, no matter how complex, has a **main** clause—the clause containing the main idea, subject, and verb of the sentence.

A main clause, also known as an **independent** clause, can always stand alone as a sentence.

Phrases are word groups lacking a subject or verb—or both—and they cannot stand alone (although exceptions to this rule are often allowed in works of fiction). They are used within sentences, usually as adjectives, adverbs, or nouns.

9-3A: PREPOSITIONAL PHRASES

Prepositional phrases are groups of words that begin with a preposition, such as *at, across, by, beside, for, from, in, into, off, on, over, to,* or *without*. (See 9-1g.) Prepositional phrases always include a noun or a pronoun, which serves as the object of the preposition.

Prepositional phrases usually act as adverbs or adjectives. When a prepositional phrase is used as an adjective, it appears right after the noun or pronoun that it modifies.

A bird in the hand is worth two in the bush.

When a prepositional phrase is used as an adverb, it may or may not directly follow the verb it modifies.

We ate with gusto the picnic she had brought for us.

You can't judge a book by its cover.

9-3B: VERBAL PHRASES

Verbal phrases are formed from parts of the verb, but they function as nouns, adjectives, or adverbs. There are three kinds of verbal phrases: those formed with infinitives, present participles, and past participles.

INFINITIVE PHRASES

The **infinitive** is *to* + the base form of the verb: for example, *to be, to do, to love*. The infinitive often functions as a noun in a sentence, but it can also be an adjective or an adverb.

S

To be or not to be is the question. [infinitive phrase as subject]

Donating food to help those in need feels good. [infinitive phrase as adjective]

He swims laps to relieve stress. [infinitive phrase as adverb]

PARTICIPIAL PHRASES

Participial phrases can use either present participles or past participles. **Present participles** are formed with *-ing* and act like adjectives.

Standing there among the gardenias, the gardener could see what the problem was.

The baby, crying in the dark, had been abandoned.

Past participles are forms of regular verbs that end in *-ed* or the equivalent forms of irregular verbs. They, too, operate like adjectives in a sentence.

Exhausted, Geoffrey finished the application at midnight.

The envelope, sent by express courier, arrived just in time.

Gerunds and infinitives, when used as objects, sometimes pose problems for ESL students. See 15-2g for a discussion of gerunds and infinitives.

9-3C: APPOSITIVE PHRASES

Appositives and **appositive phrases** are used to rename nouns or pronouns. They function like nouns.

Sanitary engineers, otherwise known as garbage collectors, are going on strike.

9-3D: ABSOLUTE PHRASES

An **absolute** phrase modifies a clause or a sentence. It usually is made up of a noun followed by a participial phrase.

Her head spinning with confusion, Ethel left the exam room.

The participial phrase *spinning with confusion* refers to the noun *head*.

9-3E: SUBORDINATE CLAUSES

Subordinate clauses (SC), like main clauses, contain a subject and a verb, but they cannot stand alone as complete sentences, and instead function in sentences as adjectives, adverbs, or nouns. Subordinate clauses are usually indicated by the presence of a subordinate conjunction or a word beginning with *wh-*.

ADJECTIVAL CLAUSES

An adjectival subordinate clause modifies a noun or a pronoun. Adjectival clauses often start with a relative pronoun (*who, whom, whose, which,* or *that*) or with a word like *when* or *where.*

Sc

The boat that I am rowing has sprung a leak.

ADVERBIAL CLAUSES

Subordinate clauses can act as adverbs by modifying adjectives, adverbs, or verbs. They usually answer at least one of the questions *when? where? why? how? under what conditions?* or *to what degree?* These clauses usually begin with a subordinate conjunction, such as one of the following: *after, although, as, as if, because, before, even though, if, in order that, provided that, rather than, since, so that, than, though, where, wherever, whereas, whether.*

Sc

If I had a hammer, I'd hammer in the morning.

Sc

Whether you like it or not, it's your turn.

NOUN CLAUSES

Subordinate noun clauses are used as subjects, objects, or complements. They usually begin with one of these words: *how, that, which, who, whoever, whom, whomever, what, whatever, when, where, whether, whose, why.*

Sc

Whatever frog she kisses will become a prince.

9-4: SENTENCE TYPES

There are two approaches to the classification of sentences.

Sentences may be categorized according to their structure or their function.

9-4A: SENTENCE STRUCTURE

Sentences can be simple, compound, complex, or compound-complex, depending on the number and type of clauses they contain. In order to be a sentence, there must be at least one independent (or main) clause (IC). A subordinate clause, like the main clause, has a subject and a verb, but it cannot stand alone as a sentence.

Simple sentences have one independent clause with no subordinate clauses. A simple sentence has just one subject and verb.

IC
Yesterday, the dog was sick.

Compound sentences have two or more independent (or main) clauses, with no subordinate clauses. The main clauses may be joined by a comma and a coordinating conjunction (*and, or, nor, for, but, yet,* or *so*) or with a semicolon.

IC IC
Potatoes are healthy, but potato chips are not.

Complex sentences are made up of one independent clause and at least one subordinate clause.

SC IC
If you go into the woods today, you're in for a big surprise.

Compound-complex sentences are made up of at least two independent clauses and at least one subordinate clause.

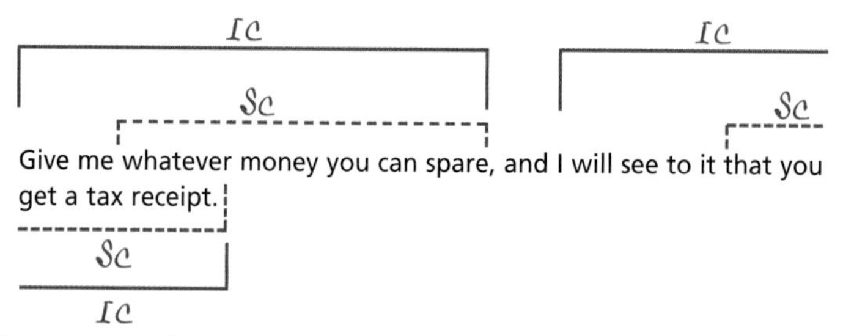

This sentence has two main clauses, and each main clause contains a subordinate clause.

9-4B: SENTENCE FUNCTION

Sentences can function in any of the following ways:

- as statements (declarative)
- as requests or commands (imperative)
- as questions (interrogative)
- as exclamations (exclamatory)

Here are examples of each.

Declarative
To err is human.

Imperative
To yourself be true.

Interrogative
What vision do I see before me?

Exclamatory
You must listen to me!

10

COMMON SENTENCE ERRORS

10

Common Sentence Errors

10 Common Sentence Errors

The following sections catalogue a number of common errors made by writers in English. Use these sections to revise your work and to respond to questions and suggestions about your use of language. If you discover that you have a tendency to make any one of these errors with some frequency, review the relevant section carefully to internalize the information you find. Doing so will improve your sense of grammar for the next piece of writing you complete. Current grammar checkers are mainly quite reliable, but it is still up to you to accept or reject the changes suggested, and to understand them. The grammar in this chapter reflects formal usage in business and academic documents, but usage is key: e-mail and instant messaging have created increasingly informal usage. Be aware of the level of formality you need in a given document.

10-1: SENTENCE FRAGMENTS

A sentence is, at the very least, one complete independent clause that contains a subject and verb. A **sentence fragment**, on the other hand, is part of a sentence that is set off as if it were a whole sentence by a beginning capital letter and a final period or other end punctuation. However, the fragment lacks essential requirements of a grammatically complete and correct sentence.

For example, the fragment may lack a main verb.

Just Phil and I.

A sentence fragment could lack a subject.

Pacing the hallway.

Note that even a phrase such as "Just Phil and I, pacing the hallway" does not have a main verb. Don't confuse the participle *pacing* with a main verb. Here the participle operates as an adjective and modifies "Phil and I"; it doesn't provide a main action for the sentence.

A sentence fragment could also be a subordinate clause commencing with a subordinating word.

When I fly a kite.

Sentence fragments give readers a fragment of a thought as opposed to a complete thought, and they interfere with writing clarity. In any type of academic writing, sentence fragments are considered a serious writing error, and they must be eliminated.

TESTING FOR SENTENCE FRAGMENTS

Fragments can be spotted easily when they appear in isolation, but they are more difficult to identify when they are near complete sentences. If you suspect a group of words is a sentence fragment, consider the following:

1. Does the word group have a verb?
   - ❑ YES. *Consider the next question.*
   - ❑ NO. The word group is a fragment and must be revised to include a verb.
2. Does the word group have a subject?
   - ❑ YES. *Consider the next question.*
   - ❑ NO. The word group is a fragment and must be revised to include a subject.
3. Does the word group start with a subordinating word, making it a subordinate clause?
   - ❑ YES. The word group is a sentence fragment and must be revised to create a complete sentence that is an independent clause.
   - ❑ NO. *If you answered yes to the two previous questions and no to this one, the word group is a complete sentence and does not require revision for sentence completeness.*

Make sure to consider all three questions when reviewing your sentence, since a fragment could be missing more than one essential sentence element. If your evaluation indicates that you have a sentence fragment, use the following strategies to transform it into a complete sentence.

ELIMINATING SENTENCE FRAGMENTS

To fix the sentence fragment and make it a complete sentence, do one of the following:

1. Attach the sentence fragments to an independent clause or a clause that contains the essential element lacking in the fragment (e.g., a subject or a verb).

   Just Phil and I were pacing the hallway.

2. Compose an independent clause from the fragment.

   At the emergency ward, the parents were pacing the hallway.

3. Drop the subordinating word.

   ~~When~~ I fly a kite.

Subjects may not be omitted in English, except in the case of imperative sentences. Verbs may not be omitted either. If English is not your first language, consult 15-2i and 15-3a for further information.

10-1A: SUBORDINATE CLAUSES

A subordinate clause contains a subject and a predicate, or verb, but the clause begins with a subordinating word or phrase (e.g., *after, although, if, until*) or a relative pronoun (*that, which, what, who*). Therefore, the clause is not independent.

You can make a subordinate clause into an independent clause in one of two ways.

1. Merge the subordinate clause with a nearby sentence.

> because
> Many of Elmore Leonard's novels have been made into movies~~. Because~~ he is an amazingly popular crime writer.

2. Delete the subordinating element of the clause.

> He
> Many of Elmore Leonard's novels have been made into movies. ~~Because he~~ is an amazingly popular crime writer.

10-1B: PHRASES

A phrase is a group of words that does not have either a subject or a verb, and, therefore, cannot stand alone as an independent clause or sentence. Look at these examples:

> to go kayaking
>
> for the umpteenth time
>
> with great trepidation

Major types of phrases include noun phrases, adjective phrases, adverb phrases, and prepositional phrases. (For more information about phrases, see 9-3.)

FIXING PHRASE FRAGMENTS

You can address phrase fragment problems in two ways.

1. Incorporate the phrase into a nearby sentence.

> , which is there for
> Our community library has an amazing array of resources~~. For~~ every local citizen to use.

The phrase *for every local citizen to use* has been added to the sentence in a subordinate clause.

, a
He took part in the smudging~~. A~~ ceremony that uses smoke to purify the psychic energy field, or aura, around a person.

The writer has used the phrase beginning *A ceremony that uses smoke* as an appositive to rename *smudging.*

2. Turn the phrase into a complete sentence by adding a subject, predicate (verb), or both.

Smokejumpers land with heavy gear, including two parachutes, puncture-proof Kelvar suits, freeze-dried food, fire shelters, and personal effects.

Next, containing
^ cardboard boxes ^ ~~heaved out of the airplane~~ chain saws, shovels,

are heaved out of the airplane
and axes^.

Cardboard boxes has become the subject, and the verb has been changed to *are heaved.*

10-1C: OTHER WORD GROUPS

Other commonly fragmented word groups include

- compound predicates
- examples introduced by *for example, such as,* and *for instance*
- lists

The following section will help you identify these fragmentation problems and provides strategies for correcting them.

COMPOUND PREDICATES

The predicate is the part of the sentence that contains the verb. It indicates what the subject is doing or experiencing, or what is being done to the subject. A **compound predicate** contains two or more predicates with the same subject.

but
Joel wanted to buy a new computer and printer~~. But~~ could only afford to purchase a used laptop.

The fragment starting *But could only* has been made part of the compound predicate. Note that no comma is required between compound elements of this predicate.

EXAMPLES INTRODUCED BY FOR EXAMPLE, SUCH AS, *AND* FOR INSTANCE

Often you will need to introduce examples, illustrations, and explanations to support arguments and ideas in your academic writing. Some common words and phrases used to introduce examples, illustrations, and explanations include the following:

also	besides	as an illustration
and	such as	for example
but	namely	in particular
like	especially	furthermore
or	including	specifically
mainly	for instance	to illustrate
that is	in addition	equally important

Sometimes a fragment introduced by any one of the above words or phrases can be attached to the sentence before it to create a complete sentence.

> Any treatment of early-seventeenth-century English literature must include a discussion of the period's leading figures~~. Such~~ such as John Donne, Ben Jonson, and John Milton.

However, in some instances you may find it necessary to change the fragment containing the examples into a new sentence.

> Jan Morris's travel pieces cover many interesting cities. For instance, she explores ~~exploring~~ Beirut, visits ~~visiting~~ Chicago, and discovers ~~discovering~~ "The Navel City" of Cuzco.

The writer corrected the fragment beginning *For instance* by adding the subject *she*, creating a complete sentence.

FRAGMENTS IN LISTS

Occasionally, list elements are fragmented. This type of writing problem can usually be corrected through the use of a colon or dash.

> During my rare vacations, I work on my three R's~~. Reading~~: reading, rest, and running.

10-1D: ACCEPTABLE FRAGMENTS

Professional writers may use sentence fragments intentionally for emphasis or effect.

Creating Emphasis

A strange place it was, that place where the world began. A place of incredible happenings, splendours and revelations, despairs like multitudinous pits of isolated hells. A place of shadow-spookiness, inhabited by the unknowable dead. A place of jubilation and of mourning, horrible and beautiful.

—Margaret Laurence, "Where the World Began" in *Heart of a Stranger* (Toronto: McClelland & Stewart, 1976).

Making Transitions

Now for the con side.

In Exclamations

Not bloody likely!

Answering Questions

And should we go along with this position? Under no circumstances.

Advertising

Proven effective.

Many instructors do not accept sentence fragments, even intentional ones, in formal writing. Fragments may be acceptable in less-formal writing contexts, such as an informal personal essay or an article for a campus newspaper. Even in contexts where they are permitted, do not overuse sentence fragments.

10-2: COMMA SPLICES AND FUSED SENTENCES

Incorrectly joining two or more independent clauses within a sentence is a common writing error. An independent (or main) clause contains at least a subject and a verb, and the clause can stand on its own as a separate grammatical unit. When two independent clauses appear in a single sentence, they must be joined in one of two ways.

1. Using a comma and one of the seven coordinating conjunctions (*and, but, for, nor, or, so, yet*)
2. With a semicolon or other acceptable punctuation such as a dash or a colon

Fused sentences (also known as run-on sentences) or **comma splices** occur when two independent clauses are incorrectly joined within the same sentence.

FUSED SENTENCES

In a fused sentence, no punctuation or coordinating conjunction appears between the two independent clauses (IC).

IC IC

Canada's most famous racing ship is the *Bluenose* it was primarily designed to fish the Atlantic coast.

The first independent clause in this fused sentence is *Canada's most famous racing ship is the* Bluenose. The second independent clause is *it was primarily designed to fish the Atlantic coast.*

COMMA SPLICES

In a sentence that contains a comma splice, the independent clauses are joined (or spliced) with commas and no coordinating conjunction.

× Canada's most famous racing ship is the *Bluenose*, it was primarily designed to fish the Atlantic coast.

Often writers use conjunctive adverbs in place of coordinating conjunctions and, in doing so, create comma splice errors. A coordinating conjunction is one of these seven words: *and, but, or, nor, for, so,* and *yet.* A conjunctive adverb, on the other hand, is a word such as *furthermore, however,* or *moreover.* However, merely placing the word *however* and commas between the two independent clauses does *not* correct a comma splice error.

Comma Splice Involving Conjunctive Adverb

× Canada's most famous racing ship is the *Bluenose*, however, it was primarily designed to fish the Atlantic coast.

IDENTIFYING FUSED SENTENCES OR COMMA SPLICES IN YOUR WRITING

Use the following checklist to determine if a sentence is fused or is a comma splice.

- The sentence contains two independent clauses.
  - ❑ NO. Neither of the errors applies.
  - ❑ YES. *Proceed to the next question.*

- The independent clauses are joined by a comma and a coordinating conjunction.
  - ❑ YES. The clauses are correctly joined.
  - ❑ NO. *Proceed to the next question.*
- The independent clauses are joined by a semicolon or other acceptable punctuation, such as a colon or a dash.
  - ❑ YES. The clauses are correctly joined.
  - ❑ NO. *Use one of the revision strategies provided in the next section to correct the fused sentence or comma splice.*

STRATEGIES FOR CORRECTING FUSED SENTENCES OR COMMA SPLICES

You have four major options for correcting fused sentences or comma splices.

1. Add a comma and a coordinating conjunction (*and, but, for, nor, or, so, yet*)

   Canada's most famous racing ship is the *Bluenose,* yet it was primarily designed to fish the Atlantic coast.

2. Add a semicolon or other appropriate punctuation, such as a colon or a dash.

   Canada's most famous racing ship is the *Bluenose;* it was primarily designed to fish the Atlantic coast.

   OR

   Canada's most famous racing ship is the *Bluenose;* however, it was primarily designed to fish the Atlantic coast.

3. Revise the sentence to subordinate one of the clauses.

   Even though Canada's most famous racing ship is the *Bluenose,* it was primarily designed to fish the Atlantic coast.

4. Turn each independent clause into a separate complete sentence.

   Canada's most famous racing ship is the *Bluenose*. It was primarily designed to fish the Atlantic coast.

10-2A: REVISION WITH COORDINATING CONJUNCTION

A comma must precede the coordinating conjunction (*and, but, for, nor, or, so, yet*).

, but
It was minus 30 degrees with a wind chill factor‸ I still had to walk my dogs.

and
Mordecai Richler was a fine novelist,‸ he was also an amusing essayist.

10-2B: REVISION WITH SEMICOLON OR COLON

Use a semicolon without a conjunction if the relationship between the two independent clauses is very clear.

> The results of the chemistry experiment were disappointing; our attempt to turn salad dressing into fine cognac had failed miserably.

Use a semicolon and a comma with independent clauses that are joined with a conjunctive adverb or transitional phrase, such as the following:

also	as a result	besides
consequently	conversely	for example
for instance	furthermore	in addition
in fact	meanwhile	moreover
nonetheless	next	on the other hand
otherwise	similarly	subsequently
then	therefore	thus

> Margaret Atwood is Canada's foremost living novelist; furthermore, she is among our leading poets.

Use a colon if the first independent clause introduces the second.

> The requests are thorough and varied: a chicken or rabbit will be skinned, boned, quartered, shredded, turned into patties, prepared for stew, the liver for this, the kidney for that.

10-2C: REVISION BY SEPARATING SENTENCES

This option for correcting fused sentence and comma splices is usually the most effective, since it provides the most revision choices. You will first need to decide which of the independent clauses you would like to emphasize.

When the ,
~~The~~ ‸family visited Niagara Falls‸ we enjoyed visiting the wax museum, playing mini-golf, and taking pictures of the falls.

The rules of hockey developed in the 1870s~~, they~~ stipulated ^that there be nine players on a team instead of six as there are today.

~~There~~ *Since there* is a smog alert in south central Ontario, people with breathing difficulties are not supposed to go outside.

10-2D: REVISION BY RESTRUCTURING

Since the clauses in fused sentences and comma splices are independent, they can stand on their own as separate grammatical units.

Those who run for office are required to speak~~, the~~ *. These* speeches must be no longer than five minutes in length.

There is one council member from each region ~~the~~ *. The* chairperson is elected by the council members.

10-3: SUBJECT–VERB AGREEMENT

Every sentence has a subject (stated or implied) and a verb. **Subject–verb agreement** refers to the relationship between the subject and the verb.

In the present tense, verbs must agree with subjects in two ways.

1. In **number**. Number means the subject can be singular (e.g., *I*) or plural (e.g., *we*).
2. In **person**. Person can be first person (*I, we*), second person (*you*) or third person (*she, he, it, or they*).

If the verb is a regular verb and the subject is in the third-person singular, use the -*s* (or -*es*) form of the verb.

Amir works for his godfather.

His godfather stresses the importance of being on time.

PRESENT TENSE FORMS OF *WORK*

	SINGULAR	PLURAL
First Person	I *work*	we *work*
Second Person	you *work*	you *work*
Third person	she/he/it *works*	they *work*

Notice how the following irregular verbs achieve subject–verb agreement.

PRESENT-TENSE FORMS OF *DO*	
I *do*	we *do*
you *do*	you *do*
she/he/it *does*	they *do*

PRESENT-TENSE FORMS OF *HAVE*	
I *have*	we *have*
you *have*	you *have*
she/he/it *has*	they *have*

The verb *to be* has different forms for the present and past tense.

PRESENT-TENSE FORMS OF *BE*	
I *am*	we *are*
you *are*	you *are*
she/he/it *is*	they *are*

PAST-TENSE FORMS OF *BE*	
I *was*	we *were*
you *were*	you *were*
she/he/it *was*	they *were*

Often, if you have been speaking or writing English for a long time or know it well, problems with subject–verb agreement will be obvious to your ear or eye. For example, the sentence *James look good in his new tuxedo* immediately sounds or looks incorrect. It is obvious that the subject and verb do not agree. The sentence should be *James looks good*.

However, some subject–verb agreement problems are more difficult to spot. A number of English sentence constructions make the subject difficult to identify—often the subject is located far from the verb—and, as a result, it is easy to make verb-agreement mistakes. Information in the following section will help you to avoid the most common subject–verb agreement problems.

10-3A: WORDS BETWEEN SUBJECT AND VERB

Occasionally the modifying words between the sentence subject and verb include a noun, which might be mistaken for the subject. As a result, some writers use a verb that does not agree with the actual subject.

When evaluating any sentence for subject–verb agreement, in your mind, delete any modifying elements, such as prepositional phrases, so that only the sentence subject and verb remain. Then, assess whether or not the subject and verb agree. You might consider drawing an arrow to connect the subject with the verb, as has been done in the example below.

> The first ten minutes of a blind date are the most frightening.

> practise
> The women in my residence ~~practises~~ kung fu for hours every day.

The subject of the sentence above is *women*, not *residence*. The sentence verb is *practise*. Since the subject is in the third-person plural, the correct verb form is *practise,* not *practises.*

> is
> The objective in both cases ~~are~~ to give the students hands-on experience dealing with real-life situations.

The subject of the sentence is *objective,* not *cases*. The sentence verb is a form of the verb *to be*. The subject, *objective,* is in the third-person singular. To be correct, the verb form should be is, not *are.*

Phrases beginning *along with, as well as, in addition to,* and *together with* do not change the number of the subject because they are not really part of the subject. They are prepositional phrases used to modify the subject only.

> The prime minister, along with the cabinet, was photographed in the glamour shot.

The prime minister is the main subject of the sentence. If the writer had wanted to emphasize both the prime minister and the cabinet, he or she might have structured the sentence as follows: *The prime minister and the cabinet were photographed in the glamour shot.*

10-3B: SUBJECTS WITH *AND*

A compound subject contains two or more independent subjects joined by *and*. The compound subject requires a plural verb.

> Tina and Mauri were inseparable.

> The American bulldog's unforgettable face and amazing athletic ability
> have
> ~~has~~ helped to make Harley a star of advertising media.

However, when the parts of the subject refer to a single person or idea, they require a singular verb.

Rice and tomato is a San Francisco treat.

Spaghetti and clam sauce has been a favourite in our house for years.

The pronoun *each* is singular and requires a singular verb, even if the subjects it precedes are joined by *and*.

Each woman and man is allowed one vote.

10-3C: SUBJECTS WITH *OR* OR *NOR*

When a compound subject is joined by *or* or *nor*, make the verb agree with the part of the subject nearer to the verb.

Neither the tour guide nor his passengers know if the CN Tower is the world's tallest building.

Either the Beatles or Elvis Presley has had the most gold albums.

If my aunt or my cousins ~~is~~ are available, they will come to the quilting bee.

Neither the cabinet members nor the prime minister ~~are~~ is going to wave to the crowd.

10-3D: INDEFINITE PRONOUNS

An **indefinite pronoun** refers to an unspecified person or thing. The following are indefinite pronouns:

all	either	everybody	some
anybody	neither	everyone	somebody
anyone	nothing	everything	someone
anything	nobody	one	something
each	no one	none	

Even though many indefinite pronouns seem to refer to more than one person or thing, most require a singular verb. Note especially that *each*, *either*, and words ending in *-body* and *-one* are singular.

Everybody from our class was at the nudist colony.

smells
Something in the garage ~~smell~~ fishy.

pays
Everyone in our house ~~pay~~ bills on time.

NEITHER *AND* NONE

When used alone, the indefinite pronouns *neither* and *none* require singular verbs.

Neither is correct.

Of the guests who were sent RSVP invitations, none has deigned to respond.

When prepositional phrases with plurals follow the indefinite pronouns *neither* and *none,* in some cases a plural or singular verb may be used. However, it is best to treat *neither* and *none* consistently as singular.

Neither of those flattering adjectives applies to my parents.

None of these programs offers bonus air miles.

INDEFINITE PRONOUNS THAT CAN BE SINGULAR OR PLURAL

A few indefinite pronouns, such as *all, any, more, most, none,* and *some,* can be singular or plural, depending on the noun or pronoun to which they refer.

Singular: All of the money is in a Swiss bank account.

Plural: All of his accounts are frozen because of the terrorist connection.

In the first example, *money* is a singular noun, so a singular verb is required. In the second example, *accounts* is a plural noun, so a plural verb is required.

10-3E: COLLECTIVE NOUNS

A collective noun names a class or a group of people or things. Some examples of collective nouns include *band, committee, family, group, jury,* and *team.*

Use a singular verb with the collective noun when you want to communicate that the group is acting as a unit.

> The band agrees that it needs a new drummer.

> has
> The first-year law class ~~have~~ a test on Monday.

The *class* is considered a single unit, and individual action is not important to the sentence meaning. Therefore, a singular verb is required.

Use a plural verb when you want to communicate that members of the group are acting independently.

> The original band have gone on to pursue solo careers and spend time in rehabilitation centres.

> have
> The first-year law class ~~*has*~~ their fingerprints on file.

Each member of the class has his or her fingerprints on file.

Sometimes it is possible to better capture the idea of individual action by recasting the sentence with a plural noun.

> The original band members have gone on to pursue solo careers and spend time in rehabilitation centres.

DECIDING WHETHER TO TREAT NUMBER *AS A SINGULAR OR PLURAL*

If the collective noun *number* is preceded by *the,* treat it as a singular noun.

> The number of ways to cheat death is increasing.

If *number* is preceded by *a,* treat it as a plural.

> A number of Scrabble players have gotten a triple word score.

UNITS OF MEASUREMENT

Use a singular verb when the unit of measurement is used collectively, that is, when the thing described by the noun cannot be counted.

> One-half of the fat in those French fries is unsaturated.

Use a plural verb when the unit of measurement refers to individual persons or things that can be counted.

Only one-half of your promises are likely to be kept.

10-3F: SUBJECT AFTER VERB

Most often the verb follows the subject in sentences. However, in certain cases, the verb may come before the subject, making it difficult to evaluate subject–verb agreement.

EXPLETIVE CONSTRUCTIONS

Expletive constructions include phrases such as *there is, there are, it is,* and *it was.* When these phrases appear at the beginning of a sentence, the verb often precedes the subject.

There are significant differences among the pop stars of the '60s.

INVERTING SENTENCE ORDER

To achieve sentence variety, you may from time to time wish to invert traditional subject–verb order. Ensure that when you do this, you check that the subject and the verb agree.

are
Nestled on the couch ~~is~~ a beautiful black malamute and a spectacular red setter.

The compound subject, *a beautiful black malamute and a spectacular red setter*, requires a plural verb.

10-3G: SUBJECT COMPLEMENT

A **subject complement** is a noun or adjective that follows a linking verb and renames or describes the sentence subject, as in *Elvis Presley is a cult figure.* (See 9-2b.) Because of its relationship to the subject, the complement can often be mistaken for the subject and result in subject–verb agreement errors.

is
The socialite's central concern ~~are~~ facial lines.

The subject of the sentence is *concern*, which is singular. If the subject is singular, the sentence requires a singular verb. The plural *lines* is the complement.

are
The advice column and the comics ~~is~~ all I read in the newspaper.

The subject of the sentence is *the advice column and the comics*. Since it is plural, it requires a plural verb.

10-3H: WITH RELATIVE PRONOUNS

WHO, WHICH, *AND* THAT

A relative pronoun such as *who, which,* or *that* usually introduces an adjective clause that modifies the subject. The relative pronoun must agree with its antecedent. The antecedent is the noun or pronoun to which the relative pronoun refers. Thus, the verb in the adjective clause must agree with the antecedent.

> The wealthy industrialist <u>who</u> donates money to the food bank expects a tax deduction.

The singular noun *industrialist* is the antecedent of *who*. The verb *donates* must then be singular.

CONSTRUCTIONS USING ONE OF THE *AND* THE ONLY ONE OF THE

Subject–verb agreement mistakes are often made with relative pronouns when the sentence contains *one of the* or *the only one of the*.

Generally, use a plural verb with constructions containing *one of the*.

> The stiletto heel is one of the styles of footwear <u>that</u> ~~causes~~ cause a lot of medical problems.

The antecedent of *that* is *styles*, not *heel* or *footwear*. Since the antecedent is plural, to agree, the verb *cause* must also be plural.

Generally, use a singular verb with constructions containing *the only one of the*.

> The roller coaster is the only one of the rides <u>that</u> ~~are~~ is worth the price.

The antecedent of *that* is *one*, not *rides*. Since the antecedent is singular, to agree, the verb must also be singular: *is*.

10-3I: PLURAL FORM, SINGULAR MEANING

Some words ending in -ics or -s are singular in meaning, even though they may seem plural in appearance. These words include *athletics, economics, ethics, physics, politics, statistics, mathematics, measles, mumps,* and *news*. Nouns such as these generally require a singular verb.

> <u>The news</u> ~~were~~ was encouraging.

When nouns such as *mathematics, physics,* and *statistics* refer to a particular item of knowledge, as opposed to the collective body of knowledge, they are treated as plural.

Environment Canada statistics reveal that the area experienced record amounts of smog.

10-3J: TITLES AND WORDS AS WORDS

A work referred to by its title is treated as a singular entity, even if the title includes a plural word.

deals
Dog Days ~~deal~~ with the hilarious consequences of Peter's disenchantment with his job.

refers
In this report, "illegal aliens" ~~refer~~ to people who enter the country without following prescribed immigration procedures.

10-4: OTHER PROBLEMS WITH VERBS

The verb communicates vital information in any sentence, often by indicating what is occurring, what has occurred, or what will occur. For writers, there are several major potential trouble spots relating to verbs. You'll know from the previous section that one common problem is making sure that a sentence's subject and verb agree. Unfortunately, there are other areas where writers frequently experience problems with verb usage. Some of these potential trouble spots include the following:

- irregular verbs forms (such as *drink, drank, drunk*)
- *lie* and *lay*
- -*s* (or -*es*) endings with verbs
- -*ed* endings
- omitted verbs
- verb tenses
- the subjunctive mood
- the active versus the passive voice

Fortunately, information, models, and guidelines in this section will help you to avoid common verb problems in these areas. You might flip through the section to obtain a general sense of how its contents can help you meet your particular writing goals.

If your first language is not English, you may also wish to consult 15-2, which offers advice on working with verbs in English.

10-4A: IRREGULAR VERBS

With the exception of the verb *be,* English verbs have five forms. These forms are shown below in brief sample sentences using the regular verb *talk* and the irregular verb *ring*.

Base (Simple) Form:	Today I *(talk, ring)*.
Past Tense:	Yesterday I *(talked, rang)*.
Perfect:	I *(have talked, have rung)* many times in the past.
Progressive:	I *(am talking, am ringing)* at this moment.
-s Form:	She/he/it *(talks, rings)*.

With regular verbs, such as *talk*, the past tense and past participle verb forms are created by adding *-ed* or *-d* to the **base**, or simple, form of the verb. As you can see, this pattern is not followed for the irregular verb *ring*. In fact, many writers mix up the past tense and past participle of irregular verb forms, creating non-standard English sentences.

Non-standard: Many have rang the old church bell.

Standard: Many have rung the old church bell.

Non-standard English is language other than edited English. You may encounter and use it in very informal speaking contexts, and also in much modern literature, but it is not acceptable in formal, academic writing and speaking contexts. Standard English should be used in all formal writing and speaking situations.

CHOOSING STANDARD ENGLISH VERB FORMS

PAST TENSE FORM

Past tense verbs are used to communicate action that happened completely in the past. These verbs do not require helping verbs forms such as *was* or *were*.

> Yesterday I laughed at Donna's joke.

PAST PARTICIPLE FORM

The past participle always requires a helping verb. For the perfect tenses, these helping verbs could be *has, have,* or *had*. For the passive voice, the helping verbs are *be, am, is, are, was, were, being,* or *been*. (For a complete list of helping verbs, see 10-4e.)

Past Tense:	Last May I paid the first installment on our big-screen television set.
Past Participle:	Since that time I have paid two more installments.

HOW DO I CHOOSE?

When you want to choose the standard English verb form for formal writing, first check to see if the verb is irregular. See if it is listed on the chart of common irregular verbs on pages 279 to 283. If the verb in your sentence does not require a helping verb, select the appropriate past tense verb. If the verb does require a helping verb, use the past participle form listed in the chart. Of course, regular verbs will follow the pattern outlined above for the regular verb *talk*.

> Yesterday we were ~~shook~~ shaken by a violent tremor.

> At the pep rally I ~~sung~~ sang victory songs.

> According to the insurance agent, the windshield was ~~broke~~ broken before the accident.

> On the weekend, my grandfather ~~swum~~ swam one length of the pool.

COMMON IRREGULAR VERBS

The three-column chart below lists many of the more common irregular verbs in the base (simple), past-tense, and past-participle forms. When composing a sentence or editing your work, find the relevant verb in the first column, then determine if you have used the correct past-tense or past-participle form. If you cannot find the verb in the chart, check in a good Canadian dictionary that lists irregular verb forms.

Common Irregular Verbs

BASE (SIMPLE) FORM	PAST TENSE	PAST PARTICIPLE
arise	arose	arisen
awake	awoke, awaked	awaked, awoken
be	was, were	been
bear (carry)	bore	borne
bear (give birth)	bore	born
beat	beat	beaten, beat
become	became	become
begin	began	begun
bend	bent	bent
bet	bet	bet
bid	bid	bid
bind	bound	bound
bite	bit	bitten, bit
blow	blew	blown
break	broke	broken
bring	brought	brought

BASE (SIMPLE) FORM	PAST TENSE	PAST PARTICIPLE
build	built	built
burst	burst	burst
buy	bought	bought
catch	caught	caught
choose	chose	chosen
cling	clung	clung
come	came	come
cost	cost	cost
creep	crept	crept
cut	cut	cut
deal	dealt	dealt
dig	dug	dug
dive	dived, dove	dived
do	did	done
drag	dragged	dragged
draw	drew	drawn
dream	dreamed, dreamt	dreamed, dreamt
drink	drank	drunk
drive	drove	driven
eat	ate	eaten
fall	fell	fallen
feed	fed	fed
feel	felt	felt
fight	fought	fought
find	found	found
flee	fled	fled
fling	flung	flung
fly	flew	flown

BASE (SIMPLE) FORM	PAST TENSE	PAST PARTICIPLE
forbid	forbade, forbad	forbidden
forget	forgot	forgotten, forgot
freeze	froze	frozen
get	got	got, gotten
give	gave	given
go	went	gone
grow	grew	grown
hang (execute)	hanged	hanged
hang (suspend)	hung	hung
have	had	had
hear	heard	heard
hide	hid	hidden
hit	hit	hit
hold	held	held
hurt	hurt	hurt
keep	kept	kept
know	knew	known
lay (put)	laid	laid
lead	led	led
leave	left	left
lend	lent	lent
let (allow)	let	let
lie (recline)	lay	lain
light	lighted, lit	lighted, lit
lose	lost	lost
make	made	made
mean	meant	meant
pay	paid	paid

BASE (SIMPLE) FORM	PAST TENSE	PAST PARTICIPLE
prove	proved	proved, proven
put	put	put
quit	quit	quit
read	read	read
ride	rode	ridden
ring	rang	rung
rise (get up)	rose	risen
run	ran	run
say	said	said
see	saw	seen
seek	sought	sought
send	sent	sent
set (place)	set	set
shake	shook	shaken
shine	shone, shined	shone, shined
shoot	shot	shot
show	showed	shown, showed
shrink	shrank	shrunk, shrunken
sing	sang	sung
sink	sank	sunk
sit (be seated)	sat	sat
slay	slew	slain
sleep	slept	slept
slide	slid	slid
sling	slung	slung
sneak	sneaked	sneaked
speak	spoke	spoken
spend	spent	spent
spin	spun	spun

BASE (SIMPLE) FORM	PAST TENSE	PAST PARTICIPLE
spring	sprang	sprung
stand	stood	stood
steal	stole	stolen
sting	stung	stung
stink	stank, stunk	stunk
strike	struck	struck, stricken
strive	strove	striven
swear	swore	sworn
sweep	swept	swept
swim	swam	swum
swing	swung	swung
take	took	taken
teach	taught	taught
tear	tore	torn
tell	told	told
think	thought	thought
throw	threw	thrown
understand	understood	understood
wake	woke, waked	waked, woken
wear	wore	worn
win	won	won
wring	wrung	wrung
write	wrote	written

10-4B: *LIE* AND *LAY*

The forms of the verbs *lie* and *lay* are frequently confused.

1. *Lie,* meaning "to recline," is an intransitive verb, which means it cannot be followed by a direct object.

I am going to lie on the beach this afternoon.

2. *Lay*, meaning "to set down," is a transitive verb, which means it must be followed by a direct object.

Jack lay <u>his weary head</u> on the table.

LIE* AND *LAY

BASE (SIMPLE) FORM	PAST TENSE	PRESENT PARTICIPLE
lie	lay, lain	lying
lay	laid, laid	laying

DECIDING BETWEEN LIE *AND* LAY

Yesterday I ~~laid~~ lay in the hammock for a few hours.

Since the meaning is "to recline," the verb should be a form of *to lie*. The correct past-tense form of *lie* is *lay*.

The workers were ~~lying~~ laying the new tile floor in my bathroom.

Here the meaning is *lay*, meaning "to set down." The correct present participle of *lay* is *laying*.

The book has ~~laid~~ lain on my desk, unopened, for two days.

An additional meaning of *lie* is "to rest on a surface," so a form of the verb "to lie" is appropriate here. The past participle of *lie* is *lain*.

Other verb pairs that are easy to confuse are *sit/set* and *rise/raise*.

10-4C: *-S* ENDINGS

Use the -*s* (or -*es*) form of a verb in the present when the subject is third-person singular. Often, people who speak English dialects or who are just learning English omit verb endings such as -*s* (or -*es*) that are required in standard English. (See 10-3.)

I tell, you tell, we tell, you tell, they tell, visitors tell

BUT

Third-Person Singular
she tells, he tells, it tells, Jane tells, the parrot tells, everybody tells

As you can see, the third-person singular includes nouns such as *Jane* and *parrot;* the pronouns *she, he,* and *it;* and the indefinite pronoun *everybody.*

Although the -s verb ending may be omitted in some nonstandard English speech, it should *never* be omitted in standard English speaking and writing situations.

> Pre-production ~~involve~~ involves all the planning up to the day the camera operator ~~take~~ takes out the camera.

The sentence subject *pre-production* is third-person singular, so the verb must end in -s. In the subordinate clause, the subject is *camera operator,* which is also third-person singular and thus requires the -s ending, as in *takes.*

WHEN NOT TO ADD AN -S (-ES) VERB ENDING

If the subject is not third-person singular, *do not* add an -s (*-es*) verb ending.

> First, I ~~drafts~~ draft a script for the video.
>
> We often ~~serves~~ serve cheese and crackers instead of a dessert course.
>
> The bees ~~buzzes~~ buzz around my head whenever I go near their hive.

In the first sentence the subject is *I,* which is first-person singular; thus, the -s ending is not required. In the second sentence, the subject is *we* (second-person plural), and in the third sentence, the subject is *the bees* (third-person plural). Neither requires the -s verb ending.

USING HAS, DOES, *OR* DOESN'T *WITH A THIRD-PERSON SINGULAR SUBJECT*

> That expressway usually ~~have~~ has heavy traffic jams in the morning.
>
> ~~Do~~ Does anybody know what time it is?
>
> The stage manager ~~don't~~ doesn't think it is necessary to alter the backdrop.

10-4D: *-ED* ENDINGS

For regular verbs, the past tense and past participle are formed by adding *-ed* or *-d* to the base verb, as in *talked* and *have talked,* or *used* and *have used.*

Some speakers omit *-ed* endings from past-tense and past-participle regular verbs and also omit the endings from these words in their writing. Often it can be difficult to remember the *-ed* ending, since in some verbs it is not very distinctly pronounced (for example, *asked, learned, licensed, passed, practised, supposed to*).

Make sure to add the *-ed* or *-d* ending to the base (simple) verb for all regular past-tense or past-participle verbs.

PAST TENSE

The past tense indicates an action that has happened at a particular time in the past. To form the past tense of a regular verb, add *-ed* or *-d* to the base (simple) verb form.

> watched
> Last January we ~~watch~~ an opera by Verdi at the Four Seasons Centre.

> licensed
> Amazingly, the province ~~license~~ his great uncle to drive.

PAST PARTICIPLES

Past participles may be used in three ways.

1. TO FORM ONE OF THE PERFECT TENSES

In this case, the past participle follows *have, has,* or *had.*

> developed
> The scientist had ~~develop~~ a new technique for destroying cancer cells.

Had developed is the past-perfect tense (*had* followed by a past participle; here *developed*).

For more information on the perfect tenses, see page 289 in 10-4f.

2. TO FORM THE PASSIVE VOICE

In this case, the past participle follows *be, am, is, are, was, were, being,* or *been.*

> created
> The decorations were ~~create~~ by the social club.

Were created is in the passive voice. The subject, *the decorations,* is the receiver of the action. In the passive voice, a form of *be* (here *were*) is followed by the past participle (here *created*).

For more information on the passive voice, see 10-4h.

3. AS AN ADJECTIVE MODIFYING NOUNS OR PRONOUNS

> The medics carried the ~~weaken~~ weakened soldier to the field hospital.

Here the past participle *weakened* modifies the noun *soldier.*

For more information on using participles as adjectives, see 9-3b.

10-4E: OMITTED VERBS

In formal writing contexts, do not omit required linking verbs or helping (auxiliary) verbs.

LINKING VERBS

A linking verb is a main verb that links a subject with a subject complement (a word or words that renames or describes the subject). Linking verbs indicate a condition or state of being. They are often forms of the verb *be,* such as *am, was,* or *been.*

> After tracing the call, the police discovered that the caller was a fellow employee.

Some linking verbs appear in contractions, such as in *I'm* for *I am* or *it's* for *it is.* Especially in formal writing, do not leave out linking verbs.

For more information on linking verbs, see 9-2b.

HELPING, OR AUXILIARY, VERBS

A helping verb, also known as an auxiliary verb, is a form of *be, do, can, have, may, will, shall, could, would, might,* or *must* that combines with a main verb to express tone, and voice.

> Housing prices have escalated in recent months.

Like linking verbs, helping verbs can be contracted as in *she's going* or *they've been warned.* Especially in formal writing, do not leave out helping verbs.

For more information on helping verbs, see 9-1d.

If English is not your first language, you might consult the section on omitted verbs, 15-2i.

10-4F: TENSE

Tense indicates the time or duration of an action. The following section outlines some common writing problems associated with verb tenses and suggests strategies for avoiding these problems and ways of correcting them. One major problem connected with verb tense—shifts from one verb tense to another—is covered in detail in 12-1b. Before exploring tense problems in detail, it is important to understand English verb tenses.

OVERVIEW OF VERB TENSES

There are three basic verb tenses.

1. Present
2. Past
3. Future

Each tense has three forms, also known as aspects.

1. Simple
2. Perfect
3. Progressive

SIMPLE FORMS

The three simple tenses divide time into present, past, and future.

The **simple present tense** indicates something that happens regularly or in the present.

I wipe the counters.

The **simple past tense** indicates a completed action that happened at a particular time in the past.

She skated at the recreation centre yesterday.

The **simple future tense** indicates an action that will happen sometime in the future.

We will ask the neighbours to our housewarming party.

The table below provides the simple forms for the regular verb *to cook*, the irregular verb *to take*, and the irregular verb *to be*.

SIMPLE FORMS FOR ALL TENSES

SIMPLE PRESENT

Singular		***Plural***	
I	*cook, take, am*	we	*cook, take, are*
you	*cook, take, are*	you	*cook, take, are*
she/he/it	*cooks, takes, is*	they	*cook, take, are*

SIMPLE PAST

Singular		***Plural***	
I	*cooked, took, was*	we	*cooked, took, were*
you	*cooked, took, were*	you	*cooked, took, were*
she/he/it	*cooked, took, was*	they	*cooked, took, were*

SIMPLE FUTURE

I, you, she/he/it, we, they	*will cook, will take, will be*

PERFECT FORMS

There are perfect forms for present, past, and future tenses.

The **present perfect tense** indicates action that has happened in the past.

We have shovelled the driveway twice this morning.

The **past perfect tense** indicates an action that has been completed at some time in the past before another past action.

We had shovelled the driveway before the snowplow circled our street.

The **future perfect tense** indicates an action that will take place before some time in the future.

I will have finished carving the pumpkin before the little goblins arrive.

PERFECT FORMS FOR ALL TENSES

PRESENT PERFECT

I, you, we, they	*have cooked, have taken, have been*
she/he/it	*has cooked, has taken, has been*

PAST PERFECT

I, you, she/he/it, we, they	*had cooked, had taken, had been*

FUTURE PERFECT

I, you, she/he/it, we, they	*will have cooked, will have taken, will have been*

PROGRESSIVE FORMS

The progressive forms indicate that an action, occurrence, or state of being is ongoing, or progressive. This ongoing action can take place in the present, past, or future, and can be either completed or not yet completed (i.e., still going on). Progressive verb forms are created by combining the present participle and forms of the verb *to be* as a helping, or auxiliary, verb.

PROGRESSIVE FORMS

PRESENT PROGRESSIVE	
I	*am cooking, am taking, am going*
she/he/it	*is cooking, is taking, is going*
you, we, they	*are cooking, are taking, are going*
PAST PROGRESSIVE	
I, she/he/it	*was cooking, was taking, was going*
you, we, they	*were cooking, were taking, were going*
FUTURE PROGRESSIVE	
I, you, she/he/it, we, they	*will be cooking, will be taking, will be going*
PRESENT PERFECT PROGRESSIVE	
I, you, we, they	*have been cooking, have been taking, have been going*
she/he/it	*has been cooking, has been taking, has been going*
PAST PERFECT PROGRESSIVE	
I, you, she/he/it, we, they	*had been cooking, had been taking, had been going*
FUTURE PERFECT PROGRESSIVE	
I, you, she/he/it, we, they	*will have been cooking, will have been taking, will have been going*

Verbs that involve mental activity, such as *think*, *know*, and *imagine*, usually do not use progressive forms. (See 15-2b.)

OBSERVING SPECIAL USES OF THE PRESENT TENSE

As well as being used to indicate that something happens or can happen in the present, the present tense has several special uses in formal academic writing.

DISCUSSING CONTENT IN LITERARY WORKS

The **literary present tense** refers to the use of the present tense to discuss events that have happened in the past. Using the present tense to describe fictional events in novels, short stories, or films makes these events feel more immediate.

> seethes reaches
> In Todd Field's *In the Bedroom* the mother's grief ~~seethed~~ until it ~~reached~~ a boiling point.

GENERAL TRUTHS AND SCIENTIFIC PRINCIPLES

General truths and scientific principles should appear in the present tense.

> reduces
> According to mechanical advantage, a machine ~~reduced~~ the force necessary to move a load.

However, if a scientific principle has been disproved, the verb can be presented in the past tense.

> According to the early Greeks, the brain pumped blood through the body.

SUMMARIZING, PARAPHRASING, AND QUOTING

Often, to introduce ideas or support your own, you will need to present the views of another author. When summarizing, paraphrasing, or directly quoting an author's views as expressed in a non-literary work, use the present tense.

> contends
> John Stuart Mill ~~contended~~ that "genius can only breathe freely in an atmosphere of freedom."

Note that John Stuart Mill (1806–73) is no longer alive. The present tense is used to introduce an author's view, even if the author is dead.

Exception: If you are following the American Psychological Association style for in-text citation, use the past tense when the date and author's name are provided.

> G. Temple (1995) described the patient's way of transforming words and numbers into images.

USING THE PAST PERFECT TENSE CORRECTLY

The past perfect tense (i.e., the perfect form of the past tense) indicates an action that has been completed at some time in the past, before another action. The past perfect is formed by using the helping verb *had* before the past participle of a verb.

I had completed a draft of the essay before we learned about Britain's post-colonial involvement.

COMMON MISTAKES

1. Using the simple past tense when the sentence's meaning and grammar require the past perfect tense.

By the time I arrived at the station, the bus ~~left~~ had left.

Both actions took place in the past, but one took place before the other. The past perfect is used to indicate that one action was completed *(the bus had left)* before the other happened *(I arrived)*.

By the time the hikers came, we ^had cleared the trail.

The action of clearing the trail had been completed before the hikers arrived, so the past perfect tense is required.

2. Overusing the past perfect tense. Do not use the past perfect tense if two past actions in the sentence happened at the same time.

As the train approached the Zurich station, the conductor ~~had~~ arrived to check our tickets.

USING CORRECT TENSES WITH INFINITIVES AND PARTICIPLES

INFINITIVES

An infinitive is a verbal consisting of the simple verb form and, usually, *to*.

PRESENT TENSE INFINITIVE: Use the present tense infinitive (*to exercise, to fly*) to indicate action that takes place at the same time as, or later than, the action of the sentence's main verb.

Bert had tried to ~~have lost~~ lose weight before his vacation.

The action of the infinitive (*to lose*) took place at the same time or later than the action of the sentence verb (*had tried*).

PRESENT PERFECT INFINITIVE: The perfect form of the infinitive is created by placing the helping verb *to have* in front of the past participle (*to have exercised, to have flown*). Use the present perfect infinitive to indicate action that takes place before the action of the main sentence verb.

> have finished
> I would like to ~~finish~~ the paper on time.

The time of the main verb, *would like,* is the present. Since the paper should have been finished before the present, the present perfect infinitive is used.

PARTICIPLES

The tense of the participle is determined by the tense of the main sentence verb.

PRESENT PARTICIPLE: Use the present participle (*risking, making*) when the action occurs at the same time as that of the main sentence verb.

> Flying over British Columbia, Danielle spotted her hometown through the clouds.

The present participle is required since Danielle spotted her hometown at the same time as she was flying over British Columbia.

PAST PARTICIPLE OR PRESENT PERFECT PARTICIPLE: Use the past participle (*risked, made*) or the present perfect participle (*having risked, having made*) to indicate action that occurred before that of the main sentence verb.

> Made of cedar, the canoe floated well.

The making of the canoe took place before the canoe floated.

> Having invested all his money in a dot-com, Yuri lost it all when profits in the high-technology sector dramatically declined.

Yuri's investment took place before his unfortunate financial loss.

10-4G: MOOD

The mood of a verb indicates the manner of action. There are three moods of a verb: the **indicative**, the **imperative**, and the **subjunctive**. By using one of three verb moods, a writer can show how he or she views a thought or action. For instance, through his or her choice of mood, a writer can indicate if he or she is expressing an opinion or a wish.

The indicative mood states a fact or opinion or asks a question.

The library needs our assistance.

The imperative mood gives an order or a direction.

Be at the library by eight.

The subjunctive mood is used to express demands, recommendations, and requests in clauses using *that*. It is also used to express conditions that are contrary to fact or are wished for. Finally, it is seen in idiomatic expressions such as *be that as it may*. Note that the subjunctive mood appears more commonly in North American than in British usage. Many writers frequently use the subjunctive mood incorrectly.

FORMING THE SUBJUNCTIVE

To create the subjunctive mood with *that* clauses, use the base (simple) form of the verb (e.g., *come, decide, produce*). Do not change the verb to indicate whether the subject is singular or plural.

It is crucial that I be [not am] at the interview on time.

The judge requested that he produce [not produces] more evidence.

If you are employing the subjunctive to express a contrary-to-fact clause starting with *if* or to express a wish, use *were*, the past tense form of *be*. Do not use *was*.

I wish that I were [not was] seventeen again.

APPROPRIATE USES OF THE SUBJUNCTIVE

The subjunctive mood is used in the following writing situations:

- contrary-to-fact clauses beginning (usually) with *if* or *as if*
- contrary-to-fact clauses expressing a wish
- *that* clauses after verbs such as *ask, insist, recommend, request, require, suggest*, and *urge*
- idiomatic expressions such as *suffice it to say* or *be that as it may*

CONTRARY-TO-FACT CLAUSES BEGINNING WITH IF OR AS IF

In the subjunctive, use *were* to express a contrary-to-fact clause starting with *if* or *as if*.

were
If she ~~was~~ our class president, she would fight for the cause.

were
Denise acts as if Roger ~~was~~ her slave.

The *if* clauses express conditions that do not exist—they are contrary to fact; therefore, they require the subjunctive.

The subjunctive is not used when the *if* clause expresses a condition that does exist or may exist.

Not Contrary to Fact: If he gets a flight, he will cancel his bus ticket.

CONTRARY-TO-FACT CLAUSES EXPRESSING A WISH

In the subjunctive, use *were* to express a wish.

Formal (Writing): I wish that the reading material in Dr. Vavougis's medical office were better.

Note: In informal speech, people often use the indicative mood in place of the subjunctive.

Informal (Speech): I wish that the reading material in Dr. Vavougis's medical office was better.

In a formal writing context, when you need to express a wish, always use the subjunctive.

THAT CLAUSES AFTER VERBS SUCH AS *ASK, INSIST, RECOMMEND, REQUEST, REQUIRE, SUGGEST,* AND *URGE*

The following verbs can indicate a requirement or a request: *ask, insist, recommend, request, require, suggest,* and *urge*. These verbs often come before a clause starting with *that*. These sentences require the subjunctive. To form the subjunctive, use the base (simple) form of the verb whether the subject is singular or plural.

The memorandum requires that all employees are there.

It is suggested that the examination candidate presents himself or herself at 9:30 a.m.

The sentence is expressed in the subjunctive because it involves a request.

IDIOMS AND EXPRESSIONS SUCH AS *SUFFICE IT TO SAY*

The subjunctive mood is used in idioms and expressions such as the following:

as it were	be that as it may
come rain or shine	far be it from me
God be praised	suffice it to say

Suffice it to say, they concur.

10-4H: VOICE

Voice refers to whether the sentence subject is the actor performing the action communicated by the sentence verb or the receiver of that action. In the active voice the subject (S) performs the action, while in the passive voice the subject is acted upon. Only transitive verbs (TV)—those verbs requiring a direct object (DO)—can be active or passive.

ACTIVE VOICE

S TV DO
The guard took the prisoner to his cell.

PASSIVE VOICE

The passive voice consists of a helping, or auxiliary, verb (some form of *be*) plus the past participle, as in *was taken*.

S TV
The prisoner was taken to his cell by the guard.

For more information on the active and passive voice, see 9-2b.

CHANGING A SENTENCE FROM THE PASSIVE TO THE ACTIVE VOICE

In most cases, use the active voice in your academic writing. The active voice tends to be clearer and more concise, direct, powerful, and dramatic. Passives, by contrast, tend to be wordier, more awkward, and less direct. To change a sentence from the passive to the active voice, identify the sentence actor (who or what performs the main sentence action) and make that actor the sentence subject. Remember, most grammar checkers will point out passive voice very quickly, and you can then decide whether to make a change in wording.

Every spring, ~~gardens are planted by~~ millions of North American homeowners ^plant gardens^.

WHEN THE PASSIVE VOICE IS APPROPRIATE

Although the active voice is often preferable, the passive voice does have important functions. It is appropriate when the actor is unknown or unimportant, or when responsibility for an action should not or cannot be assigned.

The passive voice is often used in technical and scientific writing in which a process, as opposed to a person, is important.

> The solution is pumped through a special filter where harmful impurities are extracted.

When writing about historical events, you may wish to use the passive voice to avoid assigning blame for an action or to emphasize that a certain group was acted upon.

> During the 1950s in British Columbia's Kootenay region, Doukhobor parents were compelled to send their very young children to a residential school.

Do not always avoid the passive voice. It is, in many cases, appropriate. For information on how to transform the active voice to the passive, consult 15-2c.

10-5: PROBLEMS WITH PRONOUNS

A pronoun is a word that replaces a noun or another pronoun. Three major types of pronoun problems occur frequently in writing:

1. *Antecedent agreement problems:* The pronoun does not agree with the noun or pronoun to which it refers.
2. *Reference problems:* It is not clear to which noun or pronoun the pronoun refers.
3. *Case problems:* The case of a pronoun is its form in a particular sentence context—whether the pronoun functions as a subject, object, or a possessive. Writers sometimes confuse pronoun case. Two common pronoun case difficulties involve the following:
   a) When to use *I* instead of *me*, *he* instead of *him*, *they* instead of *them*, and so on (that is, the subjective and objective cases of personal pronouns)
   b) When to use *who* instead of *whom*

The following four sections provide guidance in identifying, avoiding, and—if necessary—correcting these types of pronoun errors.

10-5A: PRONOUN–ANTECEDENT AGREEMENT

The antecedent is the word the pronoun replaces. (*Ante* in Latin means *before.*) A pronoun must agree with its antecedent.

If the antecedent is singular, the pronoun that refers to it must also be singular.

The microbiologist adjusted his microscope.

Similarly, if the antecedent is plural, the pronoun must be plural.

The choir members opened their song books.

ESL Note

Pronouns like *he, she, his, her* and *its* agree in gender with their antecedents, not with the words they modify: *Lorna travelled with her* [not *his*] *chauffeur to Saskatoon.*

MAKING PRONOUNS AGREE WITH ANTECEDENTS THAT ARE INDEFINITE PRONOUNS

Indefinite pronouns do not refer to any specific person, thing, or idea:

another	everybody	no one
anybody	everyone	nothing
anyone	everything	one
anything	neither	somebody
each	nobody	someone
either	none	something

In formal English, treat indefinite pronouns as singular even though they may seem to have plural meanings.

Anyone who knows the answer should enter it using ~~their~~ his or her keyboard.

CORRECTING INDEFINITE-PRONOUN AGREEMENT PROBLEMS

Often when you are editing a piece of writing, you may find that you have used a plural pronoun to refer to a singular indefinite pronoun. In such instances, you might apply the follow strategies for correcting the pronoun agreement problem.

1. Change the plural pronoun to a singular, such as *he or she.*

> his or her
> When the airplane hit severe turbulence, everyone feared for ~~their~~ safety.

2. Make the pronoun's antecedent plural.

> the passengers
> When the airplane hit severe turbulence, ~~everyone~~ feared for their safety.

3. Recast the sentence to eliminate the pronoun agreement problem.

> safety was a common fear among all those on board
> When the airplane hit severe turbulence, ~~everyone feared for their safety~~.

Since the use of *his or her* can be awkward and wordy, especially if used repeatedly, you might consider correction strategies 2 and 3 as preferable alternatives. Do, however, be careful to use inclusive language when gender is involved.

GENERIC NOUNS

A **generic noun** names a typical member of a group, such as a typical *classroom teacher,* or a typical *dentist*. Generic nouns might appear to be plural; however, they are singular.

> Each Olympic athlete must sacrifice if he or she plans [not they plan] to win a gold medal.

If a plural pronoun incorrectly refers to a generic noun, there are three major ways to remedy the error. As you will notice, they are the same as those outlined above for correcting indefinite-pronoun agreement problems.

> he or she feels
> Although the average Canadian complains about overwork, ~~they feel~~ powerless to cut back.

> Canadians complain
> Although ~~the average Canadian complains~~ about overwork, they feel powerless to cut back.

> The but feels
> ~~While the~~ average Canadian complains about overwork~~, they feel~~ powerless to cut back.

COLLECTIVE NOUNS

A collective noun names a group of people or things. Examples of collective nouns include *audience, army, choir, class, committee, couple, crowd, faculty, family, group, jury, majority, number, pack,* and *team.*

IF THE COLLECTIVE NOUN REFERS TO A UNIT

Use the singular pronoun.

The audience stood and applauded to show its approval.

IF PARTS OF THE COLLECTIVE NOUN ACT INDIVIDUALLY

Use a plural pronoun.

The audience folded up their lawn chairs and left the park.

Often it is a good idea to emphasize that the antecedent is plural by adding a word, such as *members,* describing individuals within the group.

The audience members folded up their lawn chairs and left the park.

MAINTAIN SINGULAR OR PLURAL CONSISTENCY

Whether you treat the collective noun as singular or plural, ensure that you consistently treat references within the sentence as singular or plural respectively.

The faculty ~~have~~ has completed its review of courses for the upcoming term.

Its is a singular pronoun but *have* is a plural verb form. To be consistent, the verb should be changed to *has*. The sentence could also be revised to read: *The faculty have completed their review of courses for the upcoming term,* but in that case it might be preferable to add the word *members* after *faculty.*

COMPOUND ANTECEDENTS

TWO OR MORE ANTECEDENTS JOINED BY AND

Antecedents joined by *and* form a **compound antecedent** and require a plural pronoun whether the antecedents are plural or singular.

Dave and Michaela were hungry after their [not *his and her*] day of skiing in Whistler.

TWO OR MORE ANTECEDENTS CONNECTED BY *OR, NOR, EITHER . . . OR, NEITHER . . . NOR*

Make the pronoun agree with the nearest antecedent.

Either Melodie or the Chans will have their way.

Note: With a compound antecedent such as the one above, place the plural noun last to prevent the sentence from sounding awkward.

Neither the captain nor the other players could explain their lopsided defeat.

In a sentence with a compound antecedent in which one antecedent is masculine and the other is feminine, rewrite the sentence to avoid any gender problem.

Original: Either Michelle or Yuri will be selected to have his documentary previewed at the campus film festival.

Rewrite: The judges will select Michelle's or Yuri's documentary for a preview at the campus film festival.

10-5B: PRONOUN REFERENCE

A pronoun is a word that replaces a noun or another pronoun. Using pronouns allows you to avoid repeating nouns in speech and writing.

Once Jarod made the sandwich, he packed it in a brown bag.

The noun or pronoun that the pronoun replaces is its antecedent. Here the pronoun *he* clearly relates to the antecedent *Jarod,* and the pronoun *it* clearly relates to the antecedent *sandwich.*

However, when the relationship between the antecedent and the pronoun is ambiguous, implied, vague, or indefinite, the intended meaning can become unclear or completely lost to the reader.

AVOIDING AMBIGUITY ABOUT PRONOUN REFERENCE

When it is possible for a pronoun to refer to either one of two antecedents, the sentence is ambiguous.

?

Ambiguous: Franz told his father that his car needed a new transmission.

In this sentence the second possessive pronoun *his* could refer to *Franz* or *his father*: is Franz talking about his father's car or his own car?

To eliminate the ambiguity, either repeat the clarifying antecedent or rewrite the sentence.

> ***Option 1:*** Franz told his father that his father's car needed a new transmission.
>
> ***Option 2:*** Franz said, "Dad, your car needs a new transmission."

AVOIDING IMPLIED ANTECEDENTS

The reader should be able to clearly understand the noun antecedent of any pronoun you use. This antecedent must be stated and not implied or merely suggested.

> Before the raging fire spread too close to nearby farms, ~~they~~ the residents were ordered to leave their homes.

Although in the original sentence it is implied that the occupants of the farms were the ones ordered to leave, it is not explicitly stated. The pronoun *they* has no clear antecedent.

Make sure that antecedents refer to nouns present in, or near, the sentence.

> In ~~Naomi Wolf's~~ *The Beauty Myth*, ~~she~~ Naomi Wolf explores the relationship between gender and work.

In the original sentence, it is not clear who is doing the exploring. The wording allows the possibility that it is not *Naomi Wolf*, but a contributor to her book.

AVOIDING VAGUENESS WHEN USING PRONOUNS

Pronouns such as *this, that, which,* and *it* should refer clearly to a specific noun antecedent and not large groups of words expressing ideas or situations.

> The international figure skating organization agreed to a major overhaul of the judging process; however, ~~it~~ the change took time.

A spot forecast may state that a temperature range for a specific canyon in the forest will be between 25 and 30 degrees; the humidity between 12 and 14 percent, and the winds 15 kilometres an hour.

All of these details interest
~~This interests~~ firefighters.

AVOIDING INDEFINITE USE OF IT, THEY, *OR* YOU

The pronouns *it*, *they*, and *you* must have clear, definite antecedents.

USING IT

Do not use the pronoun it indefinitely (e.g., "In this book it says . . .").

~~In~~ Chapter 23 of the textbook ~~it~~ states that one of the most important factors in transforming Canadian culture was the change in immigration patterns.

USING THEY

Never use *they* without a definite antecedent.

the director, screenwriter(s), and actors
In a typical Hollywood movie, ~~they~~ manipulate the audience's emotions.

USING YOU

In formal writing, the use of *you* is acceptable when you are addressing the reader directly.

If you do not want the beeper on, select OFF, and if you want it loud, select HIGH.

In formal writing, do not use *you* as an indefinite pronoun.

one
In ancient Greece ~~you~~ dropped a mussel shell into a certain jar to indicate that a defendant was guilty.

10-5C: PRONOUN CASE (*I* VS. *ME*, ETC.)

Case refers to the form a pronoun takes according the function of that pronoun in a sentence. In English there are three cases.

1. The **subjective case** indicates that the pronoun functions as a subject or a subject complement.
2. The **objective case** indicates that the pronoun functions as the object of a preposition or a verb.

3. The **possessive case** indicates that the pronoun shows ownership.

PRONOUN CASES

SUBJECTIVE	OBJECTIVE	POSSESSIVE
I	me	my, mine
we	us	our, ours
you	you	your, yours
she/he/it	her/him/it	her/his/its, hers
they	them	their, theirs

The remainder of this section will help you to clearly distinguish between the subjective and the objective case; it also explains how to avoid common pronoun case errors. The final part of the section explains common uses of pronouns in the possessive case.

SUBJECTIVE CASE

The subjective case (*I, we, you, she/he/it, they*) must be used when the pronoun functions as a subject or as a subject complement.

As a Subject

Tony and I split the cost of the video.

A subject complement is a noun or adjective that follows a linking verb and renames or describes the sentence subject. Since the way pronouns are used in the subjective case often sounds quite different than the way you might use pronouns in informal speech, subjective case pronouns as subject complements frequently cause writing difficulties.

As a Subject Complement

The students who did the most work are Ivan and ~~her~~ she.

In all formal writing, ensure that you use the subjective pronoun case when the pronoun is part of the subjective complement.

The woman Anatole married is she.

The subject complement of the subject *woman* is the pronoun *she*.

If the construction sounds too unnatural, you may wish to recast the sentence.

She is the <u>woman</u> Anatole married.

OBJECTIVE CASE

An objective case pronoun (*me, us, you, her/him/it, them*) is used when the pronoun functions in any of the following ways:

- as a direct object

  The instructor asked her to read the poem.

- as an indirect object

  The invigilator gave pencils to Sam, Duncan, and me.

- as the object of a preposition

  Just between you and me, the Russian's routine was superior.

IN COMPOUND SUBJECTS AND OBJECTS

A compound subject or a **compound object** includes more than one pronoun.

Compound Subject
She and I went to the multiplex to see a movie.

Compound Object
The park proposal surprised her and me.

The fact that the subject or object is compound does not affect the case of the pronoun. However, compound structures often cause writers to confuse pronoun case.

To determine if you have selected the correct pronoun case, try mentally blocking out the compound structure and focusing on the pronoun in question. Then, decide if the pronoun case you have selected is correct.

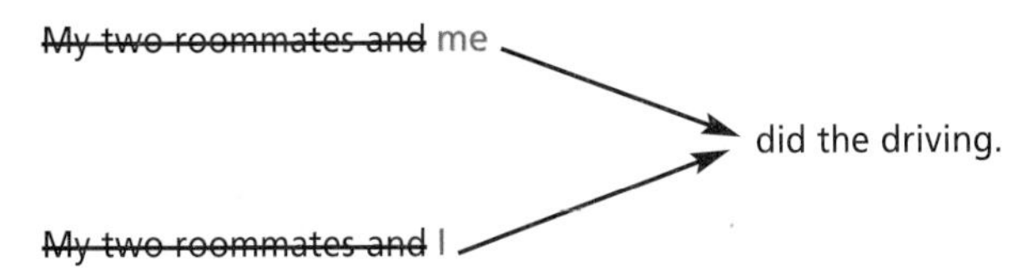

You would say *I did the driving* so the correct choice for the compound is *My two roommates and I did the driving.*

> In spite of our difficulties, my uncle and ~~me~~ *I* had a wonderful vacation in Mexico.

You wouldn't say *me had a wonderful vacation*, so the correct choice is *my uncle and I*. The pronoun is part of the subject of the sentence, so the subjective case is required.

> After the class, the librarian gave detentions to Rachel and ~~I~~ *me*.

You wouldn't say *gave detentions to I*, so the correct choice is *to Rachel and me*. The pronoun is the indirect object, so the objective case is required.

Resist the impulse to use a reflexive pronoun such as *myself* or *himself* when you are uncertain about the pronoun case.

> The contest organizers sent the entry forms to Del and ~~myself~~ *me*.

In this sentence, *Del* and *me* are the indirect objects of the verb *sent*, so the objective case (*me*) is correct.

AS APPOSITIVES

An appositive is a noun or noun phrase that renames a noun, noun phrase, or pronoun. When a pronoun functions as an appositive, it has the same function, and hence the same case, as the noun or pronoun it renames.

> Three members of the debating team—Clara, Michael, and ~~me~~ *I*—were mentioned in the article.

Clara, Michael, and I is an appositive for the sentence subject *three members*. As a result, the subjective case of the pronoun is required.

> Let's you and ~~I~~ *me* take the weekend off and go to the St. Jacob's market.

You and me is an appositive to *us* (*let's* is a contraction of *let us*). *Us* is the objective of the verb *let*; therefore, the objective case of the pronoun is required.

WHEN WE *OR* US *PRECEDES A NOUN*

Sometimes you may need to decide whether *we* or *us* should come before a noun or noun phrase. Mentally block out the noun so that only the pronoun remains. Then, decide which pronoun case is correct.

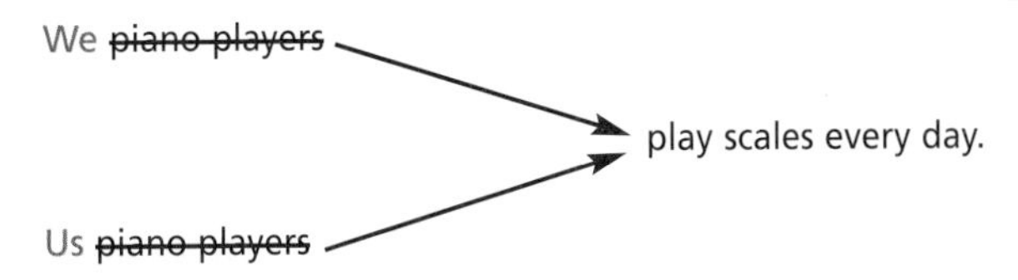

We is correct since a subjective case of the pronoun is required.

Follow the same procedure when considering pronouns that function as sentence objects.

> The teacher yells at ~~we~~ us banjo players during every practice.

You wouldn't say *The teacher yells at we*. The word *us* functions here as an indirect object, so the objective case is most appropriate.

COMPARISONS USING THAN OR AS

When making comparisons using *than* or *as*, writers frequently leave out words because these words are clearly understood by readers.

> Last year Bill Gates made more money *than* I ~~made~~.

The case of the pronoun is determined by its function in the implied part of the sentence, which has been omitted. To determine the correct pronoun case in a sentence that uses *than* or *as* to make a comparison, supply the implied or missing part of the sentence. Then, decide if the pronoun case is correct.

> The groom is a full metre taller than ~~her~~ she.

When the omitted words are supplied, the sentence reads: *The groom is a full metre taller than she [is]. She* is the subject of the verb *is*; therefore, the subjective case of the pronoun is required.

> My late grandmother left my cousin as many family heirlooms as ~~I~~ me.

When the omitted words are supplied, the sentence reads: *My late grandmother left my cousin as many family heirlooms as [she left] me. Me* is the indirect object of *left*.

WITH INFINITIVES

The infinitive is the base (simple) form of a verb, usually following *to*, as in *to jump*. Both the subject and the object of an infinitive are in the objective case.

As the Subject of an Infinitive

The minister asked her [not *she*] to sing at the wedding.

As the Object of an Infinitive

Club members decided to elect him.

POSSESSIVE CASE WHEN MODIFYING A GERUND

A **gerund** is a form of a verb that ends in *-ing* and is used as a noun; for example, *Fencing is my favourite sport*. Use a pronoun in the possessive case (*my, our, your, her/his/its, their*) to modify a gerund or gerund phrases.

his
The physical trainer disapproved of ~~him~~ eating bacon before workouts.

Nouns as well as pronouns can modify gerunds; as with pronouns, you must use the possessive case of the noun. The possessive is formed by adding an apostrophe and *-s* to the end of the noun.

Wayne's smoking is the cause of his bad breath.

Wayne's
The physical trainer disapproved of ~~Wayne~~ eating bacon before workouts.

For more information on possessives, see 11-4a.

10-5D: *WHO* AND *WHOM*

Who and *whom* are pronouns. *Who* is the subjective case; it must only be used for subjects and subject complements. *Whom* is the objective case; it must only be used for objects.

Who and *whom* are used as interrogative pronouns to open questions. They are also used as relative pronouns, to introduce subordinate clauses.

AS INTERROGATIVE PRONOUNS OPENING QUESTIONS

To decide whether to use *who* or *whom*, you must first determine the pronoun's function within the question. Does the interrogative pronoun function as a subject or subject complement, or as an object? Determine whether the subjective or objective case is required by recasting the question as a statement—that is, giving a possible answer to the question. Temporarily substitute a subjective case pronoun, such as *he*, or an objective case pronoun, such as *him*.

Who
~~Whom~~ commanded the coalition forces during the war in Afghanistan?

A possible answer would be *He commanded the coalition forces. Him commanded* would not work. *He* is the subject of the verb *commanded*. Therefore, the subjective case is required, and *who* is the correct interrogative pronoun.

> Whom
> ~~Who~~ did the human resources manager interview?

A possible answer to the question would be *The human resources manager interviewed her. Interviewed she* would not work. *Her* would be the direct object of the verb *did interview*. Therefore, the objective case is required, and *whom* is the correct interrogative pronoun.

AS RELATIVE PRONOUNS INTRODUCING SUBORDINATE CLAUSES

Use *who* and *whoever* as relative pronouns for subjects and use *whom* and *whomever* for objects. When deciding which pronoun to use, you must determine whether the relative pronoun functions as a subject or object within the subordinate clause. A good technique to employ when making this decision is to mentally block off the subordinate clause you are considering.

> whoever
> The Nobel Prize for Literature is presented to [~~whomever~~ has made the most significant contribution to literature over the course of a writing career.]

When determining the correct relative pronoun, consider only the subordinate clause. Hence, the main clause (*The Nobel Prize for Literature is presented to*) is mentally set aside. The relative pronoun of the subordinate clause is the subject of the verb *has made*. The subjective pronoun case is required; thus, the relative pronoun *whoever* is the correct choice. Notice that the entire subordinate clause functions as the object of the preposition *to*.

> whom
> We don't know [~~who~~ the university president nominated to chair the committee.]

Mentally set aside *We don't know* to enable you to focus exclusively on the subordinate clause. The relative pronoun is the object of the verb *nominated*. Thus, the objective case is required, and the correct pronoun is *whom*.

Do not be misled by interrupting expressions such as *I know, they think*, or *she believes*, which often come after *who* or *whom* in a subordinate clause.

The car dealer intends to invite only the customers [~~whom~~ who *he thinks* will want to attend.]

Mentally set aside *The car dealer intends to invite only the customers* and *he thinks*. The relative pronoun of the remaining subordinate clause is the subject of the verb *will want*. Therefore, the subjective case is required, and the correct relative pronoun is *who*.

10-6: ADVERBS AND ADJECTIVES

Adjectives and adverbs are modifiers. Adjectives modify nouns and pronouns. Adverbs can modify

- verbs

He left the examination early.

- adjectives

Her cheeks were slightly red.

- other adverbs

They ate dinner very late.

Many adverbs end in *-ly* (*quickly, oddly*); however, some do not (*often, very*). As well, a number of adjectives end in *-ly* (*lovely*).

Problems can occur when adjectives are incorrectly used as adverbs or vice versa. The best way to decide whether a modifier should be an adjective or an adverb is to determine its function in the sentence. If you are in doubt about whether a word is an adjective or an adverb, you might also consult a good Canadian dictionary.

ESL Note

Adjectives in English do not have to agree in number or gender with the words they modify. *The white* [not *whites*] *tree ornaments were purchased during my last holiday.*

10-6A: ADVERBS

In modifying a verb, another adverb, or an adjective, an adverb answers questions such as why? when? where? how? The following are some common misuses of adjectives in situations where adverbs are required:

1. Using adjectives to modify verbs

   The choir sang ~~loud~~ loudly and ~~clear~~ clearly at the concert.

2. Using the adjective *good* when the adverb *well* is required

   The minister of education indicated to the media that he wants students within the province to be able to write ~~good~~ well.

For more detail on the correct uses of *good* and *well*, see the usage glossary in section 13-1.

3. Using adjectives to modify adjectives or adverbs

   The museum in Niagara Falls has a ~~real~~ really unusual collection of artifacts.

ESL Note

For help with placement of adjectives and adverbs in English, see 15-3e.

10-6B: ADJECTIVES

Usually adjectives come before the nouns or pronouns they modify.

She watched the red dawn.

However, adjectives can also function as subject complements that follow a linking verb. The subject complement renames or describes the sentence subject.

Silence *is* golden.

Linking verbs communicate states of being as opposed to actions.

The milk at the back of the refrigerator *tasted* ~~sourly~~ sour.

She *seems* ~~happily~~ happy.

When my headache returned, I *felt* ~~badly~~ bad.

In these examples, the verbs *taste, seem,* and *feel* communicate states of being that modify the subject, so adjectives are required.

Some verbs, such as *look, feel, smell,* and *taste,* may or may not be linking verbs. When the word after the verb modifies the subject, the verb is a linking verb, and this modifying word should be an adjective. However, when the word modifies the verb, it should be an adverb.

Modifying the Subject
The girl looked curious.

Curious modifies the subject, *girl*. Here, *looked* is a linking verb and the modifier is an adjective. The adjective *curious* describes the girl's state of being.

Modifying the Verb
The girl looked curiously at the man dressed in a bunny suit.

Here, *curiously* modifies the verb, *looked*. The adverb *curiously* describes how the act of looking was done.

10-6C: COMPARATIVES AND SUPERLATIVES

Most adjectives and adverbs have three forms:

1. The positive
2. The comparative
3. The superlative

Forming Comparatives and Superlatives

ADJECTIVES

Positive	*Comparative*	*Superlative*
One- and most two-syllable adjectives		
red	redder	reddest
crazy	crazier	craziest
Longer adjectives		
intoxicating	more intoxicating	most intoxicating
selfish	less selfish	least selfish
Irregular		
good	better	best
bad	worse	worst

Positive	*Comparative*	*Superlative*
No comparative or superlative form		
unique	—	—
pregnant	—	—
ADVERBS		
Ending in *-ly*		
selfishly	more selfishly	most selfishly
gracefully	less gracefully	least gracefully
Not ending in *-ly*		
fast	faster	fastest
hard	harder	hardest
Irregular		
well	better	best
badly	worse	worst
No comparative or superlative form		
really	—	—
solely	—	—

WHEN TO USE THE COMPARATIVE FORM AND WHEN TO USE THE SUPERLATIVE FORM

When comparing two entities, use the comparative form.

Which is the ~~least~~ lesser of the two evils?

The jaguar moves ~~fastest~~ faster than the lion.

When comparing three or more entities, use the superlative.

Of all the playwrights, I feel that William Shakespeare is the greatest.

She is the ~~more~~ most selfish of the three sisters.

DO NOT USE DOUBLE COMPARATIVES OR SUPERLATIVES

Of the two playwrights, I feel that William Shakespeare is the ~~more~~ greater.

The painting is probably one of the most ~~beautifulest~~ beautiful in the museum.

DO NOT USE COMPARATIVES OR SUPERLATIVES WITH ABSOLUTE CONCEPTS

Absolute concepts by their very nature do not come in degrees and cannot be compared. Some examples of absolute concepts are *favourite, unique, perfect, pregnant, impossible, infinite,* or *priceless*. If two diamonds are perfect, one cannot be more perfect than the other. Similarly, of three perfect diamonds, one cannot be most perfect.

Incorrect: The cat looks more pregnant than she did last week.

Correct: The cat's pregnancy is more obvious than it was last week.

That painting by Leonardo da Vinci is ~~very~~ unique.

The bizarre comedy was the most ~~unique~~ [unusual] I have ever seen.

10-6D: DOUBLE NEGATIVES

Two negatives are only acceptable in a sentence if they create a positive meaning.

She was not unhappy with her ten-game hitting streak.

A **double negative** is a non-standard English construction in which negative modifiers such as *no, not, neither, none, nothing,* and *never* are paired to cancel each other. Double negatives should be avoided in any formal writing.

The government ~~never~~ does nothing to solve the problems affecting the poor.

Barry did not feel ~~nothing~~ [anything] during his hernia operation.

In standard English, the modifiers *barely, hardly,* and *scarcely* are considered negative modifiers. These words should not be paired with words such as *no, not,* or *never*.

They could ~~not~~ barely hear the tiny girl speak.

10-7: PROBLEMS WITH MODIFIERS

A modifier is a word, phrase, or clause that describes or limits another word, phrase, or clause within a sentence. Modifiers must be placed carefully and correctly or they will cloud—or, in some instances, destroy—sentence meaning. Generally, modifying words should be kept close to the words they modify.

10-7A: LIMITING MODIFIERS SUCH AS *ONLY* AND *EVEN*

Place limiting words such as *just, even, only, almost, hardly, nearly,* and *merely* directly before the verb they modify.

She nearly missed the swim team's practice.

If a limiting word modifies another word in the sentence, place the modifier in front of that word.

Incorrect: In the first quarter, Steve Nash did not even score one point.

Correct: In the first quarter, Steve Nash did not score even one point.

In this example, *even* must modify *one point* instead of *score,* so the modifier should be placed in front of *one point.*

Incorrect: Louis Cyr only weighed 250 pounds.

Correct: Louis Cyr weighed only 250 pounds.

Here, *only* must modify 250 *pounds* instead of *weighed,* so the modifier should be placed in front of 250 *pounds.*

The modifier *not* is often misplaced, a situation that can create confusing or unintended meanings.

Unintended Meaning: All snake bites are not lethal.

Intended Meaning: Not all snake bites are lethal.

In the first version, one possible meaning is that no snake bite is lethal, which could be a dangerous assumption in certain parts of the world. The correction makes the meaning clear: one does not have to worry that all snake bites are lethal.

10-7B: MISPLACED PHRASES AND CLAUSES

A **misplaced modifier** is a describing word, phrase, or clause that is incorrectly positioned within a sentence so that the modifier's meaning is illogical or unclear. The misplaced modifier relates to, or modifies, the wrong word or words in the sentence. When a modifier is misplaced, unusual misreadings can result.

× Jennifer sat waiting for her boyfriend to park the car in a slinky red dress with a plunging neckline.

√ In a slinky red dress with a plunging neckline, Jennifer sat waiting for her boyfriend to park the car.

When the modifier is placed so far from what it modifies, the reader could easily conclude that it is Jennifer's boyfriend who is wearing the slinky dress.

× The counter clerk at the soda fountain brought the sundae to the eager young boy covered in chocolate sauce.

√ The counter clerk at the soda fountain brought the sundae covered in chocolate sauce to the eager young boy.

The first sentence can be misinterpreted two ways: either the clerk or the boy was covered in chocolate sauce.

× A beautiful painting attracts the viewer's eye on the wall of the National Gallery.

√ A beautiful painting on the wall of the National Gallery attracts the viewer's eye.

The painting, not the viewer's eye, is on the wall.

Sometimes modifier placement can lead to ambiguity so that two or more revisions are possible. The correction chosen will depend on the writer's intended meaning.

Ambiguous: The fellow we interviewed at the station yesterday turned up in London.

Clear: The fellow we interviewed yesterday at the station turned up in London.

Clear: The fellow we interviewed at the station turned up in London yesterday.

In the first sentence, it is unclear whether the fellow was interviewed yesterday or turned up in London yesterday.

10-7C: AWKWARDLY PLACED MODIFIERS

Sentences should generally flow in a pattern from subject to verb to object. Keep the subject as close to the main verb as possible and, where possible, don't separate the subject from the main verb of the sentence with a modifying adverb clause.

Awkward: The dog, after chasing the mail carrier, wagged its tail and pranced triumphantly to the front porch.

Clear: After chasing the mail carrier, the dog wagged its tail and pranced triumphantly to the front porch.

There is no reason to separate the subject *dog* from the verb *wagged* with a fairly long modifying clause.

As well, keep auxiliary verbs near to the main verbs.

Awkward: I have as long as I can remember had a scar on my elbow.

Clear: I have had a scar on my elbow as long as I can remember.

The complete verb is *have had,* so the main and auxiliary verb should be placed together.

10-7D: SPLIT INFINITIVES

An infinitive consists of to and the verb, as in *to love, to leave,* and *to forget*. In a **split infinitive**, a modifier is placed between to and the verb. Frequently, including a split infinitive in a sentence will make the sentence awkward, and the sentence will need to be revised. One famous example of a split infinitive is in the opening to Star Trek, "To boldly go where no man has gone before"; it is parodied by Douglas Adams in *The Hitchhiker's Guide to the Galaxy*: "Men boldly split infinitives that no man had split before." Split infinitives are not considered grammatical errors in modern writing and are often very effective usage, but they are easy to spot, so use them at your peril.

Awkward: Financial analysts expected the stock prices to, after a period of sharp decline, dramatically rise.

Clear: Financial analysts expected the stock prices to rise dramatically after a period of share decline.

Here the phrasing is awkward because of a long intervening phrase that splits the infinitive. A similar case is illustrated below:

Awkward: Try to, if you can get it, see her latest DVD.

Clear: Try to see her latest DVD, if you can get it.

However, in some instances, split infinitives are preferable to alternative wordings. It might be argued that the following split infinitive is essential because of a slight nuance in meaning:

The audience failed to completely understand the argument.

This may mean that that the audience's understanding was incomplete, but not that their failure was complete, as it would in this example where the infinitive is not split:

The audience failed completely to understand the argument.

Generally, avoid split infinitives in formal writing. They are often pointed out as errors, even though they are quite common in informal writing. They are not errors, but it may be better to play it safe since many regard them as such.

10-7E: DANGLING MODIFIERS

A **dangling modifier** is a word, phrase, or clause that does not relate to any word within the sentence and, as a result, confuses the reader. Dangling modifiers usually appear at the start of the sentence, and the person who performs the action is not mentioned. A dangling modifier can be one of the following:

- a participial phrase

  Believed to be dangerous, an old lady was accosted on the street.

- a gerund phrase

  After eating dinner, the turkey was left sitting on the table.

- an infinitive phrase

  To win first place on a reality-TV show, a strong stomach is needed.

To repair dangling modifier problems, use one of the following revision strategies:

PROVIDE THE SUBJECT OF THE SENTENCE IMMEDIATELY AFTER THE DANGLING PHRASE

× Believed to be dangerous, an old lady was accosted on the street.

√ Believed to be dangerous, an escaped convict accosted an old lady on the street.

A new subject must be added.

× After eating dinner, the turkey was left sitting on the table.

√ After eating dinner, we left the turkey sitting on the table.

The implied subject of the gerund phrase is explicitly stated.

× To win first place on a reality-TV show, a strong stomach is needed.

√ To win first place on a reality-TV show, a contestant needs a strong stomach.

The implied subject of the infinitive phrase is explicitly stated.

Also watch out for elliptical phrases. The subject of the participle must be explicitly stated in order to avoid dangling modifiers.

× Keep stirring the meat until browned.

As it stands, this sentence implies that the person stirring the meat is being browned, not the meat.

√ Keep stirring the meat until it is browned.

In an **elliptical clause,** a word or phrase required by the rules of grammar is omitted because the clause can be understood without it. Here the elliptical clause has an implied subject and verb; it is means "the meat is," a connection that is implied but not stated in the unclear elliptical clause.

To assess whether or not a sentence you have written has a dangling modifier, apply the following questioning strategy:

1. Does the word group have a verb?
   - ❑ YES. *Consider the next question.*
   - ❑ NO. The word group is a fragment and must be revised to include a verb.
2. Does the participial phrase suggest an action without indicating who is performing the action?
   - ❑ NO. You do not have a dangling modifier problem.
   - ❑ YES. *Consider the next question.*
3. Does the subject of the independent clause indicate who performs the action?
   - ❑ YES. You do not have a dangling modifier problem.
   - ❑ NO. *Apply one of the three strategies listed above to address the dangling modifier problem.*

11

PUNCTUATION

***Let me be plain:* the semi-colon is ugly, ugly as a tick on a dog's belly, I *pinch* them out of my prose.**

— Donald Barthelme, *Not-Knowing*

11

Punctuation

11 Punctuation

This section on punctuation follows the one on grammar because so many issues of punctuation depend on a knowledge of how the language is put together grammatically. For this reason, grammar checkers cannot easily catch routine comma errors, so don't rely on them to do so. Refer to this section for advice on problem areas you encounter as you compose and revise.

11-1: THE COMMA

Frequently, a comma is essential to ensure that readers clearly understand your intended meaning. Omitting or misplacing a comma can easily lead to misreadings.

> While e-mailing,^Mary Beth spoke on the telephone with her stockbroker.

Without the comma, this sentence could be interpreted to mean that Beth was speaking on the phone with her stockbroker while e-mailing Mary.

The following sections provide rules and guidance for instances in which you must use commas.

11-1A: INDEPENDENT CLAUSES WITH A COORDINATING CONJUNCTION

In some sentences, two or more independent clauses (clauses that can stand on their own as sentences) are linked by coordinating conjunctions (*and, or, for, but, so, nor,* and *yet*). In such sentences, place a comma before the coordinating conjunction.

> I enjoy watching television, but I draw the line at World Wrestling Entertainment.

Exception: If the two independent clauses are very short, and there is no chance of misinterpreting the sentence, the comma may be omitted.

> The Greyhound bus pulled in and we boarded it.

11-1B: COMPOUND ELEMENTS

Never use a comma to separate compound elements of a sentence that are not complete independent clauses.

A good commercial pitches its wares to viewers with smooth language, and is loud enough to reach those who have left the room during the break.

The words following the comma do not form an independent clause, so the comma is not appropriate.

Margaret picked up dog food, and bought a full tank of gas.

The conjunction *and* links two elements, but the element after *and* is not an independent clause. Instead, *and* joins two parts of a compound predicate: *picked up* and *bought*.

He will not quit smoking until he takes responsibility for his own health, and until he shows responsibility for his immediate family.

In this example, *and* joins two subordinate clauses, each of which commences with *until*.

11-1C: INTRODUCTORY ELEMENTS

Introductory groups of words in sentences are often made up of the following:

- adverbial clauses
- prepositional phrases
- verbal phrases
- absolute phrases

In each case, the introductory group of words is followed by a comma, which signals to the reader that the main part of the sentences (the subject and verb) is about to begin.

Note: Another type of introductory word group is the transitional expression. For more information on punctuating with transitional expressions, see 11-1i.

COMMAS WITH INTRODUCTORY ADVERBIAL CLAUSES

An introductory adverbial clause is a construction that has a subject and a verb and that introduces a main clause.

Whenever I feel in need of cheering up, I go to the park.

Introductory adverbial clauses indicate *where, when, why, how,* or *under what conditions* the main sentence action takes place. After such clauses, use a comma to indicate that the main part of the sentence is about to start.

Whenever he hears gossip about company plans for hiring, Pedro talks about his conspiracy theory.

By a bend in the mighty Thompson River, I learned to swim.

If the adverbial phrase or clause is very brief, and there is no danger of misreading the sentence, the comma may be omitted.

In a flash it was over.

COMMAS WITH LONGER INTRODUCTORY PREPOSITIONAL PHRASES

After longer introductory prepositional phrases, use a comma to indicate that the main part of the sentence is about to start.

After appetizers and an extended family dinner, my uncle fell asleep in his chair.

COMMAS WITH INTRODUCTORY VERBAL PHRASES

Verbals include participles, gerunds, and infinitives. Place a comma after short and long introductory verbal phrases.

Participle
Elated about the court ruling, Renée phoned her probation officer.

Gerund
By studying the stock market, Rafe found a way to add excitement to his life.

Infinitive
To be considered by a casting director, an actor must demonstrate versatility as well as talent.

COMMAS WITH INTRODUCTORY ABSOLUTE PHRASES

An absolute phrase modifies the entire sentence. Follow an introductory absolute phrase with a comma.

All things considered, it was an ideal first date.

11-1D: ITEMS IN A SERIES

A series in a sentence can be made up of three or more words, phrases, or clauses that have the same grammatical form and are of equal importance. Place commas between the items in the series (e.g., *knife, fork, and spoon*). The comma before the last item, commonly called "the serial comma," is optional, and it is omitted by many writers. However, the serial comma is useful in preventing ambiguity. If you decide to use the serial comma, make sure that you use it consistently throughout your writing.

> Serena thanked her parents, Karen Kain, and Frank Augustyn, for helping her win the award for her dancing.

Without the serial comma, it is unclear: are Serena's parents Karen Kain and Frank Augustyn? With the serial comma, it is clear that she is thanking four different people.

> The woods are lovely, dark and deep.

The above line is from the famous Robert Frost poem "Stopping by Woods on a Snowy Evening." Here the punctuation is intentionally ambiguous. The speaker could mean that he considers the woods lovely because they are dark and deep, or that the woods are lovely *and* dark *and* deep.

Especially when writing a report or essay, it is wise to use the comma between all elements in a series to avoid any possibility of ambiguity or misinterpretation by the reader.

Note: Do not place a comma *before the first* or *after the last* item in a series, unless another comma rule makes using a comma necessary.

> The poets E.J. Pratt, F.R. Scott, and A.J.M. Smith played an important role in the development of uniquely Canadian poetry.

> There were two bars of soap, a box of detergent, some hamburger buns, and onions in her shopping cart.

11-1E: COORDINATE ADJECTIVES

Coordinate adjectives are two or more adjectives that separately and equally modify a noun or pronoun. The order of these adjectives can be changed without affecting the meaning of the sentence. Coordinate adjectives can be joined by *and*. Separate coordinate adjectives with commas.

> The cold, smelly, wet basement was off-limits to the children as a play area.

You can tell these adjectives are coordinate since they can easily be linked with *and* (*cold* and *smelly* and *wet*).

It was a fluffy, playful, tiny kitten.

11-1F: CUMULATIVE ADJECTIVES

A **cumulative** adjective modifies the adjective that comes after it and the noun or pronoun that follows. Cumulative adjectives increase meaning from word to word as they progress toward a noun or pronoun. They are not interchangeable and cannot be joined by *and*. Do not use a comma between cumulative adjectives.

The book talk featured three well-known English authors.

English modifies *authors, well-known* modifies *English authors,* and *three* modifies *well-known English authors.* The order of the adjectives cannot be changed, nor can the coordinating conjunction *and* be placed between the adjectives.

His résumé included various, short-term, landscaping jobs.

An exhibit of authentic, early, Incan art was on display at the Royal Ontario Museum.

The music festival featured many, Canadian, folk acts.

11-1G: RESTRICTIVE AND NONRESTRICTIVE ELEMENTS

Adjective clauses, adjective phrases, and appositives can modify nouns and pronouns. These modifying elements may be either restrictive or nonrestrictive.

WHAT IS A RESTRICTIVE ELEMENT?

A **restrictive** element limits, defines, or identifies the noun or pronoun that it modifies. The information in a restrictive element is essential to a sentence's meaning. Do not set off a restrictive element with commas.

The man who has the scar above his left eyebrow is the chief robbery suspect.

The fact that the man has a scar is essential to identifying him as the chief robbery suspect. Omitting the restrictive element would greatly alter the meaning of the sentence, turning it into a very general statement.

WHAT IS A NONRESTRICTIVE ELEMENT?

A **nonrestrictive** element adds nonessential, or parenthetical, information about an idea or term that is already limited, defined, or identified; hence, a nonrestrictive element is set off with a comma or commas.

> The man who is the chief robbery subject has a scar, which is above his left eyebrow.

The essential meaning of the sentence—that the chief robbery suspect has a scar—is not lost if the information about the location of the scar is removed; thus, this information is nonrestrictive.

CONTEXT

Often, to decide whether a modifying element is restrictive or nonrestrictive, you can simply read the sentence without the element. If the sentence doesn't make sense without the element, the element is restrictive and does not require commas; if it does make sense, the element is nonrestrictive and does require commas.

In some cases, however, you will need to know the context in which a sentence appears to decide whether a restrictive or nonrestrictive element is required.

> The man who is the chief robbery subject has a scar that is above his left eyebrow.

The writer has not used a comma to set off *that is above his left eyebrow,* so the element is restrictive. This indicates that the sentence appears in a context where knowing the location of the scar is essential information.

ADJECTIVE CLAUSES

Adjective clauses are dependent clauses that modify nouns or pronouns. An adjective clause can begin with a relative pronoun (*who, whose, whom, that, which*) or a relative adverb (*when, where*).

Adjective clauses can be nonrestrictive or restrictive. Nonrestrictive adjective clauses are set off with commas. Use *which,* rather than *that,* with nonrestrictive adjective clauses.

> ***Nonrestrictive Clause***
> Tofino, which is well over 200 kilometres from Victoria, attracts many tourists during November for storm-watching.

The information about Tofino's approximate distance from Victoria is not essential to the main idea of the sentence. The clause is therefore nonrestrictive and set off with commas.

A restrictive adjective clause should not be set off by commas since removing the clause would change the meaning of the sentence.

Restrictive Clause

Drivers who drink excessively should be banned from driving.

The *who* clause is restrictive, limiting the *drivers* to those *who drink excessively*. The clause is essential to the meaning of the sentence; therefore, it should not be set off by commas.

Use *that*, rather than *which*, with restrictive adjective clauses.

The poodle that won the trophy for Best in Show was stylishly groomed.

PHRASES THAT FUNCTION AS ADJECTIVES

Verbal and prepositional phrases can function as adjectives and may be nonrestrictive or restrictive. Whether they appear at the beginning, middle, or end of sentences, nonrestrictive adjective phrases must be set off with commas to indicate that the information is nonessential.

Nonrestrictive Adjective Phrase

Canadian tourists, especially when travelling in foreign countries, often wear a Canadian flag.

The adjective phrase beginning *especially* provides nonessential information about *Canadian tourists*. The phrase is not used to identify the tourists particularly since the adjective *Canadian* has already done that. Consequently, the phrase is nonrestrictive and must be set off by commas.

A restrictive adjective phrase should never be set off by commas, since removing the phrase would change the sentence's meaning.

Restrictive Adjective Phrase

Shoppers using debit cards to make small purchases are becoming more common today.

The phrase *using debit cards to make small purchases* restricts the meaning of *shoppers*. As a restrictive phrase, it is not set off by commas.

APPOSITIVES

An appositive renames or extends the meaning of a nearby noun or noun phrase. Many appositives are nonrestrictive and therefore must be set off with commas.

Nonrestrictive Appositive

Emmy Lou, who runs the daycare centre, is a retired karate teacher.

The appositive *who runs the daycare centre* is not information essential to the main part of the sentence. Since it is a nonrestrictive appositive, commas should be used to set it off.

Some appositives, however, are restrictive and do not require commas.

Restrictive Appositive

The Rolling Stones song "Start Me Up" is often played during football games to motivate the home team.

The appositive following *song* restricts the meaning. It is not just any Rolling Stones song that is meant; rather, it is the specific song "Start Me Up."

James Joyce's book *Ulysses* was initially banned in the United States.

The appositive *Ulysses* is restrictive. It is not another book written by James Joyce that was banned; rather, it is a particular book, *Ulysses*. Thus, no commas should be used.

11-1H: CONCLUDING ADVERB CLAUSES

Adverb clauses introducing a sentence almost always conclude with a comma. (See 11-1c.) However, when adverb clauses conclude a sentence and their meaning is essential to the sentence, they are not set off by commas. Adverb clauses that begin with the following subordinated conjunctions are usually essential: *after, as soon as, before, because, if, since, unless, until,* and *when*.

Water boils at sea level when it reaches a temperature of 100 degrees Celsius.

The concluding adverb clause commencing with *when* is essential to the meaning of the sentence, so it is not set off with a comma.

Place a comma before adverb clauses that contain nonessential information. Adverb clauses beginning with the subordinating conjunctions *although, even though, though,* and *whereas* are often nonessential.

He missed the turn for the expressway, <u>even though signs for the on-ramp were well posted</u>.

11-1I: TRANSITIONS, PARENTHETICAL EXPRESSIONS, ABSOLUTE PHRASES, CONTRASTS

TRANSITIONAL EXPRESSIONS

Transitional expressions are words or groups of words that function as links between or within sentences. A transitional expression can appear at the beginning, end, or within a sentence. Transitional expressions can be conjunctive adverbs, such as *therefore* and *however,* or transitional phrases, such as *for example, in addition,* and *on the contrary*. (For a more complete list, see 11-2b.)

If a transitional expression appears between independent clauses in a compound sentence, place a semicolon before the transitional expression. Most often, you should also place a comma after it.

Edwin did not fit in with our crowd; <u>furthermore</u>, he was openly antagonistic toward us.

The soprano was a prima donna; <u>for instance</u>, she demanded that mineral water chilled to a specific temperature be available in her dressing room before and after every performance.

Set off a transitional expression with commas if it appears at the start of a sentence or in the middle of an independent clause.

<u>As a result</u>,^the medical insurance plan will not pay for liposuction.

The dermatologist comes highly recommended; he can't give me an appointment,^<u>however</u>,^until the end of March.

In some cases, if the transitional expression is integrated with the sentence and requires no pause or a minimal one when reading, no commas are needed to set off the expression. Expressions such as the following may not always need to be set off by commas:

at least	indeed	then
certainly	of course	therefore
consequently	perhaps	undoubtedly

You have been a good child; <u>therefore</u> you will get a pet pony.

The Lord of the Rings is a Canadian musical; <u>indeed</u>, it was created and staged in Toronto in 2006.

PARENTHETICAL EXPRESSIONS

Parenthetical expressions contain additional information the writer inserts into the sentence for such purposes as to explain, qualify, or give his or her point of view. If parenthetical expressions do not appear in parentheses, they are set off with commas.

> The inarticulate politician, unfortunately, stated his contradictory views about abortion on national television.

> In most writing situations, such as this one, commas are used to set off parenthetical expressions.

While commas are required to set off *distinctly* parenthetical expressions, do *not* use commas to set off *mildly* parenthetical expressions.

> Team Canada finally scored the winning goal.

ABSOLUTE PHRASES

An absolute phrase contains a noun subject and a participle that modify an entire sentence. (See 9-3d.) Set off absolute phrases with commas.

> The war being over, the refugees returned home.

> Their profits steeply declining, many computer companies laid off employees.

EXPRESSIONS OF CONTRAST

Expressions of contrast include words such as *not, nor, but,* and *unlike*. Set off expressions of contrast with commas.

> The Toronto Raptors, unlike the Vancouver Grizzlies, flourished in Canada.

> Martin found fame as a standup comedian, not as a writer.

11-1J: NOUNS OF DIRECT ADDRESS, *YES* AND *NO*, INTERROGATIVE TAGS, INTERJECTIONS

Use commas to set off the following:

- nouns of direct address

> Your back flip, Olga, is of Olympic calibre.

- the words *yes* and *no*

  No,^you don't sound crazy.

- interrogative tags

  You did turn off the iron,^didn't you?

- mild interjections

  Of course,^incidents like that are inevitable.

11-1K: *HE SAID,* ETC.

Use commas with speech tags such as *she wrote* or *he said* to set off direct quotations. (See also 11-5f.)

> Woody Allen wrote,^"It is impossible to experience one's death objectively and still carry a tune."

> "Defining and analyzing humor is a pastime of humorless people,^" quipped Robert Benchley.

11-1L: DATES, ADDRESSES, TITLES, NUMBERS

DATES

When the date is within the sentence, use commas following the day and the year in month-day-year dates.

> On August 14,^1945,^Japan surrendered.

When the date is inverted or when just the month and year are given, commas are not required.

> Queen Victoria's birthday will be celebrated on 21 May 2007.

> January 2002 was unseasonably warm.

ADDRESSES

Use a comma between the city and province or city and country. When a sentence continues on after the city and province or city and country, also use a comma after the province or country.

> Stephen Leacock died in Toronto,^Ontario,^in 1944.

In a complete address, separate all items (except the postal code) with a comma.

I would appreciate it if you would courier the book to Ella James at 126 Mayburn Drive,^Oakville,^Ontario L6P 1K8.

TITLES

When an abbreviated title follows a name, place a comma after the name and a second comma after the title.

Philip Bacho,^Ph.D.,^taught the course on writing scripts.

NUMBERS

Canada follows the international system of metric measurement (SI), which does not use commas in numbers. Instead, spaces are used to separate sets of three digits. Four-digit numbers may be grouped together. Be aware that many U.S. style guides use the imperial system instead and hence do not conform to the international system of metric measurement.

In your reading, you may encounter commas used for numbers that are four digits or more. This system was used before Canada adopted the international metric system.

4673

233 971

6,299,381

Never use commas to separate sets of digits in years, telephone numbers, street numbers, or postal codes.

11-1M: PREVENTING CONFUSION

In many writing situations, commas are required to prevent reader confusion.

OMITTED WORDS

A comma is used to indicate that an understood word or words have been omitted.

Tasha adored jazz; Bert,^gospel.

ECHOING WORDS

When two words repeat or strongly echo each other, a comma helps to clarify sentence meaning.

Undeterred by the possibility of plane hijackings, he felt that whatever happens,^happens.

CLARIFYING A WRITER'S INTENTION

Occasionally commas are required to help readers group units of meaning as the writer intended.

> Those who can,^run every chance they get.

11-1N: INCORRECT USES OF THE COMMA

Don't use commas injudiciously or believe the old saying that commas should be inserted wherever you pause for breath. This section describes some of the ways that commas are commonly misused.

BETWEEN VERB AND SUBJECT OR OBJECT

Do not use a comma to separate a subject from its verb or a verb from its object.

> Tom Patterson originated the idea for the Stratford Festival in 1952.

The subject of the sentence, *Tom Patterson*, should not be separated from the main verb, *originated*.

> The superior boxer mercilessly punched his staggering opponent.

The verb *punched* should not be separated from the direct object, *his staggering opponent*, with a comma.

OTHER SITUATIONS IN WHICH A COMMA SHOULD NOT BE USED

- separating an adjective from a following noun

  > It was a gruesome, thankless investigation.

- separating an adverb from a following adjective

  > The party was victorious in the hotly contested riding.

- after *like* or *such as*

  > Many Canadian recording artists will be in attendance, such as Jann Arden, Sarah McLachlan, and Joni Mitchell.

- after a coordinating conjunction (*and, but, for, nor, or, so, yet*)

  > The journalist has been to some of the most dangerous trouble spots in the world, and she has lived to tell about them.

- after *although*

  > Although we are going to the bullfight, we don't plan to stay long.

- before *than*

  Visiting Cathedral Grove on Vancouver Island was more enjoyable than seeing the suspension bridge in North Vancouver.

- to set off an indirect quotation

  Pierre Trudeau once said that, for Canada, being close to the United States was like sleeping next to an elephant.

- with an exclamation mark or a question mark

  "Watch out for the logging truck!" he bellowed.

- before a parenthesis

  On the other hand, there are some Catalans (usually women who've never worked outside the home) who haven't spoken Spanish since their school days.

11-2: THE SEMICOLON

A semicolon is used to separate major elements of a sentence that are of equal grammatical rank.

11-2A: INDEPENDENT CLAUSES WITH NO COORDINATING CONJUNCTION

An independent clause expresses a complete thought and can stand on its own as a sentence. When related independent clauses appear in a sentence (as in a compound sentence), they are usually linked by a comma and a coordinating conjunction (*and, but, for, nor, or, so,* and *yet*). The conjunction indicates the relationship between the clauses.

When the relationship between independent clauses is clear without the conjunction, you may instead link the two clauses with a semicolon.

> A teacher affects eternity; no one can tell where his influence stops.
>
> —Henry Adams

Use a semicolon if a coordinating conjunction between two independent clauses has been omitted. If you use a comma, you will create a grammatical error known as a comma splice. (See 10-2.)

Provincial health insurance plans cover some medical costs when Canadians travel outside the country; they do not cover many vital health-care expenses.

Strategies for revising comma splice errors can be found in 10-2. You may wish to consider other alternatives to using a semicolon.

11-2B: INDEPENDENT CLAUSES WITH TRANSITIONAL EXPRESSIONS

Transitional expressions can be conjunctive adverbs or transitional phrases.

Transitional Expressions

COMMON CONJUNCTIVE ADVERBS

accordingly	however	now
also	incidentally	otherwise
anyway	indeed	similarly
besides	instead	specifically
certainly	likewise	still
consequently	meanwhile	subsequently
conversely	moreover	then
finally	namely	thereafter
further	nevertheless	therefore
furthermore	next	thus
hence	nonetheless	undoubtedly

TRANSITIONAL PHRASES

after all	for example	in summary
as a matter of fact	for instance	in the first place
as an illustration	in addition	in the same way
as a result	in conclusion	of course
at any rate	in fact	on the contrary
at the same time	in other words	on the other hand
equally important	in short	to be sure
even so	in spite of	to illustrate

When a transitional expression comes between independent clauses, place a semicolon before the expression and a comma after it.

> She is an authority on the West Nile virus; <u>furthermore</u>, we need someone with her expertise.

If the transitional expression is in the middle of or at the end of the second independent clause, the semicolon is placed between the independent clauses.

> Generally people who work at the biological station have advanced postsecondary degrees; Tony, <u>on the other hand</u>, acquired his knowledge and expertise through practical experience.

Do not confuse the punctuation for transitional expressions with that used with coordinating conjunctions (*and, but, for, nor, or, so,* and *yet*). When a coordinating conjunction links two independent clauses, it is preceded by a comma. (See 11-1a and 10-2a.)

11-2C: SERIES WITH INTERNAL PUNCTUATION

Usually, commas separate items in a series. However, when series items contain commas, a semicolon is placed between items to make the sentence easier to read.

> Here is the list of remaining speakers and topics: Gurdeep, the rewards of working at a student newspaper; Miles, the elements of hip-hop; and Mustapha, the wonders of wireless technology.

Without semicolons, the sentence would be difficult to read. In each series element, the speaker's name is followed by the topic of his speech. The semicolons help the reader to group information accurately.

11-2D: INCORRECT USES OF THE SEMICOLON

Never use a semicolon in the following writing situations:

- between independent clauses joined by *and, but, for, nor, or, so,* or *yet*

> The painter was very prolific during his lifetime;, yet he only achieved the fame he deserved after death.

- between a subordinate clause and the remainder of the sentence

> After she had made the lemon curd;, Leona whipped the cream she needed to ice the cake.

- between an appositive and the word to which it refers

  Raj's favourite television program is *Six Feet Under*, a dark but funny dramatic series.

- to introduce a list

  A number of great novels are covered in the course: *Bleak House*, *Pride and Prejudice*, and *Gulliver's Travels*.

11-3: THE COLON

The colon is most often used as a formal and emphatic method to introduce a word, phrase, or clause that follows it.

11-3A: BEFORE A LIST, AN APPOSITIVE, A QUOTATION

Use a colon before

- a list

  For this experiment, you will need the following materials: three small cups, a transparent sheet, a waterproof marker, an eye dropper, and three paper towels.

- an appositive

  While held hostage, the journalist had one all-consuming thought: survival.

- a quotation

  Mackenzie King summed up his position with this epigrammatic line: "Not necessarily conscription, but conscription if necessary."

For additional ways of introducing quotations, see 11-5g.

11-3B: BETWEEN INDEPENDENT CLAUSES

You can use either a capital letter or a lower-case letter to begin the independent clause after the colon.

In North America, there are two classes of travel: there is first-class travel, and then there is travel with children.

11-3C: CONVENTIONAL USES

The colon is conventionally used

- after the salutation of a formal letter

  Dear Ms. Pointman:

- to indicate hours and minutes

  6:31 a.m.

- between numbers in ratios

  The ratio of men over fifty was 5:1.

- between the title and subtitle of a book

  Dancing at the Edge of the World: Thoughts on Words, Women, Places

- to separate the city from the publisher and date in a bibliographic entry

  Toronto: Nelson, 2006.

- between Bible chapters and verses

  Psalms 23:1–3

11-3D: INCORRECT USES OF THE COLON

Except in documentation, a complete independent clause must precede a colon.

Do not use a colon in the following writing situations:

- between a verb and its complement or object

  The main ingredients in a good mushroom omelette are: eggs, mushrooms, and butter.

- between a preposition and its object

  The open-area portion of the dome house consisted of: a kitchen, living room, and master bedroom.

- after *for example, such as,* and *including/included*

  The content of the botanist's lecture included: boreal forests, a Carolinian forest, and an Amazonian rain forest.

Note, too, that it is optional to capitalize after a colon if what follows is an independent clause. If what follows is not an independent clause, do not capitalize. (See 14-3f.)

11-4: THE APOSTROPHE

11-4A: POSSESSIVE NOUNS

An apostrophe (') appears as part of a noun to indicate that the word is possessive. Often ownership is obvious, as in *Mishka's hockey stick* or *the instructor's briefcase*. Sometimes ownership is not as explicit, as in *the journey's end* or *the river's tributaries*. To test if a noun is possessive, see if you can state it as an "of" phrase, as in *the end of the journey* or *the tributaries of the river*. According to this test, both nouns, *journey's* and *river's*, are possessive.

POSSESSIVES FORMED BY ADDING AN APOSTROPHE AND -S

- a singular or plural noun that does not end in -s

  The commodore's cabin cruiser ran aground.

  It was the team's wish that the donation be made in his name.

  The women's shelter needs volunteers.

- a singular noun that ends in -s.

  Gus's father owns a single-engine plane.

Exception: For names such as Moses and Jesus, or if the noun ends in an "eez" sound, an apostrophe without an -s may be added to a singular noun. (You may see this usage with other nouns ending in -s; however, the preferred style is to add an apostrophe and -s as shown above.)

Euripides' tragedy *Medea* is his best-known work.

POSSESSIVES FORMED BY ADDING AN APOSTROPHE ONLY

- The noun is plural and ends in -s.

  Workers' rights were neglected by the military regime.

  The boys' tent was flattened in the storm.

WITH COMPOUND SUBJECTS

To show joint possession, use -'s (or -s') with the last noun only.

You should see Doug and Dino's modified stock car.

Manuela and Jesus' new house overlooks the valley.

To show individual possession, make all nouns in the compound subject possessive.

Todd's and Charles's ideas on how to decorate the home were diametrically opposed.

WITH COMPOUND NOUNS

Use -'s (or -s') with the last element in a compound noun to show possession.

My sister-in-law's film won a Genie.

My in-laws' parties are always worth attending.

11-4B: POSSESSIVE INDEFINITE PRONOUNS

An indefinite pronoun refers to a general or non-specific person or thing. Examples of indefinite pronouns are *somebody, anything*, and *anyone*. (See 9-1c.) Add -'s to the end of the indefinite pronoun to make it possessive.

It is not anybody's business what I do in my free time.

Someone's laptop was stolen from the reference library.

11-4C: CONTRACTIONS

The apostrophe takes the place of missing letters in contractions.

Who's going to do it doesn't matter.

Who's written in full is *Who is*, and *doesn't* written in full is *does not*.

The apostrophe can also indicate that the first two digits of years have been left out.

There will be a reunion for the class of '88.

Note that, when referring to a decade, the plural is formed by adding -s (no apostrophe) after the year. Be careful to use the apostrophe correctly when dealing with decades in your writing.

She lived in Paris in the 1940s.

Did you enjoy *That '70s Show*?

11-4D: PLURALS OF NUMBERS, LETTERS, ETC.

In some common writing situations, an apostrophe plus -s is used to form the plural.

- numbers

As scores for his perfect dive, he received all 10's.

- letters

Tiny X's and O's were embroidered on the scarf.

- word as words

I don't want to have to deal with any more *what if*'s.

- abbreviations

It was the Calgary-area M.P.'s responsibility to ensure the issue was addressed.

Notice that the -s is not italicized when used with italicized words or letters.

You should also note that some style guides (e.g., that of the Modern Language Association) do not use an apostrophe to form the plurals of numbers and abbreviations. Ask your instructor if there is a preferred style for your discipline.

He has trouble writing 6s. [MLA style]

I bought some new DVDs. [MLA style]

11-4E: INCORRECT USES OF THE APOSTROPHE

Do not use an apostrophe with the following:

- nouns that are not possessive

  Employee's must wear security badges at all times.

  The clients' had expected us to pick up the tab for dinner.

- the possessive pronouns *his, hers, its, ours, theirs,* and *whose*

  The dog must wear it's collar when outdoors.

Here, *its* must be the possessive, so there is no apostrophe needed. Do not mistake the contraction *it's* ("it is") for the possessive *its*.

11-5: QUOTATION MARKS

11-5A: DIRECT QUOTATIONS

Direct quotations are the exact words copied from a print source or transcribed from what a person says. Direct quotations must be enclosed within quotation marks.

"The open ocean is normally a friendly environment for a sea kayak," writes John Dowd in *Sea Kayaking: A Manual for Long-Distance Touring.*

On the other hand, indirect quotations paraphrase or summarize what has appeared in a print source or what a person has said. Indirect quotations are not placed within quotation marks.

John Dowd professes that, usually, the open ocean is a safe place to sea kayak.

QUOTING LONGER PASSAGES BY A SINGLE SPEAKER

If you are directly quoting passages by a single speaker, start each new paragraph with quotation marks, but do not use closing quotation marks until the end of the quoted material.

MARKING A CHANGE IN SPEAKER WITHIN DIALOGUE
Start a new paragraph to signal a change in the speaker.

> "I said me, not you."
> "Oh. You got a car outside?"
> "I can walk."
> "That's five miles back to where the van is."
> "People have walked five miles."
>
> —Alice Munro, "Friend of My Youth"
> in *Friend of My Youth* (Toronto: McClelland & Stewart, 1990).

11-5B: LONG QUOTATIONS

PROSE
A "long" quotation of prose is any passage that is more than four typed or handwritten lines. Start the quotation 2.5 cm (1 in.) from the left margin. You do not need to enclose the longer quotation within quotation marks because the indented format establishes for the reader that the quotation is taken exactly from a source. Usually, longer quotations are introduced by a sentence ending with a colon.

> Smoking can destroy the health of smokers and is a very real health risk to those around them, as researcher Warren Clark clearly points out:
>
> > In 1995, 4.5 million nonsmoking Canadians aged 15 and over were exposed to cigarette smoke on a daily basis. Another 2.2 million were exposed to it at least once a week, while about 840 000 were exposed to it less frequently. In terms of percentages, about 28 per cent of nonsmokers aged 15 and over breathed secondhand smoke every day, while about 19 per cent were exposed to it somewhat less often. Just over half of nonsmokers reported that they were not exposed to ETS (Environmental Tobacco Smoke). (161)

Placing the page number reference within parentheses follows the citation style prescribed by the Modern Language Association. (See Chapter 5.)

If the direct quotation had included additional paragraphs, each new paragraph would need to be indented an additional 0.75 cm (0.3 in.).

POETRY
A "long" quotation of poetry is more than three lines of the poem. Start the quotation 2.5 cm (1 in.) from the left margin. You do not need to enclose the longer quotation within quotation marks

because the indented format establishes for the reader that the quotation is taken exactly from the poem. Only use quotation marks within the quotation if they are part of the poem. (For information on how to punctuate two or three lines of poetry, see 11-6h.)

> P.K. Page is more personal in "After Rain" than in "The Stenographers." In "After Rain," she defines her own poetic sensibility through the poem-within-a-poem of stanza three:
>
> > the clothes-reel gauche
> > as the rangy skeleton of some
> > gaunt delicate spidery mute
> > is pitched as if
> > listening;
> > while hung from one thin rib
> > a silver web—
> > its infant, skeletal, diminutive,
> > now sagged with sequins, pulled ellipsoid,
> > glistening. (122)

See Chapter 5 for MLA guidelines on how to include the reference in a Works Cited page. If your paper is written according to the style of the American Psychological Association, you will need to follow slightly different guidelines for setting off long quotations. These guidelines can be found in Chapter 6.

11-5C: QUOTATIONS WITHIN QUOTATIONS

Single quotation marks are used only to enclose quotations within quotations. Some confusion arises because this is a North American convention; British usage is the reverse (i.e., single quotation marks are the norm, and double quotation marks are only used inside single quotation marks).

> According to Newman et al., Charles de Gaulle "spoke the words that jolted a nation: 'Vive le Québec libre!'"

Two different quotation marks appear at the end of the quotation. The single quotation mark completes the interior quotation, while the double quotation mark completes the main quotation.

11-5D: TITLES

Use quotation marks around titles of works that are included within other works, such as poems, short stories, newspaper and magazine articles, radio programs, television episodes, and chapters and other subdivisions of books.

His talk focused on point of view in Edgar Allan Poe's short story "The Tell-Tale Heart."

The titles of plays, books, and films and the names of magazines should be set in italics if you are typing your manuscript. (Underline them if your manuscript is handwritten.) For more information on how to present titles, see 14-6a.

11-5E: WORDS AS WORDS

Italics or underlining is preferred for setting off words used as words (see 14-6d). However, it is also acceptable to use quotation marks for this purpose.

I remember once displaying my ignorance by using the word *irregardless* when I should have used *regardless.*

I remember once displaying my ignorance by using the word "irregardless" when I should have used "regardless."

Note that double—not single—quotation marks are used.

11-5F: WITH OTHER PUNCTUATION

The following section provides rules for using punctuation with quotation marks.

COMMAS AND PERIODS

Place commas and periods inside quotation marks. (Note that this is a North American convention; British usage generally places commas and periods outside quotation marks.)

"I'm not finished yet," she said. "The books I looked at were of no help."

Also follow the above punctuation rule in the following cases:

- with single quotation marks (see 11-5c)
- for titles of works
- for words used as words

Exception: If you follow Modern Language Association style guidelines for your paper, for parenthetical in-text citations, the period follows the final parenthesis. In this case, the period is therefore outside the quotation marks.

Clarkson and McCall contend "Davis was apprehensive that Trudeau's pugnacity might scupper the possibility" (368).

SEMICOLONS AND COLONS

Place semicolons and colons outside quotation marks.

> He explained his term "in the moment": the individual focuses himself or herself on the elusive present.

> As the bank's head economist, she asserts that the economy will soon "take off"; several of her colleagues at other banks strongly disagree.

QUESTION MARKS AND EXCLAMATION MARKS

If the question mark or exclamation mark is part of the quoted material, place the question mark or exclamation mark *inside* the quotation marks.

> ***Part of the Quoted Material***
> When Parminder heard what Susan had done, he shouted, "She made the shot from centre court!"

If the question mark or exclamation mark applies to the entire sentence, place a question mark or exclamation mark *outside* the quotation marks.

> ***Applies to the Entire Sentence***
> What do you think of Napoleon's view that "history is a set of lies agreed upon"?

If your instructor requires that you follow the style of the Modern Language Association, you will need to pay particular attention to your use of question marks and exclamation marks with quotation marks. According to MLA style, the question mark or exclamation mark is placed before the final closing quotation mark; a sentence period is then placed after the final parenthesis in the parenthetical citation.

> Oliver Sacks ponders, "If this was the case in Virgil, what might happen if visual function was suddenly made possible, demanded?" (291).

11-5G: INTRODUCING QUOTED MATERIAL

You have three major punctuation options when using a group of words to introduce a quotation:

1. a colon
2. a comma
3. no punctuation

WHEN TO USE THE COLON

Use the colon if the quotation has been formally introduced. A formal introduction is a complete independent clause.

> In *The Globe and Mail*, John Stackhouse presents the following insight about political change in Africa: "The economic revolution that has swept through Africa, from the highlands of eastern Kenya to the rain forests of Ivory Coast, has affected almost every African—and altered few governments."

WHEN TO USE THE COMMA

Use a comma if a quotation is introduced with or followed by an expression such as *she said* or *he uttered*.

> With a wry smile, the firefighter remarked, "Where there's smoke, there's fire."

> "I'm a Canadian," I protested.

WHEN A QUOTATION IS BLENDED INTO A SENTENCE

Use a comma or no punctuation depending on how the quotation fits into the grammatical structure of the sentence.

> She walked with an awkward jerky gait, as though she were not at home on her own legs, and as she passed by, the other kids would whisper, "Pigeon-Toed Cochran!"

> In summertime, all expeditions were planned tentatively; sentences ended with the phrase "if it doesn't rain."

WHEN A QUOTATION BEGINS A SENTENCE

Use a comma to set off a quotation at the beginning of a sentence.

> "I'll be back in a moment," I told my students, and half out of my mind with anxiety, I went down in the lift, dashed across the street, and burst into Jai Lu's house.

However, a comma is not needed if the opening quotation ends with a question mark or an exclamation mark.

> "What are you doing?" I demanded.

WHEN A QUOTED SENTENCE IS INTERRUPTED BY EXPLANATORY WORDS

Use commas to set off the explanatory words.

> "No," he called back, "I can see it breathing!"

WHEN TWO SUCCESSIVE QUOTED SENTENCES ARE INTERRUPTED BY EXPLANATORY WORDS

Use a comma within the quotation marks of the first quotation. End the explanatory words with a period.

> "We are simply not well prepared for the rapid development that we have been experiencing," Dr. Muangman said. "Politicians and decision-makers think that if we make a lot of money, that is enough."

11-5H: INCORRECT USES OF QUOTATION MARKS

Do not use quotation marks around indirect quotations.

> My mother always said longingly that she'd "like to visit Greece."

Do not use quotation marks to call attention to a word or expression. Never use quotation marks to distance yourself from an expression or to call attention to slang. Quotation marks used in this way are often called *scare quotes*. They are best avoided because they send an ambiguous message. Trust your words to speak for you, without the addition of quotation marks. Relying on such artificial devices is like explaining a joke; it reduces the effect, rather than increasing it.

> Some might say the mechanic went on a "busman's holiday."

> Many academics find the language of "political correctness" objectionable.

Finally, do not use quotation marks to set off the title of your document.

11-6: OTHER MARKS

11-6A: PERIOD

Periods are commonly used to indicate the end of a sentence. They are also used in abbreviations.

ENDING SENTENCES

Use the period after statements, indirect questions, and mild commands.

STATEMENT

Use a period after a statement.

> Rock climbing on the Bruce Trail can be dangerous.

INDIRECT QUESTION

After a **direct question**, use a question mark.

> Do you want to walk the Gun Point Loop section of the trail?

However, if the question is **indirect**, use a period to end the sentence.

> The hike leader inquired if they wanted to walk the Gun Point Loop section of the trail.

MILD COMMAND

After a strong command, use the exclamation mark. (See 11-6c.)

> Please, call an ambulance now!

However, after a **mild command**—an imperative or declarative sentence that is not an exclamation—use a period.

> Please pick up the groceries.

ABBREVIATIONS

Use periods in abbreviations such as the following:

a.m.	p.	B.A.	Dr.	Inc.
p.m.	etc.	M.A.	Ms.	Ltd.
B.C. (or B.C.E.)	e.g.	M.B.A.	Mrs.	Dec.
A.D. (or C.E.)	i.e.	Ph.D.	Mr.	St.

Do not use periods with Canada Post abbreviations, such as SK, ON, and NB.

Widely recognized abbreviations for organizations, companies, and countries do not require periods.

CBC	CSIS	NFB	UK	USA
IBM	UN	NBA	CFL	

If you are in doubt about whether or not an abbreviation requires a period, check in a good Canadian dictionary or encyclopedia. To check the abbreviation of a name of a company, you might consult that company's website.

Do not add a second period if the sentence ends with an abbreviation's period.

He always wanted to complete his M.A.

11-6B: QUESTION MARK

FOLLOWING A DIRECT QUESTION

Use a question mark after any direct questions.

Are you coming or going?

Also use a question mark after a polite request.

Would you please forward me a copy of the article for my files?

Use a period after an indirect question.

Selby asked if she could go home.

FOLLOWING QUESTIONS IN A SERIES

Use a question mark to end each question in a series, even if series questions are not complete sentences.

We are curious to hear what Justin's career goal will be this week.
Maybe a brain surgeon? A stock broker? Or perhaps a travel agent?

11-6C: EXCLAMATION MARK

Use the exclamation mark with an emphatic declaration or a strong command.

The plane will hit the mountain!

Get out of the way, quickly!

Do not overuse the exclamation mark.

× We climbed the mountain on Hornby and had an incredible view! On one side was the snowcapped Coastal Range! On the other side, we could see majestic Mt. Washington!

√ We climbed the mountain on Hornby and had an incredible view. On one side was the snowcapped Coastal Range. On the other side, we could see majestic Mt. Washington.

If every sentence ends with an exclamation mark, the mark loses its effectiveness in communicating emphasis. Communicate strong impressions through the powerful use of words, not through overuse of the exclamation mark.

11-6D: DASH

The dash marks a strong break in the continuity of a sentence. It can be used to add information, to emphasize part of a sentence, or to set part of the sentence off for clarity.

To make a dash using your computer, enter two unspaced hyphens (--). Do not leave a space before the first hyphen or after the second hyphen. Many computer programs automatically format dashes when you enter two consecutive hyphens. This kind of dash is called an em dash (—). You can also select it in Word by going to the Insert menu, choosing Symbol and then selecting Em Dash from the Special Characters option.

Dashes are used for the following purposes:

- to enclose a sentence element that interrupts the flow of thought, or to set off parenthetical material that deserves emphasis

> Our civilization is decadent and our language—so the argument runs—must inevitably share in the general collapse.
>
> —George Orwell, "On Politics and Government" in *Shooting an Elephant and Other Essays* (London: Secker and Warburg, 1950).

- to set off appositives that contain commas (for more information on appositives, see 11-1g)

> Teachers—those educators, parents, entertainers, babysitters, and counsellors—are undervalued and underpaid by society.

- to show a dramatic shift in tone or thought

> At the NBA All-Star Game, Michael Jordan took the pass, eluded the defender, hit full stride, soared—and missed an uncontested dunk.

- to restate

> Although they are close together—living only a few kilometres apart—they may as well be on different sides of the planet.

- to amplify

> Peanut butter was everywhere—in their hair, on their clothes, smudged on their glasses.

- to introduce a list

In the storage room are all the paint supplies—paints, paint thinner, drop cloths, brushes, rollers, and paint trays.

Do not overuse dashes. If overused, dashes can lose their effectiveness and make writing disjointed. The Modern Language Association manual suggests limiting the number of dashes in a sentence to two paired dashes or one unpaired dash.

× Three students—Anwar, Sanjah, and Pete—won prizes—scholarships, books, and medallions. This is quite an achievement—especially for Pete since he studies only minimally—if at all.

√ Three students—Anwar, Sanjah, and Pete—won prizes, which included scholarships, books, and medallions. This is quite an achievement, especially for Pete, since he studies only minimally, if at all.

11-6E: PARENTHESES

Parentheses are used to set off helpful, nonessential, additional information. While dashes usually call attention to the information they enclose, parentheses often de-emphasize the information they enclose.

Parentheses can be used for the following purposes:

- to enclose supplemental information, such as a definition, an example, a digression, an aside, or a contrast

Calgary is second among cities in Canada for number of head offices located within its city limits (92 in 1995).

Kenner taught at Assumption College (now University of Windsor) from 1946 to 1948.

- to enclose letters or numbers that label items in a series

Follow these directions to make a puppet: (1) put your hand inside a white sock, (2) form the puppet's mouth with your thumb and fingers, and (3) draw a face on the sock with a felt-tipped marker.

Do not overuse parentheses. Including too much parenthetical information can make your writing seem choppy and awkward. Often, you can integrate information from parentheses into your sentences so they flow more smoothly.

The second phase of railway building in Canada ~~(starting 1867)~~ came with Confederation ^in 1867^.

11-6F: BRACKETS

Brackets (also called square brackets—not to be confused with parentheses) are used to enclose any words you have inserted into quoted material. You may need to add or change a word so a quotation will fit more smoothly into the structure of your sentences, or to clarify information or ideas for readers. As well, square brackets might be used to indicate an error in the original quoted material.

TO ADD OR SUBSTITUTE CLARIFYING INFORMATION IN A QUOTATION

> "I rode swiftly toward Sitting Bull's camp. Then I saw the white soldiers [Reno's men] fighting in line."

The short passage is from *Bury My Heart at Wounded Knee* and offers oral accounts from a Native perspective of fighting between Native Americans and soldiers. Within the context of the book, the information in square brackets clarifies which white soldiers were doing the fighting.

TO INDICATE ERRORS IN ORIGINAL MATERIAL

The Latin word *sic* means "so" or "thus." The word *sic* is placed in square brackets immediately after a word in a quotation that appears erroneous or odd. *Sic* indicates that the word is quoted exactly as it stands in the original. The term is always in italics to indicate that it is a foreign word.

> "Growing up on the small island [*sic*] of Nanaimo, British Columbia, Diana Krall has made a name for herself as a jazz singer."

[*Sic*] indicates to the reader that the writer who is quoting the sentence realizes the author of the original article is wrong in calling Nanaimo an "island," when in fact it is a city.

11-6G: ELLIPSIS MARK

An ellipsis mark consists of three spaced periods (. . .). The ellipsis is used to indicate that you have omitted material from the original writer's quoted words.

WHEN DELETING MATERIAL FROM A QUOTATION

> Gagnon states that "as much as 65% to 70% of semen volume originates from the seminal vesicles . . . and about 5% from the minor sexual glands."

The Modern Language Association used to recommend placing brackets around an ellipsis inserted by the quoting writer. The brackets indicated to the reader that the ellipsis did not appear in the original material. Though the MLA no longer recommends using brackets in this way, many instructors like the idea. You may wish to check with yours to clarify which style he or she would like you to follow.

An ellipsis is not required at the beginning of a quotation. Do not place an ellipsis at the end of the quotation, unless you have omitted content from the final quoted sentence.

WHEN DELETING A FULL SENTENCE FROM THE MIDDLE OF A QUOTED PASSAGE

Use a period before the three ellipsis points if you need to delete a full sentence or more from the middle of a quoted passage.

> Priestly's ideas on nationalism are not flattering. He says, "If we deduct from nationalism all that is borrowed or stolen from regionalism, what remains is mostly rubbish. . . . Almost all nationalist movements are led by ambitious, frustrated men determined to hold office."

WHEN QUOTING POETRY

Use a full line of spaced dots to indicate that you have omitted a line or more from the quotation of a poem.

> Death, be not proud, though some have called thee
> Mighty and dreadful, for thou art not so;
> . . . .
> From rest and sleep, which but thy pictures be,
> Much pleasure; then from thee much more must flow,
>
> —John Donne

WHEN INDICATING INTERRUPTION OR HESITATION IN SPEECH OR THOUGHT

Often in story dialogue or narration, an ellipsis is used to indicate hesitation or interruption in speech or thought.

> "Well . . . I couldn't make it. I didn't get to the exam."

11-6H: SLASH

USING THE SLASH TO INDICATE LINES OF POETRY

The slash is used most often in academic writing to mark off lines of poetry when these have been incorporated into the text. Up to three lines from a poem can be quoted in the text.

Atwood's "Death of a Young Son by Drowning" opens with the haunting lines, "He, who navigated with success / the dangerous river of his own birth / once more set forth."

Leave one space before and one space after the slash. For quoted passages of poetry that are four or more lines in length, start each line of the poem on its own line, indented in the style of block quotations.

USING THE SLASH TO INDICATE OPTIONS OR PAIRED ITEMS

Sometimes the slash is used between options or paired items. Examples include *actor/producer, life/death, pass/fail*. In these cases, do not leave a space before and after the slash.

Since the orchestra was short of funds, he served as artistic director/conductor.

Avoid the use of *he/she, his/her,* and *and/or,* as they are informal and awkward in writing.

12

SENTENCE STRUCTURE AND STYLE

FIRST you write a sentence,
AND then YOU CHOP IT SMALL;
Then mix the bits, and sort them out
JUST AS THEY CHANCE TO FALL:
THE ORDER OF THE PHRASES MAKES
NO DIFFERENCE AT ALL.
— Lewis Carroll

12

Sentence Structure and Style

12 Sentence Structure and Style

Chapter 10, Common Sentence Errors, is designed to deal with the nuts and bolts of putting a sentence together. At a later stage in revision, you may give more thought to why you structured a sentence in a particular way. This section provides you with information on how to make your sentences work better for you in your efforts to persuade the reader of the point you are making.

12-1: SHIFTS

A **shift** is a sudden and unnecessary change in point of view, verb tense, mood, or voice, or a change from indirect to direct questions or quotations. Shifts can occur within and between sentences. They often blur meaning and confuse readers.

12-1A: POINT OF VIEW

In writing, **point of view** is the perspective from which the work is written. Often this is indicated by the pronouns the writer uses.

1. First person: *I, we*
2. Second person: *you*
3. Third person: *he/she/it/one* or *they*

You have probably noticed the following in the course of your own writing and reading:

- The first-person point of view often appears in more informal types of writing, such as journals, diaries, and personal letters.
- The second-person point of view is often found in directions or instructional types of writing, such as this handbook.
- The third-person point of view emphasizes the subject. It is used in informative writing, including the writing you do in many academic and professional contexts.

Shifts in point of view occur when a writer begins his or her piece of writing in one point of view, then shifts carelessly back and forth to other points of view. To prevent needless shifts, think about the most appropriate point of view for your writing situation, establish the point of view in your writing, and keep to that point of view.

Shifts in Point of View

Some hikers have their dogs carry the food pack on longer trips. As
their
~~our~~ journey progresses and stops are periodically made for meals, the dog's pack becomes lighter.

The writer started the passage in the third person, then shifted to the first person with *our*.

Your fax machine supports both tone and pulse dialling. The default
you do
setting is TONE, so ~~one does~~ not need to change the setting if
you use
~~he or she uses~~ that kind of line. If you are using a pulse dial line, change the setting to PULSE by following these steps.

In these instructions, the writer began in the second person, then shifted to the third person before returning to the second person.

A common problem among student writers is shifting from the third-person singular to the third-person plural or vice versa.

Shift from Singular to Plural

they prefer
Since malamutes have very heavy fur coats, ~~it prefers~~ to sleep outside even in extremely cold temperatures.

The writer shifted from third-person plural (*malamutes*) to third-person singular (*it*).

12-1B: VERB TENSE

The verb tense tells the reader when the action in the piece of writing is taking place. Shifting from one verb tense to another without a sound reason only confuses the reader.

Tense Shift

He is so vain that he always sits at a restaurant table facing the
thinks
sunlight, since he ~~thought~~ the rays might add to his precious tan.

The sentence begins in the present tense (*sits*) then shifts to the past tense (*thought*).

The convention in essays about literature is to describe fictional events consistently in the present tense. Sometimes, of course, shifts in tense are necessary if you are discussing literature in its historical context.

D.H. Lawrence's use of profane language was a departure from the conventions of the novel in the early twentieth century.

Shift from Literary Present

As an egocentric, Gabriel has "restless eyes" early in "The Dead." However, when he displays empathy near the end of the story, he ~~possessed~~ possesses "curious eyes."

The writer begins using the literary present tense convention, then erroneously shifts into the past tense with *possessed*.

12-1C: VERB MOOD AND VOICE

MOOD

Shifts can also occur in the mood of verbs. The mood of the verb indicates the manner of action. There are three moods in English.

1. The indicative mood is used to state facts or opinions, or to ask questions.

He wrote a short story.

Did he win a prize for the story?

2. The imperative mood is used to give a command or advice, or make a request.

Don't do that!

Rewind the videotape before returning it.

3. The subjunctive mood is used to express doubt, wishes, or possibility.

If I were lucky, I might have won the lottery.

The subjunctive mood also expresses conditions contrary to fact.

If wishes were horses, beggars would ride.

Mood Shift

Include more foreground by focusing in front of your main subject while keeping the subject within the depth of field. ~~The reverse is also true~~. To include more background, do the reverse.

The writer's purpose is to give advice on photography. He or she appropriately begins in the imperative mood, but erroneously shifts into the indicative mood.

VOICE

Voice refers to whether a verb is active or passive. A verb is active when the subject is the doer of the action. A verb is passive when the subject of the verb receives the action. If the writer suddenly shifts between voices, it can be jarring and confusing to the reader.

> ***Shift in Voice***
>
> I could immediately comprehend the devastation of the avalanche
>
> I reached
>
> as soon as^ the peak overlooking the valley ~~was reached~~.

The subordinate clause is in the passive voice, while the main clause is in the active voice.

12-1D: DIRECT AND INDIRECT QUESTIONS OR QUOTATIONS

DIRECT AND INDIRECT QUOTATIONS

In a direct quotation, the writer repeats a speaker's words exactly, placing those words within quotation marks. In an indirect quotation, the writer summarizes or paraphrases what the speaker has said.

> ***Direct:*** U.S. General William C. Westmoreland said, "We'll blow them back into the Stone Age."
>
> ***Indirect:*** U.S. General William C. Westmoreland said his forces would bomb the enemy so relentlessly that they would be blown back into the Stone Age.

> ***Shift from Indirect to Direct***
>
> not
>
> The dog trainer told me to keep Pepé by my side and ~~don't~~ give the dog more than a foot of slack on his lead.

The writer shifts from indirect quotation to direct quotation with *don't give the dog more than a foot of slack on his lead*. The revision makes the quotation consistently indirect. An alternative revision would be *The dog trainer said, "Keep Pepé by your side and don't give the dog more than a foot of slack on his lead."* In this version, the quotation is consistently direct.

DIRECT AND INDIRECT QUESTIONS

A direct question stands alone as a question. It is not introduced or included in any statement.

Which road do you take to get to Lions Head?

An indirect question reports that a question was asked, but does not actually ask the question.

I asked which road to take to get to Lions Head.

Shifting from indirect to direct questions can make writing awkward and confusing.

Shift from Indirect to Direct

whether you'd like

I'm asking you if you'd like to hike the Bruce Trail, and if so, ~~would you like~~ to start at Tobermory or St. Catharines.

The revision presents both questions indirectly. An alternate revision would be to pose both questions directly: *Would you like to hike the Bruce Trail, and if so, would you like to start at Tobermory or St. Catharines?*

12-2: MIXED CONSTRUCTIONS

A sentence with a **mixed construction** incorrectly changes from one grammatical construction to another incompatible one, thereby confusing the sentence's meaning.

12-2A: MIXED GRAMMAR

When you draft a sentence, your options for structuring that sentence are limited by the grammatical patterns of English. (See 9-2 and 9-3.) You must consistently follow the pattern you choose within the sentence. You cannot start the sentence using one grammatical pattern and then abruptly change to another. *Don't switch horses* [grammatical structures] *in the middle of a stream* [sentence] is an idiom that can help you remember this key grammatical guideline.

Mixed: By multiplying the number of specialty stations available to viewers via digital television increases the chance that cultural communities within Canada's diverse cultural mosaic will be better served.

Revised: Multiplying the number of specialty stations available to viewers via digital television increases the chance that cultural communities within Canada's diverse cultural mosaic will be better served.

OR

Revised: By multiplying the number of specialty stations available to viewers via digital television, satellite and cable companies increase the chance that cultural communities within Canada's diverse cultural mosaic will be better served.

The mixed construction, which begins with *By*, cannot serve as the subject of the sentence. In the first revision, *by* is dropped, so the opening is no longer a participial phrase but is now a gerund and hence the subject. In the second revision, the participial phrase is retained, but a subject is added so that the phrase is not a dangling modifier.

Another mixed construction is incorrectly combined clauses.

Satellite
~~Although satellite~~ dishes have become popular in many northern Canadian communities, but many viewers still prefer local stations.

Here the clause beginning *although* is a subordinate clause. Hence, it cannot be linked to an independent clause with the coordinating conjunction *but*.

From time to time, when revising your own work, you may encounter a sentence that can't be fixed grammatically. In instances such as this, it is often wise to rethink what you want to say, and then completely recast the sentence so it is clear, straightforward, and logical.

Mixed: In communicative language teaching, students' errors are corrected only when they interfere with comprehension rather than by the direct method in which students' errors are corrected immediately to avoid habit formation.

Revised: In communicative language teaching, students' errors are corrected only when they interfere with comprehension; in the direct method, students' errors are corrected immediately to avoid habit formation.

Often, trying to pack too much information into a sentence causes confusion.

ESL Note

Double subjects do not exist in English; similarly, objects or adverbs may not be repeated in an adjective clause. See 15-3b and 15-3c.

The museum you want to visit ~~it~~ is not open on Sunday.

Upset at the news, she ran to the school that her son was attending ~~it~~.

12-2B: ILLOGICAL CONNECTIONS

A number of sentence faults can occur when elements of the sentence do not logically fit together. **Faulty predication** is one example of such a problem. In faulty predication, the subject and predicate do not make sense together. To remedy this problem, either the subject or the predicate must be revised.

> Originally,
> ~~The original function of~~ the Internet was created to exchange academic and military information.

The function was not created to exchange academic and military information. In this instance, the subject is refined so that it connects more logically with the predicate.

> The decisions on who would make Canada's 2002 Olympic hockey team
> were made
> ~~was chosen~~ by a management committee headed by Wayne Gretzky.

The decisions didn't do the choosing. The management committee headed by Wayne Gretzky made the decisions.

An appositive is a noun or noun phrase that renames or explains a noun or noun phrase immediately before it; for example

> November, <u>the month of my birth</u>, . . .

The appositive must logically relate to the noun or noun phrase that precedes it; otherwise **faulty apposition** occurs.

> speculation
> Stock ~~speculators~~, <u>a very risky business</u>, demands nerves of steel and a healthy bank account.

Stock speculation, not stock speculators, is a very risky business.

12-2C: AVOIDING *IS WHEN, IS WHERE, REASON . . . IS BECAUSE*

In formal writing, avoid the following constructions:

1. *Is when* or *is where*

> In computer dating,
> ~~Computer dating is when~~ the computer is used to match potential romantic partners according to their compatibility, interests, and desirability.

Computer dating is not a time but a service.

2. *The reason . . . is because*

> ~~The reason~~ I watch horror movies ~~is~~ because I need a release from the tensions of life.

Notice that the revised sentence is much tighter. The writer might also have avoided the awkward *reason . . . is because* construction by replacing *because* with *that.*

These constructions are not grammatical and often add unnecessary words to a sentence. If you find such constructions in your drafts, revise the sentences that contain them.

12-3: COORDINATION AND SUBORDINATION

Coordination and **subordination** allow you to communicate the relationships between ideas in sentences. You can use coordination to give equal emphasis to ideas; use subordination to give unequal emphasis.

COORDINATION

Coordination balances two or more equal ideas in a sentence, giving equal emphasis to each idea. You can coordinate ideas at the level of words, phrases, or clauses by using the coordinating conjunctions *and, but, for, nor, or, so,* and *yet.*

> Nelson Mandela spent 28 years in a South African jail, but the great dignity with which he endured imprisonment made him a symbol of the struggle against apartheid.

When coordinating words or phrases, you need only use the coordinating conjunction. When coordinating independent clauses (remember that a clause is a group of words that can stand on its own as a sentence), join the clauses with a comma and a coordinating conjunction or a semicolon alone. In some cases, the semicolon is followed by a conjunctive adverb, such as *however, therefore, moreover, hence,* and *indeed.*

> Nelson Mandela spent 28 years in a South African jail; moreover, the great dignity with which he endured imprisonment made him a symbol of the struggle against apartheid.

SUBORDINATION

Subordination allows you to communicate the relative importance of ideas within sentences. You can emphasize important ideas by making them independent clauses or give ideas less emphasis by making them subordinate clauses, which cannot stand on their own as sentences. Usually subordinating clauses begin with one of the following subordinating conjunctions:

after	since	when	while
although	than	whenever	who
as	that	where	whom
because	though	wherever	whose
before	unless	whether	
if	until	which	

When drafting a sentence, you must decide which idea you would like to emphasize. Subordinating a clause within the Nelson Mandela sentence can give it a very different meaning.

> Although Nelson Mandela spent 28 years in a South African jail, the great dignity with which he endured imprisonment made him a symbol of the struggle against apartheid.

If you want to emphasize that the great personal price of spending 28 years behind bars might have been somehow worth it to become a symbol against apartheid, you might use the following subordination pattern.

> While Nelson Mandela spent 28 years in a South African jail, the great dignity with which he endured imprisonment made him a symbol of the struggle against apartheid.

Or, perhaps your intended meaning is to look at events from a more temporal perspective, suggesting that it was the dignity he displayed in the latter years of his long imprisonment that made him very noble.

> After Nelson Mandela spent 28 years in a South African jail, he became a symbol of the struggle against apartheid because of the great dignity with which he endured imprisonment.

No version is right or wrong. However, one of versions might be closer to the meaning that you, as a writer, intend.

12-3A: CHOPPY SENTENCES

Too many consecutive short sentences in a passage can make your writing seem mechanically repetitive and choppy. As well, probably not all of the ideas in the string of short sentences are equally important. Some sentence ideas you might wish to emphasize, some you might want to de-emphasize, and some ideas in pairs of sentences you might consider balancing. Subordination and coordination allow you to combine sentences and thus eliminate the problem of choppy writing.

> ***Choppy:*** Tennyson called lightning a "flying flame." Lightning travels at between 100 000 and 300 000 kilometres per second. Lightning reaches temperatures of 24 000 to 28 000 degrees Celsius. It kills 20 people each day.

> ***Revised:*** Lightning, which Tennyson called a "flying flame," travels at between 100 000 and 300 000 kilometres per second and reaches temperatures of 24 000 to 28 000 degrees Celsius, killing 20 people each day.

These four very short sentences have become one by using the subordinator *which* and the coordinator *and*. Also note the use of the modifier *killing* to replace *it kills*.

> ***Choppy:*** The basketball team huddled on the sidelines. The players were drenched in sweat. They looked dejected.

> ***Revised:*** The basketball team, drenched in sweat and looking dejected, huddled on the sidelines.

Here, the two final sentences have been subordinated into an adjective clause modifying the basketball team.

> After illness, I
> ^I received a call from the doctor about my dad's serious ~~illness. I~~ immediately booked the first possible flight to Victoria.

The subordinating word *after* has been used to turn the first sentence into an adverbial clause.

> , student,
> Harjeet^ ~~was~~ my adult literacy ~~student. Harjeet~~ was fighting a valiant battle against multiple sclerosis.

A less-important idea has been turned into an appositive describing Harjeet.

> ***Choppy:*** The marathon swimmer was coated with grease, and she listed as she made her way to the shore. She seemed a symbol of determination.

> ***Revised:*** Coated with grease and listing as she made her way to the shore, the marathon swimmer seemed a symbol of determination.

Less significant details about how the swimmer looked are placed in the participial phrase beginning *Coated*.

While these sentences serve as examples, you can also use them as models for strategies to improve your own writing. For example, you might consider combining sentences by turning a shorter sentence into an appositive or an adjectival phrase.

> ***Choppy:*** Miners in Nanaimo-area coal mines had to worry about shafts under the harbour collapsing. They had to be concerned about deadly gases. The miners also had to be worried about fires or explosions.
>
> ***Revised:*** Miners in Nanaimo-area coal mines had to worry about shafts under the harbour collapsing, deadly gases, and fires or explosions.

The three sentences have been combined into one sentence containing ideas of equal importance.

ESL Note

Do not repeat the subject when you combine sentences. Also do not repeat an adverb when it occurs in an adjective clause. See 15-3b and 15-3c.

> The work that he completed ~~it~~ was sloppy.
>
> The spot where the accident occurred ~~there~~ is dangerous.

12-3B: INEFFECTIVE COORDINATION

Coordination is effective when you want to point out to the reader that two ideas are of equal importance.

> Speak softly and carry a big stick.

U.S. president Theodore Roosevelt quoted this adage in a speech in 1901. The balance of the sentence is central to Roosevelt's meaning. He thought American foreign policy should employ diplomacy (*speak softly*) but at the same time be backed up by military might (*a big stick*). Coordination is extremely effective here.

However, coordination problems arise when you attempt to coordinate ideas that are unrelated or unequal.

> Since cell
> ~~Cell~~ phones became very popular in the 1990s, ~~and~~ many users have experienced car accidents.

In the coordinated version of the sentence, the two ideas could be unrelated. By adding the subordinating word *Since* and turning the opening independent clause into a subordinate one, the cause–effect relationship between the ideas is foregrounded.

> , observing
> The doctor^ ~~observed~~ that there were an abnormal number of patients
>
> ,
> from the Walkerton area with gastrointestinal disorders^ ~~and~~ alerted authorities that they could have a major health crisis on their hands.

The key idea that the doctor concluded there might be a crisis is given prominence in the sentence. The less significant idea is given less prominence as a participial phrase modifying the subject, the doctor.

> ***Coordinated Unequal Ideas:*** Poet P.K. Page studied art in New York and Brazil, and then in the 1940s she was a filing clerk and historical researcher, but it was during the '40s that she became a founding member of the literary periodical *Preview*.

> ***Revised:*** After studying art in New York and Brazil, in the 1940s poet P.K. Page worked as a filing clerk and historical researcher, but it was also during this time that she became a founding member of the literary periodical *Preview*.

The original sentence contained too many coordinated independent clauses. In the revision, the opening clause has become dependent, which is appropriate since that clause contains less important information.

12-3C: INEFFECTIVE SUBORDINATION

Main sentence ideas should be given emphasis within the sentence; do not relegate them to subordinate status. Structure your sentences so that important ideas appear in independent clauses, while less important ideas or information appears in subordinate dependent clauses.

> While
> ^Raginder was riding the bus along West Hastings Street, listening on his iPod to the Steve Miller song "Take the Money and Run," ~~when~~ he saw two bank robbers fleeing a TD Canada Trust branch on foot.

The fact that Raginder was listening to a song is not as important as the fact that he saw a bank robbery in progress.

12-3D: EXCESSIVE SUBORDINATION

Sometimes subordination can be overused. If you have more than two dependent clauses in a sentence, determine whether or not excessive subordination has made the sentence unclear or otherwise ineffective. Usually there are two ways to address the excessive subordination problem.

1. Recast the sentence.
2. Divide the sentence in two.

Unclear: While jogging is good aerobic exercise, as you get older, since running adversely affects deteriorating knees, it is advisable to do it in moderation.

Revision: Jogging is good aerobic exercise. However, as you get older, since running adversely affects deteriorating knees, it is advisable to do it in moderation.

Too many secondary, subordinate ideas were packed into one sentence.

12-4: PARALLELISM

Parallelism in writing means that equal grammatical structures are used to express equal ideas. Errors in parallelism, known as **faulty parallelism**, occur when *unequal* structures are used to express equal ideas. Words, phrases, and clauses should all be parallel when they express a similar idea and perform a similar function in a sentence. When using parallelism for effect, balance single words with single words, phrases with phrases, and clauses with clauses.

The following three quotations from Winston Churchill all demonstrate parallel, balanced elements:

Words: I have nothing to offer but blood, toil, tears and sweat.

Phrases: Victory at all costs, victory in spite of all terror, victory however long and hard the road may be; for without victory there is no survival.

Clauses: You do your worst, and we will do our best.

12-4A: WITH ITEMS IN A SERIES

When the reader encounters items in a series, he or she expects that parallel grammatical pattern to continue within the sentence. However, when one or more items do not follow the parallel grammatical pattern, the sentence seems jarring and awkward to the reader.

× Anatole liked the lawn, the hedge, and to garden.

√ Anatole liked the lawn, the hedge, and the garden.

All items in the corrected version are nouns.

× Ace may not be the cutest or the largest dog in existence, but he's also very smart.

√ Ace may not be the cutest or the largest dog in existence, but he may be one of the smartest.

Items in the corrected sentence are all comparative adjectives with the *-est* (or superlative) ending.

× Being outdoors, feeling the winds off the ocean, and to smell the Douglas fir are what I like about hiking British Columbia's West Coast Trail.

√ Being outdoors, feeling the winds off the ocean, and smelling the Douglas fir are what I like about hiking British Columbia's West Coast Trail.

To smell must be in the *-ing* participial form to be consistent with *being* and *feeling*.

12-4B: WITH PAIRED ITEMS

Parallel ideas are often connected in one of three ways:

1. With a coordinating conjunction, such as *or, and,* or *but*
2. With a pair of correlative conjunctions, such as *not only . . . but also* or *either . . . or*
3. With comparative constructions using *than* or *as*

Whenever you relate ideas using one of these methods, always emphasize the connection between or among ideas by expressing them in parallel grammatical form.

USING PARALLEL FORMS WITH COORDINATING CONJUNCTIONS
Coordinating conjunctions (*and, but, or, nor, for, yet,* and *so*) are words that connect ideas of equal importance. Avoid faulty parallelism by ensuring that all elements joined by coordinating conjunctions are parallel in grammatical form.

× Alfred, you may go by train, boat, car, bus, or a jet will take you there.

√ Alfred, you may go by train, boat, car, bus, or jet.

In the original sentence, all elements in the series before the conjunction are nouns, but a clause is used for the last item, which is therefore not parallel.

× Our debating team read Jordan's ideas, were discussing her arguments, and have decided they are not relevant to our debate position.

√ Our debating team read Jordan's ideas, discussed her arguments, and decided they are not relevant to our debate position.

The verb tenses *were discussing* and *have decided* are not consistent with the simple past tense *read*.

USING PARALLEL FORMS WITH CORRELATIVE CONJUNCTIONS

Correlative conjunctions are pairs of words that join equal grammatical structures. Examples include *not only . . . but also*, *either . . . or*, and *both . . . and*. Avoid faulty parallelism by ensuring that each element linked by correlative conjunctions is parallel in its grammatical form.

× When the staff met the sales target, the manager not only ordered new chairs, but also new desks, potted plants, and a microwave for the lunchroom.

√ When the staff met the sales target, the manager ordered <u>not only</u> new chairs, <u>but also</u> new desks, potted plants, and a microwave for the lunchroom.

OR

√ When the staff met the sales target, the manager <u>not only</u> ordered new chairs, <u>but also</u> provided new desks, potted plants, and a microwave for the lunchroom.

In the first revision, a noun follows *not only*, so a noun must follow *but also*. In the second, a verb follows *not only*; similarly, a verb must follow *but also*.

× Viewers either criticized the television station for its inflammatory views, or it was criticized for its political stance.

√ Viewers <u>either</u> criticized the television station for its inflammatory views <u>or</u> criticized it for its political stance.

OR

√ Viewers criticized the television station <u>either</u> for its inflammatory views <u>or</u> for its political stance.

The verb used with *either* must match the verb used with *or*, but in the original sentence, one is in the active voice, and the other is in the passive voice. The first revision corrects this problem; however, the second revision is more economical, and the connection between related ideas is even clearer.

COMPARISONS LINKED WITH THAN *OR* AS

Often you will use *than* or *as* to make comparisons. To avoid faulty parallelism, make sure the elements being compared are expressed using parallel grammatical structure.

× Having great wealth is not as satisfying as the completion of charitable works.

√ Having great wealth is not as satisfying as completing charitable works.

Use the matching *-ing* form on both sides of the comparison.

× It is better to give than do the receiving.

√ It is better to give than to receive.

Use the matching form—in this case, the infinitive form of the verb (with *to*)—on both sides of the comparison.

Note: With many of the corrections shown above, there are equally acceptable alternatives. In some instances, faulty parallelism corrections that occur to you may be improvements over what appears in the handbook.

12-5: NEEDED WORDS

In your efforts to write concisely by deleting words, be careful not to cut essential words.

This is especially true in the following situations:

- when using compound structures
- when *that* is required, if there is danger of misreading sentences
- when using comparisons

Provide all words needed to make such sentences grammatically and logically complete.

Other languages have different rules about which words can be omitted. Watch especially for missing articles, verbs, subjects, or expletive pronouns. See 15-1, 15-2i, and 15-3a.

12-5A: IN COMPOUND STRUCTURES

In compound constructions, two or more elements (e.g., words, phrases, clauses) have equal importance and function as a unit.

In the Big Sur event, some competitors will run in the marathon and some [will run] in the 10 km race.

It is acceptable to omit *will run* since the omitted words are common to both parts of the compound structure.

However, when the parts in a compound structure differ in any way, all words must be included in each part of the compound construction.

× A funeral lasts for hours; some wakes for days.

√ A funeral lasts for hours; some wakes last for days.

You cannot omit the verb *last* from the compound, since in one-half of the compound the verb is singular and in the other half it is plural.

× I have and will continue to support your right to remain silent.

√ I have supported and will continue to support your right to remain silent.

In the incorrect version *have . . . support* is not grammatically acceptable.

× Many little tots believe and leave milk and cookies for Santa Claus.

√ Many little tots believe in and leave milk and cookies for Santa Claus.

Believe . . . for is not correct. English idiom requires different prepositions for *believe* and *leave.*

12-5B: *THAT*

Sometimes when the word *that* introduces a subordinate clause it may be omitted, but only if the omission does not present a danger of misreading the sentence.

The movie [that] I saw most often when I was young was *The Mummy*.

BUT

× Edgar noticed his brand new television, which he had purchased on credit, didn't match his new carpet.

√ Edgar noticed that his brand new television, which he had purchased on credit, didn't match his new carpet.

The second sentence makes it clear that Edgar *noticed his television didn't match his new carpet* as opposed to simply *noticed his brand new television.*

12-5C: IN COMPARISONS

Make comparisons only between like items. Comparisons between unlike items are illogical and jarring to the reader.

× I compared my short stories to Ernest Hemingway.

√ I compared my short stories to Ernest Hemingway's.

OR

√ I compared my short stories to those of Ernest Hemingway.

The incorrect version compares short stories with Ernest Hemingway—two distinctly different items. The sentence requires that short stories be compared with short stories.

× In terms of special effects, James Cameron's version of the *Titanic* story is more stunning than any other director.

√ In terms of special effects, James Cameron's version of the *Titanic* story is more stunning than any other director's.

In the incorrect sentence, version and director—two very different items—are compared. By adding the possessive director's, which implies version, you are comparing two like items: versions of the *Titanic* story.

USING ANY *AND* ANY OTHER

Comparisons using *any* and *any other* can be confusing. Writers sometimes omit *other*, making comparisons illogical. Follow these guidelines:

1. Use *any other* when comparing an item with other items in the same group.

other
Toronto has a larger population than any ^ city in Ontario.

Without *other,* the sentence suggests that Toronto has a larger population than itself.

2. Use *any* when comparing an item with other items in a different group.

Toronto has a larger population than any ~~other~~ city in Quebec.

The incorrect sentence suggests that Toronto is in Quebec, which is untrue.

USING AS TO MAKE GRAMMATICALLY CORRECT COMPARISONS

Insert *as* when it is needed to make a comparison grammatically correct.

> Canada's best authors are as renowned^as, and probably more renowned than, those of any other small country.

The construction *as renowned . . . than* is grammatically incomplete.

Comparisons must be complete so that it is clear to the reader just what is being compared.

× Sudsaway is a better dishwashing detergent.

√ Sudsaway is a better dishwashing detergent than Dentoxanol.

Leave no chance for ambiguity in the comparisons you make. For example, the following sentence can be interpreted in a number of ways.

× I gave him more soup than you.

√ I gave him more soup than I gave to you.

OR

√ I gave him more soup than you gave him.

12-6: SENTENCE VARIETY

After you complete an essay or report draft, chances are you're relieved just to have the ideas on paper. When you carefully review the draft, you may find that many sentences are very similar in structure and length. By revising and crafting your work to create sentences of varied structures and lengths, you can make your writing livelier. However, when striving for sentence variety, be sure that you do not detract from your intended meaning or sentence clarity.

12-6A: SIMPLE, COMPOUND, AND COMPLEX SENTENCES

Too many of any one type of sentence structure can make your writing repetitive and monotonous. Recall that sentences come in three basic structures—simple, compound, and complex—and that sentence structures can be combined to create, for example, compound-complex sentences. Guard against overuse of one sentence type: too many simple sentences can make your ideas sound simplistic, and too many complex sentences, if not required because of difficult content, can make your writing seem tedious or pretentious. For a discussion on sentence types, see 9-4.

12-6B: SENTENCE OPENINGS

The majority of English sentences begin with the subject first, followed by the verb, and then the object. If this subject-verb-object pattern appears too often in your writing, it can create a monotonous effect.

To add variety and interest to your writing, as you revise, consider beginning some sentences differently.

ADVERBIAL MODIFIERS

You can easily place an adverbial modifier in front of the sentence subject, if such a construction is needed to achieve sentence variety. These modifiers can be single words, phrases, or clauses.

Soon the ferrets
~~The ferrets soon~~ returned from their sanctuary at the wildlife habitat.

For seven days, the
~~The~~ students stayed in their rooms ~~for seven days~~, where they were deprived of sleep, overwhelmed by assignments, and driven to distraction with worry.

ADJECTIVAL AND PARTICIPIAL PHRASES

Often adjectival phrases and participial phrases can be moved to the start of the sentence without affecting meaning.

Broken the boxer
~~The boxer, broken~~ and battered, ^ relinquished his heavyweight crown.

Draft: The provincial government employees, expecting to be terminated, dusted off their résumés.

Revision: Expecting to be terminated, the provincial government employees dusted off their résumés.

When using adjectival or participial phrases, ensure that the subject is clearly identified, or you may be creating a dangling modifier. For information on repairing dangling modifiers, see 10-7e.

12-6C: INVERTED ORDER

Changing the common subject-verb-object sentence pattern may not only create sentence variety but also—in some instances—add emphasis. In an inverted sentence, the subject appears at the end of the sentence.

> ***Subject-Verb-Object:*** The world-famous painting rested against the far wall.
>
> ***Inverted Order:*** Against the far wall rested the world-famous painting.

Use inverted sentences in moderation. They often sound awkward and artificial.

> ***Subject-Verb-Object:*** The movie star sauntered into the suite for the press conference.
>
> ***Inverted Order:*** Into the suite sauntered the movie star for the press conference.

12-7: WORDINESS

Effective writing is concise, clear, and direct. Concise writing does not necessarily mean fewer words or shorter sentences. It means words that function clearly and sentences that express their point without empty words. A longer sentence may be considered extremely succinct if it is required to express a sophisticated idea. As well, many shorter sentences can be even more economically written. When revising, review each sentence you write with an eye to eliminating any phrase or word that is not absolutely necessary to your intended meaning.

12-7A: REDUNDANCIES

Redundancy is the use of unnecessary words in a sentence. Often the same idea is expressed twice or more.

> It is 6:30 a.m. in the morning.

Other common redundancies include *final completion, important essentials, close proximity, consensus of opinion,* and *actual fact.*

> ~~The reason~~ Nebuchadnezzar stopped his conquest ~~was~~ because he heard of his father's death and his own succession to the throne.
>
> The board members did not want to repeat the debate ~~again~~, so they had a frank ~~and honest~~ discussion during which they identified some basic ~~essential~~ ideas.

When people are in ~~situations of~~ conflict at a meeting, they should circle ~~around~~ the speaker and try to attempt to ~~form~~ achieve a consensus ~~of opinion~~.

The bridge ~~that people cross to get~~ to Burlington is ~~sort of~~ rectangular ~~in shape~~, and it is made of strong materials such as reinforced steel ~~,~~ and concrete~~, etc~~.

12-7B: UNNECESSARY REPETITION OF WORDS

Sometimes you may wish to repeat words or phrases to create an effect or for emphasis, as in parallel constructions. However, when words are repeated for no apparent reason, they make writing seem sloppy and awkward. As you revise, eliminate unnecessary repeated words.

The quarterback passed the football, but the lineman raised his meaty ~~,~~ ~~heavy~~ hand and batted ~~the football~~ it away.

The houses ~~where the people live~~ are not far from ~~the city of~~ Moncton.

12-7C: EMPTY OR INFLATED PHRASES

Occasionally, to make your writing sound more important, you may be tempted to include certain phrases you've heard others use. When you examine your sentences carefully, you'll find these padded phrases only increase your word count and contain little or no meaning. Effective writers state what they mean as simply and directly as possible. As you revise your work, trim sentences of any wordy, empty, or inflated phrases. These can often be easily spotted when you edit for conciseness. You don't need words like "I think" or "I feel" or "in my opinion," for example, because your ownership as an author is established without them. Expressions like "in today's society" are also meaningless and should be avoided.

~~By virtue of the fact~~ Because ~~that at the current time~~ currently we do not have sufficient funding, the skateboard park will not be built.

You can use concise words or phrases without affecting your meaning.

Eliminating Wordy or Inflated Phrases

WORDY/INFLATED	CONCISE
along the lines of	like
as a matter of fact	in fact
at all times	always
at the present time	now, currently, presently
at this point in time	now, currently, presently
because of the fact	because
being that	because
by means of	by
by virtue of the fact that	because
due to the fact that	because
for the purpose of	for
for the simple reason that	because
have a tendency to	tend
have the ability to	be able to
in the nature of	like
in order to	to
in spite of the fact that	although, even though
in the event that	if
in the final analysis	finally
in the neighbourhood of	about
in the world of today	today
it is necessary that	must
on the occasion of	when
prior to	before
until such a time as	until
with regard to	about

12-7D: SIMPLIFYING STRUCTURE

The following word-trimming strategies will help you make your sentences simple, clear, and direct.

STRENGTHEN THE VERB

Often nouns derived from verbs can be turned back into verbs to make the sentence more direct and active.

> accumulated
> During the strike, the ~~accumulation of~~ garbage ^ ~~carried on~~ for fifteen days.

The noun phrase *the accumulation of garbage* has been turned into the subject and active verb *garbage accumulated.*

AVOID COLOURLESS VERBS

The verbs forms *is/are, was/were,* and *has/have/had* are weak and often create wordy sentence constructions.

> recommends
> The budget proposal before the legislature ~~is to do with~~ tax cuts and massive reductions in public-sector spending.

The weak verb is has been replaced with the more active verb *recommends.*

REVISE EXPLETIVE CONSTRUCTIONS

An expletive construction uses *there* or *it* and a form of the verb *to be* in front of the sentence subject. Often these constructions create excess words. You might remove the expletive and revise the sentence to make it more concise and direct.

> A
> ~~There is a~~ picture of Pierre Trudeau playing baseball ~~that~~ shows the energy he brought to the prime minister's office.

> Most importantly,
> ~~It is important that~~ you should remain calm if your kayak capsizes in rough water.

WHERE POSSIBLE, USE THE ACTIVE VOICE

The active voice is generally more concise and direct than the passive voice. Use the active voice when you want to be direct and to focus on the action of a sentence. (See 10-4h.)

Passive: The research was conducted by senior students who plan to enter graduate school.

Active: Senior students who plan to enter graduate school conducted the research.

Note: A grammar checker can easily find instances of the passive voice, but it is up to you to decide whether or not to make the suggested changes, based on your knowledge and the context of the document you are working on.

12-7E: REDUCING CLAUSES AND PHRASES

In many instances, modifying clauses and phrases can be tightened. Where possible, reduce clauses to phrases and phrases to single words.

As basketball fans, we journeyed to Almonte, Ontario, ~~which is~~ the birthplace of Canadian John Naismith.

The powerful
~~Loaded with power, the~~ car was considered unbeatable.

13

USAGE

THE ill & unfit CHOICE OF WORDS wonderfully obstructs the UNDERSTANDING.

—Francis Bacon

13

Usage

13 Usage

Many questions of style relate to a writer's use of words, since word choice determines the attitude, or **tone**, of writing, its length and level of repetition, and its degree of formality. If you are careful about word choices, your writing will be clearer and more distinctly your own, and these are goals to strive for as you learn to express yourself in more public and professional ways. Knowing when to use a word—and when not to use it—can make all the difference.

13-1: GLOSSARY OF USAGE

HOW CAN THE GLOSSARY OF USAGE HELP YOU?

The glossary will help you to make correct word choices in both your formal and informal writing and speaking. It will do this by providing the following information:

- definitions of words
- sample sentences using words correctly in context
- preferred formal usage for academic writing
- commonly confused words (*explicit, implicit*)
- nonstandard vocabulary (*anyways*)
- colloquialisms (*flunk*)
- jargon (*finalize*)
- non-inclusive language (*mankind*)
- redundancies (*and etc.*)
- parts of speech for many words
- cross-references to other relevant handbook sections
- homophones (*night, knight*)
- common abbreviations
- prefixes (*dis-*) and suffixes (*-ness*)

Note: Red text indicates terms that, while acceptable in some contexts, should be used with caution or not at all in formal writing (nonstandard vocabulary, colloquialisms, jargon, non-inclusive language, and redundancies).

a, an. Use *a* before a word that begins with a consonant sound, even if the word begins with a vowel: *a computer, a desk, a unique individual, a university*. Use *an* before a word that begins with a vowel sound, even if the word begins with a consonant: *an iguana, an oak, an hour, an honour*. Words beginning with the letter *h* often present problems. Generally, if the initial *h* sound is hard, use *a*: *a hot dog, a heart attack*. However, if the initial *h* is silent, use *an*: *an honest mistake*. If the *h* is pronounced, Canadian writers generally use *a* with the word: *a history, a hotel*.

accept, except. *Accept* is a verb meaning "to receive" or "take to (oneself)." *He accepted the lottery prize. Except* is very rarely a verb; usually, it is a preposition meaning "to exclude." *Everyone except Jerome received a penalty.*

adapt, adopt. *Adapt* means to "adjust oneself to" or "make suitable," and it is followed by the preposition *to*. *The lizard will adapt to its surroundings*. The word *adapt* can also mean "revise," in which case it is used with the preposition *for* or *from*. *They will adapt the novel for the silver screen. Adopt* means "to take or use as one's own." *They plan to adopt the idea for their computer game.*

adverse, averse. *Adverse* means "unfavourable." *Smoking has an adverse effect on your health. Averse* means "opposed" or "having an active distaste"; it can also mean "reluctant," in which case it is followed by the preposition *to*. *She was averse to fighting of any kind.*

advice, advise. *Advice* is a noun that means "an opinion about what should be done." *Take my advice and sell while you can. Advise* is a verb that means "to offer advice." *The high-priced lawyer will advise us on what course of action to take.*

affect, effect. *Affect* is a verb that most commonly means "to influence." *Water pollution affects the health of fish. Effect* is often a noun meaning "result." *The artist flicked paint on the canvas but could not achieve the effect he wanted. Effect* can also be used as a verb meaning "to bring about or execute." *The cost-cutting moves will effect a turnaround for the business.*

aggravate, irritate. *Aggravate* is a verb that means "to make worse or more severe." *The boy's cold was aggravated by the dry air. Irritate*, a verb, means "to make impatient or angry." Note that *aggravate* is often used colloquially to mean *irritate*. Do not substitute *aggravate* for *irritate* in formal writing. *His constant complaining irritated* [not *aggravated*] *me.*

agree to, agree with. *Agree to* means "to consent to." *The two sides will agree to the proposal. Agree with* mean "to be in accord with." *The witness's version of events agrees with theirs.*

ain't. *Ain't* means "am not,“ "are not," or "is not." It is nonstandard English and should not be used in formal writing.

all ready, already. *All ready* means "completely prepared." *The sprinter is all ready for the starter's gun. Already* is an adverb that means "before this time; previously; even now." *They have already seen* The Lion King.

all right, alright. *All right* is always written as two words. *Alright* is nonstandard English for *all right* and should not be used in formal writing. *It's all right* [not *alright*] *to eat dinner if Desmond is late.*

all together, altogether. See *altogether, all together.*

allude, elude. *Allude* means "to refer to indirectly or casually." Do not use it to mean "to refer to directly." *In his presentation, Freud specifically referred to* [not *alluded to*] *the importance of the subconscious. Elude* means "to evade or escape from, usually with some daring or skill," or "to escape the understanding or grasp of." *I eluded my pursuers, but why they were chasing me eluded me.*

allusion, illusion, delusion. *Allusion* is an "implied or indirect reference." *The prosecuting attorney made an allusion to her criminal past.* The word *illusion* means "an appearance or feeling that misleads because it is not real." *When the bus beside ours backed up, it created the illusion that we were moving.* This should be distinguished from *delusion,* which means "a false and often harmful belief about something that does not exist." *The paranoid reporter had the delusion that every e-mail contained a virus.*

alot, a lot. *A lot* is always written as two words. *We have not had a lot of snow this winter.* Avoid using *a lot* in formal writing.

altogether, all together. *Altogether* means "completely, entirely." *Altogether there were eight novels assigned for the course.* The phrase *all together* means "together in a group." *We found the litter of puppies all together in the garage.*

a.m., p.m., A.M., P.M. Use these abbreviations only with specific times, when numerals are provided: 10 *a.m.* or 1 *p.m.* Do not use the abbreviations as substitutes for *morning, afternoon,* or *evening. The mother had to get up early in the morning* [not *the a.m.*] *to take her daughter to the hockey game.*

among, between. See *between, among.*

amoral, immoral. *Amoral* means "not having any morals; neither moral nor immoral." *The cabinet adopted an amoral perspective when they considered tax cuts.* The word *immoral* means "morally wrong or wicked." *It is immoral to steal food from the food bank.*

amount, number. *Amount* is used to refer to things in bulk or mass. These things cannot be counted. *A large amount of litter can be found along the highway. Number* is used to refer to things that can be counted. *He gobbled down a number of bedtime snacks every evening.*

an, a. See *a, an.*

and etc. *Etc. (et cetera)* means "and so forth." Do not use *and etc.* because it is redundant. See also *etc.*

and/or. *And/or* is sometimes used to indicate three possibilities: one, or the other, or both. It is occasionally acceptable in business, technical, or legal writing. Avoid this awkward construction when writing for the humanities.

ante-, anti-. *Ante-* is a prefix that means "before; earlier; in front of." *The reporter waited in an anteroom until the politician could see her.* The prefix *anti-* means "against" or "opposed to." *Thousands of supporters turned out for the antipoverty rally.* Use *anti-* with a hyphen when it is followed by a capital letter *(anti-American)* or a word beginning with i *(anti-intellectual)*. Otherwise, consult a dictionary.

anxious, eager. *Anxious* means "nervous," "troubled," or "worried." *The looming, dark clouds made Tim anxious. Eager* means "looking forward" and is often followed by the preposition *to. Stella was eager to receive the Christmas parcel.* Do not use *anxious* to mean "eager." *I'm eager* [not *anxious*] *to spend my gift certificate.*

anyone, any one. *Anyone* is an indefinite pronoun that means "any person at all." *Anyone* is singular. (See 10-3d and 10-5a.) *Can anyone tell me what to do?* In *any one*, the pronoun *one* is preceded by the adjective *any*. Here the two words refer to any person or thing in a group. *Once the last of the patrons has left, you can jump into any one of the bumper cars.*

anyplace. *Anyplace* is informal for *anywhere*. Do not use *anyplace* in formal writing.

anyways, anywheres. *Anyways* and *anywheres* are nonstandard for *anyway* and *anywhere,* respectively. Always use *anyway* and *anywhere* in formal speaking and writing.

as. Substituting *as* for *because, since,* and *while* may make a sentence vague or ambiguous. *Since* [not *as*] *we were stopping for gas, we decided to use the restroom.* If *as* were used in this sentence, the cause–effect relationship would be unclear.

as, like. See *like, as.*

averse, adverse. See *adverse, averse.*

awful, awfully. In formal English usage the adjective *awful* once meant "filled with awe" or "inspiring awe." Now, *awful* is more commonly used to mean "bad" or "terrible." *It was an awful day when I was fired.* The adverb *awfully* is sometimes used colloquially as an intensifier to mean "extremely" or "very." *He was awfully upset when he opened the bill.* Avoid such colloquial usage in formal writing.

awhile, a while. *Awhile* is an adverb. *Stay awhile, if you wish.* Use the article and noun, *a while,* as the object of a preposition. *We had obviously arrived too early, so we circled the block for a while.*

bad, badly. *Bad* is an adjective. *They felt bad about leaving the party early.* The word *badly* is an adverb. *His infected hand hurt badly.*

being as, being that. Both *being as* and *being that* are nonstandard expressions used in place of the subordinate conjunctions *because* or *since. Since* [not *Being that*] *vandals had written on the walls, tough security measures were put in place.*

beside, besides. *Beside* is a preposition meaning "by the side of" or "next to." *Grass grows beside the stream. Besides* is an adverb meaning "moreover," or "furthermore." *Jeff did not want to fight; besides, he was injured. Besides* can also be a preposition meaning "in addition to," "except for," or "other than." *Besides me, there is no one working on the project.*

between, among. Use *among* when referring to relationships involving more than two people or things. *You can choose among fifteen sports.* Use *between* when referring to relationships involving two people or things. *When deciding which band is better, you need to take into account the difference in record sales between the two.*

bring, take. Use *bring* when something is being moved toward the speaker. *Please bring the thermometer to me.* Use *take* when something is being moved away. *I ask that you take the pizza to the Simpsons.*

burst, bursted; bust, busted. *Burst* is an irregular verb meaning "to fly apart suddenly with force; explode; break open." *The water-filled balloon burst when it hit the pavement. Bursted* is the nonstandard past-tense form of *burst;* use the standard past tense (*burst*) instead. *Bust* and its past-tense form *busted* are slang.

can, may. *Can* means "know how to" or "be able to." *Mai-Ling can play the piano. May* means "be allowed to" or "have permission to." *Ted, you may go now.* The distinction in meaning between *can* and *may* is still made in formal writing. In informal English, *can* is widely used to mean "be able to" and "be allowed to."

capital, capitol. *Capital* refers to a city where the government of a country, province, or state is located. *Edmonton is the capital of Alberta. Capital* can also mean "the amount of money a company or person uses in carrying on a business." A *capitol* is a building in which American lawmakers meet. When referring to the building in which the U.S. Congress meets, capitalize the first letter, as in *Capitol.*

censor, censure. The verb *censor* means "to edit or remove from public view on moral or other grounds." *They will censor the violent movie before it can be seen in theatres.* The verb *censure* means "to express strong disapproval." *The House will censure the minister for giving misleading information.*

cite, site. The verb *cite* means "to quote, especially as an authority." *Doug cited the poet's use of allusion in his essay.* The noun *site* often means "a particular place." *The vacant field will be the site of a new shopping centre.*

climactic, climatic. *Climactic* is an adjective derived from *climax*; *climax* means "the highest point; point of highest interest; the most exciting part." *The scene in which the boy is reunited with his father is the climactic moment of the movie.* The adjective *climatic* means "of or having to do with climate." *In order for a tornado to occur, there must be certain climatic conditions.*

coarse, course. *Coarse* usually means "heavy and rough in texture" or "crude." *Shelley used a coarse sandpaper to finish the table. Course* means "a line of movement," "a direction taken," "a way, path, or track," or "a playing field." *Seeking help for your drinking problem is the right course of action.*

compare to, compare with. *Compare to* means "to represent as similar." *Shall I compare thee to a summer's day? Compare with* means "to point out how two persons or things are alike and how they differ." *I will compare Millay's poem with Eliot's.*

complement, compliment. The verb *complement* means "to reinforce, add to, or complete something." *The scarf complements his wardrobe.* As a noun, *complement* is something that completes.

Compliment as a verb means "to say something in praise." *I must compliment you on your fine enunciation.* As a noun, *compliment* means "a remark of praise."

conscience, conscious. *Conscience* is a noun meaning "the sense of moral right and wrong." *His conscience would not let him shoplift the DVD. Conscious* is an adjective that means "aware; knowing." *Nancy Drew was conscious of a shadowy figure sneaking up behind her.*

consensus of opinion. *Consensus* means "general agreement." As a result, the phrase *consensus of opinion* is redundant. *A consensus* [not *consensus of opinion*] *is required before the motion will be passed.*

contact. *Contact* is often used informally as a verb meaning "to communicate with." In formal writing, use a precise verb such as *e-mail, telephone,* or *write. I will telephone* [not *contact*] *you for directions to the plant.*

continual, continuous. *Continual* means "repeated many times; very frequent." *When the roofers were here, there was continual hammering. Continuous* means "without a stop or a break." *During rush hour, there is a continuous line of cars.*

could care less. *Could care less* is nonstandard and should not be used in formal writing. Use *couldn't care less* in its place. *Daphne couldn't care less how much the job pays, as long as it gives her satisfaction.*

could of. *Could of* is nonstandard for *could have. If not for his injury, Mr. Martin could have* [not *could of*] *become a professional basketball player.*

council, counsel. *Council* is a noun used to describe "a group of people called together to talk things over, or give advice"; it also applies to "a group of people elected by citizens to make up laws." *A tribal council will decide the appropriate punishment.* A *councillor* is a member of the *council. Counsel* as a noun means "advice." *The chief gives wise counsel. Counsel* can also mean a lawyer. A *counsellor* is someone who gives advice or guidance.

course, coarse. See *coarse, course.*

criteria, criterion. *Criteria* are rules for making judgments. *Criteria* is the plural form of *criterion. The major criteria for the job are a background in multimedia and a readiness to work overtime.*

data, datum. *Data* are "facts or concepts presented in a form suitable for processing in order to draw conclusions." *Data* is the plural form of *datum*, which is rarely used. Increasingly *data* is used as a singular noun; however, careful writers use it as a plural. *The new data reveal* [or, increasingly, *reveals*] *that the economy is rebounding.*

defuse, diffuse. *Defuse* means "to take the fuse out" or "to disarm." *The counsellor managed to defuse the volatile family situation.* *Diffuse* as a verb means "to scatter" or "to spread out," but *diffuse* is more commonly used as an adjective to describe something spread out or, in the context of language, something wordy or verbose. *The smell of cologne diffused after we opened the windows. His speech was diffuse and did not focus on a particular point.*

delusion, illusion. See *allusion, illusion, delusion.*

differ from, differ with. *Differ from* means "to be unlike." *The brothers differ from each other only in their girlfriends. Differ with* means "to disagree with." *I used to differ with my stepmother on what time I should be home on Saturday night.*

different from, different than. In standard English the preferred form is *different from. The new edition of* Ulysses *is very different from the previous one.* However, *different than* is gaining wider acceptance, especially when *different from* creates an awkward construction. *He is a different person today than* [as opposed to the more awkward *from the person*] *he used to be.*

discreet, discrete. *Discreet* means "prudent and tactful in speech and behaviour." *The mayor was very discreet when talking about the manager's personal life. Discrete* means "separate; distinct." *There are discrete parts of the cell that perform specialized functions.*

disinterested, uninterested. *Disinterested* means "impartial." *The premier appointed a disinterested third party to mediate the dispute. Uninterested* means "lacking in interest," or "bored." *Shelley is uninterested in soap operas.*

don't. *Don't* is a contraction for *do not. Don't slam the door.* Do not use *don't* as a contraction for *does not*; the correct contraction is *doesn't. Selma doesn't* [not *don't*] *want to shovel the walk.*

due to. *Due to* means "caused by" or "owing to." It should be used as an adjective phrase following a form of the verb *to be. The inquest ruled that the death was due to driver error.* In formal writing, *due to* should not be used as a preposition meaning "because of." *Classes were cancelled because of* [not *due to*] *the heavy snowstorm.*

each. *Each* is singular. (See 10-3d and 10-5a.)

eager, anxious. See *anxious, eager.*

effect, affect. See *affect, effect.*

e.g. This is the Latin abbreviation for *exempli gratia,* which means "for example." In formal writing, avoid *e.g.* and use phrases such as *for example* or *for instance* instead. *Many fish—for example, salmon and trout—will be affected.*

either. *Either* is singular. (See 10-3d and 10-5a.) For *either . . . or* constructions, see 10-3c.

elicit, illicit. *Elicit* is a verb meaning "to draw forth" or "bring out." *Listening to a great symphony will elicit strong emotions.* The adjective *illicit* means "unlawful." *The neighbours had an illicit growing operation in their basement.*

elude, allude. See *allude, elude.*

emigrate from, immigrate to. *Emigrate* means "to leave one's own country or region and settle in another"; it requires the preposition *from. The Bhuttos emigrated from Pakistan. Immigrate* means "to enter and permanently settle in another country"; it requires the preposition to. *Mr. Bhutto's cousin now plans to immigrate to Canada.*

eminent, immanent, imminent. *Eminent* means "distinguished" or "exalted." *The eminent scientist delivered the lecture. Immanent* is an adjective that means "inherent" or "remaining within." *I believe most Canadians have an immanent goodness. Imminent* is an adjective meaning "likely to happen soon." *Given the troop movements, the general felt that an attack was imminent.*

enthused, enthusiastic. *Enthused* is sometimes informally used as an adjective meaning "having or showing enthusiasm." Use *enthusiastic* instead. *He becomes enthusiastic* [not *enthused*] *about Oilers playoff games.*

-ess. Many readers find the *-ess* suffix demeaning. Write *actor,* not *actress; singer,* not *songstress; poet,* not *poetess.*

etc. *Etc.* is an abbreviation that in English means "and other things." Do not use *etc.* to refer to people. In formal writing, it is preferable to use the expression *and so on* in place of *etc*. See also *and etc.*

eventually, ultimately. *Eventually* often means "an undefined time in the future." *Ultimately* commonly means "the greatest extreme or furthest extent." *Eventually* and *ultimately* are frequently used interchangeably. It is best to use *eventually* when referring to time and *ultimately* when referring to the greatest extent. *Eventually the robber will be found. I find it ultimately the most reasonable alternative.*

everybody, everyone. *Everybody* and *everyone* are both singular. (See 10-3d and 10-5a.)

everyone, every one. *Everyone* is an indefinite pronoun meaning "every person." *Everyone wanted to purchase a ticket. Every one* is a pronoun, *one*, modified by an adjective, *every*; the two words mean "each person or thing in a group." *Every one* is frequently followed by *of*. *Every one of the merchants in Kamloops is participating in this promotion.*

except, accept. See *accept, except.*

except for the fact that. Avoid this wordy, awkward construction. Instead, use *except that*. *Alex would be a good candidate for office, except that he is unreliable.*

explicit, implicit. *Explicit* means "clearly expressed; directly stated." *The coach gave everyone but Keon explicit orders not to shoot. Implicit* means "meant but not clearly expressed or directly stated." *My mother-in-law's silence was implicit consent to pour her another glass of wine.*

farther, further. In formal English *farther* is used for physical distance. *On the map, Courtenay is farther than Ladysmith. Further* is used to mean "more" or "to a greater extent." *He took the teasing further than would be appropriate under any circumstances.*

female, male. *Female* and *male* are considered jargon if substituted for "woman" and "man." *Sixteen men* [not *males*] *and seventeen women* [not *females*] *made the team.*

fewer, less. Use *fewer* only to refer to numbers and things that can be counted. *There are fewer houses up for sale than there were last year at this time.* Use *less* to refer to collective nouns or things that cannot be counted. *Generally, there is less traffic congestion at midday.*

finalize. *Finalize* is a verb meaning "to bring to a conclusion." The word, though often used, is considered jargon by many people. Use a clear, acceptable alternative. *The football coach completed* [not *finalized*] *plans for the game.*

flout, flaunt. *Flout* is a verb that means "to treat with contempt." *Magdalena flouted the rules of the road until she became one of the worst drivers in Canada. Flaunt* means "to show off." *Agnes flaunted her new MP3 player.*

flunk. *Flunk* is colloquial for *fail*, and it should be avoided in formal writing.

folks. *Folks* is informal for "one's family; one's relatives." In academic writing, use a more formal expression than *folks*. *My mother and father* [not *folks*] *are organizing the family reunion.*

fun. When used as an adjective, *fun* is colloquial; it should be avoided in formal writing. *The Jawbreaker was an exciting* [not *fun*] *ride.*

further, farther. See *farther, further.*

get. *Get* is a common verb with many slang and colloquial uses. Avoid the following uses of *get*: "to become" (*He got cold*); "to obtain revenge" (*Gillian got back at Ted for the rumours he spread*); "to annoy" (*His constant complaining finally got to me*); "to elicit an emotional response" (*The final scene in the movie really got to her*).

good, well. *Good* is an adjective. *Michael is a good skier. Well* is nearly always an adverb. (See 10-6.) *The racing team skis well.*

hanged, hung. *Hanged* is the past tense and past participle of *hang*, which means "to execute." *The man was convicted of treason and hanged. Hung* is the past tense and past participle of *hang*, which means "to fasten or be fastened to something." *Decorations for the dance hung from the ceiling.*

hardly. Avoid double negative expressions such as *not hardly* or *can't hardly*. (See 10-6d.) *I can* [not *can't*] *hardly find words to express myself.*

has got, have got. Avoid using *have got* or *has got* when *have* or *has* alone will communicate the intended meaning. *I have* [not *have got*] *two more books to finish reading to complete the course requirements.*

he. Do not use only *he* when the complete meaning is "he or she." In modern usage, this is not inclusive. See 10-5a and 13-2e for alternative constructions.

he/she, his/her. Use *he or she*, or *his or her* in formal writing. For alternative, more concise constructions, see 10-5a and 13-2e.

hisself. Nonstandard for *himself.*

hopefully. *Hopefully* is an adverb meaning "in a hopeful manner." *Hopefully* can modify a verb, an adjective, or another adverb. *They waited hopefully for news from the surgeon on how the operation had gone.* In formal writing, do not use *hopefully* as a sentence modifier with the meaning "I hope." *I hope* [not *Hopefully*] *the operation will be a success.*

hung, hanged. See *hanged, hung.*

i.e. The abbreviation *i.e.* stands for the Latin *id est*, which in English means "that is." In formal writing, use the English equivalent, *that is.*

if, whether. *If* is used to express conditions. *If there is sufficient snow, we will go skiing at Whistler.* Use *whether* to express alternatives. *The couple was not sure whether to take the holiday in St. Lucia or in Aruba.*

illicit, elicit. See *elicit, illicit.*

illusion, allusion. See *allusion, illusion, delusion.*

immanent, imminent, eminent. See *eminent, immanent, imminent.*

immigrate to, emigrate from. See *emigrate from, immigrate to.*

immoral, amoral. See *amoral, immoral.*

implement. *Implement* means "to carry out." It is often unnecessary and pretentious. *The president carried out* [not *implemented*] *the board's recommendations.*

implicit, explicit. See *explicit, implicit.*

imply, infer. *Imply* means to "express indirectly." *Angie's grin implied that she knew Jo had a crush on Bono. Infer* means "to conclude by reasoning." *You could infer that the man was poor by his tattered clothes.*

in, into. *In* generally indicates a location or condition. *She is hiding in the house. Into* indicates a direction, a movement, or a change in condition. *He went into the house to look for her.*

individual. *Individual* is sometimes used as a pretentious substitute for *person. The person* [not *individual*] *sitting next to me slept through the entire play.*

ingenious, ingenuous. *Ingenious* means "clever" or "skillful." *The criminal devised an ingenious plan to rob the bank. Ingenuous* means "frank" and "simple." *His country manner was quite ingenuous.*

in regards to. *In regards* to confuses two phrases: *in regard* to and *as regards.* Use either one of these alternatives instead. *Talk to your counsellor in regard to the application.*

irregardless. *Irregardless* is nonstandard English. Use *regardless* instead.

irritate, aggravate. See *aggravate, irritate.*

is when, is where. Do not use *when* or *where* following is in definitions. *Photosynthesis is the process by which* [not *is when*] *plant cells make sugar from carbon dioxide and water in the presence of chlorophyll and light.*

it is. It is becomes nonstandard when used to mean "there is." *There is* [not *It is*] *a glowing disc in the night sky.*

its, it's. Its is a possessive pronoun. *The cat will come in its own good time. It's* is a contraction for it is. *It's the perfect time to buy a house.* (See 11-4c.)

kind, kinds. *Kind* is singular and should not be treated as a plural. *This* [not *These*] *kind of painting was popular in that era. Kinds* is plural. *These kinds of paintings were popular in that era.*

kind of, sort of. *Kind of* and *sort of* are colloquial expressions meaning "rather" or "somewhat." Do not use these colloquialisms in formal writing. *I was somewhat* [not *kind of* or *sort of*] *disappointed by the low mark.*

lay, lie. See *lie, lay.*

lead, led. *Lead* is a soft heavy metal. *Led* is the past tense of the verb *lead. His accurate directions led me to the correct address.*

learn, teach. *Learn* means "to gain knowledge of or a skill by instruction, study, or experience." *I learned how to play chess. Teach* means "to impart knowledge or a skill." *I will teach* [not *learn*] *my little cousin to play the game.*

leave, let. *Leave* means "to go away." *Let* means "to allow or permit." Do not use *leave* with the nonstandard meaning "to permit." *Let* [not *leave*] *me help you trim the fruit trees.*

led, lead. See *lead, led.*

less, fewer. See *fewer, less.*

liable. *Liable* means "legally responsible." Avoid using it to mean "likely." *Jeff will likely* [not *is liable to*] *catch many fish on this trip.*

licence, license. *Licence* is a noun meaning "legal permission by law to do something." *Joe's business licence hung prominently on the wall. License* is a verb meaning "to permit or authorize." *A veterinarian is licensed to practise animal medicine.*

lie, lay. *Lie* means "to recline." It is an intransitive verb, which means it does not take a direct object. The principal forms of the verb are *lie, lay,* and *lain. Lie down now.* Lay means "to put" or "to place." It is a transitive verb, which means it always requires a direct object. The principal parts of the verb are *lay, laid,* and *laid. Lay the guests' coats on the bed in the spare room.* (See 10-4b.)

like, as. *Like* is a preposition, and it should be followed by a noun or a noun phrase. *Daniel looks like a million dollars. As* is a subordinating conjunction and should be used to introduce a dependent clause. *As I predicted, he is late again.*

loose, lose. *Loose* is an adjective meaning "not firmly fastened." *He has a loose tooth as a result of biting into the hard candy. Lose* is a verb meaning "to misplace" or "to be defeated." *He predicted that the Stampeders would lose the Grey Cup.*

lots, lots of. *Lots* and *lots of* are colloquial substitutes for *many, much,* and *a great deal.* They should not be used in formal writing.

male, female. See *female, male.*

mankind. *Mankind* is not an inclusive term, as it excludes women. Avoid it in favour of terms such as *humans, humanity, the human race,* or *humankind.*

may, can. See *can, may.*

may of, might of. *May of* and *might of* are nonstandard English for *may have* and *might have. Mona might have* [not *might of*] *taken the chicken out of the oven too early.*

maybe, may be. *Maybe* is an adverb meaning "perhaps." *Maybe we should build the outdoor rink tomorrow. May be* is a verb phrase. *Since the temperature will be lower on Tuesday, that may be a better day.*

media, medium. *Media* is the plural of *medium. The media are offering too much coverage of sensational stories.*

moral, morale. *Moral* is a noun meaning "an ethical conclusion." *Morale* means "the attitude as regards courage, confidence, and enthusiasm." *Team morale was low after the twentieth defeat.*

most. When used to mean "almost," *most* is colloquial. This usage should be avoided in formal writing. *Almost* [not *Most*] *every student went to the party.*

must of. *Must of* is nonstandard English for *must have.* See *may of, might of.*

myself. *Myself* is a reflexive pronoun. *I hurt myself. Myself* can also be an intensive pronoun. *I will go myself.* Do not use *myself* in place of *I* or *me. Jeremy and I* [not *myself*] *are going on a trip.* (See also 10-5c.)

neither. *Neither* is most often singular. (See 10-3d and 10-5a.) For *neither . . . nor* constructions, see 10-3c.

none. *None* is usually singular. (See 10-3d and 10-5a.)

nowheres. *Nowheres* is nonstandard English for *nowhere.*

number, amount. See *amount, number.*

of. *Of* is a preposition. Do not use it in place of the verb *have* after *could, should, would, may, must,* and *might. The Johnsons might have* [not *of*] *left their garage door open.*

off of. Omit *of* from the expression as *off* is sufficient. *The young boy fell off* [not *off of*] *the table.*

OK, O.K., okay. All three forms are acceptable in informal writing and speech. However, avoid these colloquial expressions in formal writing and speech.

parameters. *Parameter* is a mathematical term that means "a quantity that is constant in a particular calculation or case but varies in other cases." It is sometimes used as jargon to mean any limiting or defining element or feature. Avoid such jargon and use precise English instead. *The whole project had very vague guidelines* [not *parameters*].

passed, past. *Passed* is the past tense of the verb *pass*, which means "to go by." *Uncle Theo passed by our front window.* Never use *past* as a verb. *Past* can be an adjective that means "gone by; over." *They overcame their past misunderstanding. Past* can also be a noun meaning "the time before the present." *Canada has a rich and glorious past.* Finally, *past* can be a preposition. *Past the exit on the highway, there was a service station.*

people, persons. Use *people* to refer to a group of individuals who are anonymous and uncounted. *The people of South Africa have a long history of apartheid.* Generally, you may use *persons* or *people* when referring to a countable number of individuals. *Only five persons* [or *people*] *attended the town meeting.*

percent, per cent, percentage. Always use *percent* (also spelled *per cent*) with specific numbers. *The survey revealed that 48 percent of Canadians want their country to become a republic. Percentage* means "part of" or "portion," and it is used when no number is provided. *A large percentage of the population favoured the Liberals.*

phenomenon, phenomena. *Phenomenon* means "a fact, event or circumstance that can be observed." *Phenomena* is the plural of *phenomenon. There were all sorts of paranormal phenomena taking place in the haunted house.*

plus. *Plus* is a nonstandard substitute for *and*. Do not use *plus* to join independent clauses. *He has a driver's license; however* [not *plus*], *it has expired.*

p.m. See *a.m., p.m.,* A.M., P.M.

pore, pour. *Pore* is an intransitive verb meaning "to read or study carefully" or "to ponder." *Ahmed has been poring over his chemistry notes to prepare for his exam. Pour* means "to cause to flow in a stream." *It has been pouring rain for days.*

practice, practise. *Practice* is a noun meaning "an action done several times over to gain a skill." *Practice will improve your dribbling.*

Practise is a verb meaning "to do something again and again in order to learn it." *Su Li practises the violin twice a day*. In American spelling, both the noun and verb are spelled *practice*.

precede, proceed. *Precede* means "to go or come before." *A mild gust preceded the hurricane. Proceed* means "to go on after having stopped" or "to move forward." *After a family meeting about finances, we proceeded with the wedding plans.*

principal, principle. The noun *principal* means "a chief person" or "a sum of money that has been borrowed." *After Mr. Toutant's retirement from Dauphin Elementary School, a new principal was appointed.* The noun *principle* means "a fact or belief on which other ideas are based." *The constitution is based on the principles of equality and justice.* Note, too, that *principal* can be an adjective, meaning "main." *The principal reason I didn't vote was my disagreement with all the candidates' platforms.*

proceed, precede. See *precede, proceed.*

quote, quotation. *Quote* is a verb meaning "to repeat the exact words of." *She quoted the precise line from "Leda and the Swan" to illustrate her point. Quotation* is a noun meaning "a passage quoted." Do not use *quote* as a shortened form of *quotation. Using a relevant quotation* [not *quote*] *is often a good way to begin a speech.*

raise, rise. *Raise* means "to move to a higher level; to elevate." It is a transitive verb, which means it requires a direct object. *The stage manager raised the curtain. Rise* means "to go up." It is an intransitive verb, which means it does not require a direct object. *The smoke rises.*

real, really. *Real* is an adjective. Occasionally, in informal speech and writing, it is used as an adverb, but this usage should be avoided in formal writing. *Really* is an adverb. *Don was really* [not *real*] *excited.* (See 10-6.) In informal writing and speech, *real* and *really* are used as intensifiers to mean "extremely" or "very"; such usage should be avoided in formal writing and speech.

reason is because. *Reason is because* is a redundant expression. Use *reason is that* instead. *One reason we moved from Moose Jaw is that* [not *is because*] *Mom got a teaching job at a community college.*

reason why. *Reason why* is a redundant expression. In its place use either *reason* or *why. I still do not know why* [not *the reason why*] *she rejected my invitation.*

regretfully, regrettably. *Regretfully* means "full of regret." It describes a person's attitude of regret. *Regretfully, he wrote to apologize. Regrettably* means that circumstances are regrettable. *Regrettably, the circus was rained out today.*

rein/reign. *Rein* refers to the restraint a driver uses to control an animal or any kind of restraint in general. *The equestrian champion reined in his horse forcefully. Reign* means "royal authority." *Shakespeare wrote* Hamlet *during the reign of James I.* Be careful not to confuse them in certain idiomatic phrases, such as "give free rein [not reign] to."

relation, relationship. *Relation* is used to describe the association between two or more things. *The scientist studied the relation between lung cancer and smog. Relationship* is used to describe the association or connection between people. *Peter and Olga had a professional relationship that soon blossomed into a personal one.*

respectfully, respectively. *Respectfully* is an adverb meaning "showing or marked by proper respect." *She respectfully presented her counterargument in the debate. Respectively* is an adverb meaning "singly in the order designated or mentioned." *Chand, Doug, and Lenore are a plastic surgeon, bus driver, and company vice-president respectively.*

rise, raise. See *raise, rise.*

sensual, sensuous. *Sensual* is an adjective meaning "relating to gratification of the physical senses." *The chef obtains sensual pleasure from cooking. Sensuous* is an adjective meaning "pleasing to the senses." *Sensuous* is always favourable and often applies to the appreciation of nature, art, or music. *She obtains a sensuous delight from Mozart's music.*

set, sit. *Set* means "to put in place or put down, or to position." It is a transitive verb, requiring a direct object, and its principal parts are *set, set, set. Ali set the book on the ledge. Sit* means "to be seated." It is an intransitive verb, not requiring a direct object, and its principal parts are *sit, sat, sat. Set* is sometimes a nonstandard substitute for sit. Avoid this usage in formal writing. *The dog* sat [not set] *down.*

shall, will. *Shall* was once used with the first-person singular and plural as the helping verb with future-tense verbs. *I shall visit my* *grandfather on Wednesday. We shall deliver the results on Thursday.* In modern usage *will* has replaced *shall*. *I will see you on Friday.* The word *shall* is still often used in polite questions. *Shall I bring the newspaper to your door?*

she/he, her/his. See *he/she, his/her.*

should of. *Should of* is nonstandard for *should have*. *He should have* [not *should of*] *submitted the essay on time.*

since. *Since* should mainly be used in situations describing time. *We have been waiting for the bus since midnight.* Do not use *since* as a substitute for *because* in cases where there is any chance of confusion. *Since we lost the division, we have been playing our second-string players.* Here *since* could mean "from that point in time" or "because."

sit, set. See *set, sit.*

site, cite. See *cite, site.*

somebody, someone. *Somebody* and *someone* are singular. (See 10-3d and 10-5a.)

something. *Something* is singular. (See 10-3d and 10-5a.)

sometime, some time, sometimes. *Sometime* is an adverb meaning "at an indefinite or unstated time." *Let's meet sometime on Thursday.* In *some time* the adjective *some* modifies the noun *time*. *We haven't seen the Jebsons for some time.* *Sometimes* is an adverb meaning "at times; now and then." *Sometimes I'm not sure what major to pursue.*

sort of, kind of. See *kind of, sort of.*

sneaked, snuck. *Sneaked* is the correct past participle. *Sameer sneaked* [not *snuck*] *into his parents' closet looking for his birthday presents.*

stationary, stationery. *Stationary* means "not moving." *At the club, he rode on a stationary bike.* *Stationery* refers to paper and other writing products. *I will need to buy the stationery at the business supply store.*

suppose to, use to. See *use to, suppose to.*

sure and. *Sure and* is nonstandard. Instead, use *sure to*. *Please be sure to* [not *sure and*] *edit your work carefully.*

take, bring. See *bring, take.*

teach, learn. See *learn, teach.*

than, then. *Than* is a conjunction used to make comparisons. *I would rather have cheesecake than pie. Then* is an adverb used to indicate past or future time. *My husband will do the vacuuming, and then he will wax the floors.*

that, who. See *who, which, that.*

that, which. Most North American writers use *that* for restrictive clauses and *which* for non-restrictive clauses. (See 11-1g.) Note, however, that in some circles *that* and *which* are increasingly treated as grammatically identical. Most grammar checkers still distinguish between them. Your instructor may or may not observe this distinction.

theirselves. *Theirselves* is nonstandard English for *themselves. They amused themselves* [not *theirselves*] *by going to the drive-in.*

them. *Them* is nonstandard when it is used in place of *those. Please place those* [not *them*] *flowers on the kitchen table.*

then, than. See *than, then.*

there, their, they're. *There* is an adverb meaning "at or in that place." *I'll call home when I get there. There* can also be an expletive, a phrase at the beginning of a clause. *There are two beautiful dogs in the garage. Their* is a possessive pronoun. *It was their first house. They're* is a contraction for *they are. They're first in line for tickets.*

this kind. See *kind, kinds.*

thru. *Thru* is a colloquial spelling of *through*. Do not use *thru* in formal academic or business writing.

to, too, two. *To* can be a preposition. *They swayed to the rhythm. To* can also be part of an infinitive. *We need to talk. Too* is an adverb. *There are too many people in the city. Two* is a number. *I have two red pens.*

toward, towards. Both versions are acceptable; however, *toward* is preferred in Canadian English.

try and. *Try and* is nonstandard English. Instead use *try to*. *Try to* [not *Try and*] *be polite.*

ultimately, eventually. See *eventually, ultimately.*

uninterested, disinterested. See *disinterested, uninterested.*

unique. Like *straight, round,* and *complete, unique* is an absolute. There are not degrees of uniqueness. Especially in formal writing, avoid expressions such as *more unique* and *most unique*. (See 10-6c.)

usage, use. *Usage* refers to conventions, most often of language. *Placing "ain't" in a sentence is nonstandard usage. Use* means "to employ." Do not substitute *usage* when *use* is required. *I do not think surfing the Internet is the proper use* [not *usage*] *of your study time.*

use to, suppose to. *Use to* and *suppose to* are nonstandard for *used to* and *supposed to*. *We used to* [not *use to*] *have roast beef for dinner every Sunday night.*

utilize. *Utilize* means "to put to use." Often *use* can be substituted, as *utilize* can make writing sound pretentious. *He will use* [not *utilize*] *the best material to tile the bathroom.*

wait for, wait on. *Wait for* means "to await." *The girls are waiting for the commuter train. Wait on* means "to serve." It should not be used as substitute for *wait for*. *The owner of the bistro waited on our table. We will wait for* [not *wait on*] *the morning bus.*

ways. *Ways* is colloquial in usage when designating distance. *Edmonton is quite a way* [not *ways*] *from Vancouver.*

weather, whether. *Weather* is a noun describing "the state of the atmosphere at a given time and place." *The weather in central Canada has been unseasonably warm. Whether* is a conjunction that signals a choice between or among alternatives. *Grif did not know whether to stay or to go.*

well, good. See *good, well.*

where. *Where* is nonstandard in usage when it is substituted for *that* as a subordinate conjunction. *I read in the newspaper that* [not *where*] *Arundhati Roy will be giving a reading at the university.*

whether, if. See *if, whether.*

which. See *that, which* and *who, which, that.*

while. Do not use *while* as a substitute for "although" or "whereas" if such usage risks ambiguity. *Although* [not *While*] *Jennifer's grades got worse, Jack's got better.* If *while* were used, it could mean "although" or "at the same time."

who, which, that. Use *who* not *which* to refer to persons. Most often *that* is used to refer to things. *There is the boy who* [not *that*] *took the candies.* However, *that* may be used to refer to a class or group of people. *The team that scores the most points wins.*

who, whom. *Who* is used for subjects and subject complements. *Who is coming to dinner? Whom* is used for objects. *He did not know whom to ask.* (See 10-5d.)

who's, whose. *Who's* is a contraction for *who is. Who's going to the dinner? Whose* is a possessive pronoun. *Whose life is it anyway?*

will, shall. See *shall, will.*

would of. *Would of* is nonstandard English for *would have. He would have* [not *would of*] *achieved a perfect score if he had obtained one more strike.*

you. Avoid using *you* in an indefinite sentence to mean "anyone." (See 10-5b.) *Any collector* [not *You*] *could identify it as a fake.*

your, you're. *Your* is a possessive pronoun. *Your bicycle is in the garage. You're* is a contraction for *you are. You're the first person I contacted about the job.*

13-2: DICTION AND AUDIENCE

The effectiveness of your writing will in large measure depend on the appropriateness of the language you decide to use for your audience. Choose the wording that best suits the context and the audience of your writing. Consider these elements as you choose your words:

- subject
- audience (their needs, expectations, and feelings)
- purpose
- voice (as reflected in your unique writing style)

The following section provides guidance and information that will help you to select appropriate language for your writing assignments.

13-2A: JARGON

Jargon is the specialized language of a particular group or occupation. In some instances you may need to use jargon; for example, if your audience is the particular group or occupation that uses the jargon, or you can reasonably assume your audience will understand this specialized language. Generally, though, avoid jargon and use plain English in its place.

> ***Jargon:*** Positive input into the infrastructure impacts systematically on the functional base of the organization in that it stimulates meaningful objectives from a strategic standpoint.
>
> ***Revised:*** Positive feedback to the organization helps it formulate concrete, strategic objectives.

Notice that the jargon made the meaning of the original sentence virtually incomprehensible; the writer needed to rethink his or her ideas completely, and then recast the sentence.

In addition to very specialized language, jargon often includes language that is intended to impress readers rather than to communicate information and ideas effectively. Jargon-filled language is often found in business, government, education, and military documents.

Sentences containing jargon are difficult to read and extremely unclear.

> ***Jargon:*** The Director of Instruction implemented the optimal plan to ameliorate poor test scores among reading-at-risk students.
>
> ***Clear:*** The Director of Instruction carried out the best plan to improve poor test scores among students having trouble reading.
>
> ***Jargon:*** We will endeavour to facilitate a viable trash recovery initiative for all residences in the neighbourhood.
>
> ***Clear:*** We will try to create a workable garbage pickup plan for all neighbourhood homes.

If you encounter inflated words or phrases in your writing draft, consider alternative words that are simple, clear, and precise in meaning.

Eliminating Jargon

WORDS DESIGNED TO IMPRESS	SIMPLE ALTERNATIVE(S)
ameliorate	fix, improve
commence	begin, start
components	parts
endeavour	attempt, try
exit	go, leave
facilitate	help
factor	cause, consideration
finalize	complete, finish
impact on	effect
implement	carry out
indicator	sign
initiate	start, begin
optimal	best
parameters	boundaries, limits
prior to	before
prioritize	order, rank
utilize	use
viable	workable

13-2B: PRETENTIOUS LANGUAGE, EUPHEMISMS

AVOID PRETENTIOUS LANGUAGE

When writing for academic audiences and purposes, it is tempting to opt for elevated language. However, using uncommon or unnecessarily long words can highlight rather than obscure deficiencies in content—and make the writing seem pretentious. Academic writing does not require that you use longer, difficult words for their own sake. State your ideas in words that *you* and your audience understand.

Pretentious: It is *de rigueur* to expound on reification in Timothy Findley's fictional tome *The Wars.*

Plain Language: It is necessary to discuss the treatment of people as objects in Timothy Findley's novel *The Wars.*

AVOID EUPHEMISMS

A **euphemism** is a word or expression intended to lessen the impact of harsh or unacceptable words or phrases. An example of a euphemism in a military context is *collateral damage,* a term sometimes used to describe civilian casualties. In a few writing situations, using euphemisms is acceptable. For instance, when expressing condolences to a friend you might use the euphemism *passed away* as a substitute for *died*. Generally, however, avoid euphemisms; they are highly indirect and blur meaning.

Avoiding Euphemisms

EUPHEMISM	PLAIN ENGLISH
chemical dependency	drug addiction
correctional facility	jail
declared redundant	fired, laid off
developing nations	poor countries
downsizing	laying off or firing employees
economically deprived	poor
incendiary device	bomb
laid to rest	buried
leather-like	vinyl
military solution	war
misleading phrase	lie
pre-owned automobile	used car
starter home	small house
strategic withdrawal	defeat or retreat

13-2C: SLANG, REGIONALISMS, NONSTANDARD ENGLISH

SLANG

Slang is the informal, colourful vocabulary that is often unique to and coined by subgroups such as teenagers, college students, musicians, skateboarders, computer programmers, street gangs, rap artists, and soldiers. Slang is often used to communicate the unique common experiences of these subgroups, and it is frequently not understood by all segments of society. Most often, slang attempts to be current and trendy, but such language is soon overused and quickly becomes dated. For instance, in the early part of the twentieth century, the expression *the cat's pyjamas* was the fashionable way to call something or someone *excellent*; more recently, a *cool dude* might use the slang terms *bad* and *wicked*. Other more modern examples of slang include *bummer, grunt, rip-off, wired,* or *preppie.*

Slang can often make story dialogue sound lively and authentic. However, it is inappropriate in formal writing such as academic essays and business letters.

> Jeff ~~flunked~~ failed his final history ~~exam~~ examination, and now his semester ~~is a total write-off~~ has been completely wasted.

> ***Slang:*** Mel and her gang are coming over, and we're going to watch the tube and pig out.

> ***Formal:*** Melanie and her friends are coming over. We are going to watch television and eat snacks.

REGIONAL EXPRESSIONS

A regional expression is an expression that is common to a particular area of the country. For instance, in Atlantic Canada, a *barachois* is "a tidal pond partly obstructed by a bar" (*Nelson Canadian Dictionary*, p. 108).

> Murray could see the skiff beyond the barachois.

Regional expressions, like slang, can add colour and authenticity; however, they may not be familiar to a general audience and should be avoided in formal academic writing.

> After he caught the winning salmon, they threw the fisherman in the ~~salt chuck~~ ocean.

Salt chuck is a regional expression used in British Columbia and the U.S. Pacific Northwest. It might not be known to all Canadians.

Many Canadian dictionaries have labels indicating if a word or expression is regional.

NONSTANDARD ENGLISH

Nonstandard English is acceptable in informal social and regional contexts, but it should be avoided in any formal writing. Examples of nonstandard English include the following words and phrases from the Glossary of Usage: *anyways, bursted, nowheres,* and *theirselves.*

Standard English, on the other hand, is the written English commonly expected and used in educational institutions, businesses, government, and other contexts in which people must formally communicate with one another. Use standard English in all of your academic writing. If you are in doubt about whether a word or phrase is standard or nonstandard English, check in the Glossary of Usage in this handbook or in a good Canadian dictionary.

> ***Nonstandard:*** The guy was nowheres in sight. He could of left town, but she didn't care anyways.
>
> ***Standard:*** The man was nowhere in sight. He could have left town, but she did not care anyway.

You may speak a nonstandard dialect. If so, try to identify how your dialect differs from standard English. In the following handbook sections, you will find language areas that often present writing problems for speakers of nonstandard dialects.

- *10-4a:* Misuse of verb forms
- *10-3 and 10-4c:* Omission of -s endings on verbs
- *10-4d:* Omission of *-ed* endings on verbs
- *10-4e:* Omission of necessary verbs
- *10-6d:* Double negatives

13-2D: LEVELS OF FORMALITY

Informal writing is casual in language and tone, and it is appropriate for communication in such forms as notes, friendly letters, e-mails, journal entries, and brief memorandums to people you know very well.

Formal writing is formal in tone and language, and it is appropriate for academic and business writing such as essays, research reports, job application letters, and business letters and reports.

When deciding which level of formality to employ in a piece of writing, you should consider two key factors:

1. Subject
2. Audience

As you draft and revise your work, ask the following questions about the level of formality you select.

SUBJECT

- Is my choice of words appropriate to the seriousness of my subject?

AUDIENCE

- What type of language will my audience expect?
- Is my choice of words appropriate for the intended audience?
- Does my choice of words and the tone these words create make me seem too close or too distant from my readers?

In any academic or business writing you do, use a formal level of writing and assume a serious tone. The following opening line of a career application letter is too informal.

× I'm just dropping you a few lines to put my name in for that fisheries biologist's assistant job I saw somewhere in the *Free Press* a few weeks back.

√ I am writing to apply for the fisheries biologist's assistant position advertised in the June 16 edition of the *Free Press.*

The level of language can also seem highly inappropriate when too formal.

Too Formal: When the illustrious Maple Leafs exited from the frozen playing surface trailing their less renowned opponents, the Wild, by the modest score of 1–0, the assembled spectators vigorously voiced their disapproval. The officials in charge of the National Hockey League were authentic demons for having the audacity to schedule these mismatched contests between the annual All-Star Game and the hockey tournament that is part of Olympic competition.

More Appropriate: When the Leafs left the ice trailing the Wild 1–0, a smattering of boos rained down from the crowd. The NHL was the real culprit for slipping lopsided games like these between the All-Star Game and the Olympics.

13-2E: NONSEXIST LANGUAGE

Sexist language is biased in attributing characteristics and roles to people exclusively on the basis of gender. Sometimes sexist language is very obvious, but often it is less so. Sexist language can be explicit, as in calling an attractive young woman a *hot chick*. It can be patronizing by referring to a mature woman as a *girl Friday*. It can reflect stereotypical thinking by unnecessarily drawing attention to a person's gender, as in *a female university president*. And sexist language can be subtle, yet still highly biased, by including only male pronouns when more inclusive language is needed; for example, *an athlete always needs to maintain his composure.*

Sexist language can apply to men as well as women; for instance, if a writer describes *a male kindergarten teacher.*

There are a number of strategies you can use to avoid sexist language.

1. Treat all people equally in your descriptions of them.

   × Mr. Delmonico, Mr. Habib, Mr. Dawson, and Tillie, the secretary, arrived for the meeting.

   √ Mr. Delmonico, Mr. Habib, Mr. Dawson, and Ms. Lord arrived for the meeting.

2. Avoid stereotypes.

   Stereotyping: Like all men, he hates to cook.

3. Use pairs of pronouns to indicate inclusive gender references.

   × A professor is motivated by his students.

   √ A professor is motivated by his or her students.

4. Rewrite the sentence as a plural.

   √ Professors are motivated by their students.

5. Rewrite the sentence so there is no gender problem.

   √ A professor is motivated by students.

6. Make gender-neutral word choices.

Avoiding Sexist Language

INAPPROPRIATE	GENDER-NEUTRAL
alderman	city council member, councillor
anchorman	anchor
businessman	businessperson, entrepreneur
chairman	chairperson, chair
clergyman	member of the clergy, minister
coed	student
craftsman	artisan, craftsperson
fireman	firefighter
forefather	ancestor
foreman	supervisor
freshman	first-year student
housewife	homemaker
mailman	mail carrier, letter carrier, postal worker
male nurse	nurse
mankind	people, humankind, human
manpower	personnel, human resources
newsman	journalist, reporter
policeman	police officer
salesman	salesperson, sales clerk
stewardess	flight attendant
to man	to staff, to operate
weatherman	weather forecaster
waitress	server
workman	worker, labourer, employee

13-3: PRECISION IN LANGUAGE

When trying to choose the most precise word to communicate your meaning, you may find a number of language reference books helpful. Among the most useful will be a good Canadian dictionary and a book of synonyms and antonyms such as *Roget's Thesaurus*, *Gage Canadian Thesaurus*, or *Fitzhenry and Whiteside's Canadian Thesaurus*. (See 13-4.)

13-3A: CONNOTATIONS

Many words have two levels of meaning: a **denotative** meaning and a **connotative** meaning. The denotative meaning of a word is its common, literal, dictionary meaning. The connotative meaning is the emotional meaning of the word, which includes experiences and associations you make when you see a word in print or hear it spoken. For example, the dictionary meaning of *eagle* is "a large bird of prey." However, the word *eagle* also carries additional emotional and associative meanings such as "power," "pride," "majesty," and "fierceness."

When considering any word for a piece of writing, you should consider both its denotative and connotative meanings. Sometimes by using a word with certain connotations, you could imply a meaning you do not intend. Conversely, you can enhance your intended meaning by selecting the word with the most appropriate connotations for your subject, purpose, and audience. Often, reviewing all listed meanings in a dictionary entry will give you a sense of a word's connotations. Take special care when using a thesaurus to be sensitive to the connotations of a word. A word like "dissipated," for example, means "scattered" when applied to clouds, but "drunken or disorderly" when applied to people. Context affects connotation and can profoundly affect meaning.

> The young women ~~giggled~~ laughed at all the right parts of the Restoration comedy.

Giggled has an association with immaturity, and since the women were *young*, the sentence implies the women were immature. The intended meaning of the sentence was that the women appreciated the humour of the play, so *laughed* is more appropriate.

> Ethel ~~is a victim of~~ has rheumatoid arthritis and has ~~suffered from~~ had it for ten years.

It would be even better to use this sentence instead: *Ethel was diagnosed with rheumatoid arthritis ten years ago.* Other emotional language related to suffering is best avoided since this kind of language adds an inappropriate slant to the meaning.

13-3B: CONCRETE NOUNS

There are many types of nouns.

GENERAL AND SPECIFIC NOUNS

Nouns can be very general or very specific. Suppose a friend asks, *What did you do on Saturday?* You respond: *I watched a comedy. Comedy* is a very broad, general noun. Your response could refer to a sophisticated Shakespearean comedy, a television situation comedy, or a particular movie, such as *Ace Ventura, Pet Detective*. All of these individual alternatives within the general category *comedy* are specific nouns.

ABSTRACT AND CONCRETE NOUNS

Nouns can be abstract or concrete. Abstract nouns refer to concepts, ideas, qualities, and conditions. Examples include *love, charity, kindness, humanism, youth,* and *integrity*. Concrete nouns name things that are detectable by your senses, such as *snake, dill, sunset, coffee, caramel,* and *harp*.

Many professional creative writers, especially poets and novelists, spend a great deal of time selecting the most appropriate and precise word to communicate an idea or feeling. Similarly, in your own writing, try to select the most effective word for your writing purpose. Of course, in the range of your writing assignments, you will frequently need to describe, explain, and evaluate general and abstract content. At these times, general and abstract language will be most appropriate. But wherever possible, use specific and concrete nouns to make your writing clear and evocative.

> ~~Hazy city air~~ Toronto's smog made it difficult to breathe as we ~~put the boat in the water~~ launched the sailboat onto Lake Ontario.

General abstract nouns, such as *things, considerations,* and *aspects,* are extremely vague and lacking in colour.

have several renovations done

We plan to ~~do a number of things~~ to improve our home.

issues to discuss

There are several ~~considerations to be addressed~~ before we allow the new subdivision.

13-3C: ACTIVE VERBS

Where possible, choose precise verbs that give your writing impact and power.

WHICH VERBS ARE WEAK?

Weak verbs are forms of the verb *be* (*be, am, is, are, was, were, being, been*). None of these verb forms communicates a specific action. As well, verbs in the passive voice tend to be lacking in power and can lead to lifeless, uninspiring writing: *An acceptable job was done by her.* (See 9-2b and 10-4h for more information on verbs and voice.) Watch for static verbs like "seem," "appear," and "feel" as well as forms of "be." They can make writing less dynamic.

HOW CAN I USE VERBS TO MAKE MY WRITING LIVELY?

Choose precise, vigorous, emphatic, expressive, or descriptive verbs in the active voice. In the following examples, the sentence has been revised from one that uses the verb *be* in the passive voice to a precise verb in the active voice.

Passive Voice: The eager young actors *were trained* by the dynamic acting coach.

Active Voice: The dynamic acting coach *trained* the eager young actors.

Use the most precise and descriptive verbs to communicate vividly the action(s) performed in your sentence.

approached — lunged for

As she ~~got near to~~ the finish line, the marathon runner ~~leaned toward~~

grimaced — collapsed

the tape, ~~crinkled her face~~, and ~~fell down~~.

WHEN SHOULD I REPLACE THE VERB BE?

Change the form of the verb *be* when it creates a wordy construction. Look in the phrase that follows the verb for a word that could be turned into a verb.

infringe on

Keeping the prisoners in cages would ~~be an infringement of~~ their human rights.

Using the verb *infringe* is more dynamic—and more economical—than using *be an infringement of.*

WHEN SHOULD I NOT REPLACE THE VERB BE?

Keep forms of the verb *be* in the following circumstances:

- when you want to link the subject of a sentence with a noun that renames the subject or an adjective that describes it

  Life is a bed of roses.

  Bed-and-breakfast proprietors are usually hospitable.

- when they function as helping verbs before present participles

  The elk are vanishing.

- when expressing ongoing action (see 10-4f)

  I was driving to work when I heard that several buildings were burning in the downtown core.

WHEN SHOULD I REPLACE A PASSIVE VERB?

With sentences in the active voice, the subject performs the action.

Active Voice: José hammered the nail.

With sentences in the passive voice, the subject receives the action.

Passive Voice: The nail was hammered by José.

In some passive sentences the performer of the action is not mentioned.

The nail was hammered.

Strong writing clearly states who or what performs the action. Use the active voice by making the person or thing that performs the action the subject of the sentence.

The class selected
^"Canada's Ethnic Diversity" ~~was selected by the class~~ as the theme for the panel discussion.

The sentence is more direct and vigorous in the active voice. The class clearly performs the action—selecting—and it is the subject of the sentence.

WHEN SHOULD I NOT REPLACE A PASSIVE VERB?

Use the passive voice in the following situations:

- when you want to emphasize who or what receives the action
- when you want to give less emphasis to the person or thing performing the action
- when the person or thing performing the action is not known

For example, in the example involving José and the nail (above), you would choose the active voice if you wished to emphasize José's importance. If you wanted to emphasize the importance of the nail being hammered, you would use the passive voice. And if hammering the nail was of central importance and José of no importance whatsoever, or you didn't know who did the hammering, you would use *The nail was hammered.*

13-3D: MISUSED WORDS

Often when working on a draft, you may want to use a word but may be unsure of the word's meaning or spelling. Always check the meaning of such words in a good dictionary. Misusing words can confuse your overall meaning and create unintentional humour.

> conscious
> Burns is ~~conscience~~ of his own powers of destruction.

> censored
> The provincial review committee ~~censured~~ the pornographic movie.

> cited
> In a definitive book on Gorbachev, the author ~~sighted~~ the main reasons for the collapse of the Soviet Union.

Many writers incorrectly use a noun when the meaning and sentence structure require an adjective. For instance, they might use *abhorrence, indulgence,* or *independence* in sentences that require the adjective forms *abhorrent, indulgent,* or *independent*, respectively.

> abhorrent
> It is an ~~abhorrence~~ practice when advertisers target viewers under five years of age.

13-3E: STANDARD IDIOMS

An idiom is an expression whose meaning can't be determined by simply knowing the definition of each word within the idiom. Many idioms are very colourful and easy to spot: *kill two birds with one stone, read between the lines, the last straw.*

An idiom always appears in one particular form, one that may not necessarily be taken literally. An example of an idiom is *beside himself* [or *herself*]. *She was beside herself* means "She was in a state of extreme excitement or agitation."

Using idiomatic expressions with prepositions can be tricky. An unidiomatic expression may make better literal sense, but the idiomatic expression is used because it is accepted English usage. If you are in doubt, check a good Canadian dictionary by looking up the word before the preposition.

Avoiding Unidiomatic Expressions

UNIDIOMATIC	IDIOMATIC
according with	according to
angry at	angry with
capable to	capable of
comply to	comply with
desirous to	desirous of
different than	different from
go by	go to
intend on doing	intend to do
off of	off
plan on doing	plan to do
preferable than	preferable to
prior than	prior to
recommend her to do	recommend that she do
superior than	superior to
sure and	sure to
try and	try to
type of a	type of
wait on a person	wait for a person
wait on line	wait in line
with reference in	with reference to

13-3F: CLICHÉS

A **cliché** is an overused phrase or expression that has become tired and predictable and, hence, is ineffective for freshly communicating writing ideas.

Selected Clichés to Avoid in Your Writing

add insult to injury	easier said than done	in the long run
at long last	few and far between	in this day and age
a word to the wise	finishing touches	it stands to reason
cool as a cucumber	first and foremost	narrow escape
cold as ice	good as gold	red-letter day

You might wish to create a computer file of these and other clichés to avoid.

Clichés, by being so predictable, deprive writing of any sense of surprise. However, in some rare instances, you might inject freshness into a cliché by giving it an unexpected twist.

He is as strong as an ox; unfortunately, that describes his odour, too.

13-3G: FIGURES OF SPEECH

In figurative language, words carry more than their literal meaning. **Figures of speech** are particular types of figurative language. Common examples of figures of speech are **similes**, **personification**, and **metaphors**. In a simile, a comparison is made between two different ideas or objects, using *like* or *as*. In personification, human traits are assigned to something that is not human. And in a metaphor, a comparison is made between two otherwise dissimilar ideas or objects; here, the comparison does not use *like* or *as*.

Used effectively, figures of speech can add colour and emphasis to your writing and enrich meaning. However, used without care, they can make writing clumsy. A common writing problem is mixing metaphors. In a **mixed** metaphor, two or more incongruous images are mingled.

She was able to ~~take a firm foothold~~ keep focus while in the eye of public opinion.

~~The Grand Canyon of Harry's depression~~ Harry reached the ~~pinnacle~~ depth of depression when his pet died.

13-4: THE DICTIONARY AND THESAURUS

13-4A: THE DICTIONARY

A student at the postsecondary level needs at least one good Canadian dictionary in his or her personal reference library. Canadian dictionaries provide correct spelling and usage in Canada and are not mere adaptations of American or British dictionaries. Standard volumes include the following:

- *ITP Nelson Canadian Dictionary*
- *The Canadian Oxford Dictionary*
- *Gage Canadian Dictionary*
- *Funk & Wagnalls Canadian College Dictionary*

Online dictionaries are also available; however, if they are British or American in origin, be aware that they may not always apply Canadian standards of spelling or usage. For American usage, try the Merriam-Webster online dictionary. For British usage, try the Cambridge or Oxford online dictionaries.

A sample entry from the *ITP Nelson Canadian Dictionary* appears on page 419. The labels indicate the range of information you can obtain from a typical dictionary entry.

SPELLING, WORD DIVISION, PRONUNCIATION

The main entry (*poor* in the sample entry) shows the correct spelling of the word. When there are two spellings of a word (*pickaxe* or *pickax*, for example) both spellings are given, with the preferred Canadian spelling provided first.

If the word is a multi-syllabic word (as in *poor•ly*), the entry shows how to divide the word into syllables. The dot between *poor* and ly separates the word's two syllables. If a word is a compound word, the main entry shows how to write it: as one word (*poolroom*), as a hyphenated word (*pooper-scooper*), or as two words (*poop deck*).

The pronunciation of the word is given just after the main entry. If the word is a multi-syllabic word, accents indicate which syllables are stressed. Other marks help the reader pronounce the word. These marks are explained in a pronunciation key. In this dictionary, the pronunciation key is in the lower far right-hand corner of the two-page spread. The placement of this feature varies from dictionary to dictionary.

FIGURE 13.1
Sample Dictionary Entry

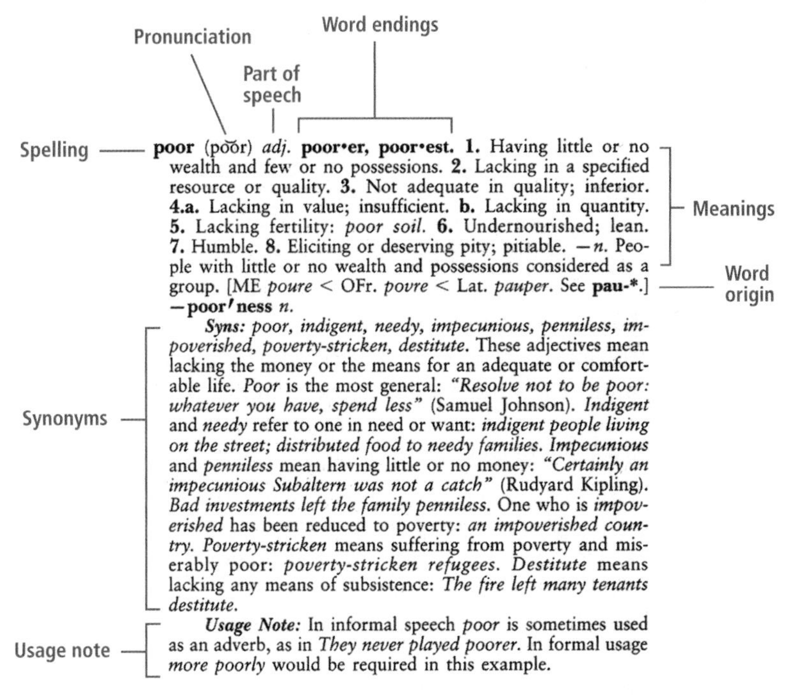

poor (po͝or) *adj.* **poor•er, poor•est. 1.** Having little or no wealth and few or no possessions. **2.** Lacking in a specified resource or quality. **3.** Not adequate in quality; inferior. **4.a.** Lacking in value; insufficient. **b.** Lacking in quantity. **5.** Lacking fertility: *poor soil.* **6.** Undernourished; lean. **7.** Humble. **8.** Eliciting or deserving pity; pitiable. —*n.* People with little or no wealth and possessions considered as a group. [ME *poure* < OFr. *povre* < Lat. *pauper.* See **pau-***.] —**poor′ness** *n.*

Syns: *poor, indigent, needy, impecunious, penniless, impoverished, poverty-stricken, destitute.* These adjectives mean lacking the money or the means for an adequate or comfortable life. *Poor* is the most general: *"Resolve not to be poor: whatever you have, spend less"* (Samuel Johnson). *Indigent* and *needy* refer to one in need or want: *indigent people living on the street; distributed food to needy families. Impecunious* and *penniless* mean having little or no money: *"Certainly an impecunious Subaltern was not a catch"* (Rudyard Kipling). *Bad investments left the family penniless.* One who is *impoverished* has been reduced to poverty: *an impoverished country. Poverty-stricken* means suffering from poverty and miserably poor: *poverty-stricken refugees. Destitute* means lacking any means of subsistence: *The fire left many tenants destitute.*

Usage Note: In informal speech *poor* is sometimes used as an adverb, as in *They never played poorer.* In formal usage *more poorly* would be required in this example.

Source: *ITP Nelson Canadian Dictionary of the English Language: An Encyclopedic Reference,* by Nelson Canada, p. 1068.

WORD ENDINGS AND GRAMMATICAL LABELS

When a word takes endings to indicate grammatical functions, which are called **inflections**, the endings are listed in boldface. In the *poor* entry, three inflections are listed: poor•er, poor•est, and poor•ness.

The labels for the parts of speech and for other grammatical terms used in entries are abbreviated. Here are the most commonly used dictionary abbreviations:

n.	noun
pl.	plural
sing.	singular
v.	verb
tr.	transitive (as in *transitive verb*)
intr.	intransitive (as in *intransitive verb*)

adj.	adjective
adv.	adverb
pron.	pronoun
prep.	preposition
conj.	conjunction
interj.	interjection

MEANINGS, WORD ORIGIN, SYNONYMS, AND ANTONYMS

Each word meaning is given with a separate number, and the most common meanings are listed first.

Some words can function as more than one part of speech (*positive*, for example, can be a noun or an adjective). In such cases, all meanings for one part of speech are given, then all meanings for another part of speech, and so on. After the final meaning, any idioms containing the word are given. For example, with the entry for *pop*, the idiom *pop the question* is listed; as well, the idiom's meaning is provided. In square brackets at the end of the entry appears the *etymology*, or information about the origins of the word. According to the etymology for *poor*, the word originated from the Middle English word *poure*, as well as from Old French and Latin.

Synonyms, or words with similar meaning to the main entry word, are listed for some dictionary entries. *Indigent* is listed as one of seven synonyms for *poor*.

Antonyms are words that have a meaning opposite to that of the main entry word. For example, *poor* is an antonym of *rich*.

USAGE

Usage notes follow many entries in this dictionary. These notes present important information and guidance on matters of grammar, diction, pronunciation, and nuances of usage.

This particular dictionary also includes labels, which provide guidance regarding levels of usage. For the *Nelson Canadian Dictionary*, status labels indicate that an entry word or an entry is limited to a particular level or style of usage. These labels include *nonstandard, usage problem, offensive, vulgar, obscene, slang,* and *informal*. Usage labels can vary among dictionaries.

Dictionaries also vary in their content and features. It's a good idea to explore the front matter of any dictionary you own for information on what it has to offer and how to use this invaluable resource.

13-4B: THE THESAURUS

You may find yourself in a writing situation in which you know a word but want to find a more precise or colourful word with the same or a similar meaning. Or, you have repeatedly used a word within a paragraph or even a sentence and don't want your writing to sound mechanical. The *Gage Canadian Thesaurus* is an excellent resource for finding synonyms, or words with a similar meaning. It is available in hardcover, paperback, and software format.

HOW DO I USE THE THESAURUS?

Suppose you want to find a synonym for *abundance*. Your first step is to find *abundance* in the extensive index at the back of the thesaurus.

Of the possibilities listed in the entry, the closest to the meaning and part of speech you want is *plenty*. Turn to the Abstract Relations section at the front of the thesaurus to the number listed in the index beside *plenty*, under *abundance*.

One possibility you could use as an alternative to *abundance* is *cornucopia*. Or you might explore other word choice options in the thesaurus. Before you actually include a word in your manuscript, double-check its meaning in the dictionary.

Use the thesaurus to locate the best word. Some writers use a thesaurus to find the most difficult or exotic synonym possible. Always strive for simplicity and clarity when writing. If you use the thesaurus to find inflated vocabulary, you'll risk misusing words and make your writing seem pretentious.

FIGURE 13.2
Sample Thesaurus Entry for "Plenty"

plenty *n* abundance, affluence, a fund, a plethora, a profusion, copiousness, enough, fertility, fruitfulness, heap(s), lots, luxury, mass, masses, milk and honey, mountain(s), oodles, opulence, overabundance, pile(s), plenitude, plenteousness, plentifulness, prosperity, quantities, stack(s), ton(s), volume(s), wealth.
antonyms lack, need, scarcity, want.

Source: *Gage Canadian Thesaurus*, p. 485. Copyright © 1998 Gage Learning Corporation.

FIGURE 13.3
Explanation of Terms and Format of a Thesaurus Entry

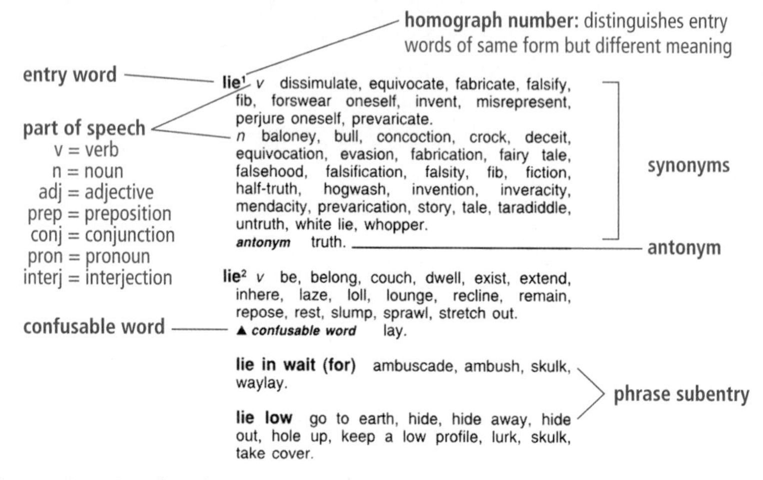

Source: *Gage Canadian Thesaurus*, p. ix. Copyright © 1998 Gage Learning Corporation.

Note that the thesaurus in Microsoft Word can be found under the Language heading in the Tools menu. If you do not have access to a printed thesaurus, you may find it somewhat useful. Unlike print sources, though, it does not give you insight into the subtle nuances of word choice and therefore may be less than wholly satisfactory for your writing purposes.

14

MECHANICS AND SPELLING

Spel chekers, hoo neeeds em?

-Alan James Bean

14

Mechanics and Spelling

14 Mechanics and Spelling

Spelling and mechanics often make or break a document. Referring to "Robert Bondar" in a fundraising letter when you meant to refer to Canadian astronaut Roberta Bondar may have serious repercussions for your fundraising campaign and will certainly make the reader think twice about your credibility as a writer. Little things mean a lot.

14-1: SPELLING

Checking spelling should be one of the final steps in your writing process, and it is an extremely important step. Presenting error-free written work is vital to creating a good impression in academic and business contexts. Spelling errors distract readers and, at their worst, can cause them to lose your meaning; when misspellings suggest entirely different meanings, they can completely confuse readers.

Spell checkers in word-processing programs can be useful tools for helping you spot *some* potential spelling problems. However, spell checkers have limitations that allow many spelling errors to be missed. These limitations include the following:

- Many spell checkers, in their default setting, do not include Canadian spellings. It is, however, often possible to select Canadian spelling. As well, dictionaries such as *The Canadian Oxford Dictionary* are available in CD-ROM and can be installed and used to do the spell checking.
- Countless words, such as new or marginal words or very specialized vocabularies, are not included. For instance, if you type *tchotchkes* (meaning "cheap, showy trinkets"), the spell checker may offer you "crotches" as a correction—not what you had in mind at all.
- Spell checkers cannot distinguish between commonly confused words that have entirely different meanings (e.g., *allusion* and *illusion*).
- They cannot intuit that you have made a simple typographical error, such as using *do* when you meant *to*.
- The majority of proper nouns are not included.

Rumour has it that, in one early spell checker, a common misspelling of *inconvenience* ("inconvinence") was corrected to read *incontinence*; well-meaning people who didn't proofread carefully ended up with *Sorry for the incontinence* instead of *Sorry for the inconvenience.* Mistakes of this kind could prove very embarrassing, to say the least.

Checking writing drafts for spelling errors demands your complete attention, and a computer spell checker is just one of many tools and strategies at your disposal.

Good spelling is a challenge in English since sound and letter patterns frequently do not correspond and many spelling rules have exceptions. Still, you can greatly improve your spelling by concentrating on the following:

- knowing basic spelling rules and their exceptions
- recognizing words that sound alike but have entirely different meanings and spellings
- identifying and remembering commonly misspelled words

Once you have mastered these spelling strategies, there are three more you can apply to help ensure that any manuscript you submit is free of spelling errors.

1. Proofread drafts meticulously to identify and fix any spelling problems.
2. Keep a dictionary nearby to check the spelling of words you do not know; have access to specialized dictionaries or other resources to check concerns you have about spelling specialized vocabulary.
3. Make and maintain a list of your own recurrent spelling problems; focus on list items as you proofread your draft so you don't repeat these errors.

14-1A: SPELLING RULES

Know the major spelling rules.

PATTERNS OF IE *AND* EI *WORDS*

Use *i* before *e* except after *c* or when *ei* sounds like *ay*, as in *weigh*.

i before *e*:	believe, chief, niece, yield, fierce, grieve
e before *i* after *c*:	ceiling, deceive, perceive, receive
ei sound like *ay*:	eight, vein, neighbour, freight, reign
exceptions:	either, leisure, weird, foreign, seize

DROPPING OR KEEPING A FINAL SILENT E *WHEN ADDING A SUFFIX*

Usually, drop the final silent *e* when adding a suffix that begins with a vowel and keep the final *e* when the suffix begins with a consonant.

DROP FINAL E

love + able = lovable

race + ing = racing

fame + ous = famous

Exceptions: dyeing, changeable, hoeing

KEEP FINAL E

achieve + ment = achievement

hope + ful = hopeful

love + ly = lovely

Exceptions: judgment, truly, argument

ADDING -ED OR -S TO WORDS ENDING IN Y

When adding *-ed* or -s to words ending in y, you usually change the y to i when y is preceded by a consonant. However, do not change the y when it is preceded by a vowel.

PRECEDED BY A CONSONANT

try + ed = tried

melody + s = melodies

If you need to spell a proper name ending in y and preceded by a consonant, do not change the y to i when adding s. For example, when referring to the Dunwitty family, you would use *the Dunwittys.*

PRECEDED BY A VOWEL

stay + ed = stayed

donkey + s = donkeys

DOUBLING CONSONANTS WHEN ADDING SUFFIXES

Double the final consonant before a suffix starting with a vowel and ending with a consonant preceded by one vowel.

bet + ing = betting

fit + ed = fitted

Double the final consonant when the word ends in an accented syllable.

commit + ing = committing

occur + ed = occurred

Double the final consonant when the word ends in the consonant *l* (Canadian spelling).

travel + ed = travelled

ADDING -S TO FORM PLURALS OF NOUNS

Add -*s* to make most nouns plural. However, if the noun ends in -*s*, -*sh*, -*ch*, -*x*, or -*z*, add -*es*.

MOST NOUNS

plant + s = plants

fork + s = forks

satellite + s = satellites

NOUNS ENDING IN -S, -SH, -CH, -X, OR -Z

stress + s = stresses

bush + s = bushes

peach + s = peaches

fax + s = faxes

quiz + s = quizzes

CREATING OTHER PLURALS

Usually, add -*s* to nouns ending in -*o* when -*o* follows a vowel. However, add -*es* when -*o* follows a consonant.

FOLLOWING A VOWEL

studio + s = studios

video + s = videos

FOLLOWING A CONSONANT

echo + s = echoes

hero + s = heroes

When making a plural of a hyphenated compound word, add -*s* to the main word of the compound, even if that word does not appear at the end of the compound.

father-in-law + s = fathers-in-law

Some English words come from other languages, such as French and Latin. These words are usually made plural as they would be made plural in the original language.

SINGULAR	PLURAL
criterion	criteria
château	châteaux
datum	data
phenomenon	phenomena

BRITISH AND U.S. VARIATIONS

In your reading, you might notice variations in spellings for certain words. For instance, if you are reading an American article, you might encounter *traveled*, while in a Canadian article you would see *travelled*. Similarly, in a British article you might find *apologise*, while a Canadian article would use *apologize*. Consistently use Canadian spellings in your writing. Generally, Canadian spelling follows British usage in its treatment of *-our* words (*colour* not *color*) and *-re* words (*centre* not *center*), as well as doubling certain consonants before a suffix beginning with a vowel (*counsellor* not *counselor*), but follows American style for *-ize* words (*organize* not *organise*). Check the preferred spelling in a good Canadian dictionary, where the Canadian spelling will be listed first.

14-1B: WORDS THAT SOUND ALIKE

Words that sound the same but have different meanings and spellings are called **homophones.** Homophones are often the source of spelling problems. As you proofread your work, look carefully for homophones you may have used or spelled incorrectly.

Commonly Confused Words

accept a verb meaning "to receive"
except a preposition meaning "other" or verb meaning "to exclude"

affect a verb meaning "to cause change"
effect usually a noun meaning "the result of change"

cite a verb meaning "to quote"
site a noun meaning "location"
sight a noun meaning "vision"

desert a verb meaning "to abandon"
dessert a noun meaning "sweet course after the main course of a meal"

its possessive pronoun meaning "belonging to it"
it's contraction of *it is*

loose adjective meaning "not well attached"
lose verb meaning "to misplace" or "to part with"

principal noun meaning "the chief person" (as in a school), or adjective meaning "main"
principle noun meaning "a basic truth"

their possessive pronoun meaning "belonging to them"
they're contraction of *they are*
there adverb meaning "in that place"

who's contraction of *who is* or *who has*
whose the possessive form of *who*

your possessive form of *you*
you're contraction of *you are*

The Glossary of Usage (13-1) contains many homophones, as well as words that sound nearly the same and can cause spelling problems. There you will also find definitions for each word in the following sets of words.

Homophones and Similar-Sounding Sets of Words in the Glossary of Usage

accept, except
adapt, adopt
adverse, averse
advice, advise
affect, effect
aggravate, irritate
all ready, already
all together, altogether
allude, elude
allusion, illusion
amoral, immoral
anyone, any one
awhile, a while
beside, besides

capital, capitol
censor, censure
cite, site
climactic, climatic
coarse, course
complement, compliment
conscience, conscious
continual, continuous
council, counsel
discreet, discrete
disinterested, uninterested
elicit, illicit
emigrate, immigrate
eminent, imminent
everyone, every one
explicit, implicit
farther, further
ingenious, ingenuous
its, it's
lead, led
licence, license
loose, lose
maybe, may be
moral, morale
passed, past
practice, practise
precede, proceed
principal, principle
respectfully, respectively
sometime, some time, sometimes
stationary, stationery
than, then
there, their, they're
to, too, two
weather, whether
who's, whose
your, you're

14-1C: COMMON SPELLING ERRORS

Following is a list of words commonly misspelled by students. Check that they are spelled correctly in your writing drafts.

Commonly Misspelled Words

abbreviate	abhor	absence	absorption
absurd	abysmal	acceptable	accidentally
accommodate	accomplish	accumulate	acquaintance
acquire	address	aggressive	all right
almost	amateur	analyze	annual
apology	apparently	appearance	appropriate
arctic	argument	arrangement	ascend
association	attendance	attorney	audience
awkward	bachelor	barbarous	basically
becoming	beginning	behaviour	believe

beneficial	boundary	brilliant	Britain
bureau	burial	business	cafeteria
calendar	candidate	canister	carburetor
career	Caribbean	category	cemetery
changeable	characteristic	choose	chosen
column	commission	committee	comparative
competitive	compulsory	concede	conceivable
conference	conqueror	conscience	conscientious
conscious	consensus	courteous	criticism
criticize	curiosity	curriculum	cylindrical
dealt	decision	definitely	descend
description	despair	desperate	diarrhea
dictionary	dilemma	disagree	disappear
disappointment	disastrous	discipline	dissatisfied
dissipate	dominant	dormitory	ecstasy
efficient	eighth	eligible	elimination
embarrassment	eminent	enthusiastic	entirely
entrance	environment	equipped	equivalent
erroneous	especially	exaggerated	exceptionally
exercise	exhaust	exhilarate	existence
experience	explanation	extraordinary	extremely
fallacy	familiar	fascinate	February
fictitious	foreign	foreseen	forty
frantically	friend	fundamental	further
gauge	genealogy	generally	grammar
guarantee	guard	guerrilla	guidance
harass	height	hereditary	heroine
hindrance	humorous	hungrily	hypocrisy
hypothesis	illiterate	imaginary	imagination
imitation	immediately	impromptu	incidentally
incredible	indefinitely	independent	indispensable
inevitable	infinite	ingenious	initiation
inoculate	intelligence	interesting	interpretation
involve	iridescent	irrelevant	irresistible

jealousy	knowledge	laboratory	legitimate
liaison	license (verb)	lightning	literature
liveliest	loneliness	luxury	magazine
maintenance	manoeuvre	marriage	marshal
mathematics	medieval	miniature	mischievous
misspell	moccasin	mortgage	mysterious
necessary	negotiation	nevertheless	noticeable
obligation	obstacle	occasion	occasionally
occur	occurred	occurrence	omission
opinions	opportunity	optimistic	original
outrageous	pamphlet	parallel	paralyze
particularly	pastime	peer	perform
performance	permanent	permissible	perseverance
perspiration	Philippines	physically	picnicking
playwright	politics	practically	precedence
preference	preferred	prejudice	preparation
prevalent	primitive	privilege	probably
proceed	professor	prominent	pronunciation
propaganda	psychology	quantity	quiet
quite	quizzes	recede	receive
recommendation	reference	referred	regard
religious	reminiscent	repetition	resistance
restaurant	rhythm	ridiculous	roommate
sacrifice	sandwich	schedule	secretary
seize	separate	sergeant	several
siege	similar	simultaneous	sincerely
soliloquy	sophomore	specimen	strictly
subtly	succeed	supersede	surprise
syllable	tariff	temperament	temperature
tendency	thorough	threshold	tragedy
transferred	tries	truly	typical
tyranny	unanimous	unnecessarily	until
usually	vacuum	vengeance	villain
weird	whether	written	

14-2: THE HYPHEN

14-2A: COMPOUND WORDS

A **compound word** is made up of two or more words that combine to express one concept. It may be written in one of three ways:

1. As separate words (*half sister*)
2. As one word (*stepfather*)
3. As a hyphenated word (*mother-in-law*)

Check in the dictionary to determine whether to write a compound word as separate words, one word, or a hyphenated compound. If a compound word does not appear in the dictionary, treat it as separate words.

The tractor ‸ trailer swerved and almost hit us.

He has an extensive resource library on the ~~book shelf~~ bookshelf in his dormitory room.

Each time the Davidsons went to the CNE, they made a point of having candy floss.

14-2B: HYPHENATED ADJECTIVES

When two or more words function as an adjective before a noun, they are hyphenated.

Vladimir is a well ‸ known tenor in opera circles.

Because the thief was a fourteen ‸ year ‸ old girl, her picture could not be shown on the evening news.

In most cases, do not use a hyphen when the compound follows the noun.

She would go to any type of publicity event in the hope of becoming well known.

To qualify for the league team, Adam had to be seventeen years old.

Hyphens are suspended if the modifying words are in a series.

The family could not decide whether to purchase a one-, two-, or three-day pass to the theme park.

14-2C: FRACTIONS AND COMPOUND NUMBERS

Use a hyphen with compound numbers from twenty-one through ninety-nine and with fractions.

Faisal dreaded the thought that he would be sixty-five on his next birthday.

I use one-third of my basement as an office.

14-2D: WITH CERTAIN PREFIXES AND SUFFIXES

Use a hyphen with the prefixes *all-*, *ex-*, *great-*, *quasi-*, and *self-* and with the suffix *-elect*.

The ex-premier always has a difficult time because he is frequently asked his position on controversial issues.

The mayor-elect was impatient to begin implementing her agenda.

Note that U.S. dictionaries suggest that the prefix *non* be used without a hyphen, but Canadian and British style tends to hyphenate *non-*, if not consistently, then at least frequently.

14-2E: TO AVOID AMBIGUITY AND AWKWARDNESS

A hyphen is used in some words to eliminate awkward double or triple letters—for example, *co-opt*.

Some pairs of words are spelled the same but have entirely different meanings and could cause confusion. In such cases, a hyphen is traditionally used in one of the words to distinguish it from the other. For example, *recount* means "to tell a story," while *re-count* means "to count again."

My uncle used to recount terrible stories about life in a concentration camp during the Second World War.

The candidate for council requested a re-count after her opponent received only marginally more votes.

14-2F: WORD DIVISION AT THE END OF A LINE

Most word-processing programs automatically break between words at the end of a line. However, you will likely encounter some occasions (e.g., when proofreading printed material or handwriting a test) when it will be important to know end-of-line hyphenation rules.

1. Divide words only between syllables.

   pro-
   If you want to write well, you must follow a systematic ~~proc-~~
   cess
   ~~ess~~ that includes more than one draft.

2. Do not divide one-syllable words.

   death
   Wounded in the extremely heavy fighting, the officer knew ~~dea-~~
   ~~th~~ was approaching, and he accepted it with great dignity.

3. Do not divide a word so that only one or two letters remain at the end of the line.

   opened
   She found the stale air in the room oppressive, so she ~~o-~~
   ~~pened~~ the window and turned on the fan.

   alone
   Neighbours of the accused man told reporters that the man lived ~~a-~~
   ~~lone~~ and was very quiet.

4. Divide a hyphenated word at the hyphen, and divide a closed compound only between complete words.

   self-
   He is not naive in any way; most people consider him a very ~~sel-~~
   aware
   ~~f-aware~~ individual.

   base-
   The next step, after installing the new carpet, is to nail on the ~~ba-~~
   boards
   ~~seboards~~ where they are required.

14-3: CAPITALIZATION

Capitalize the first word of every sentence. You will also need to capitalize specific types of words within sentences. Use the following rules as general guidelines for capitalization. Consult your dictionary to determine which words must be capitalized.

14-3A: PROPER VS. COMMON NOUNS

Capitalize proper nouns, and words derived from them, but do not capitalize common nouns. Proper nouns are the names of specific people, places, and things. Common nouns include all other nouns.

Usually, capitalize the following:

- names of religions, religious practitioners, holy books, special religious days, and deities
- geographic place names
- people's names and nicknames
- words of family relationship used as names (e.g., Uncle Bill)
- nationalities, tribes, races, and languages
- names of historical events, periods, movements, documents, and treaties
- political parties, organizations, and government departments
- educational institutions, departments, degrees, and specific courses
- names of celestial bodies
- names of ships, planes, and aircraft
- parts of letters (e.g., Dear John)
- names of specific software

Capitalizing Nouns

PROPER NOUNS	COMMON NOUNS
Zeus	a god
Book of Mormon	a book
Kamloops	a city
Marcel	a man
Aunt Agnes	my aunt
French	a language
Romanticism	a movement
New Democratic Party	a political party
Mars	a planet
the *Formidable*	a ship
Microsoft Word	a software program

Months, days of the week, and holidays are considered proper nouns. The seasons and numbers of days of the month are not considered proper nouns.

Every spring, Victoria Day falls on a Monday in May.

The meeting is held on the second Tuesday of January, June, and December.

Capitalize the names of school subjects only if they are languages, but capitalize the names of specific courses.

In his final year, he will need to take microbiology, chemistry, biology, English, and Spanish.

Professor Woodman teaches Nineteenth-Century Literature to all students majoring in English.

14-3B: TITLES WITH PROPER NAMES

Capitalize the title of a person when it is part of a proper name.

Dr. Norman Bethune

Rev. David Rooke

Pat McLauglin, P.Eng.

Douglas Fairbanks Sr.

Judge Shepperd gave his decision on the appeal.

Do not capitalize the title when it is used alone.

A judge presided over the inquiry.

Note: In some cases, if the title of an important public figure is used alone, the first letter can appear as either a capital letter or a lowercase letter. Conventions vary.

The prime minister [or Prime Minister] dodged the protester's pie.

14-3C: TITLES OF WORKS

Capitalize the first, last, and all other important words in the titles of works such as books, articles, films, and songs.

IMPORTANT WORDS

These important words should be capitalized in titles and subtitles:

- nouns
- verbs
- adjectives
- adverbs

LESS IMPORTANT WORDS

These less important words should not be capitalized *unless* they are the first or last word of the title or subtitle:

- articles
- prepositions
- coordinating conjunctions

Book Title: *A Feminist Dictionary*

Article Title: "A Turkey with Taste"

Film Title: *From Earth to the Moon*

Song Title: "Do You Know the Way to San Jose?"

Also use the guidelines above to capitalize chapter titles and other major divisions in a work.

"Phantom of the Canadian Opera: *Trudeau's Revenge*" is Chapter 11 in Peter C. Newman's *The Canadian Revolution.*

For information on using italics and quotation marks in titles, see 14-6a.

14-3D: FIRST WORD OF A SENTENCE

Capitalize the first word of a sentence.

It's Monday morning, time for the weekly editorial meeting at a mass-market publishing house.

If a sentence appears within parentheses, capitalize the first word of the sentence. However, do not capitalize the first word if the parentheses are within another sentence.

The effects of plaque on the heart valves are significant. (See Figure 6.)

The effects of plaque on the heart valves are significant (see Figure 6).

14-3E: FIRST WORD OF A QUOTED SENTENCE

Capitalize the first word of a direct quotation, but do not capitalize it if the quotation is blended into the sentence in which the quotation is introduced.

The department chair defended the embattled professor, arguing, "He is an outstanding teacher, and the evidence against him is flimsy at best."

In his article "Eco-tourism Boom: How Much Can Wildlife Take?" Bruce Obee says that "tour boats . . . are a fraction of the traffic."

If you need to interrupt a quoted sentence to include explanatory words, do not capitalize the first word following the interruption.

"She goes by bus," the mother exclaimed with anger, "and I'm not very happy about that."

If you need to quote poetry in an essay, use the capitalization employed by the poet.

Season of mists and mellow fruitfulness,
Close bosom-friend of the maturing sun;
Conspiring with him how to load and bless
With fruit the vines that round the thatch-eves run; . . .

—John Keats, "To Autumn"

Many modern poets do not follow the conventions of capitalization. When quoting their work, copy the text exactly.

so much depends
upon
a red wheel
barrow

—William Carlos Williams, "The Red Wheelbarrow"

14-3F: FIRST WORD AFTER A COLON

When an independent clause appears after a colon, capitalizing the first word is optional; if the content after the colon is not an independent clause, do not capitalize.

We were told to bring the following items for the hike: a compass, a sleeping bag, a tent, and enough food to last seven days.

There is one major reason that Phillip doesn't want Kathleen for a friend: he [*or* He] doesn't trust her.

14-3G: ABBREVIATIONS

Capitalize the abbreviations for government departments and agencies, names of organizations and corporations, trade names, and call letters of television and radio stations.

CSIS CIA NATO CTV Loblaws Inc. CHCO-TV CKNW

14-4: ABBREVIATIONS

In most cases, abbreviations should not be used in formal writing, such as academic essays, unless the abbreviations are very well known; for instance, *CBC* or *UN*. Abbreviations are more widely used in science and technical writing than in writing for the humanities.

Always consider your reader when deciding whether or not to use any abbreviation. Will he or she understand the abbreviation Otherwise, you run the risk of confusing the reader. If the type of writing that you are doing requires abbreviations, be consistent in your use of them.

14-4A: TITLES WITH PROPER NAMES

Abbreviate titles and degrees immediately before and after proper names.

Do not abbreviate a title or degree if it does not accompany a proper name.

professor
The ~~prof.~~ gave an inspiring lecture last Thursday.

Do not use titles and degrees redundantly:

× Dr. Steven Edwards, M.D.

√ Dr. Steven Edwards

OR

√ Steven Edwards, M.D.

Abbreviated Titles

BEFORE PROPER NAMES	AFTER PROPER NAMES
Rev. R.W. McLean	Edward Zenker, D.V.D.
Dr. Wendy Wong	Paul Martin Jr.
Asst. Prof. Tom Simpson	Margaret Barcza, M.B.A.
Ms. Germaine Greer	John Bruner, LL.D.
Mrs. Sodha Singh	Eleanor Semple, D.D.
Mr. Wil Loman	Roy Shoicket, M.D.
St. John	Barbara Zapert, Ph.D.

14-4B: ORGANIZATIONS, CORPORATIONS, AND COUNTRIES

Use standard abbreviations for names of countries, organizations, and corporations.

UK (or U.K.) FBI NORAD RCMP CIDA
TSN RCA IBM

To save money, she got a room at the YWCA.

If you need to use a less familiar abbreviation in your paper (e.g., COMECON, for the Council of Mutual Economic Assistance) do the following:

1. Write the full name of the organization, followed by the abbreviation in parentheses.
2. For each subsequent reference to the organization, use the abbreviation on its own.

14-4C: *B.C., A.D., A.M., P.M., NO.*

Use the standard abbreviations *B.C., A.D., a.m., p.m.,* and *no.* only with particular years, times, numbers, or amounts.

The abbreviation *B.C.* ("before Christ") or the acceptable alternative *B.C.E.* ("before the Common Era") always appears after a specific date.

156 B.C. (or B.C.E.)

The abbreviation *A.D.* (*Anno Domini*) appears before a specific date. *C.E.*, an acceptable alternative meaning "Common Era," always appears after a specific date.

A.D. 65

65 C.E.

Use *a.m., p.m.,* or *no.* only with a particular figure.

5:15 a.m. (or A.M.)

8:30 p.m. (or P.M.)

no. 16 (or No.)

In formal writing, do not use these abbreviations without particular figures.

afternoon.
We arrived for the dance in the early ~~p.m.~~

It is impossible to estimate the ~~no.~~ number of fish in the stream during spawning season.

14-4D: LATIN ABBREVIATIONS

Since some readers may be unfamiliar with Latin abbreviations, keep use of these abbreviations to a minimum or use the English equivalent.

Latin Abbreviations

ABBREVIATION	LATIN	ENGLISH MEANING
c.	*circa*	approximately
cf.	*confer*	compare
e.g.	*exempli gratia*	for example
et al.	*et alii*	and others
etc.	*et cetera*	and the rest
i.e.	*id est*	that is
N.B.	*nota bene*	note well
P.S.	*postscriptum*	postscript
vs.	*versus*	versus

In informal writing, such as personal e-mails, it is acceptable to use Latin abbreviations.

Jennifer wants to go the Raptors game this Tuesday. It's the Raptors vs. the Sonics. After the game let's grab a burger, etc. N.B. Dominique and her gang will be there.

In formal writing, use the full English words or phrases.

The Sumerians came down to the bank of the Euphrates and Tigris rivers ~~c.~~ around 3500 B.C.E. Many artifacts—~~e.g.,~~ for example, the headdress of Queen Sub-ad and the bronze mask portrait of King Sargon—provide evidence of their cultural advancement.

14-4E: MISUSES

Abbreviations are generally not appropriate in formal writing.

> Canadian literature
> Margaret Atwood is a popular author in ~~Can. lit.~~ classes because she has written so many outstanding novels.

Types of Abbreviation to Avoid in Formal Writing

CATEGORY	√ FORMAL	× INFORMAL
Names of Persons	Jennifer	Jen
Holidays	Christmas	Xmas
Days of the Week	Tuesday to Thursday	Tues. to Thurs.
Months	from January to August	from Jan. to Aug.
Provinces and Countries	Saskatchewan	Sask. or SK
Academic Subjects	Biology and English	Bio. and Engl.
Units of Measurement*	6 ounces	6 oz.
Addresses	Madison Avenue	Madison Ave.
Subdivision of Books	chapter, page	ch., p.**

* except metric measurements
** except as part of documentation

Metric abbreviations are often permitted in formal writing, as in 25 *kg* or 15 *mm*. However, do not use a number written in words with an abbreviation, as in *twenty cm*.

Abbreviations are acceptable in company or institution names only if the abbreviation is part the company's or institution's official name, as in *Jack's Windows & Roofing Co.*, or *Writers Inc. Consulting*. Never arbitrarily abbreviate a company's name. For example, if a company's name is *Randolph Architectural Group,* do not shorten it to *Randolph Arch. Gr.* When corresponding with any company, use the full company name that appears on company stationery or in the firm's advertising, or on its website.

14-5: NUMBERS

14-5A: SPELLING OUT

Spell out numbers of one or two words, or any number that starts a sentence; use figures for all other numbers and amounts.

eight
It has been ~~8~~ years since we last heard from him.

356
In a single section of Biology 101 there are ~~three hundred and fifty-six~~ first-year students.

Seven hundred and twenty-one
~~721~~ folding chairs are required for the wedding reception.

You might also consider recasting the sentence if it begins with a figure.

For the wedding reception, we require 721 folding chairs.

In some instances, if numbers follow one another, you may wish to write one as a figure.

During the Olympic trials, she swam four 100-metre heats.

Note: In business and technical writing, figures are sometimes preferred for all numbers except one to nine because they provide clarity and brevity. However, usage varies, so it is best to check with your instructor.

14-5B: USING FIGURES

Figures are acceptable in the following writing situations:

DATES

January 16, 1952   21 B.C.E.   A.D. 400

TIME

3:51 a.m.   7 p.m.

If *a.m.* and *p.m.* are not used, write the time in words.

one o'clock in the morning

midnight

eight-thirty in the evening

ADDRESSES

31 Bloor Street West

75 West Broadway

EXACT AMOUNTS OF MONEY

$15.99 $30 $72 300.68

I was stunned to learn that the price of a movie ticket had gone up to $12.76 ~~twelve dollars and seventy-six cents~~ with tax.

PERCENTAGES, FRACTIONS, DECIMALS

92 percent 1/5 3.75

The poll indicates that the premier has a 93 ~~ninety-three~~ percent approval rating.

If a paper is heavily statistical, however, use the % sign. It is appropriate with a list of figures, but not in a paper where words predominate.

STATISTICS, SCORES, SURVEYS

In Canada, 14 babies are born each year for every 1000 people.

Team Canada won the game against Sweden by a score of 3–2.

According to the study, 1 out of every 10 residents was out of work.

MEASUREMENTS AND COUNTS

4.5 metres clearance

19 800 people at the game

DIVISIONS OF BOOKS

Chapter 7, page 381

DIVISIONS OF PLAYS

Act V, Scene ii, lines 10–15

IDENTIFICATION NUMBERS

Highway 427 Room 311 Channel 2 #73321

14-6: ITALICS (UNDERLINING)

Italics is the typeface in which letters slant to the right and appear like handwritten script. Italics is a typeface option on word-processing programs. When writing by hand, use underlining to indicate italics.

Note: The *MLA Handbook* recommends that students use underlining, not italics, in their papers. Check with your instructors to determine their preferences.

14-6A: TITLES OF WORKS

Convention requires that you use italics (or underlining) when making reference to certain types of works or materials. These are listed in the table below.

Titles of Works in Italics (or Underlined)

PRINT	
Books, Plays, Long Poems	*In the Skin of a Lion*
Journals, Magazines	*Journal of Reading*
Newspapers	*Winnipeg Free Press*
Conference Proceedings	*Women in Physics*
Published Dissertations	*Serial Murder and Leyton's "Proletarian Rebellion"*
Maps, Charts	*Southern Arabian Peninsula*
Comic Strips	*Peanuts*
ART	
Visual Works of Art	*The West Wind*
Musical Compositions, Scores	*Symphony in B Major*
Ballets, Operas	*Don Giovanni*
Performances	*Nothing Sacred*

ELECTRONIC	
Films, Videotapes	*The Sweet Hereafter*
Sound Recordings	*Sgt. Pepper's Lonely Hearts Club Band*
Radio and Television Programs	*Cross Country Checkup, Venture*
Computer Games, Video Games	*Tomb Raider: Chronicles*
ONLINE	
Websites	*The Canada Council for the Arts*
Books, References	*The Martyrology*
Projects, Services, Databases	*Canadian Periodical Index*
Discussion Lists, Newsgroups	*Alliance for Computers and Writing Listserv*
GOVERNMENT PUBLICATIONS	
Acts, Statutes	*The Income Tax Act*
Court Cases	*Norberg v. Wynrib*
Debates	*Debates, Hansard, Congressional Record*
Papers, Hearings, Reports	*Agenda: Jobs and Growth*

Use quotation marks (*not* italics) to identify the titles of the following:

- short stories, essays, and poems (except long poems published independently)
- journal, magazine, or newspaper articles, including titles of reviews, interviews, and editorials
- unpublished material such as theses, dissertations, or papers read at meetings or published in conference proceedings; lectures, speeches, or readings
- manuscripts in collections; published letters
- chapters in a book
- laws and treaties
- songs
- television episodes

Do not italicize, underline, or place in quotation marks the following:

- names of sacred works, such as the Bible or names of books within it
- laws
- unpublished letters
- the title of your own essay or report

14-6B: NAMES OF SHIPS, PLANES, AND SPACECRAFT

Italicize (or underline) the names of ships, planes, and spacecraft.

Lusitania *Spirit of St. Louis* *Columbia*

During the *Apollo 11* lunar-landing mission, Mission Commander Neil Armstrong became the first person to walk on the moon.

14-6C: FOREIGN WORDS

Italicize (or underline) foreign words that have not become part of the English language.

Their relationship is a classic case of *omnia vincit amor.*

You do not need to italicize or underline words that have become part of the English language, such as café au lait, bon voyage, per se, and habeas corpus.

Remember that English is an evolving language and new words borrowed from other languages are regularly accepted into common English usage. If you are unsure about whether or not to italicize or underline, check in a recent edition of a comprehensive Canadian dictionary.

14-6D: WORDS, LETTERS, NUMBERS AS THEMSELVES

Italicize (or underline) words, letters, or numbers mentioned as themselves.

Erika said she could be late, but for her *could* means *will.*

The *W* and the *S* had blown off of the restaurant's sign so that customers couldn't tell what the special was.

When the *–7* went up next to Tiger Woods' name, the whole crowd cheered wildly.

It is also acceptable to use quotation marks to set off words mentioned as words.

14-6E: MISUSE

Writers occasionally use italics or underlining to emphasize important words in their work. Such an emphatic technique is only effective if it is not overused. Allow emphasis to come from the words and structure of the sentence itself, rather than from overuse of italics, underlining, or exclamation marks.

× Residential development in the Golden Horseshoe of southern Ontario was *rampant*.

Italics do not add anything to the above sentence. The word *rampant* is strong enough to stand on its own and does not need any enhancement.

15

ESL

A different language is a different vision of life.

-Federico Fellini

15

ESL

15 ESL

This section is written especially for readers whose first language is not English. Some specific features of English are typically problematic and may cause errors in usage; these features are dealt with below.

15-1: ARTICLES

The articles in English are *a*, *an*, and *the*. They are determiners, which signal that a noun will follow and that any modifiers appearing before that noun refer to that noun. A and *an* are the indefinite articles; *the* is the definite article.

Indefinite Article: a cat, a Siamese cat

Definite Article: the television, the portable television

Other determiners that may mark nouns include the following:

- possessive nouns

  Beenish's car, Mom's birthday

- numbers

  two cats, 102 balloons

- pronouns

  each Canadian, several items, a lot of experience, those colours, my dream

For further information, see 9-1a, Nouns; 9-1b, Articles; 9-1c, Pronouns.

15-1A: WHEN TO USE *A* (OR *AN*)

If the noun is a singular count noun, use *a* or *an* before the noun. To decide whether the noun is a singular count noun, consult the box on page 450.

✔ Use *a* if a consonant sound follows the article.
✔ Use *an* if a vowel sound follows the article, remembering that *h* or *u* may make either vowel or consonant sounds.

H, U *as Consonants:* a horse, a historic trip, a union, a useful tool

H, U *as Vowels:* an hour, an honest man, an ugly face, an umbrella

How to Tell If a Noun Is a Singular Count Noun

1. It is a common noun (rather than a proper name).
2. The noun refers to a person, place, or thing that can be counted, such as *one woman, two cities, three bowls.*
3. The noun names something unknown to the reader because it is being used for the first time or because its specific identity is not known even to the writer.

If the answer to all three of these questions is yes, then use *a* or *an* before the noun.

Note: A or *an* usually means "one among many" but may simply mean "any."

Note also: Some collective nouns (nouns that name a group of things) are always treated as plural. These include *clergy, military, people, police.* To refer to one member of the group, use a singular noun with these collective nouns, such as *a member of the clergy, a military officer, a man of the people, a police officer.*

For further information, see 9-1a, Nouns.

15-1B: WHEN NOT TO USE *A* (OR *AN*)

If the noun is a noncount noun, do not use *a* or *an* before the noun. To decide whether a noun is a noncount noun, ask if it satisfies this statement:

✔ The noun refers to an entity that cannot be counted, such as *philosophy, ice,* or *fatigue.*

To express a particular amount of a noncount noun, you can modify it by using another determiner, such as *some, any,* or *more.* Remember these guidelines:

- *A few* or *a little* means "some," whereas *few* and *little* mean "almost none."
- Use *much* with noncount nouns and *many* with count nouns.
- Use *an amount of* with noncount nouns and *a number of* with count nouns.
- Use *less* with noncount nouns (*less money*) and *fewer* with count nouns (*fewer hours*).

Noncount Nouns

GROUPS OF ITEMS THAT MAKE UP A WHOLE

baggage, money, silver, research, furniture, mail, clothing, real estate

ABSTRACT NOUNS

wealth, awareness, joy, discord, esteem

LIQUIDS

tea, milk, water, beer

GASES

smoke, steam, oxygen, air, fog

MATERIALS

wood, steel, wool, gold

FOOD

pork, pasta, butter, salmon

GRAINS OR PARTICLES

wheat, dust, rice, dirt

SPORTS OR GAMES

rugby, hockey, chess, poker

LANGUAGES

French, English, Mandarin, Farsi

FIELDS OF STUDY

chemistry, engineering, nursing

NATURAL EVENTS

lightning, cold, sunlight, darkness

You can also add a count noun in front of a noncount noun to make it more specific (*a jug of wine, a piece of jewellery, a game of bridge*).

I ate a bowl of porridge for breakfast.

Note: Some noncount nouns can also be used as count nouns, depending on their meaning. This is usually the case when the noun can be used individually or as part of a larger whole made up of individual parts.

Tim bought me a coffee this morning; he knows I love coffee.

Invest in a dictionary that tells you whether a noun is noncount or count.

15-1C: WHEN TO USE *THE*

Use *the* in the following circumstances:

✔ when the noun has been previously mentioned

A woman entered the emergency room of the hospital. The woman began to cry.

The noun *woman* is preceded by A when first named. When named again, it is preceded by *the* since you now know its specific identity.

Note: A may be used after the first mention of a noun if a descriptive adjective comes between the article and the noun.

Rachel wore a *new* dress to the prom. It was a *silk* dress.

✔ when a modifying word, phrase, or clause after the noun restricts its meaning

The program *you are about to see* has been edited for television.

The clause *you are about to see* restricts the meaning of the word *program*. In other words, it identifies the specific program.

✔ when a superlative makes *the* specific

Bill Gates is the *richest* man in the world.

The superlative *richest* restricts the identity of the noun *man*.

✔ when the noun is a unique person, place, or thing

Some people still maintain that the Earth is flat.

The Earth refers to this specific planet.

✔ when the context makes the noun's specific identity clear.

Feed the dog before you leave the house.

The context makes clear which dog is to be fed.

Note: In phrases beginning with *one of the,* the noun that follows must be in the plural.

She is one of the candidates (not candidate) most likely to get the job.

For further information, see 9-1e, Adjectives; 9-1f, Adverbs; and 9-3, Phrases and Clauses.

15-1D: WHEN NOT TO USE *THE*

Elephants are mammals.

The is not needed because the statement refers to all elephants, that is, to elephants in general.

DON'T USE* THE *WITH MOST PROPER NOUNS

Proper nouns name specific persons, places, and things and begin with a capital letter. *The* is not used with proper names, except in the following cases.

Exceptions:

✔ nouns that follow the pattern *the . . . of . . .*

the Prime Minister of Canada, the province of Manitoba

✔ plural proper nouns

the Mulroneys, the Toronto Blue Jays, the United States

✔ collective proper nouns

the Canadian Opera Company, the Royal Canadian Mounted Police, the Supreme Court

✔ some proper names of geographical features, such as large areas, deserts, mountain ranges, peninsulas, oceans, seas, gulfs, canals, and rivers

the West Coast, the Sahara Desert, the Pyrenees, the Iberian Peninsula, the Pacific Ocean, the St. Lawrence Seaway, the Gulf of Mexico, the Suez Canal, the Ganges

✔ names of ships

the *Hesperus,* the *Black Pearl*

15-2: VERBS

All writers in English encounter problems with verbs. In addition to the material below, helpful information will be found in the following sections: 9-1d, Verbs; 9-2b, Verbs, Objects, and Complements; 9-3b, Verbal Phrases; and 9-3e, Subordinate Clauses.

15-2A: MAIN VERBS AND HELPING VERBS (*BE*, *DO*, AND *HAVE*)

The verb in a sentence may be one verb or a phrase made up of a main verb and a helping verb. Every main verb (with the exception of *be*) has five forms that are used to create tenses.

Base (Simple) Form: work, eat

Past Tense: worked, ate

Past Participle: worked, eaten

Present Participle: working, eating

-s ***Form:*** works, eats

The -s form is used with the third-person singular in the present tense.

Work is an example of a regular verb; *catch* is an example of an irregular verb. (For a list of frequently used irregular verbs, see 10-4a.)

HELPING VERBS

Helping (auxiliary) verbs always come before main verbs.

The snake *has* eaten the frog.

Don't you find nature fascinating?

Some helping verbs—*be*, *do*, and *have*—are used to conjugate verbs into their various tenses. *Be*, *do*, and *have* thus change form.

FORMS OF *BE*, *DO*, AND *HAVE*

be, am, is, are, was, were, being, been

do, does, did

have, has, had

MODALS

Other helping verbs, called modals, usually do not change form to indicate tense or to indicate singular or plural.

- One-word modals do not change form. These include *can*, *could*, *may*, *might*, *must*, *shall*, *should*, *will*, and *would*.

- Most two-word modals do change form to indicate tense or to indicate singular or plural; examples include *need to* and *has to.*

Modals do not require the word *to* in front of the base verb, except in the case of *need to, has to,* and *ought to.* Note that *ought to* is a two-word modal that does not change form.

15-2B: USE OF *BE* TO FORM THE PROGRESSIVE ASPECT

The progressive aspect is used to indicate action that is in progress. Create the progressive aspects of the past, present, or future tense by using *am, is, are, was, were, have been, has been, had been, will have been,* or *will be* followed by the present participle of the main verb. (See 10-4f.)

Present Progressive: Anne is sitting in the waiting room while her husband sees the doctor.

Past Progressive: Anne was sitting in the waiting room when the doctor rushed from the examining room.

Future Progressive: Anne will be sitting in the hospital lounge tomorrow during her husband's surgery.

Present Perfect Progressive: Anne has been sitting in the lounge since early this morning.

Past Perfect Progressive: Anne had been sitting in the lounge for two hours before the nurse came to tell her about the delay.

Future Perfect Progressive: By the time the surgery is finished, Anne will have been sitting in the lounge for seven hours.

Always make sure to use the *-ing* form to create the progressive aspect.

× Martin Short is plan to visit Hamilton, where he was born.

√ Martin Short is planning to visit Hamilton, where he was born.

Note: *Been* and *be* need other helping verbs to form the progressive tense. *Been* requires either *have, has,* or *had* to form the tense. *Be* forms the future progressive tense with one of the modal verbs.

I have been worrying about you. (present perfect progressive)

The teacher will be watching you. (future progressive)

Some verbs are not commonly used in the progressive tense in English. These are considered **static** verbs, which describe a state of being or a mental activity (e.g., *appear, believe, belong, contain, know, seem, think, understand, want*)

× The canister is not containing any sugar.

√ The canister does not contain any sugar.

There are, however, many exceptions that do normally use the progressive tense, such as *I have been thinking about you.* Keep notes for future reference about the exceptions that you hear and read.

For more information, see 9-3b, Verbal Phrases.

15-2C: USE OF *BE* TO FORM THE PASSIVE VOICE

A verb is in the passive voice when its subject is the receiver of the action, rather than the performer of the action.

The road to hell is paved with good intentions.

The passive voice is formed with one of the forms of the verb *be* and the main verb's past participle.

Passive Voice, Present Tense: Aleksandar Antonijevic and Xiao Nan Yu are acclaimed for their recent work with the National Ballet of Canada.

Passive Voice, Past Tense: *Generation X* by Douglas Coupland has been recognized as a groundbreaking work of fiction.

Passive Voice, Future Tense: Many Canadians will be pleased by the results of the hockey game.

The passive voice can occur in any tense of a transitive verb (that is, a verb that takes an object to complete its meaning). However, if a verb is intransitive, it cannot be used to form the passive voice. Hence, the following examples cannot be made into the passive voice.

The accident happened last night.

The accident was last night.

Note: When *be, being,* or *been* is used to form the passive voice, it must be preceded by another helping verb. *Been* must be preceded by a form of *have; being* must be preceded by a form of *to be,* and *be* must be preceded by a modal verb.

15-2D: USE OF *DO* TO FORM QUESTIONS AND FOR EMPHASIS

The auxiliary forms of the verb *do* (*do, does, did*) are used to indicate questions, negatives, and emphasis. The verb *do* is always used with base forms of the main verb that do not change.

It does not look like rain.

Did you look in the glove compartment?

I didn't believe it until I saw it.

I do believe that you will succeed in your endeavours.

In these examples, *look* and *believe* are base forms of the main verb.

15-2E: USE OF *HAVE* TO FORM THE PERFECT ASPECT

After the helping verbs *have, has,* or *had*, use the past participle to form the perfect aspect. (See 10-4f.) Note that past participles frequently end in *-d, -en, -n,* or *-t*. (See 9-3b.)

Though Yuen has never lived in China, Cantonese is his native language.

We had never paid any attention to their suggestions before.

Have, has, and *had* may also be preceded by modal verbs, such as *will*, used in forming the future perfect.

By next week, the class will have done most of the assignments for the course.

15-2F: MODAL VERBS BESIDES *BE, DO,* AND *HAVE*

Use modal auxiliary verbs before main verbs to express the following:

- ability
- necessity
- advisability or expectation
- probability or possibility
- promise or agreement
- preference
- a plan or obligation
- an action now past

ABILITY

Can is used to express ability in the present or future tense. *Could* is used to express ability in the past tense.

Popeye can lift his own weight, or at least he could when he was younger.

NECESSITY

Must, have to, and *need to* express the necessity of doing something. *Must* is used in the immediate present and the future tense; therefore, you cannot use an auxiliary verb before *must*. The others are used in all verb tenses.

I must insist that you leave.

I will have to call the police if you refuse.

I needed to clear the room as quickly as possible.

ADVISABILITY

Should and *ought to* indicate that a certain action is advisable or expected in the present or the future. The past tenses are *should have* and *ought to have*. Note that *had better* implies advice with a warning.

You should take my advice.

He ought to buy a watch of his own.

It should snow tomorrow.

She should have said something at the time.

I ought to have told you earlier.

You had better listen to me this time.

PROBABILITY OR POSSIBILITY

May, might, could, and *must* sometimes express probability or possibility. To form the past tense, add *have* and the past participle of the main verb after the modal. *Could* or *might* are also used for polite requests.

We may regret skipping class.

We could pretend we overslept.

We might have missed something important.

We must have lost our minds.

PROMISE OR AGREEMENT

Will and *would* suggest promise or agreement. *Would* may also be used for polite requests.

All of us will be on our best behaviour.

Would you be so kind as to attend?

PREFERENCE

Would rather is used to express preference. To form the past tense, add *have* and the past participle of the main verb after the modal.

He would rather die than live with his parents again.

I would rather have made the meal myself than have eaten her cooking.

PLAN OR OBLIGATION

Be supposed to indicates that the subject has a plan or an obligation. This modal can be used in the present and in the past tense.

He was supposed to arrive at work by 8:30.

AN ACTION NOW PAST

Used to and *would* indicate that a repeated action or habit is now past. Only *used to* can express an action that lasted a length of time in the past.

I used to smoke.

I would light a cigarette as soon as I woke up in the morning.

× I would live in the Middle East.

√ I used to live in the Middle East.

15-2G: VERBS FOLLOWED BY GERUNDS OR INFINITIVES

A **gerund** is a verb form that ends in *-ing* and is used as a noun.

My cat likes sleeping sixteen hours a day.

George spends his days moping around the house.

Smoking is dangerous to your health.

Eating before you go to bed may contribute to weight gain, or so Oprah tells us.

An **infinitive** is the base form of the verb preceded by *to*, which marks its use as an infinitive. *To* in front of the base form of a verb is not a preposition, but an indication of the infinitive use.

My cat likes to sleep sixteen hours a day.

When will that child learn to behave?

To succeed in sports, you must practise.

To be honest, that dog could use a bath.

A few verbs, such as *like*, used above, may take either a gerund or an infinitive after them, although they sometimes change their meaning as a result. Other verbs take a gerund, but never an infinitive; others may take an infinitive (some with an intervening noun phrase), but not a gerund.

VERBS THAT TAKE EITHER GERUNDS OR INFINITIVES

Some common verbs may take either a gerund or an infinitive, with negligible or no differences in meaning. Here are just a few examples:

begin	go	love
can't bear	hate	prefer
can't stand	like	start
continue		

Infinitive: Elvis Stojko started *to skate* at three years old.

Gerund: Elvis Stojko started *skating* at three years old.

Some other verbs (e.g., *forget, remember, stop, try*) can take both gerunds and infinitives, but their meaning changes significantly depending on which is used.

Gerund: He remembers *going* to visit his grandparents when he was little.

Infinitive: Remember *to eat* your vegetables.

VERBS THAT TAKE ONLY GERUNDS

acknowledge	detest	miss
admit	discuss	object to
adore	dislike	postpone
advise	dream about	practise
anticipate	enjoy	put off
appreciate	escape	quit
avoid	finish	recall
be left	give up	recommend
can't help	have trouble	resent
complain about	imagine	resist
consider	include	risk
consist of	insist on	suggest
contemplate	keep	tolerate
delay	mention	understand
deny	mind	

Gerund: David and Nate avoided *talking* about the funeral.

Note that some of these verbs can also take an infinitive, but only if there is an intervening noun or pronoun.

I imagine you *to have* big ambitions.

I consider you *to be* a fine person.

We advise clients *to seek* a second opinion.

VERBS THAT TAKE ONLY INFINITIVES

afford	decline	plan
agree	demand	prepare
aim	deserve	pretend
appear	expect	promise
arrange	fail	refuse
ask	give permission	say
assent	have	seem
attempt	hesitate	struggle
be able	hope	tend
beg	intend	threaten
care	know how	volunteer
claim	learn	wait
consent	manage	want
dare	mean	wish
decide	offer	would like

Infinitive: My parents plan *to attend* the graduation ceremony.

VERBS THAT TAKE INFINITIVES BUT NEED A NOUN OR PRONOUN IN BETWEEN

Some verbs in the active voice usually require an infinitive, but a noun or pronoun must come between the verb and infinitive. The noun or pronoun usually names a person affected by the action in the sentence.

admonish	forbid*	persuade
advise	force	remind
allow	have	request
cause	instruct	teach
challenge	invite	tell
command	hire	urge
convince	oblige	warn
dare	order	
encourage	permit	

*can also take gerund

Infinitive: She encouraged Paolo *to stay* in school.

Note: There are a few verbs (*ask, need, would like, expect, want*) that can take an infinitive either directly or with a noun or pronoun in between.

Direct Infinitive: She expected *to leave* the party early.

Pronoun between Verb and Infinitive: I expected her *to decline* the invitation.

"SENSE VERBS" THAT TAKE AN UNMARKED INFINITIVE OR A GERUND WITH A NOUN OR PRONOUN

Some verbs that are sometimes called "sense verbs" take either an **unmarked infinitive** (the base form of the verb without *to*) or a gerund, with a noun or pronoun in between.

feel	listen to	notice
have	look at	see
hear	make (meaning "force")	watch
let		

Unmarked Infinitive: We watched the goalie *defend* the net.

Gerund: We watched the goalie *defending* the net.

Note: The verb *help* may be used either with a marked or unmarked infinitive.

Marked Infinitive: He helps the homeless *to find* shelter.

Unmarked Infinitive: He helps the homeless *find* shelter.

15-2H: PHRASAL VERBS

Phrasal, or two-word, verbs consist of verbs with prepositions or adverbs, known as particles. Phrasal verbs have distinctive idiomatic usage that requires careful study since they cannot be understood literally. Look at the verbs in these sentences:

Matt will call *back* later in the evening.

Matt and Khiet called *off* the wedding.

Matt calls *up* his friends every day to discuss what happened.

Most phrasal verbs can be separated to allow a noun or pronoun object to come between them. Others cannot be separated.

× The professor went the homework *over* with the class.

√ The professor went *over* the homework with the class.

With verbs that can be separated from their particles, a pronoun object must always be placed between them. (A noun object can be placed either before or after the particle.)

× The chef threw *away* them.

√ The chef threw them *away*.

√ The chef threw *away* the leftovers.

√ The chef threw the leftovers *away*.

COMMON PHRASAL VERBS

Here is a list of common phrasal verbs. If the particle (preposition or adverb) cannot be separated from the verb by a direct object, it is marked with an asterisk (*). Check meanings of phrasal verbs carefully in the dictionary if you have doubts about their usage.

Common Phrasal Verbs

ask out	get away with*	leave out
break down	get back	look after*
bring about	get off	look around*
bring up	get up *(intr.)*	look into*
burn down	give away	look out for*
burn up	give back	look over
call back	give in *(intr.)*	look up
call off	give up	make up with*
call up	go out of	pick out
clean up	go over*	pick up
come across*	grow up *(intr.)*	play around*
cut up	hand in	point out
do over	hand out	put away
drop in	hang on *(intr.)*	put back
drop off	hang on to*	put off
figure out	hang up	put on
fill out	help out	put out
fill up	keep on	put together
get along with*	keep up with*	put up with*

quiet down	take off	throw out
run across*	take out	try on
run into	take over	try out
run out of*	take up	turn down
see off	talk about*	turn on
shut off	talk to*	turn out
speak to*	talk with*	turn up
speak up *(intr.)*	talk over	wake up
speak with*	think about*	wear out
stay away from*	think over	wrap up
stay up*	think up	
take care of*	throw away	

15-2I: OMITTED VERBS

All English sentences must have a verb. In some languages, verbs such as *to be* can be omitted. This is not true of English. Always include the verb.

× Dolores very industrious.

√ Dolores is very industrious.

× Wayne Gretzky in Manhattan.

√ Wayne Gretzky lives in Manhattan.

× Roads in Saskatchewan wide.

√ Roads in Saskatchewan are wide.

15-2J: CONDITIONAL SENTENCES

Conditional sentences state a relationship between one set of circumstances and another. Conditional sentences can be used for the following purposes:

- to express a cause-and-effect relationship that is factual
- to predict future possibilities or express plans
- to speculate about unlikely future events
- to speculate about events that didn't happen
- to speculate about things that are hypothetical or contrary to fact

EXPRESSING FACTUAL RELATIONSHIPS

Such sentences may express scientific truths, or they may simply describe something that usually or habitually happens.

Present Conditional: When a leap year occurs, there are 366 days in the year. [simple present tense]

Past Conditional: Whenever Joe petted the cat, he broke out in hives. [simple past tense]

PREDICTING FUTURE POSSIBILITIES OR EXPRESSING PLANS

Normally, use the present tense in the subordinate clause and the future tense in the main clause.

If that child sees a snake, she will scream.

Sometimes a modal verb, such as *may, might, can, could,* or *should* is used in the main clause instead of a future tense.

If you smoke heavily, you *might* develop lung disease.

SPECULATING ABOUT UNLIKELY FUTURE EVENTS

The verb in the main clause is usually a modal verb, such as *will, can, could, may, might,* or *should,* followed by the base form of the main verb.

If I won the lottery, I *could* finally quit my job.

If I had time, I *might* travel round the world.

If I were you, I *would* trade in that old car.

Note: The subjunctive mood is used in the *if* clause; the subjunctive is used when you are describing unlikely events. (See 10-4g.)

SPECULATING ABOUT EVENTS THAT DID NOT HAPPEN

If I had listened to my friends, I would have taken a vacation last summer.

If my mother had been here, she would have helped me clean the house.

SPECULATING ABOUT THINGS THAT ARE HYPOTHETICAL OR CONTRARY TO FACT

Hypothetical: If he only had a heart, he would have friends.

Contrary to Fact: If your story were true, you could sell it to the *National Enquirer*.

Note: The subjunctive mood is used in the *if* clause; the subjunctive is used when you are describing a hypothetical case or something contrary to fact. (See 10-4g.)

15-2K: INDIRECT QUOTATIONS

An indirect quotation reports what someone said or wrote but with slight changes in verb tense and without quotation marks. Indirect quotations usually occur in subordinate clauses.

When the present tense is used in the main clause, the verb in the subordinate clause is in the same tense as the original quotation.

Indirect Quotation: Sasha Trudeau says the Pierre Trudeau fellowships will change the country.

Original Quotation: "The Pierre Trudeau fellowships will change the country."

When the past tense is used in the main clause, the verb in the subordinate clause changes tense from the original quotation. Subordinate clause verbs in the past tense and the present perfect tense change to the past perfect tense; those in the simple present tense change to the simple past tense. The past perfect tense [*had been*] does not change.

Indirect Quotation: Trudeau said that he had never been president and wondered what it would be like.

Original Quotation: "I have never been president and wonder what it would be like."

In the example above, the present perfect *have never been* changes to the past perfect *had never been*. The simple present *wonder* becomes the simple past *wondered*.

When the direct quotation states a general truth, or reports a situation that is still true, use the present tense in the indirect quotation regardless of the verb in the main clause.

Indirect Quotation: Trudeau said that the state has no place in the nation's bedrooms.

Original Quotation: "The state has no place in the nation's bedrooms."

Note: In indirect quotations, the pronoun forms of *I* and *we* change to forms of *he, she* or *they*. Note also that indirect quotations are usually introduced by *that*.

For further information on direct and indirect quotations, see 11-5a; on subordinate clauses, see 9-3e.

15-3: MORE ESL ADVICE

15-3A: OMITTED SUBJECTS; OMITTED *THERE* OR *IT*

English requires a subject in all sentences except for commands, in which the subject *you* is understood. (See 12-1c.) If your first language does omit subjects in some cases, pay particular attention to this usage in English.

× Have a diploma in accounting.

√ I have a diploma in accounting.

× Your daughter is accomplished; seems very gifted.

√ Your daughter is accomplished; she seems very gifted.

If a subject is not placed in its usual position in front of a verb, it requires an expletive pronoun (*there* or *it*) at the beginning of the clause. *There* used in this way points to the location or existence of something.

× Is a letter in the mailbox.

√ There is a letter in the mailbox.

× As I have explained, are many reasons for my decision.

√ As I have explained, there are many reasons for my decision.

Note that the verb after *there* agrees with the subject that follows it: *letter is*, *reasons are*.

The word *it* may also function as an expletive, calling attention to something and introducing it in an impersonal way.

× Is important to get a good education.

√ It is important to get a good education.

× Is clear that he must arrive on time.

√ It is clear that he must arrive on time.

The word *it* is also used as the subject in sentences that

- describe temperature or weather conditions

It snows less in Canada than people think.

In the summer, it can be extremely warm.

- state the time

  It is midnight.

- indicate distance

  It is a long way from Victoria to St. John's.

- state a fact about the environment

  It gets busy on the highways on long weekends.

15-3B: REPEATED SUBJECTS

Do not restate a subject as a pronoun before the verb. State the subject only once in the clause.

× The temperature it reached thirty degrees Celsius.

√ The temperature reached thirty degrees Celsius.

× The professor she gave a lecture on globalization and the new media.

√ The professor gave a lecture on globalization and the new media.

Note that there is no need for a pronoun even if other words intervene between the subject and the verb.

× The letter I received today it brought good news.

√ The letter I received today brought good news.

15-3C: REPEATED OBJECTS AND ADVERBS IN ADJECTIVE CLAUSES

Adjective clauses begin with relative pronouns: *who, whom, whose, which, that, where(ever)*, or *when(ever)*. The first word of an adjective clause replaces another word, either the subject, an object, or a pronoun.

Make sure not to restate the word being replaced in the adjective clause. Such repetition occurs in other languages, but never in English.

× He usually works at the desk that I am sitting at it.

× He usually works at the desk I am sitting at it.

√ He usually works at the desk that I am sitting at.

√ He usually works at the desk I am sitting at.

The pronoun *that* replaces *desk* in the adjective clause; hence *it* is not needed as the object after the preposition *at*. Even when the pronoun *that* is left out, it is still understood.

Adverbs in adjective clauses, like relative pronouns, do not need to be repeated.

× The city where she lives there is accessible by bus or train.

√ The city where she lives is accessible by bus or train.

The adverb *there* is not needed in an adjective clause beginning with *where*.

For further information see 9-3e, Subordinate Clauses; 9-1c, Pronouns; and 10-3h Subject–Verb Agreement with Relative Pronouns.

15-3D: GENDER IN PRONOUN–ANTECEDENT AGREEMENT

In English, the gender of a pronoun should match its antecedent (that is, the noun to which it refers) and not a noun that the pronoun may modify.

× Andrew gave the diamond ring to her fiancée.

√ Andrew gave the diamond ring to his fiancée.

Note: Nouns in English are neuter unless they specifically refer to males or females. Hence, nouns such as *chair, newspaper, moon,* and *ring* take the pronoun it.

× Andrew gave him to his fiancée.

√ Andrew gave it to his fiancée.

15-3E: PLACEMENT OF ADJECTIVES AND ADVERBS

PLACEMENT OF ADJECTIVES

In English, adjectives normally precede the noun, though they may also follow linking verbs. The box on page 470 shows the proper word order for cumulative adjectives (those not separated by commas); for example, *I ate another five beautiful round ripe black Spanish olives.* Note that some exceptions do occur. (For more information on linking verbs, see 9-2b; on cumulative adjectives, see 11-1f.)

Remember that long lists of adjectives in front of a noun may be awkward. Try to use no more than two or three of them between the determiner and the noun itself.

Word Order for Cumulative Adjectives

DETERMINERS, IF THERE ARE ANY
a, an, another, the, my, your, Canada's, those

EXPRESSIONS OF ORDER, INCLUDING ORDINAL NUMBERS, IF ANY
first, second, next, final

EXPRESSIONS OF QUANTITY, INCLUDING CARDINAL NUMBERS, IF ANY
one, two, five, each, some, all

ADJECTIVES OF OPINION, IF ANY
beautiful, fascinating, ugly, dull

ADJECTIVES OF SIZE OR SHAPE, IF ANY
tiny, huge, tall, rotund, triangular, round

ADJECTIVES OF AGE AND CONDITION, IF ANY
brand-new, ancient, ripe, rotten

ADJECTIVES OF COLOUR, IF ANY
yellow, purple, magenta, chartreuse, black

ADJECTIVES OF NATIONALITY, IF ANY
Chinese, Portuguese, German, Spanish

ADJECTIVES OF RELIGION, IF ANY
Muslim, Jewish, Protestant, Catholic

ADJECTIVES OF MATERIAL, IF ANY
gold, mahogany, silk, wood

ADJECTIVES THAT CAN ALSO BE USED AS NOUNS, IF ANY
business, English, government

THE NOUN BEING MODIFIED

PLACEMENT OF ADVERBS

Adverbs and adverbial phrases are flexible in English, and they can appear at the beginning, middle, or end of a clause.

Tomorrow afternoon, we're leaving for China.

She opened the door hesitantly.

Ansel always beats me at checkers.

We have repeatedly asked for assistance.

An adverb may not be placed between a verb and a direct object, however.

× She opened hesitantly the door.

√ Hesitantly, she opened the door.

√ She opened the door hesitantly.

√ She hesitantly opened the door.

Here, the adverb *hesitantly* must be placed either at the beginning or the end of the sentence or immediately before the verb. It cannot appear directly after the verb because the verb is followed by the direct object *the door*.

Placement of adverbs in English sentences depends on the type of adverb.

MANNER

Adverbs of manner describe how something is done. They usually appear in the middle of the clause or at the end.

Jules successfully crossed the bridge.

She sneezed violently.

TIME

Adverbs of time describe when an event takes place or how long it lasts. They usually go at the beginning or end of a clause.

Then she searched for her allergy medication.

I saw that film last year.

PLACE

Adverbs of place describe where an event occurs. They usually go at the end of a clause.

She found it in her purse.

FREQUENCY

Adverbs of frequency describe how often an event occurs. They usually appear in the middle of a clause or at the beginning of a clause to modify the whole sentence.

He always knows the right thing to say.

Every evening, we meditate for half an hour.

DEGREE OR EMPHASIS

Adverbs of degree or emphasis describe how much or to what degree and are used with other modifiers. They come immediately before the word they modify.

> She is also very uncomfortable when there are pets around.

SENTENCE MODIFIERS

Some adverbs modify an entire sentence, using transitional words and words like *however, therefore,* and *doubtless*. These usually appear at the beginning of a clause.

> As a result, she often turns down invitations to visit.

15-3F: PRESENT AND PAST PARTICIPLES AS ADJECTIVES

Both present and past participles may be used as adjectives in English.

> ***Present Participles:*** fascinating, exciting
>
> ***Past Participles:*** fascinated, excited

To decide whether to use the present participle or past participle, ask whether the noun modified is causing or experiencing what is being described.

PRESENT PARTICIPLES

✔ always end in *-ing*
✔ modify a noun or pronoun that is the cause of the action

> Oman told us about his fascinating project.

The *project,* the noun modified, causes fascination; hence, the present participle, which causes the feeling, is correct.

> Your trip sounds very exciting.

The *trip,* the noun modified, causes excitement; therefore, the present participle is correct.

PAST PARTICIPLES

✔ usually end in *-ed, -d, -en,* or *-t,* though many other endings are possible
✔ modify a noun or pronoun that experiences what is being described

> The speakers were fascinated by Oman's project.

The noun *speakers* experience the fascination; hence, the past participle, which describes something experiencing the feeling, is correct.

She was very excited about her trip.

The pronoun *she* experiences the excitement; therefore the past participle is correct.

Note: In English, both the past-tense and past-participle forms of regular verbs (such as *talk, work, play, love*) are created by adding *-ed* or *-d* to the base (simple) form of the verb. But this pattern is not followed for all irregular verbs (for example, *ring, rang, rung*). For a list of the past tense and past participles of some common irregular verbs, see 10-4a.

Although the present and past participles of a verb sound similar, they can mean very different things. *He is annoying* (present participle) means "He is causing an annoyance"—the verb is in the active voice. *He is annoyed* (past participle) means "He is experiencing annoyance"—the verb is in the passive voice.

Participles That May Cause Confusion

PRESENT PARTICIPLE	PAST PARTICIPLE
amazing	amazed
amusing	amused
annoying	annoyed
appalling	appalled
astonishing	astonished
boring	bored
confusing	confused
depressing	depressed
disgusting	disgusted
embarrassing	embarrassed
exciting	excited

PRESENT PARTICIPLE	PAST PARTICIPLE
exhausting	exhausted
fascinating	fascinated
frightening	frightened
frustrating	frustrated
insulting	insulted
interesting	interested
offending	offended
overwhelming	overwhelmed
pleasing	pleased
reassuring	reassured
satisfying	satisfied
shocking	shocked
surprising	surprised
tiring	tired
worrying	worried

15-3G: PREPOSITIONS: *AT, ON, IN . . .*

Idiomatic uses of verbs with prepositions must be memorized since no particular rules apply.

TIME

At a specific time: at 9:00 a.m., at midnight, at breakfast

On a specific day or date: on Friday, on June 16

In part of a 24-hour period: in the morning, in the daytime (*but* at night)

In a year or month: in 2003, in June

In a period of time: in two weeks

PLACE

At a specific location: at home, at school

At the edge of something: at the corner

At a target: aim the dart at the board

On a surface: on the wall, on the floor, on the road (*but* in the newspaper)

On a street: the school on my street

In an enclosed place: in the room, in the camera, in the car (*but* on a plane)

In a geographic location: in Winnipeg, in the Northwest Territories

Prepositions used with verbs vary widely in meaning. Check in an ESL dictionary for the meanings of verbs in combination with different prepositions. Keep track of their meanings in a notebook as you discover them in different contexts.

p. 10: David Adams Richards, "My Old Newcastle" in *A Lad from Brantford and Other Essays* (Fredericton, NB: Broken Jaw Press, 1994); p. 15: Carla Thorneloe, student; p. 15: Dave Barry, humorist; p. 19: Rex Murphy, "Pierre Trudeau: He Has Gone to His Grace," http://www.cbc.ca/national/rex/rex20000928.html, September 28, 2000; p. 21: Janet Takefman, "Psychological Issues in Male Factor Infertility," *Journal of the Infertility Awareness Association of Canada.* Reprinted by permission of the Infertility Awareness Association of Canada; p. 22: Lorna Crozier, "What Stays in the Family" in *Dropped Threads: An Anthology of Women's Writing*, edited by Marjorie Anderson and Carol Shields (Toronto: Vintage Canada, 2000): p. 23: Andrew Ward, "Oil and Water" in *Out Here: A Newcomer's Notes from the Great Northwest* (Harmondsworth, UK: Penguin, 1991); p. 24: Marie Winn, "Television Addiction" in *The Plug-in Drug: Television, Computers, and Family Life* (New York: Viking, 1977); p. 24: Pico Iyer, *Falling Off the Map: Some Lonely Places of the World* (New York: Vintage Departures, 1993); p. 25: Isabelle Mills. "Choral Music," *The Canadian Encyclopedia.* The Historica Foundation of Canada. 2006. http://www.thecanadianencyclopedia.com; p. 25: Peter Gzowski, "And the Best Damn Stew-Maker Too" from *Selected Columns from Canadian Living* (Toronto: McClelland & Stewart, Inc., 1993); p. 26: Ian Fraser, "Dearly Disconnected," *Mother Jones* (January-February 2000), http://www.motherjones.com/new/feature/2000/01/disconnected.html; p. 26: Hugh MacLennan, "If You Drop a Stone..." from *The Other Side of Hugh MacLennan: Selected Essays Old and New*, edited by Elspeth Cameron (Toronto: Macmillan of Canada, 1978); p. 27: Derek Boles, "Disaster as Popular Culture" from *Deconstructing the Titanic: A Teaching Unit for Middle & Secondary Students* (Media Awareness Network, http:///.media-awareness.ca/english/resources/educational/teachable_moments/deconstructing_titanic_5.cfm); p. 28: Todd Mercer, "'April is the Cruelest [Magazine] Month': Hoaxes in Canadian Magazines"; p. 28: Eric Fromm, "Symbolic Language of Dreams" from *Language: An Inquiry into Meaning and Function*, edited by Ruth Nanda Anshen (New York: Harper & Row, 1957); p. 29: Morris, Desmond. "Territorial Behaviour." Excerpted from *Manwatching: A Field Guide to Human Behaviour*. 1977. Published by Harry N. Abrams, Inc. New York. By permission of the publisher; p. 30: Charles Darwin, "The Formation of Vegetable Mould through the Action of Worms and the Soil" (London, John Murray, 1881); p. 32: Joyce Carol Oates, from *On Boxing* (New York: Doubleday, 1987); p. 33: Elie Wiesel, "The Perils of Indifference" (speech given at the White

House, April 12, 1999. See http://www.historyplace.com/speeches/wiesel.htm); p. 35: Barbara Ehrenreich, "Where the Wild Things Are" from "Civilization" June/July 2000.

Chapter 2

p. 64: "Family Budget Work Sheet," adapted from Statistics Canada website http://www.statcan.ca/english/kits/pdf/censu7.pdf; p. 65: "Family Structure, 2001 Census," adapted from Statistics Canada website "2001 Census Results Teacher's Kit, Activity 6: Families," http://www12.statcan.ca/english/census01/teacher's_kit/activity6_emptygraph.cfm; p. 66: "Number of Marriages and Divorces in Canada, 1921 to 2001," adapted from Statistics Canada publication "The Daily," Catalogue 11-001, Released May 4, 2004, page 2, http://www.statcan.ca/Daily/English/040504/d040504a.htm; p. 67: "Immigrants," adapted from Statistics Canada publication Canada at a Glance, 2006, Catalogue 12-581, page 4, Released March 10, 2006, http://www.statcan.ca/english/freepub/12-581-XIE/12-581-XIE2005001.pdf; p. 67: "Television Viewing by Type of Program, Fall 2003," Canada at a Glance, 2006, Catalogue 12-581, page 8, Released March 10, 2006, http://www.statcan.ca/english/freepub/12-581-XIE/12-581-XIE2005001.pdf; p. 68: Hydroelectric Power Generation, http://atlas.gc.ca/site.english/english/maps/freshwater/consumption/hydro_generation.jpg/image_view, Environment Canada, 2006. Reproduced with the permission of the Minister of Public Works and Government Services, 2006.

Chapter 3

p. 107: Software designed by Innovative Interfaces, Inc. Reprinted by permission of Western Libraries, University of Western Ontario; p. 108: Software designed by Innovative Interfaces, Inc. Reprinted by permission of Western Libraries, University of Western Ontario; p. 109: Software designed by Innovative Interfaces, Inc. Reprinted by permission of Western Libraries, University of Western Ontario; p. 110: Software designed by Innovative Interfaces, Inc. Reprinted by permission of Western Libraries, University of Western Ontario.

Chapter 4

p. 135: John Stackhouse, "Okay, You Can Take Her" p. A1; p. 136: Henry David Thoreau, *Civil Disobedience*, p. 361.

Chapter 7

p. 223: Carla Thorneloe.

Chapter 10

p.264: Margaret Laurence, "Where the World Began" from *Heart of a Stranger* (Toronto: McClelland & Stewart, 1976).

Chapter 11

p. 342: Alice Munro, "Friend of My Youth" from *Friend of My Youth* (Toronto: McClelland & Stewart, 1990); p. 343: Reprinted from *The Hidden Room* (in two volumes) by P.K. Page by permission of the Porcupine's Quill. Copyright (c) P. K. Page, 1997; p. 350: George Orwell, "On Politics and Government" in *Shooting an Elephant and Other Essays* (London: Secker and Warburg, 1950); p. 353: John Donne.

Chapter 13

p. 419: From the *ITP Nelson Canadian Dictionary of the English Language: An Encyclopedic Reference*, by NELSON CANADA, 1997. Reprinted with permission of Nelson, a division of Thomson Learning: www .thomsonrights.com. Fax 800 730-2215; p. 421: From *Gage Canadian Thesaurus* (Trade) by GAGE. 1998. Reprinted with permission of Nelson, a division of Thomson Learning: www.thomsonrights.com. Fax 800 730-2215; p. 422: From *Gage Canadian Thesaurus* (Trade) by GAGE. 1998. Reprinted with permission of Nelson, a division of Thomson Learning: www.thomsonrights.com. Fax 800 730-2215.

Chapter 14

p. 438: John Keats, "To Autumn"; p. 438: By William Carlos Williams, from COLLECTED POEMS: 1909-1939, VOLUME I, copyright (c) 1938 by New Directions Publishing Corp. Reprinted by permission of New Directions Publishing Corp.